Phonology: Applications in Communicative Disorders

by
Mary Louise Edwards, PhD
Syracuse University

Lawrence D. Shriberg, PhD
University of Wisconsin-Madison

College-Hill Press, Inc.
San Diego, California

College-Hill Press, Inc.
4284 41st. Street
San Diego, CA 92105

© 1983 by College-Hill Press

Library of Congress Cataloging in Publication Data

Edwards, Mary Louise, date
  Phonology.

  Includes bibliographical references and index. 1. Grammar, Comparative
and general—Phonology. 2. Language acquisition. 3. Communicative
disorders. I. Shriberg, Lawrence D., date. II. Title.
P217.3.E39   1983   414   82-25299
ISBN 0-933014-80-5

Printed in the United States of America

To our life partners . . . .

My husband, Kent H. Lindstrom
My wife, Linda K. Shriberg
MLE
LDS

Contents

HISTORY OF PHONOLOGY

APPLICATIONS OF PHONOLOGY

APPENDIXES

List of Figures

List of Tables

Preface

A basic foundation in phonological theory is necessary to understand the contemporary literature in phonological disorders. Our primary task was to make available in one place, systematic summaries of original sources in phonology and the applied assessment procedures that have been developed from these ideas. Management issues are noted only in passing reference. We hope that the text will prove useful to majors in communicative disorders, as well as to students and others interested more generally in phonological theory and child phonology.

The eight chapters and four appendixes have been structured to allow for maximum flexibility within and across instructional settings. For example, certain materials are placed in appendixes rather than within chapters, so that instructors can more readily tailor selected readings to existing curricula. We have tried to provide detailed discussions of issues and data that will be of interest in various courses in phonology. Much of this material is controversial, which required frequent literature citations and suggestions for additional readings. Our experience in the classroom is that undergraduate and graduate students will need to know exactly which discussions are testable and which can be skipped entirely or read for only more general content.

We have several people to thank for their contributions to this project.

First, the authors thank each other for an enjoyable dialogue that began in 1978. At that time, the junior author was attempting to piece together for himself and for his students, basic readings in phonological theory and child phonology. Tutelage by the senior author proved so valuable that it seemed useful to try to provide for other latecomers to the phonology literature, a systematic treatment of the topic. Our working format has been clearly divided, with the senior author providing nearly all the original writing, while the junior author has handled the editorial tasks.

Second, we thank our teachers. Among those who have influenced our thinking on issues discussed in this book are Charles Ferguson, Dorothy Huntington, Will Leben, Ilse Lehiste, David Stampe, Elizabeth Traugott and Arnold Zwicky.

Third, through the years we have benefited from discussions with friends and co-workers too numerous to mention. However, we must acknowledge at least a few: Barbara Handford Bernhardt, Mel Greenlee, David Ingram, Marlys Macken, Lise Menn, Kim Oller, and Carol Stoel-Gammon.

Finally, we wish to thank the following people for their time and expertise. Harold Clumeck and Laurence Leonard offered extremely thorough and useful comments on an earlier draft of the manuscript. Steve Ebert, Emily Kessler, and Alison Teeter provided careful typing and word processing assistance. A comprehensive index was efficiently accomplished by Christine Dollaghan. A special note of thanks is due to Kit Hoffmann, who was an expert and tireless editorial assistant. Throughout all phases of this project, the staff at College-Hill Press has been responsive and supportive.

MLE

LDS

Part I

TERMS
AND
CONCEPTS

Introduction
to Phonology

Phonology is concerned with *sound systems* and *sound patterns*. A *phonologist* may study sound systems as diverse as those found in African languages, varieties of American English, such as the speech of people living in the Greater Boston area or the sound systems of children with developmental speech disorders. Before looking at the types of questions phonologists ask about sound systems, we need to look briefly at relationships between phonology and other components of language.

PHONOLOGY: A
LANGUAGE COMPONENT

Language can be defined as *a conventionalized and arbitrary system of symbols by which human beings communicate on an abstract level*. It has become traditional to study language as though it were divided into three somewhat independent components or systems: the semantic, syntactic, and phonologic. The *semantic* system of language involves the meanings of words and how these combine to form the meanings of longer utterances. The *syntactic* system concerns how words are put together to form phrases and sentences. Finally, the *phonologic* system of a language, as just introduced, concerns its sound patterns. All three systems of language interact with one another and we will have occasional need to discuss syntactic and semantic relationships to phonology in this text. *Pragmatics*, which is concerned with how language is used to communicate, has been the focus of considerable recent study. However, we will make only passing reference to relationships between phonology and pragmatics. For reasons of convenience, we will be dealing with the phonological component of language rather in isolation in this book, as has been done historically.

The purpose of this book is to describe the many phonological terms (Chapter 2), theories (Chapters 3-5), and applications (Chapters 6-8) that are important for speech-language pathologists to understand. In teaching this information, we have found it useful to have in mind a basic conception of the phonological component of language. Figure 1-1 is a scheme upon which we will be elaborating throughout this text. It represents a minimal conception of a phonological system and we will modify this conception as required. In this chapter, we will use this scheme only to introduce a few basic notions about the phonological component of language. With the understanding of these few notions, we can then proceed to list some of the questions phonologists pursue.

TWO LEVELS
OF PHONOLOGY

One important concept about the phonological component of language is that it has a minimum of two *levels*, as shown in Figure 1-1. The "bottom" level consists of the speech sounds we hear and produce, or *overt speech*. The other, "top" level, represents the formulation of sequences of sounds based on our knowledge of the phonological system of our language. We have become so used to hearing and producing speech that we need to be reminded that there is a *covert* level of knowledge that guides overt speech.

> *To enhance your appreciation of the complexity of speech processing, read aloud the following sentence: "I like to ride a bike." Now read it backwards and listen to the speech sounds you produce: "kib a dir ot kil I."*

FIGURE 1-1
A basic scheme illustrating the two levels of phonology: the underlying, covert level of phonological knowledge and the manifest, overt level of speech production

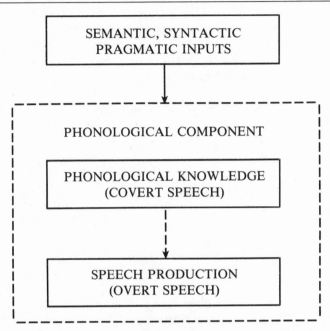

The first sentence in this example probably took you less than one second to read. The first time through the second sentence, however, probably took you three seconds or more. The sounds you heard yourself making were, in both cases, overt speech. Speech sounds are simply the product of muscular forces that generate noises. But the second sentence posed problems because you were required to do a lot more speech processing at the covert level (Figure 1-1). The written "words" were nonsense to you, e.g., *kib, dir*, and you were probably not sure how to pronounce the vowels. That is, should the *i* be pronounced as in *eat* or as in *kid*? The point to emphasize here is that we get so used to hearing and speaking that it is only when we are taxed in some way that we become aware of the speech processing involved. And for now we want to underscore that the processing of speech has to be viewed as a task that is associated with other levels of language. This covert level of speech formulation precedes what we hear and produce as manifest speech. It is the description of this covert level of processing that is the concern of much of phonology.

TWO COMPONENTS OF
COVERT PHONOLOGY

Two features of the covert level of speech processing have been described and are fairly well established as basic concepts among phonologists. The underlying phonology of any language apparently consists of at least (1) a set of meaningful sounds, and (2) rules for how these sounds may be used to make words. As the next example shows, all of us are quite familiar with the rules of English phonology if pressed to use them.

> *Suppose you have a word game wherein you are using letter tiles to spell words. You shake a container and spill out the following five tiles: R, T, A, S, T. How many words can you make using only these letters?*

Notice that here you are pressed to use your knowledge of the rules for making words in English. In particular, you must use your knowledge of which sounds are permitted to follow one another in English phonology. For example, a word can begin and end with the two consonants *st*, but English has certain rules for the sequencing of these two consonants. The sequence *ts* can occur at the end of a word, as can the sequence *st*. At the beginning of a word, however, only the sequence *st* may occur. That is, one of the rules of English phonology is that no words may begin with the sound sequence *ts*. Another language may have both sounds and may also allow particular words to begin with the sequence *ts*. Such "rules" are part of the covert knowledge possessed by speakers of a language, as represented in Figure 1-1 and as demonstrated in the example above. (For your interest, we made 10 common words from the letter combinations available in the example: *at, rat, rats, sat, tar, art, tart, tarts, star, start.*)

SYNCHRONIC AND
DIACHRONIC PHONOLOGY

One other pair of terms that it is convenient to introduce here are the terms *synchronic* and *diachronic*. When applied to the study of a language, or a person using a language, these terms refer to concepts of time. Synchronic phonology describes the phonology of a language or a person at one point in time, whereas diachronic phonology is concerned with two or more points in time. As we will see below, phonologists may be interested in one or both questions in the particular phonological phenomenon under study.

REASONS FOR STUDYING PHONOLOGY

There are many reasons for studying phonology; consequently, people from many different disciplines become involved in phonological research. Let us look briefly here at some common concerns and questions.

(1) Some linguists study phonology in order to work with "exotic" languages, for example, American Indian (Amerindian) languages, African languages, or Asian languages. These linguists often are concerned with analyzing a newly discovered language—determining its sound system and rules for use of that sound system. Moreover, phonologists may take on the task of giving a new language a written system by formulating an alphabet for it.

(2) Another reason that some linguists study phonology is to understand and describe language change and variation, for example, *synchronic* variation among regional and social dialects. When linguists study how sound systems change over time, this is a *diachronic* concern. Another type of language change that is studied concerns *pidgins* and *creoles*. Some linguists investigate the modifications (grammatical and lexical as well as phonological) that arise when pidginization and creolization take place. A pidgin is a simplified language that arises when speakers of two different languages need to communicate, for instance, for trade purposes. Pidgins based on English are found in Hawaii (Hawaiian Pidgin English), West Africa (West African Pidgin English), and numerous other areas. When a pidgin becomes a native language, that is, when children learn it as their first language, it is said to be creolized. For example, we find Jamaican Creole, and Gullah, which is the language

spoken by a group of Blacks living in the coastal areas and on the islands off the coast of South Carolina, Georgia, and Northeastern Florida. A creole based on French and Spanish is spoken by many people living in Southern Louisiana.

(3) Another reason for studying phonology is to understand phonological acquisition by children. For example, since the early 1970s a considerable amount of research concerning phonological acquisition by English-speaking, Spanish-speaking, and Chinese-speaking children has been conducted at Stanford University under the guidance of Charles Ferguson and others. Child phonologists are now investigating individual differences in phonological acquisition and are concerned with the relationship between phonological acquisition and other aspects of language development, cognitive development, and personality.

(4) In the late 1960s and early 1970s, a relatively small group of linguists and speech pathologists began studying phonological theory in order to describe severe articulation disorders from the viewpoint of phonology. This endeavor has become increasingly popular in recent years. Now, many people are attempting to increase our understanding of *phonological disorders* and to develop fairly sophisticated ways of analyzing the speech of unintelligible children so that such analyses may be used in planning management. More will be said about the normal acquisition of phonology and about phonological disorders later in this book.

(5) Phonology also is useful in foreign language teaching. Linguists have found that if they analyze and study the phonological system of the language they are teaching and compare it to the native language of the students, they are able to teach the foreign language more effectively and efficiently. Contrastive analysis allows them to focus on the ways in which the phonological systems of the two languages differ (Sloat, Taylor, & Hoard, 1978, p. 8). For instance, a person teaching English to native Japanese speakers knows from comparing the phonological systems of the two languages that the Japanese-speaking students are likely to have problems with the *l-r* distinction in English (because [l] and [r] are not distinctive sound units in Japanese). Armed with such knowledge, a teacher can anticipate potential problems and can save valuable time by arranging appropriate teaching materials.

(6) Another application of phonology is in the teaching of reading and spelling. Learning to read and write requires that the child establish a correspondence between sound units (phonemes) and written units (graphemes) (Dale, 1976, p. 224). Decoding (in reading) and encoding (in writing) involves knowledge of the phonological rules of a language. For example, it is necessary to know that *g* may have either of two different sounds, depending on the following vowel, and that the "soft *g*" sound may be written with either *g* or *j*, as in *Gene* and *jam*. Although English does not have a one-to-one correspondence between phonemes and graphemes, fairly consistent rules govern the variations. It is these rules that children must master as they learn to read and write. (See Dale, 1976 for a more detailed discussion.)

CONCLUSION

Phonology is the study of the sound component of language. Phonologists may study languages or language users. Some major questions that phonologists ask concern the sound system of a language: Which sounds are used and what are the rules for combining sounds to make words? Speech-language pathologists recently have become interested in these activities, particularly as phonological insights lead to more effective assessment and management techniques. As with so many other topics about which people interested in applied linguistics must be informed, the subdiscipline of linguistics termed *phonology* must be approached in a systematic fashion. The purpose of this text is to provide the reader with a thorough introduction to phonology and related concerns.

2

Structures and General Concerns of Phonology

The purpose of this chapter is to introduce some basic terms and concepts in phonology. First, four components of phonology are discussed—segments, suprasegmentals, syllables, and phonotactics. Next some general concerns of phonology are posed. Information in this chapter provides the foundation for materials in Part II, History of Phonology, and Part III, Applications of Phonology.

PHONOLOGICAL COMPONENTS

Segments

The term *segment*, as used by linguists and speech scientists, is usually equivalent to *speech sound*. However, in some contexts, the term segment denotes only a section of a speech sound. For example, the acoustic phonetician (to be described) uses the term segment to refer to a specific portion of a sound wave or a section of audio tape. In other contexts, the phonologist may wish to talk about an abstract hypothetical segment. Such abstract segments are usually called *phonemes*. In this book we use segment to refer to both phonetic segments (phones) and phonological segments (phonemes).

Segments or speech sounds constitute the fundamental structure or component of the phonology of a language. Although theorists disagree as to whether the segment is the basic unit of perception or production, there is general agreement that the segment is a central construct in the study of phonology. Phonologists are interested in learning the answers to at least five questions concerning the segments of a language:

(1) Which segments are "meaningful" in a language?

(2) How are meaningful segments represented at the underlying (covert) level of phonology?

(3) How are meaningful segments in a language permitted to combine to make syllables and words?

(4) How are meaningful segments described as they occur at the manifest (overt) level of phonology?

(5) What are the rules that derive overt segments from covert segments?

It is convenient to arrange discussion of these questions by first considering the task of describing manifest speech (the fourth question above). This task has traditionally been in the province of a companion discipline to phonology called *phonetics*.

Phonetics

The discipline of phonetics is concerned with describing and classifying speech sounds as they are actually produced. At least three ways to pursue these objectives can be distinguished.

Perceptual phonetics describes speech by means of phonetic transcription systems and involves training people to transcribe speech. Linguists who attempt to describe the speech patterns of a language must be highly skilled in phonetic transcription. Similarly, speech-language pathologists must learn to transcribe reliably the speech of people with communication disorders. In this book we will be using a phonetic transcription system described by Shriberg and Kent (1982). The phonetic symbols in the Shriberg and Kent system are primarily those of the International

Phonetic Alphabet. However, all symbols, including special *diacritic markings* (symbols that modify phonetic symbols) were selected and arranged to meet the transcription needs of speech-language pathologists.

Acoustic phonetics describes the acoustic components of speech by means of instruments that store and display sound waves. Acoustic records of speech have many desirable features. For example, some important speech events last only a few milliseconds, far too short for reliable phonetic transcription. With a device such as a sound spectrograph, measurements at this level of sensitivity can be made. Present-day computers can be programmed to complete with a high degree of reliability a variety of acoustic analyses of speech events.

Articulatory phonetics, the third approach to the description of speech sounds, focuses on the positions and movements of the speech structures as speech is produced. What follows is a highly condensed articulatory description of the consonant and vowel/diphthong segments of American English. This discussion and the accompanying illustrations are considered in detail in Shriberg and Kent (1982). (See MacKay, 1978, for a discussion of other subdisciplines within phonetics.)

Consonant Segments in English. Speech sounds generally are classified according to the amount of obstruction in the *vocal tract* (the cavities between the vocal folds and the lips) during their production. Consonant sounds are produced with a relatively large amount of blockage or obstruction. Vowel sounds are produced with a more open vocal tract. As illustrated in Figure 2-1, consonants traditionally have been described according to place of articulation, manner of articulation, and voicing.

Place of articulation. Place or point of articulation refers to the place in the vocal tract (usually in the mouth) at which the greatest constriction is found. For example, in the production of a *bilabial* sound (e.g. /b/; see Figure 2-1) the closure is at the lips, while for a *velar* sound (e.g. /g/) the place of constriction is at the *velum* or soft palate. As shown in Figure 2-1, English consonants require constriction at one of seven places along the vocal tract, from the lips to the glottal area, which includes the vocal folds.

Manner of articulation. Manner of articulation (see the vertical axis, Figure 2-1) refers to the way in which a sound is produced. This is generally described in terms of the amount of blockage in the vocal tract during sound production. Sounds produced with complete blockage are called *stops* or *plosives*. English has a set of six (phonemic) oral stops /b, p, d, t, g, k/, and a (nonphonemic) glottal stop [ʔ] that occurs in certain speech contexts. Sounds produced with the articulators close enough together to cause friction in the air stream are called *fricatives* or

FIGURE 2-1
The consonant sounds of English. Place of articulation is described along the horizontal axis, and manner of articulation and voicing are indicated along the vertical axis. Reproduced from L. D. Shriberg and R. D. Kent, *Clinical Phonetics*. New York: John Wiley & Sons, 1982.

PLACE

MANNER			Bilabial	Labiodental	Dental	Alveolar	Palatal	Velar	Glottal
Obstruents	Stops	voiced	b			d		g	ʔ
		voiceless	p			t		k	
	Fricatives	voiced		v	ð	z	ʒ		
		voiceless		f	θ	s	ʃ		h
	Affricates	voiced					dʒ		
		voiceless					tʃ		
Nonobstruents or sonorants		nasal	m			n		ŋ	
		lateral				l			
		rhotic					r		
		glide	w[a]				j	w[a]	

[a]This sound has constrictions in both the bilabial and velar places, as does its voiceless cognate /ʍ/.

spirants. English has nine fricative sounds: /v, f, ð, θ, z, s, ʒ, ʃ, h/ (/h/ is sometimes classified as a glide). The fricatives /z, s, ʒ, ʃ/ are called *sibilants*. They are characterized by more high frequency energy (or noisiness), giving the hissing sound characteristic of their production. English has two *affricates*, or sounds that begin like stops but are released with frication, /dʒ, tʃ/. These affricates are also classified as sibilants.

Nasal sounds /m, n, ŋ/ are produced with complete closure somewhere in the oral cavity; thus they are actually *nasal stops*, but the passage into the nasal cavity is open. That is, the velum is lowered and air passes into the nasal cavity.

Sounds that are produced with some narrowing or approximation in the vocal tract, but not enough to cause friction are called *approximants* or *frictionless continuants* (MacKay, 1978, p. 122). Linguists differ as to the classification of the four English sounds of this type, /l, r, w, j/. /l/ is the only English sound that is made by emitting the air laterally over the front of the tongue, and /r/ is the only consonant sound that has a "rhotic" quality. In some systems /l/ and /r/ are called *liquids*, in distinction to /w/ and /j/ which are called *semivowels* or *glides*. Whereas /l/ and /r/ have static positions during production, there is transition or movement (i.e., gliding) from one articulatory position to another during the production of /w/ and /j/. Approximants (liquids and glides) along with nasals and vowels are sometimes referred to as *sonorants*.

Voicing. Voicing refers to the vibration of the vocal folds during sound production. If the vocal folds are vibrating, the sound is *voiced* and if they are not vibrating, the sound is *voiceless* or *unvoiced*. *True consonants* or *obstruents* (stops, affricates, and fricatives) occur in voiced/voiceless cognate pairs produced at the same place of articulation and with the same manner of production. For example, the voiced stops in English are /b, d, g/ and the corresponding voiceless stops are /p, t, k/ (see Figure 2-1). The more vowel-like consonants, the sonorants (nasals, liquids, and glides), nearly always are voiced.

English voiced stops are produced with less *intraoral air pressure* (pressure in the mouth) than the corresponding voiceless stops. Thus English voiced stops are sometimes called *lenis*, and English voiceless stops are termed *fortis* (MacKay, 1978, p. 118). (However, the lenis/fortis distinction does not correspond to the voiced/voiceless distinction in all languages.)

Vowel and Diphthong Segments in English. *Vowels*, speech sounds produced with little obstruction in the vocal tract, traditionally have been classified by tongue height, tongue position, and lip rounding. Figure 2-2 illustrates how vowels are classified by means of these three parameters. Tongue height—high, mid, or low—refers to the degree to which the highest part of the tongue approaches the roof of the mouth. This also corresponds to the degree of jaw opening. The highest vowels in English are /i/ and /u/. Tongue position—front, central, or back—refers to the point along the roof of the mouth at which the highest part of the tongue is found during the production of a vowel. For instance, /i/ is produced in the palatal region (front) while /u/ is produced in the velar region (back). Lip rounding in English is associated mainly with the high and mid back vowels /u, ʊ, o, ɔ/.

FIGURE 2-2
The vowel sounds of English. Tongue position is indicated along the horizontal axis and tongue height along the vertical axis. Reproduced from L. D. Shriberg and R. D. Kent. *Clinical Phonetics.* **New York: John Wiley & Sons, 1982.**

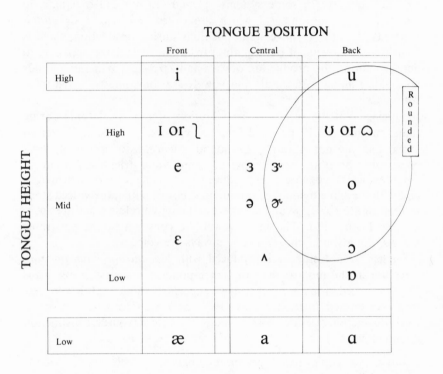

Vowels also may be classified according to the degree of muscular tension involved in their production. *Tense* vowels (for example /i, e, o, u/) are said to be produced with more tension in the muscles of the vocal tract, especially the tongue, while *lax* vowels such as /ɪ, ɛ, ʊ/ are produced with less muscular tension. (This view has, however, been challenged e.g., see Ladefoged, 1968; MacKay, 1977.) Tense vowels generally are held for a longer period of time and are perceptually more distinct than lax vowels. For instance, the tense vowel /i/ (as in the word *seat*) is longer than the corresponding lax vowel /ɪ/ (as in the word *sit*). Ladefoged (1975, pp. 203–204) uses the terms *narrow* and *wide*, which refer to the width of the pharynx, with wide corresponding somewhat to tense, at least for high vowels.

English also has five *diphthongs* or sequences of two vowel sounds together in the same syllable: /aɪ, aʊ, ɔɪ, eɪ, oʊ/. As discussed later, only the first three diphthongs are used to differentiate words in English, whereas the last two are stressed variants of the vowels /e/ and /o/, respectively.

Diacritic Marking of English Consonants and Vowels/Diphthongs. During production of sounds there may be a different degree of obstruction, a slight change in place of obstruction, a secondary articulation, or some other change in production. For example, a vowel could be nasalized or accompanied by lip rounding. To describe such changes, and to provide for more phonetic detail about normally articulated segments, phoneticians use *diacritic* marks. Figure 2-3 is a complete list of the diacritic marks used to describe the speech of people with both normal and disordered speech (Shriberg & Kent, 1982). For example, the diacritic [ʰ] (aspirated) is added to a voiceless stop symbol to represent the slight air escape (or "puff" of air) that is normally heard after the release of a word-initial voiceless stop, as in the word *to* [tʰu]. Notice that in the word *stew* [st⁼u] the diacritic [⁼] (unaspirated) is added to indicate that there is no such air release following the stop in this phonetic environment. In perceptual phonetics, the transcriber has the option of using *broad phonetic transcription*, which ignores such detail, or *narrow phonetic description*, which captures this information by means of diacritics.

Coarticulation. This overview of the articulatory phonetics of English phonology would be incomplete without brief mention of speech segments in the context of continuous speech. *Coarticulation* concerns interactions among sounds during speech production. Although speakers of English think of words as being separated into discrete sound segments (e.g., *cat* /k/ + /æ/ + /t/) we do not in reality merely produce one sound, pause, and then quickly produce another (Schane, 1973, p. 4). There is actually "a continuous flow of activity," so that adjacent articulatory movements merge or overlap (Dew & Jensen, 1977, p. 116). As we produce one sound, we are getting ready for and moving toward the position for the next sound. The result is that the sounds influence each other. For instance, the /k/ in *cool* is produced with *labialization* because of the following rounded vowel. Coarticulation increases as our rate of speech increases. Indeed, children acquiring speech must learn to maintain intelligible phonetic "targets" while increasing the length, complexity, and speed of their utterances in conversational speech.

FIGURE 2-3
Diacritic marks for phonetic transcription. The numbers 1 to 4 indicate the placement of each diacritic around the consonant, vowel, or diphthong symbol it modifies. Reproduced from L. D. Shriberg and R. D. Kent, *Clinical Phonetics.* **New York: John Wiley & Sons, 1982.**

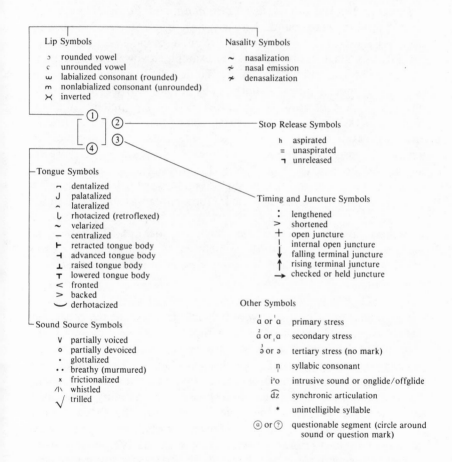

Phonology

In the introduction to this chapter, five questions about segments were said to be of interest to phonologists. We have just considered one question—ways to describe speech sounds as they occur in manifest speech. We now take up two of the other questions: Which segments are "meaningful" in a language, and how are segments represented at the underlying, covert level of phonology? In later sections we will discuss the remaining questions: How are segments permitted to combine to form syllables and words, and what are the rules that derive overt segments from covert segments?

Phonemes and Allophones. In every language some sound differences are "linguistically significant" and some are not (Schane, 1973, p. 5). Out of the many sound differences available for use in contrasting words, only a few are actually used in any one language to make lexical contrasts, i.e., to keep vocabulary items apart (Hyman, 1975). For example, in English the difference between /t/ and /d/—one of voicing—is a *distinctive* difference that keeps many pairs of words apart. So we find *minimal pairs* (words that differ in just one sound and also differ in meaning) such as *toe/doe, tip/dip*, and *tie/die*. However, as described in an earlier example, a phonetic difference such as that between aspirated /t/ ([tʰ]) and unaspirated /t/ ([t⁼]) is not significant in English. Instead, it is *redundant*; we can predict where aspiration will occur: Voiceless stops (/p, t, k/) are aspirated only in certain contexts or environments, primarily in word-initial position preceding a stressed vowel, as in *tell* [tʰɛl], *pill* [pʰɪl], and *kick* [kʰɪk]. In many languages, however, aspiration is *distinctive* or *significant*. There are pairs of words that differ in meaning and differ phonetically only in the presence or absence of aspiration on a voiceless stop. This is the case in Thai, for instance. To illustrate, [tʰam] means "to do" and contrasts minimally with [t⁼am], which means "to pound" (Ladefoged, 1975, p. 126). Thus /tʰ/ and /t⁼/ are separate *phonemes* in Thai, but in English they are *allophones* of the phoneme /t/. That is, in Thai, each variant is used distinctively, whereas in English both phonetic variants belong to the phoneme /t/ (i.e., they are allophones of /t/).[1]

Because languages differ in their inventories of meaningful sounds, second language acquisition is easier if the new language has phonemic distinctions that are similar to those in the first language. For example, native speakers of Spanish typically consider English /d/ and /ð/ to be only allophones of /d/, as they are in Spanish. In Spanish, [d] occurs only after /n/ or in a phrase-initial position, and [ð] occurs elsewhere (although this varies somewhat in different dialects). In English, we find *minimal pairs* such as *den* [dɛn] and *then* [ðɛn]; hence /d/ and /ð/ are separate phonemes. Similarly, native Japanese speakers have trouble learning to consistently keep English /l/ and /r/ apart in their speech, for example saying [pirōū] for *pillow* and [rʌk] for *luck*. This is because [l] and [r] are not distinctive sound units or phonemes in Japanese, as mentioned earlier, while they are separate phonemes in English, as shown by minimal pairs such as *lip/rip* and *pilot/pirate*.

Representation of Phonemes. If manifest speech sounds (phones) are represented by the phonetician using phonetic transcription and place-manner-voicing systems, how are phonemes represented? Recall that this is a question about speech segments that earlier we said was a major concern of phonologists. The answer is not straightforward, for unlike the rather universal acceptance of some type of place-manner-voicing system to describe manifest speech sounds, representation of abstract phonemes varies greatly among phonological approaches. For this reason, it is more convenient to take up such questions in Part II, directly within historical reviews of the many approaches to phonology.

Summary

Segments are assumed to exist at two levels. The lower, or manifest speech level, is described by phoneticians who use perceptual phonetics, acoustic phonetics, and articulatory phonetic descriptions to describe and classify each sound. The upper level consists, in part, of an inventory of sounds that are distinctive in a language, and a set of rules for sequencing those sounds to make syllables and words. "Phonotactics," which concerns the rules for sequencing sounds, is more conveniently discussed later in this chapter after we have examined some information about suprasegmentals and syllables.

Suprasegmentals

Suprasegmentals or *prosodic elements* are said to differ from sound segments in that they are "superimposed on" or "distributed over" a string of segments, syllables, or words, hence the term, suprasegmentals (Lehiste, 1970). Length, tone (and intonation), and stress customarily have been classified as suprasegmentals.

Length

Length is a perceptual term, while *duration* refers to the actual amount of time that a sound lasts. Absolute duration can be measured easily on a spectrogram or some other visual representation of the acoustic characteristics of speech. Some sounds are naturally longer than others. Lehiste (1970) calls this *intrinsic duration*. For example, low vowels tend to be longer than high vowels, and fricatives are longer than stops. The duration of a sound also may be influenced by neighboring sounds. To illustrate, English vowels are longer before voiced consonants than before voiceless consonants and are longer before fricatives than stops. Thus, /i/ is longer in *seed* than in *seat* and is still longer in *seize*. In English a vowel is longer when it is stressed than when it is not stressed, indicating that suprasegmentals may interact.

Many languages have short and long vowels and/or consonants, and the differences in length affect the meanings of the words. That is, length is *contrastive* or *phonemic*. For example, Finnish has long and short vowels, and Italian has a length contrast for consonants as in [fóla] *fable* vs. [fól:a] *crowd* (Ladefoged, 1975, p. 223). Long consonants and vowels may be represented in feature notation as [+ / − long] or by other means, such as V̄, C̄; VV, CC; or V:, C:.[2]

Tone and Intonation

Tone and intonation are related to the rate of vibration of the vocal folds, which can be controlled by the rate of airflow through the *glottis* (the opening between the vocal folds) and by the tension of the muscles of the larynx. The acoustic correlate of tone and intonation is the fundamental frequency of the sound wave, or the number of complete cycles (openings and closings of the vocal folds) in a unit of time (Lehiste, 1970, p. 60). Frequency is measured in cycles per second, called hertz (Hz). For example, the average fundamental frequency of adult female voices is about 220 Hz or 220 openings and closings of the vocal folds per second.

The perceptual term related to frequency is *pitch*. The relationship between frequency and perceived pitch is not a simple one, but in general, the higher the frequency, the higher the perceived pitch. Our ears respond to relative differences in frequency. This means that the same tonal patterns and intonation signals can be used by people with high voices and people with low voices (Lehiste, 1970).

There are several phonetic factors that may influence pitch. For example, high vowels such as /i/ and /u/ have an intrinsically higher pitch than the lower vowels because of the connections between the muscles of the tongue and the larynx. In some languages, stressed vowels are produced with a higher fundamental frequency than unstressed vowels, again indicating an interaction among suprasegmentals (Lehiste, 1970).

Tone refers to the function of fundamental frequency on the word level (Lehiste, 1970). That is, pitch differences may be used to signal differences in word meaning. Languages that use pitch this way are called *tone languages*. Such languages include many Asian languages, like Thai, Vietnamese, and Chinese, and many African languages, such as Hausa, Nupe, and Igbo. Some tone languages have *register tones*. This means that they use flat tones on different levels (e.g. high, mid, and low). If a language uses contrastive tonal movements, such as rising, falling, and rising-falling, it is said to have *contour tones*. Most tone languages use a combination of register and contour tones.

The function of fundamental frequency on the phrase, sentence, or discourse level is called *intonation* (MacKay, 1978). According to Ladefoged

(1975, p. 225) all languages use intonation. A change in intonation changes the meaning of an entire utterance. For example, the words *You're going* constitute a statement or command if they are said with a falling intonation, but if they are said with a rising intonation, *You're going?*, they make up a question that requires an answer of "yes" or "no" (a *yes-no question*). So intonation is often related to syntactic structure. The last sentence in a discourse has a relatively large drop in pitch, indicating that the speaker has finished talking (MacKay, 1978, p. 218).

Stress

Stress (sometimes called *accent* or *emphasis*) is a complicated phonetic phenomenon that appears to be related to increased muscular effort and subglottal pressure (Lehiste, 1970). Among other things, increased effort increases the intensity of the sound wave, which is measured in decibels (dB). Thus stressed syllables are perceived as being louder than unstressed syllables. However, the relationship between stress and *loudness* is not a simple one, because physically equal increases in effort do not result in equal increases in loudness. As with all suprasegmentals, stress depends on comparison (Lehiste, 1970). So, we need at least two syllables in order to talk about stress. Stressed syllables are produced with greater articulatory precision and are more "prominent" than unstressed syllables, and vowels in unstressed syllables tend to be "reduced" (MacKay, 1978, p. 142). Duration is an important clue to the identification of stress in English because stressed vowels, as just noted, are generally longer than unstressed vowels. Aspiration is another clue to stress in English, due to the fact that voiceless stops (not preceded by /s/) are quite heavily aspirated when they precede a stressed vowel.

It is often possible to distinguish at least three levels of word stress: *primary* (or main stress), *secondary*, and *tertiary* (or weak). There are several systems for marking word stress. Stressed vowels may be indicated by the use of accent marks as follows: V́, V̀, and V̂ represent primary, secondary, and tertiary stress, respectively. Another system (which is a part of the International Phonetic Alphabet) involves the use of a short vertical line to the left of the stressed syllable, ['] for primary stress and [ˌ] for secondary stress. Tertiary stress is not marked. To illustrate, a word like *diminish* could be marked in either of the following ways: [də́mínìʃ] or [dəˈmɪnˌɪʃ]. As this example shows, a disadvantage of the IPA system is that it necessitates dividing a word into syllables. In the Shriberg and Kent system (see Figure 2-3) stress is marked by writing the number corresponding to the stress level above the syllable. The example above would be written [dəmínɪʃ]. In this system, words do not have to be divided into syllables.

Word stress has several possible linguistic functions, and it is used differently in different languages. Languages in which syllables differ in prominence are called *stress languages* (Sloat, et al., 1978, p. 71). In some languages, stress is fixed on a certain morpheme or is determined by rules that stress a particular syllable. German has fixed morphological stress to a large extent; verb stems are stressed and generally remain stressed even when prefixes and suffixes are added (Lehiste, 1970, p. 149). Spanish has primarily rule-governed stress. If stress falls on a syllable other than the one predicted by the rule, it has to be marked (MacKay, 1978, p. 149), as in dialectal *quió*, but not *quiero*. In some languages stress signals word boundaries. This is true of Polish, which has stress on the penultimate (next-to-the-last) syllable of a word, and Turkish, in which the last syllable of a word is usually stressed (Hyman, 1975, p. 204).

In some languages, such as English, stress is largely unpredictable and must be learned for each separate word. In such languages, stress can be phonemic. In other words, the primary phonetic difference between two words that differ in meaning may be a difference in stress. English has a fairly large group of words which may be used either as nouns or verbs that illustrate this point. For this group of words, the stress falls on the first syllable (a prefix such as *con-*, *pro-*, *re-*, *de-*, etc.) if the word is a noun, but if the word is a verb, the stress falls on the second syllable (or stem). So we find many noun-verb pairs such as convict-convict, progress-progress, insert-insert, rebel-rebel, desert-desert, permit-permit, etc. (The vowel differences that also appear are directly related to the stress differences, as unstressed vowels in English are nearly always reduced to [ə].)

Sometimes a syllable other than the one that is usually stressed is given *contrastive stress* in order to differentiate the word from a similar sounding word with which it could be confused, for example, "I said *reform* not *deform*."

Stress also functions on the phrase level and on the sentence level as well as on the word level in English. Short phrases often have distinctive stress patterns related to the relations between the words that constitute the phrase (MacKay, 1978, p. 210). For instance, phrases made up of an adjective plus a noun usually have primary stress on the noun and secondary stress on the adjective, as in *black bird* and *English teacher*. This stress pattern differs from the stress pattern of compound nouns such as *blackbird* and *English teacher* in which the first element has primary stress and the second has secondary or tertiary stress (MacKay, 1978).

In English sentences, content words (nouns, verbs, etc.) are usually stressed more heavily than function words (prepositions, conjunctions, etc.). Four levels of sentence stress can sometimes be distinguished: primary ('), secondary (`), tertiary (â), and weak (unmarked) (MacKay, 1978, p. 211). Changes in sentence stress affect the meaning of the sentence but not the meaning of the individual words. Sentence stress, like word stress, can be *contrastive*. For example, the meaning of the sentence, "Tom didn't hit Bill" changes considerably depending on which word receives the primary stress, e.g., "Tom didn't hit Bill. (He hit Jáck)." A word may also be stressed simply for emphasis as in "Look at that moon!"

The Syllable

Description

The role of the syllable as a phonological unit is difficult to define because linguists disagree regarding its status and importance in phonology. Structurally, however, it can be described easily. A syllable may have three parts: an *onset* (or *releasing consonant*), a *peak* or *nucleus*, and a *coda* or *offset*, also called the *arresting consonant* (Hyman, 1978, p. 188). The *peak* and *coda* are often considered together as the *core* (Pike & Pike, 1947). The only part of a syllable that must be present is the *nucleus* or *peak*. In other words, every syllable must have one or more vowels. The vowel is the most prominent part of the syllable and it takes the stress. Although consonants often may initiate and/or terminate a syllable, they are not essential. A syllable may be made up of just one vowel but not one consonant alone under ordinary circumstances (although under some conditions, a nasal or liquid can form the peak of a syllable). The indefinite article *a* is an example of a word that consists of just one syllable made up of a single vowel. Such a syllable may be represented as V. A word like *do* (/du/) is also *monosyllabic* (having just one syllable), but this syllable contains a consonant onset plus a vowel. This type of syllable is represented as CV. Syllables that end in a vowel, such as V, CV, and CCV are called *open syllables*.

A syllable that ends in one or more consonants is called a *closed syllable*. The vowel nucleus is "arrested" by a consonant or *consonant cluster*, a sequence of two or more consonants in the same syllable (or *tautosyllabic*). The word *bit* [bɪt] is made up of one closed syllable and can be represented as CVC. *Belt* [bɛlt] and *fork* [fɔrk] each contain one syllable of the shape CVCC. The syllable is closed by a consonant cluster. (As these examples show, C may represent a liquid, nasal, or glide as well as a true consonant.) The word *ask* [æsk] is made up of a VCC syllable; there is no consonant onset, but the coda is made up of two consonants. A word such as *black* [blæk] or *creep* [krip] has one syllable of the shape CCVC; the onset consists of a consonant cluster.

Technically, all syllables must contain a vowel, but this vowel may be reduced, especially in connected speech, being produced as a schwa ([ə]). Occasionally, a nasal or a liquid alone may constitute a syllable. For instance, the word *button* may be produced as [bʌʔn̩] and *little* is often [lɪtl̩]. In these cases, the nucleus of the second syllable is a *syllabic nasal* or *liquid*.

Words such as *apple* and *playing* that contain two syllables are called *disyllabic*, and words with three or more syllables are called *polysyllabic* or *multisyllabic* (e.g., *elephant, telephone, incomprehensible*).

It is possible to distinguish *strong* and *weak syllables* and also *strong* and *weak positions* within syllables. For example, a strong syllable is one whose core contains a long vowel and optional coda, or a short vowel and a long consonant, or a short vowel plus two consonants. A weak syllable, on the other hand, is one whose core contains a short vowel followed by not more than one short consonant (Sloat, et al., 1978, pp. 64–65). To illustrate, *bay* (CV:), *bead* (CV:C), and *bend* (CVCC) would be strong syllables, while the last syllable in *tuba* (CV) would be a weak syllable.

A similar distinction that is sometimes made is between *heavy* and *light* syllables. A heavy syllable is one whose core contains a long vowel, a sequence of vowels, or a vowel plus a consonant (or some combination of these elements). A light syllable is one whose core contains only a short vowel. In many languages, only heavy syllables can be stressed (Hyman, 1975, p. 206).

A vowel immediately following a stressed syllable in English (a *posttonic* vowel) is said to be in a weak position (e.g., see Schane, 1973, p. 57). Vowels in such positions are often deleted. For example, we find [fæmlɪ] for *family* and [ɪntrɪst] for *interest*. Similarly, children often drop the posttonic syllable of a multisyllabic word, as in [ɛfət] for *elephant*. (It should be noted that children also may drop an unstressed *pretonic* syllable, i.e. one that precedes a stressed syllable, as in [nænə] for *banana*.) Word-final position is also said to be a weak position. Thus, word-final consonants are more likely to be lost than are word-initial consonants (Hyman, 1975, p. 18). For example, children acquiring speech normally might produce [kæ] for *cat* or [dɑ] for *dog*; only rarely might they produce these words as [æt] or [ɑg], respectively, with the initial consonant deleted.

Evidence for CV as
the Basic Syllable Structure

Many different syllable shapes are possible, for example, CVC, VC, CCVCC, VCCC, and so forth. The "basic" or "most natural" syllable shape is said to be CV, presumably because the ideal articulatory contrast is between a closed and an open vocal tract (Hyman, 1975).

Various types of evidence may be cited to show that CV is the preferred or basic syllable structure. First, it is acquired earliest by children. Children's earliest words are often simple CV or CVCV *reduplicated* forms, such as *mama, dada,* etc. At early stages, children usually simplify adult words with more complex syllable shapes to produce CV or CVCV sequences. As noted above, for example, *dog* may be produced as [dɑ] and *cat* as [kæ], with omission of the final consonant. *Clown* may be [kaʊ], *block* [bɑ], and *spoon* [pu], with reduction of the consonant cluster to one element, and loss of the final consonant, giving a CV syllable. Somewhat later, children may insert an *epenthetic* vowel, usually [ə], to break up a consonant cluster, as in [bəlu] for *blue* and [gərɪn] for *green* (Greenlee, 1974).

Evidence regarding the "favored" status of CV syllables is also found in diachronic change and in synchronic variation among social or geographical dialects. For instance, in modern English, the *t* in *hasten* is not pronounced. The *st* sequence has been simplified to [s], giving a CV sequence. In some dialects of English, people may insert an epenthetic vowel between two adjacent consonants, as in /fɪləm/ for *film* and [æθəlit] for *athlete*, again giving the preferred CV shape (see also Schane, 1973, p. 54).

Other cases can be cited in which consistent sound changes operate to simplify a more complex syllable structure to a sequence of consonant plus vowel or vowel plus consonant. For example, when two vowels would come together as in *you are*, one is often omitted; so we find *you're*, etc. Similarly, when an *-ist* ending is added to a noun that ends in a vowel, the final vowel of the noun is lost, as in *pianist* and *cellist*, rather than *pianoist and *celloist (Schane, 1973, p. 53).[3] The indefinite article in English has variant forms, *a* ([ə] or [eɪ]) and *an* ([ən] or [æn]). The V form is used before a noun that begins with a consonant, while the VC form is used before a vowel-initial noun, so we find *a boy*, but *an ear*. Again a sequence of consonant plus vowel is produced.

In dialects of English that drop word-final or preconsonantal *r*'s or "*r-less dialects,*" (e.g. in parts of New England and the Southeastern United States), /r/ is most likely to be dropped at the end of an utterance or when it precedes a word with an initial consonant, and it is less likely to be dropped when it precedes a vowel-initial word. Thus we find, "I met his *brother*" [brʌðə], but "His *brother* [brʌðɚ] is leaving." In some of these dialects we also find intrusive *r*'s being inserted where they do not belong to break up a sequence of final /ə/ followed by an initial vowel, as in "Cuba [kjubɚ] is less than 100 miles from Florida [flɔrɪdə] " (Schane, 1973, p. 54).

Another piece of evidence indicating that CV is the most basic syllable shape is the fact that it is the most widespread in phonological systems. In fact, one of Roman Jakobson's (1941/1968) "universals" to be discussed later in this chapter, is that all languages have CV syllables. This is not true of any other syllable shape, such as VC, CVC, etc. So, there is considerable evidence that CV is the most "natural" or "basic" syllable shape (e.g., see Hyman, 1975, pp. 161–164).

Phonotactics

Recall that the phonological component of a language contains an inventory of distinctive sound segments and rules for combining those segments. Having discussed issues related to three of the questions posed at the onset of this section on phonological structures, we now can proceed to consider another question: How are distinctive segments permitted to combine to make syllables and words?

In any given language, there are constraints or restrictions on where certain sounds can occur in a syllable or word and on the sequences of sounds that can occur. Several different terms are used in this connection: *syllable structure conditions* or *constraints, sequential constraints, morpheme structure conditions* (MSC), *phonotactic constraints*, or just *phonotactics*. It should be pointed out that these terms are not equivalent, although they are very similar in meaning. *Phonotactics* and *phonotactic constraints* are the most general terms referring to constraints on the position of occurrence of sounds, as well as on combinations and possible orders. *Sequential constraints*, as the name implies, involve restrictions on sequences of phonemes or sounds. The other terms listed here are more complicated. *Syllable structure conditions* or *constraints* are constraints on the number and combination of phonemes that can occur in a syllable, as well as constraints on the position of occurrence of a phoneme. The syllable structure constraints of English are discussed in more detail below. There has been some disagreement as to whether sequential constraints should be stated in terms of morphemes (meaning units) or syllables. In many cases, it does not matter whether sequential restrictions are stated in terms of syllables or morphemes. In the following sections, restrictions are generally stated in terms of syllable structure constraints.

It should be noted that phonologists also talk about *segmental constraints*, which "rule out" certain segments in a particular language. Such constraints can be phonetic and/or phonological. For instance, English has a segmental constraint that prohibits velar fricatives from occurring phonetically. Nasal vowel phonemes are prohibited in English, but nasalized vowels do occur phonetically (see Hyman, 1975, p. 10).

English Phonotactics

English has several constraints concerning where specific sounds can occur. For instance, /ŋ/ in English is always in syllable-final position as in *thing* and *singer*.⁴ (Stampe 1972a noted the difficulty that native English speakers have with foreign words such as *Nguyen* that have /ŋ/ in initial position.) In contrast, /h/ occurs only in syllable-initial position, as in *hanger* and *ahead*. The voiced alveolo-palatal fricative /ʒ/ is also limited in its occurrence in English, as it cannot occur in word-initial position (although it may be produced in initial position in words borrowed from French, such as *genre*). English also has an important vowel restriction; only tense vowels can occur word-finally in stressed open syllables. So we have, for example, *me* [mi] and *who* [hu], but not [mɪ], [mʊ] or [hɪ], [hʊ]. When lax vowels are stressed, they can occur only in closed syllables, as in *admit* and *pudding* (Schane, 1973, p. 13).

There are also restrictions on the number of consonants that can occur in syllable-initial position and syllable-final position in English. A syllable may begin with up to three consonants, but not four or more. In addition, there are restrictions on the types of consonants that can occur in the same syllable (*tautosyllabic*) and the order in which they can occur. If a sequence of two consonants releases (begins) a syllable, the consonant cluster can be made up of (1) a stop plus a liquid or glide, such as /pl, tr, bj/, (2) /s/ plus a voiceless stop /sp, st, sk/ or a front nasal /sm, sn/, (3) a fricative (usually voiceless) plus a liquid or glide e.g., /fl, fr, θr, sl, fj, sw/, (4) a front nasal plus /j/ (e.g., /mj/), (5) in rare cases, /ʃ/ plus a liquid, as in *shrimp* (MacKay, 1978, pp. 202–203).

If a syllable-initial cluster has three elements, the first must be /s/, the second must be a voiceless stop, and the third must be a liquid or glide (/l, r, w, j/). However, glides are more restricted than liquids in such clusters and not all possible combinations can occur. For instance, if the stop is /t/, only /r/ can occur as the third element as in *string*. And in most dialects of American English, if the glide in the third position is [j], the stop is [p] or [k], and the vowel is [u], as in *spew* and *skewer* (however, compare British English [stju]). If the glide is [w], the stop is [k], as in *squid* and *squash*. Whereas initial /skr/, as in *scream* and *scratch*, is common in English, initial /stl/ does not occur and /skl/ is not considered to be "well-formed," although it does appear in a few "learned" words such as *sclerosis* (Hyman, 1975, p. 11). Note that children learning English and also people with articulation problems may produce sequences that do not occur in standard adult English, such as *[tw] for /tr/ in *string, stripes*, etc.

If a word obeys the syllable structure conditions of a given language, it is said to be "well-formed," while a word that does not adhere to the constraints is said to be "ill-formed." A few words that are technically ill-formed may, however, be found in a language. *Sphere*, with its initial /sf/ cluster and *sclerosis*, mentioned above, are examples from English (Hyman, 1975, p. 20).

If a form obeys the phonotactic constraints of a language, and yet is not a real word in that language, there is an *accidental gap*. For example, *flig* is a "possible" English word because it obeys the phonotactic constraints of English. If a form is not allowed by the phonotactics of a language (i.e. is ill-formed), there is said to be a *systematic gap*. For example, */tlʌm/ and */svab/ could not be English words because English does not allow initial */tl/ or */sv/ clusters. (Again, children may occasionally break the phonotactic rules of English, producing, for instance, [tlʌm] for *thumb*.)

There are fewer restrictions on syllable-final consonant clusters than on initial clusters in English, as in many other languages. Although no more than three consonants can release a syllable, as many as four consonants can occur at the end of a syllable. *Pints* is an example of a word ending in a sequence of three consonants, and *sixths* [sɪksθs] ends in four consonants. However, in conversational speech, some of these consonants are usually omitted. The longest syllable that can occur phonetically in English can be represented as CCCVCCCC. *Strengths* [strɛŋkθs] exemplifies this syllable structure (MacKay, 1978, p. 201).

Combinations of consonants that occur across syllable boundaries are not as restricted as those that occur within syllables in English (MacKay, 1978, p. 203). For instance, the word *dogmatic* has an internal sequence of /gm/ that would not be allowed within one syllable in English. Children also may allow longer sequences across syllable boundaries. For instance, a child's first nasal plus stop sequences may occur in *finger, monkey*, etc. where there is a syllable boundary between the consonants. Such sequences may be called *abutting consonants* (e.g., see Grunwell, 1982).

Even if the native speakers of a language have never thought about the sequential constraints of their language and cannot verbalize them, they have still "internalized" them and can be said to "know" them. These constraints are part of each person's *competence* or individual grammar. A few experiments have demonstrated this. For example, Greenberg and Jenkins (1964) found that native speakers of English were able to judge "nonsense words" on a continuum from well-formed to completely unacceptable. For example [tʃwʊp], which violates the syllable structure constraints of English, was judged to be a less acceptable English word than [glʌk], which was judged to be "more English-like" (Hyman, 1975, p. 20). If we look at the names that are made up for new products or inventions, we again find evidence that native English speakers are aware of the phonotactic constraints of their native language. However, as noted above, children's early productions occasionally violate the phonotactic rules of the language, as illustrated by Amahl Smith's (Smith, 1973) rendition of *snake* [ŋēɪk].

Phonotactics and Syllabification Issues

The process of dividing words into syllables and deciding where syllable boundaries fall is called *syllabification* or *syllabication*. It is usually assumed that words can be syllabified based on the sequential constraints of the language in question and that the same constraints hold for the beginning of syllables as for the beginning of words (Hyman, 1975, p. 189). However, syllabification is not as straightforward for English as for some other languages. In fact, there is no completely agreed upon way of dividing words into syllables in English. Although native speakers generally agree as to the number of syllables in a word, they do not necessarily agree on where the syllable boundaries should be placed (Sloat, et al., 1978, p. 57).

Some linguists have attempted to formulate principles to use in determining syllable structure. For instance, Pulgram (1970) put forward three principles for syllabication discussed by Hyman (1975, pp. 189, 190). According to the first principle, a syllable boundary (represented as $) is inserted after every vowel or diphthong of a word (except the last), so that at least the first syllable is open. However, if this results in a violation of the sequential constraints, such as a stressed lax vowel occurring in syllable-final position in English, then the second principle must be applied.

According to the second principle, a consonant can be transferred from the beginning of one syllable to the end of the preceding syllable in order to give a permissible sequence. If the syllables that result after the application of the second principle still do not obey the phonotactic constraints of the language, additional consonants can be transferred from the beginning of one syllable to the end of the preceding syllable until the second syllable begins with a permissible word-initial sequence. If it is still necessary to violate the sequential constraints of the language, the disallowed sequence is left at the end of a syllable, because longer sequences are often allowed in that position rather than at the onset of a syllable. This corresponds to Pulgram's third principle, i.e., the idea of irregularities occurring at the coda.

The following example illustrates Pulgram's (1970) principles. The first principle would place the syllable boundary after the /æ/ in *candy* /kæ$ndi/. However, /æ/ is a lax vowel that, when stressed, cannot occur in word-final position in English, and /nd/ is not a permissible initial sequence in English. So, the second principle allows us to transfer the /n/ to the coda of the first syllable, giving /kæn$di/. As this results in two syllables that obey the sequential constraints of English, no further principles are applied.

In certain cases, it may be necessary to syllabify words in such a way that a medial consonant is put with both the preceding syllable and the following syllable. Such consonants are called *ambisyllabic*. For instance, the word *meadow* may be syllabified as [mɛd̆o͞u], with the syllable boundary falling within the medial consonant. This is necessary because the first syllable, which is stressed, cannot end with [ɛ], a lax vowel (Hyman, 1975, p. 191).

CONCERNS OF PHONOLOGY

The preceding description of some basic terms and concepts in phonology has included reference to many theoretical concerns, such as *distinctiveness*. The following discussion describes in general terms six concerns in the study of phonology. In Part II (History of Phonology) and Part III (Applications of Phonology) these concerns will be discussed in considerably more detail.[5]

Universals

Some phonologists are mainly concerned with discovering linguistic *universals* or *universal tendencies*. These are ways in which all languages (or most languages) are similar. Linguists are interested in sound systems. Thus they look for common characteristics among sound systems, for example, the CV syllable shape or specific sounds (such as the /a/ vowel) that are common across languages. According to Hyman (1975, p. 15) one major goal of phonology is to discover universals.

The linguist that we associate most with the concept of universals is Roman Jakobson. In his monograph titled *Child Language, Aphasia and Phonological Universals* (written in 1941 and translated into English from German in 1968), Jakobson postulated several *implicational universals* (or *laws of irreversible solidarity*) such as: "nasalized vowels imply oral vowels" and "voiced stops imply voiceless stops." Jakobson intended for his implicational universals to make predictions about languages of the world, language acquisition by children, and language loss in aphasia. To illustrate, the implicational universal "voiced stops imply voiceless stops" predicts that a language will not have voiced stops unless it also has the corresponding voiceless stops. It also predicts that children will learn (phonemic) voiceless stops before voiced stops, and before children acquire the contrast between voiced and voiceless stops, they will use voiceless stops for both. Similarly, in aphasia voiced stops should be lost before voiceless stops.

Another linguist we associate with universals is Joseph H. Greenberg. For several years, Greenberg, along with Charles A. Ferguson, directed a research project at Stanford University that was concerned specifically with universals. (See Greenberg, 1966a, 1966b, and Greenberg, Ferguson, & Moravscik, 1978, as well as Stanford University's *Working Papers in Language Universals*.) The original goals of the Project on Language Universals, as described in the preface to Volume 1 of *Universals of Human Language* (1978), J. H. Greenberg (Ed.), C. A. Ferguson and E. A. Moravscik (Associate Eds.), were to formulate cross-linguistic generalizations about language structures and to collect, organize, and store information about diverse languages of the world in order to verify those generalizations. The long-range goal was to formulate "increasingly general laws" to accou.t for observed similarities (and differences) among languages. Greenberg, as well as Jakobson, discussed the fact that all languages have CV syllables, and he also proposed a universal concerning the types of consonant clusters that can occur in certain kinds of syllables (Ferguson, 1977).

Segmentation

Another major concern of phonology is *segmentation*, which refers to the idea that spoken language can be segmented or broken down into discrete units—phoneme-length segments. As acoustic records of speech show, speech is not made up of discrete units, but rather is continuous, and is characterized by overlap between adjacent sounds, as noted earlier. However, humans are able to quite reliably segment the stream of speech as though it were composed of separate units (Dew & Jensen, 1977).

The assumption here is that segments have some perceptual reality, i.e. that utterances are actually perceived in terms of segments and that language is acquired, changes, and is also lost in segment-sized units. Evidence supporting this assumption is found in research on *slips of the tongue* (speech errors), e.g., see Fromkin, 1971, 1973a, 1973b. In spoonerisms it is often separate segments that are interchanged, as in "May I *s*ew you to a *sh*eet?" where the /ʃ/ of *show* and the /s/ of *seat* are interchanged (Schane, 1973, p. 4). The "rules" of secret languages such as pig Latin also generally involve the movement of segments, as in pig Latin [ɪtseɪ] for *sit*, where the initial segment is moved to the end of the word, and the diphthong *ay* ([eɪ]) is added.

It should be mentioned that there is also some evidence that we process language in larger "chunks" (e.g. syllables). For instance, coarticulation may involve segments that are not adjacent, and if speakers of unwritten languages are asked to divide a word, they usually divide it into syllables (Sloat, et al., 1978, p. 56).

Patterning

A third main concern of phonology is *patterning*. The assumption is that the distinctive sound differences of a language form a "coherent system." Generally, similar sounds in a given language pattern together and behave in the same way and have similar allophones. For example, in English the three voiceless stops (/p, t, k/) are each aspirated in word-initial position before a stressed vowel.

Some alphabets, although not the English alphabet, are arranged in such a way that the order shows the patterns or sound classes—for instance, voiceless stops before voiced stops, then voiceless and voiced affricates and fricatives, and so forth (C. A. Ferguson, personal communication).

Phonological Processes

Among the major aims of phonology in recent years has been the discovery and explanation of *phonological processes* and the comparison of phonological processes across languages, language families, and language varieties. The term *phonological process*, as it is used here, refers to any systematic sound change that affects a class of sounds (e.g. velars, fricatives) or a sound sequence, such as /s/ plus sonorant clusters

(/sw, sl/, etc.). For example, many languages have a process of *final devoicing*, by which obstruents (stops, fricatives, and affricates) are devoiced in word final position, so that [t] replaces /d/, [p] replaces /b/, etc., with a voiceless obstruent replacing its voiced cognate. However, the details of this process differ in different languages. In one language it may affect all word-final voiced obstruents, while in another it affects only a certain subset of voiced obstruents.

Linguists who are concerned with phonological processes necessarily assume that there is a *basic* or *underlying form*, which is called the *phonological representation*. This form is modified by a process, resulting in a new or changed form. If this is the actual spoken form, it is called the *surface form* or the *phonetic representation*.

To illustrate just one group of phonological processes, linguists often discuss processes of *cluster reduction* that are exhibited by young children. Typically, one element of the cluster is deleted, usually the more "difficult" one, resulting in a CV syllable structure. In word-initial /s/ plus stop clusters, the /s/ is usually deleted by a process of /s/ - *cluster reduction* or /s/ - *loss*. So, for example, we find [pun] for *spoon*. This assumes that the child's basic or underlying form is /spun/, which is also the adult surface form. This underlying form is then modified by the phonological process, giving the child's surface form [pun].

A phonological *derivation* represents an attempt to describe how surface forms may become considerably different from underlying forms. If more than one phonological process applies in getting from an underlying form to a surface form, a derivation displays all the intermediate steps. So if *dog* was produced by a child as [gɔ], the derivation would be as follows:

Child's underlying form	/dɔg/
Velar assimilation	/gɔg/
Final consonant deletion	/gɔ/
Child's surface form	[gɔ]

In this case, the processes have to apply in the order listed; velar assimilation must precede final consonant deletion. If deletion applied first, the final /g/ would not be present at the time when velar assimilation would apply, and the child's form would be [dɔ]. More will be said later about processes and ordering and also about the nature of underlying representations.

Variation

A major concern of some phonologists is to describe and understand phonological *variation*. It is the primary concern of sociolinguists like

William Labov who are interested in linguistic variation that is conditioned by sociological factors. These linguists attempt to write rules that describe the variable features or characteristics being studied. In one of his early and classic investigations, Labov (1963) studied the centralization of the first element of the diphthongs [a͡ɪ] and [a͡ʊ] by natives of Martha's Vineyard, an island off the coast of Massachusetts. In this study, the phonetic variants were considered in relation to various social groups.

We can differentiate *synchronic variation*, which is variation within a language at any given time, from *diachronic variation*, which concerns how sounds and sound systems change over time. We also can distinguish *regional* or *geographical variation* from *social variation*. Thus, we can talk about *regional dialects* and *social dialects*, a *dialect* being a variant of a language, with characteristic sound patterns (in addition to characteristic grammatical patterns and lexical items).

Another type of language variation that is of concern to some linguists is called *register variation*. A *register* is a language variety that is related to how the language is being used. One register that has been studied quite extensively (especially by Ferguson 1964, 1974) is called *baby talk*. Baby talk is the specialized register that is used for talking to infants and young children (and by extension, for other purposes, such as talking to pets). Baby talk includes prosodic and segmental characteristics, such as higher pitch and the substitution of glides for liquids (e.g., [w] for /r/), as well as grammatical characteristics and special lexical items. Other registers that have been studied include *foreigner talk*, which is the variety of language used for talking to "foreigners" or people who do not have a good command of the language, and *teacher talk*, which is the variety of a language used in instructional settings.

Variation is not of great interest to most *generative phonologists*, such as Noam Chomsky and Morris Halle. Generative phonologists are mainly interested in *linguistic competence*, or what the native speakers of a language have "internalized" (what they "know") about how their language works. They are generally not interested in *performance* or language behavior, that is, how language is actually used.

Alternations

Finally, a main aim of generative phonologists is to account for relationships between sounds that alternate in pairs of related words, or in their terminology, to account for *alternations* in *allomorphs* (variants) of one *morpheme* (Hyman, 1975, p. 195). For instance, in the pair of related words *electric/electricity*, there is an alternation between [k] and

[s], with [k] occurring in word-final position, and [s] occurring before the *-ity* suffix. Similarly, in *vane/vanity* and *sane/sanity*, etc. there is an alternation between [ēɪ] and [æ]. Generative phonologists are particularly concerned with accounting for such alternations and with positing an underlying form from which all the related surface forms can be derived. For example, generative phonologists would want to posit a common stem (/hɑ̄rmɔ-/) from which related forms like *harmony, harmonic, harmonious*, etc. could be derived by the addition of suffixes (endings) and the application of phonological rules establishing stress and modifying the quality of the /ɔ/ vowel. Underlying forms are often similar to historically earlier forms, and alternations among allomorphs are said to be remnants of sound changes that occurred in the history of a language. Alternations are found only when a sound change took place in some, but not all, environments (Schane, 1973, pp. 83, 91).

Some of the underlying forms that are proposed by generative phonologists are quite abstract and do not closely resemble the surface forms that result from the application of the rules. These abstract underlying forms are called *systematic phonemic representations*. To illustrate, in *The Sound Pattern of English* (Chomsky & Halle, 1968, p. 235) the underlying form of *religious* is given as /religᵈ + i + ɔs/. The surface form [rəlídʒəs] is derived by the application of several *phonological rules*, each making one modification. For example, a rule called *velar softening* changes /gᵈ/ to [dʒ]. Most other schools of phonology have not been as concerned with this particular aspect of language (alternations among allomorphs) as have generative phonologists.

THE PHONOLOGICAL
COMPONENT OF LANGUAGE

Having just discussed six general concerns in phonology—universals, segmentation, patterning, phonological processes, variation, and alternations, we now can revise and amplify our original general sketch of the phonological component of language. Figure 2-4 provides this representation, which can be summarized as follows.

The phonological component of a language is that portion concerned with sounds. It interacts with the other components of language—the semantic and the syntactic, and also with pragmatic functions. These

FIGURE 2-4
A general scheme illustrating the phonological component of a language or a language user.

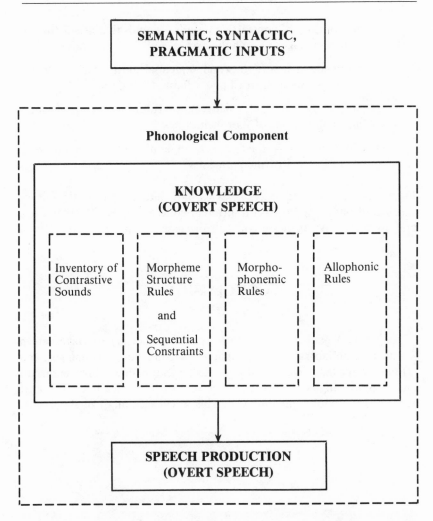

other components and functions are concerned with choice and ordering of words in accordance with appropriate social contexts and individual histories, needs, and intentions. These inputs to the phonological component provide the message. The task of the phonological component is to translate this message into manifest speech.

As modeled in Figure 2-4, the underlying level of the phonological component has at least four parts. For convenience here, they are listed as though they were "real" operations performed by a language user. We can say that the language user has:

(1) an inventory of contrastive sounds—sounds that are distinctive in the language, i.e., phonemes;

(2) morpheme structure rules and sequential constraints—rules that dictate permissible word and syllable formation;

(3) morphophonemic rules—alternation rules for correctly producing combinations of morphemes;

(4) allophonic rules—the feature change rules for correctly producing allophones of the phonemes.

Figure 2-4 is provided only as a learning aid. Different schools or theories of phonology focus on different concerns, have different aims, and do not always agree on concepts discussed in this chapter.

CONCLUSION

The general goals of phonology appear to be: (1) to formulate a satisfactory phonological theory that will account for all languages, and (2) to describe language behavior as exactly as possible with reference to one or more languages (Ferguson, personal communication). The next section of this book is an abbreviated historical account of such pursuits.

FOOTNOTES

¹Notice that we have been using both virgules (/ /) and brackets ([ ]) around sound symbols. Following the usual convention, virgules (or slashes) are used to set off presumed phonemes or abstract sound segments in a language, whereas brackets are used for manifest speech sounds.

²When referring to any vowel or consonant, the general symbols V and C, respectively, can be used. The other symbols in this example, [ˉ] and [:], are alternative diacritics sometimes used for marking a lengthened sound. In this book length is indicated by a colon ([:]) immediately after the lengthened sound.

³Following the standard practice in linguistics, we are using an asterisk to indicate nonoccurring forms.

⁴Children learning English may, however, produce forms that disobey this constraint of adult English, for example, Amahl Smith's [ŋēīk] for *snake* (Smith, 1973), and Leslie's [ŋɑŋɑ] for *(song)book* (Ferguson, 1979a).

⁵This section on the concerns of phonology owes a great deal to the influence of Professors C. A. Ferguson and W. R. Leben of Stanford University, whose phonology course was attended by the first author in 1977.

Part II

HISTORY
OF PHONOLOGY

3

Forerunners
Through the
Structuralists

In this chapter we present a chronology of the major approaches to phonological study.

FORERUNNERS
OF PHONOLOGY

Phonology can be said to date back to the second millenium B.C. when the *alphabetic principle* (one symbol for every distinctive sound) was "discovered." In order to come up with an alphabetic form of writing, in which only *distinctive* sound differences are represented, the ancient Akkadians, a Semitic people of central Mesopotamia (in southwestern Asia), must have been aware of the sound system of their language; that is, they had to identify certain sound entities in order to classify them systematically (C. A. Ferguson, personal communication).

One fascinating ancient phonology was provided by Pāṇini, an Indian grammarian. In about the fifth century B.C., Pāṇini approached the phonology of Sanskrit (an ancient Indian language) in a very systematic way. His goal was a practical one—to preserve the language of the religious rituals. People were starting to pronounce Sanskrit "incorrectly."

Pāṇini wanted to describe the language very carefully and understand how it worked in order to preserve it. Pāṇini's grammar of Sanskrit still stands as a detailed and sophisticated description of the language. (See Robins, 1967 for a more detailed discussion of Pāṇini's grammar.)

A concept similar to the 20th century phonemic concept was formulated in about 150 B.C. by other Indian grammarians, who argued that the smallest linguistic entity was a unit of "distinctive sound" capable of distinguishing among words. A similar concept was also formulated independently by the Greek grammarians (Fischer-Jørgensen, 1975, p. 4). In the middle of the 12th century A.D., an anonymous Icelandic scholar, often called the "First Grammarian," presented his views concerning how the Roman alphabet could be adapted to make it more suitable for Icelandic. For instance, he indicated which letters could be eliminated, and he stated that the same letter could be used for sound variations that were environmentally conditioned. It is clear that he was aware of the notion of *distinctiveness*. Although his proposal was rejected, his description of Icelandic, presented in *The First Grammatical Treatise* is still considered to be an excellent phonological description (Robins, 1967, pp. 72–73; Fischer-Jørgensen, 1975, pp. 4–5).

These early "phonologists" were not interested in theory, but in solving practical problems. Thus, they can be called *applied* rather than *theoretical phonologists*.

Developments in the history of phonology that took place between the 12th century and the 19th century will not be discussed here. For detailed accounts of this period, the interested reader is referred to Fischer-Jørgensen, 1975; Robins, 1967; Hughes, 1966.

MODERN APPROACHES TO PHONOLOGY

Historically, there have been many different approaches to phonology. Only a few warrant the status of a *theory*, hence, the use of terms such as *approach* and *view*. As noted by Fischer-Jørgensen (1975, p. 2), it is not completely accurate to divide phonology into separate schools, because different trends developed simultaneously in different places, but it is possible to arrange modern views of phonology into a general chronological sequence according to when each one was most prevalent. We have followed that practice here. Only movements that are relevant to the development of phonology in the United States are discussed. (See Fischer-Jørgensen, 1975 for a discussion of additional views of phonology.) It should be noted that earlier approaches have not necessarily been abandoned with the advent of newer approaches.

The 19th Century: Comparative and Historical Linguistics

The 19th century was the period of *comparative* and *historical linguistics*, also called *comparative philology*. Although other aspects of linguistics were not completely neglected, historical studies, especially concerning the Indo-European languages, dominated linguistics during this time. Even as late as 1922, Otto Jespersen, a famous linguist, wrote that linguistics was primarily a historical study (Robins, 1967, p. 164). Work on the history of languages was undertaken to some extent before the 19th century, but after 1800, historical studies became the focus of linguistics. A major stimulus was the discovery, by Sir William Jones in the late 18th century (1786), of the relationship between Sanskrit (the classical language of India) and the major languages of Europe, specifically Latin and Greek. For this reason, 1786 is often said to mark the beginning of linguistics as a science.

Most of the important linguists during this period were Germans or people who were trained in Germany. Rasmus Rask, who was a Dane, and the Germans Jakob Grimm and Franz Bopp are sometimes called the "founders of scientific historical linguistics" (Robins, 1967, p. 171). Rask was one of the first linguists to show systematic relationships among words in different languages, and his "comparative grammar" of the Scandinavian languages was the earliest such work (Hughes, 1966, p. 52). Grimm is famous for his comparative grammar of the Germanic languages and for what is called *Grimm's law*, the first "sound law" to be stated. Grimm's law is actually a set of "sound shifts" involving (word-initial) labial, alveolar, and velar consonants that took place in the history of the Germanic languages. Grimm's law can be summarized as follows. Proto Indo-European (PIE) voiceless stops (*p, *t, *k) became voiceless fricatives in the history of the Germanic languages. (Proto Indo-European is the reconstructed [hypothetical] parent language from which all the Indo-European languages developed.) In many other Indo-European languages, they remained as voiceless stops. So, for instance, we find correspondences such as Latin *pater* and English *father*, and Latin *trēs*, English *three*, etc. (In general, Latin kept the values of the PIE stops.) Proto Indo-European voiced stops (*b, *d, *g) became voiceless stops in Germanic. Thus we find parallels such as Latin *duo* and English *two*, Latin *genus* and English *kin*, etc. Finally, the Proto Indo-European "voiced aspirates" (*bh, *dh, *gh) became voiced stops in the history of the Germanic languages, while in other Indo-European languages they became spirants or aspirates. Resulting correspondences include Latin *frater* and English *brother* (from *bh), and Latin *hortus*, English *garden* (from *gh) (Wardhaugh, 1972, p. 177).

Early
19th Century

The early 19th century linguists worked out the concept of historically related language families derived from a "parent" language no longer in existence (Robins, 1967, p. 178). A basic principle of comparative or historical linguistics is that comparison of similar words in the synchronic descriptions of several related languages can provide evidence regarding the nature of an earlier parent language. For example, we can learn many things about Latin (as it was spoken) by comparing the Romance languages, which developed from it.

Middle
19th Century

The middle of the 19th century was marked by the influence of August Schleicher. Schleicher probably is best known for his *Stammbaumtheorie* or *family tree model*, describing how the Proto Indo-European language developed into the various languages that are derived from it (Hughes, 1966, p. 57). This was a way of capturing relationships among language "families." He used a family tree model to show the relationships among the Indo-European languages and between these languages and the parent language from which they descended. Languages were grouped into sub-families, such as Germanic, Italo-Celtic and so forth, according to shared characteristics, and these families were traced back to a single original language (*Ursprache*) that possessed all the characteristics shared by its descendants (Robins, 1967, p. 178-179). Although Schleicher's classification has been changed many times, his type of family tree model still is used. Figure 3-1 is a family tree diagram showing some of the Indo-European languages. Schleicher also developed the practice of using asterisks to distinguish reconstructed forms (hypothetical elements of a language) from actual forms (Hughes, 1966, p. 55). This practice still is used today.

Schleicher's student, J. Schmidt, is known for his *Wellentheorie* or *wave theory*, which describes how linguistic changes spread in Indo-European. According to this model, innovations (e.g., sound changes) spread in a wave-like fashion from dialect to dialect or language to language (Robins, 1967, p. 179).

FIGURE 3-1
Family tree diagram showing the main branches of the Indo-European language family, with English and the Romance languages shown in more detail. Based on L. M. Myers (1966) and R. Wardhaugh (1972)

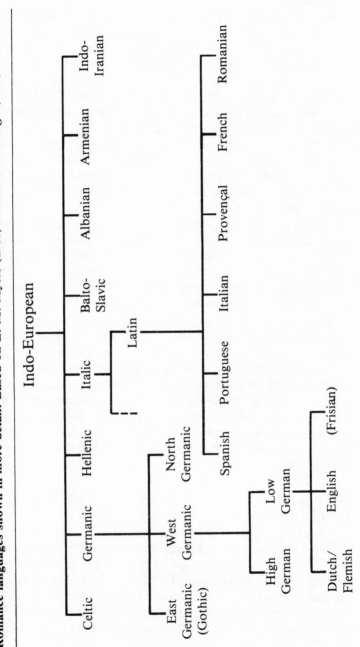

Late 19th Century

The last quarter of the 19th century and the first part of the 20th century was the period of the *neogrammarians*. *Junggrammatiker* (*neogrammarian*) was a nickname given to a group of young linguists in Leipzig. (Thus it is also called "the Leipzig school.") The major points of the "neogrammarian doctrine" were put forth, for example, by H. Osthoff and K. Brugmann in a journal called *Morphologische Untersuchungen* and also by Hermann Paul in his *Principles of the History of Language* (*Principien der Sprachgeschichte*) (Robins, 1967). Although the principles expounded by the neogrammarians were not new, they have had a significant effect on the field of comparative and historical linguistics, which they attempted to make an exact science. The model that they worked out for studying the history of languages has been applied to many different language families since their era. Perhaps most important, the neogrammarians formalized the concept of "sound law." Their view can be summarized as follows: "Sound laws have no exceptions." In other words, they assumed the regularity of sound change; the same sound in the same phonetic environment (and the same dialect) always changes in the same way (Myers, 1966, p. 43). Earlier, K. Verner, who was not a neogrammarian, stated that even apparent exceptions to rules follow rules, and he showed that the "exceptions" to Grimm's Law could be explained by taking word accent into account (Robins, 1967, p. 184).

The work of the neogrammarians stimulated later research and had an effect on the fields of phonetics, foreign language teaching, and dialectology as well as historical linguistics. The neogrammarian's emphasis on living languages and the insight they could provide into linguistic change encouraged dialectologists, and consequently the study of dialects became a serious pursuit in the last part of the 19th century (Robins, 1967, p. 186).

Development of
Descriptive Phonetics

Descriptive phonetics developed along its own path in the 19th century in both France and Great Britain. Phonetics, with its practical applications (e.g. to spelling reform and language teaching), had been studied in England since the Renaissance. The study of phonetics was reinforced by the phonetic work of Indian scholars (particularly Sir William Jones) at the end of the 18th century, and synchronic linguistics in Great Britain during the 19th century involved primarily phonetics (Robins, 1967, pp. 202–203).

British "classical phoneticians" were concerned with articulation and with classifying speech sounds. Another major concern was developing a symbolic system to represent speech sounds. (The International Phonetic Alphabet dates back to the late 19th century.) One of the most important British phoneticians was Henry Sweet (after whom Henry Higgins in *Pygmalian* was probably modeled). Sweet's *Handbook of Phonetics* was published in 1877 and his *Primer of Phonetics* in 1880. Although Sweet did not use the term *phoneme*, he distinguished environmentally conditioned nondistinctive sounds from sounds that distinguish separate words, and he argued that it was only necessary to represent distinctive sound differences in a "broad" transcription for a particular language (Robins, 1967, p. 204). Similarly, Paul Passy, the French linguist who founded the International Phonetic Association, wrote in 1888 that each distinctive sound should be represented by a separate letter (Fischer-Jørgensen, 1975, pp. 6–7).

The 20th Century:
Structuralism

Early 20th Century:
European Structuralism

European Structuralism, which began to have an impact during the first 25 years of the 20th century, was founded by Ferdinand de Saussure, a Swiss linguist. It began as a reaction to the 19th century view of language, in which historical description was the main concern. In de Saussure's theory, language is seen as a *structure* or *system* in which the *relations* among the elements are of primary importance (Fischer-Jørgensen, 1975, p. 10). Although de Saussure did not discuss phonemic systems in detail, his structural view of language includes the concept of the phoneme and is the basis for later phonemic theories.[1] After de Saussure's death, some of his students published a compilation of his lectures on linguistics, reconstructed from students' notes. This book, published in 1916, is called *Cours de Linguistique Générale*. One of the many things that de Saussure is known for is his *langue/parole* dichotomy, which is roughly parallel to the later *competence/performance* distinction.

Early 20th Century:
The Prague School

The Prague School of Phonology was founded in 1926 and was most active in the late 1920s and the 1930s. Nikolai S. Trubetzkoy, a Russian linguist and professor in Vienna, was one of the founders, as was Roman Jakobson, another Russian linguist who was a professor in Prague. The members of the Prague School met regularly and published the *Travaux du Cercle linguistique de Prague [Works of the Linguistic Circle of Prague]*. These linguists were interested primarily in structure and system, and they wished to establish phonology as a separate discipline, apart from phonetics (Fischer-Jørgensen, 1975, p. 22). The main statement of their views is Trubetzkoy's *Gründzuge der Phonologie (Principles of Phonology)* published in German in 1939. Because of the work of the Prague School in developing the concept of the phoneme, it became a basic element of linguistics. The Prague phonologists applied parts of de Saussure's theory in their expansion of the phoneme concept. Specifically, they were influenced by de Saussure's distinction between *langue*—the system of language, and *parole*—how that system is applied. In their view, speech sounds belong to *parole*, but the phoneme belongs to *langue*. They considered the phoneme to be a "complex phonological unit" realized by speech sounds (Robins 1967, pp. 204–205).

A major concern of the Prague School was *distinctiveness* (or *opposition*). This involves differences between and among sounds. Oppositions or distinctive differences were described in terms of *relations*. Trubetzkoy (1939) classified oppositions along three parameters according to the relation between the members, the relation of the opposition to the entire system, and the "distinctive force" of the opposition. To illustrate each of these parameters, the opposition between /t/ and /d/ in English would be called *privative*, because one member has a "mark" that the other does not have, i.e., /d/ is "marked" for voicing (Trubetzkoy, 1969 translation by C. A. M. Baltaxe, p. 75). The distinction between /h/ and /ŋ/ in English would be classified as an *isolated* opposition because the relation between the two phonemes does not occur elsewhere in the language. Finally, the opposition between voiced and voiceless stops in German is a *suspendable* opposition (rather than a *constant* one) because it is "neutralized" in word-final position where only voiceless stops occur. (See Fischer-Jørgensen, 1975, pp. 28–29 for a more in-depth discussion of these concepts.)

Neutralization of contrasts was an important concept in Prague School phonology. In the position of neutralization (e.g., word-final position in the German example) an *archiphoneme* was used by the Prague phonologists to represent the features shared by the two neutralized sounds. Capital letters represented archiphonemes. For instance, T or D would be used if the t/d distinction was neutralized in a certain position (Hyman, 1975, p. 70).

Markedness (see Appendix B for a discussion of this term) was also important to the phonologists of the Prague School. Markedness was related to neutralization in that the unmarked member of an opposition was said to occur in the position of neutralization (Hyman, 1975, p. 143).

As mentioned above, the idea of opposition was central to the Prague School phonologists, and they derived their definition of the phoneme from it. The Prague phonologists believed that it was not sufficient to treat phonemes as indivisible units. Instead, they analyzed phonemes into their component distinctive properties and arranged them into systems based on these properties or *features* (Fischer-Jørgensen, 1975, pp. 48–49). Because of the work of the Prague School, particularly Trubetzkoy, linguists began to look at sounds as being plus (+) or minus (−) some phonetic property. This paved the way for Jakobson's distinctive feature theory, discussed in a later section (C. A. Ferguson, personal communication).

Some Prague phonologists were interested in applying a phonological (phonemic) point of view to sound change. Linguists such as Jakobson and Martinet were concerned with how phonemic systems change over time (rather than individual phonetic segments). Thus the work of the Prague School led to changes in the field of historical linguistics (Robins, 1967, pp. 223–224).

Roman Jakobson. Roman Jakobson was a member of the Prague School who eventually immigrated to the United States. Jakobson, one of the most famous linguists, is known for his theory of phonological acquisition and universals, as well as distinctive feature theory. His classic book *Kindersprache, Aphasie und allgemeine Lautgesetze (Child Language, Aphasia and Phonological Universals)* was published in German in 1941 and was translated into English in 1968. In his book, Jakobson attempted to formulate general laws (*laws of irreversible solidarity* or *unilateral implication*) concerning the structure of sound systems. He believed that these laws would account for universals of phoneme inventories. In addition, they were said to govern language acquisition by children and language loss in aphasia. The following discussion highlights only a few of Jakobson's influential writings in phonology; his views also will be discussed in Chapter 6, Normal Phonological Development.

Jakobson's conception of the development of the basic phonemic system is illustrated in Figure 3-2. Jakobson argued that the first phonemic opposition is between a "maximally closed" consonant (e.g., /p/) and a "maximally open" vowel (e.g., /ɑ/). The second opposition is between an oral consonant (e.g., /p/) and a nasal consonant (e.g., /m/). The next contrast is between labial (e.g., /p/) and dental (e.g., /t/). The first vocalic opposition is between a low vowel and a high vowel (e.g., /ɑ/ − /i/). Then the high vowel splits into a front vowel and a back vowel (e.g., /i/ − /u/). Thus, the *principle of maximal contrast* accounts for the development of the basic phonemic system, e.g., /p, m, t, ɑ, i, u/.

FIGURE 3-2
Schematic representation of the development of the basic phonemic system, as described by Jakobson (1968).

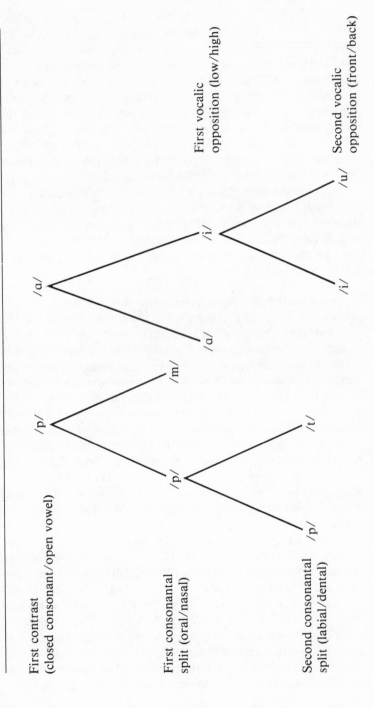

First contrast
(closed consonant/open vowel)

First consonantal
split (oral/nasal)

Second consonantal
split (labial/dental)

First vocalic
opposition (low/high)

Second vocalic
opposition (front/back)

Jakobson claimed that the order in which phonemes are acquired by children is the same across all languages and is determined by these general laws. Thus, the name "universal order" for his theory of phonological acquisition. After the basic phonemic system is acquired, the *laws of irreversible solidarity* or *unilateral implication* make specific predictions about acquisition and also about language loss in aphasia and about phoneme inventories of languages of the world.

Jakobson's *implicational universals* include the following (⊃ means "imply"):

fricatives ⊃ stops

back consonants ⊃ front consonants

rounded front vowels ⊃ unrounded front vowels and rounded back vowels

These implicational rules predict that during acquisition, the implied member (on the right of the ⊃ symbol) is acquired before the implying member (on the left of ⊃), and before the implying member is acquired, the implied member will substitute for it.

To illustrate, the first rule presented above generally is taken to mean that stops should be acquired before the corresponding fricatives (i.e., fricatives produced at approximately the same point of articulation and having the same voicing quality). Moreover, before fricatives are acquired, stops should substitute for them. Similarly, /s/, which is a front consonant, should be acquired before /ʃ/, which is a back consonant, and /s/ should also be substituted for /ʃ/. Likewise /t/ should be acquired before /k/.

In aphasia, Jakobson predicts that phonemic distinctions will be lost in the reverse order from the order in which they are acquired. That is, distinctions that are acquired late by children should be among the first to be lost in aphasia. For example, the distinction between /p/ and /a/ should be lost latest. Concerning Jakobson's implicational universals, the implying member should be lost in aphasia before the implied member, e.g., /ʃ/ should be lost before /s/, and fricatives should be lost before the corresponding stops.

The distinctions acquired earliest by children and lost latest in aphasia are also the most likely to be universals (found in all or nearly all languages), according to Jakobson's theory. On the other hand, the phonemes that are acquired latest by children (and are lost earliest in aphasia) are likely to be rare – found in fewer languages. For example, the interdental fricatives /θ/, /ð/ are acquired late by children and are also quite rare in languages of the world. Jakobson's implicational universals also predict that the implied member will be more widespread in languages of the world than the implying member. For instance, front consonants should be more common than back consonants, and no language should be found to have back consonants without also having front consonants.

Middle 20th Century: American Structuralism (The Bloomfield School)

American Structuralism, also called *the Bloomfield School* or *descriptive linguistics*, began in the 1920s and was the dominant approach to phonology in the United States from the middle 1930s until the middle 1950s. The development of descriptive linguistics in the United States can be related to several factors, but the primary factor was probably the growth of interest in American Indian languages. One of the founders of American descriptive linguistics was Edward Sapir, an anthropologist (born in Europe) who became an expert in American Indian languages. Sapir is known for his view of language as being closely related to the life and thought of the people who speak it—the Sapir-Whorf hypothesis—and also for his view of the phoneme as having "psychological reality" (Robins, 1967, p. 207). Sapir's (1921) book titled *Language* is still thought of as a good introduction to linguistics.

Leonard Bloomfield, who gave his name to this school, was trained in neogrammarian linguistics. He originally was concerned with the history of Indo-European languages, specifically the Germanic languages. However, due to the influence of the anthropologist Franz Boas (who also was trained in neogrammarian linguistics), Bloomfield became interested in American Indian (*Amerindian*) languages (Fischer-Jørgensen, 1975, pp. 64–65). Bloomfield was impressed by how different the Amerindian languages were from each other and from the Indo-European languages with which he was familiar. Therefore, he and his followers did not try to relate the languages to each other or to search for universals. Each language was treated as a separate entity, and there was no attempt to make generalizations.

Bloomfield was greatly influenced by *behaviorism*, the predominant psychological view at that time. Like other social scientists who subscribed to the tenets of behaviorism, Bloomfield was concerned only with the observable facts, in this case, facts of language behavior. As an *antimentalist*, he was not concerned with what goes on in speakers' or hearers' minds (Fischer-Jørgensen, 1975, p. 66).

Bloomfield wanted to make synchronic description an exact science (as historical linguistics was), and thus he stressed that linguistics should concentrate on formal analysis, using objective procedures and concepts. Precise scientific description was the goal (Robins, 1967, pp. 208-209). Martin Joos, one of Bloomfield's followers, stated specifically (in Joos, 1950) that their goal was not to explain. So, American Structuralism was primarily descriptive. It was not actually a theory, but a set of discovery procedures.

The main aim of Bloomfieldian linguists was to describe the synchronic state of American Indian languages as precisely as possible and to invent writing systems for them. They needed new methods for this endeavor; the methods of historical linguistics were not suitable because the histories of these languages were not known. In fact, in most cases, the linguists were learning the languages while describing them. As a consequence, they developed an elaborate set of procedures to be followed in analyzing a previously unknown language (Robins, 1967, p. 208).

Bloomfield's primary interest was not phonology, and he did not indicate how to find the phonemes or significant sound units of a language. However, several Bloomfieldians, such as Bernard Bloch, George Trager, Kenneth Pike, Charles Hockett, and others expanded the phonological aspect of descriptive linguistics. Their type of phonological analysis is often called *taxonomic* or *autonomous phonemics*.[2] Their main concern was setting up *phoneme inventories*, i.e., finding the phonemes used in a particular language. Most of them viewed the phoneme (rather than the feature) as the smallest unit of sound. They did not make a sharp distinction between phonetics and phonology, but regarded phonology, the study of significant speech sounds, as "practical phonetics" (Fischer-Jørgensen, 1975, p. 75). These linguists defined the phoneme in various ways, e.g., as a fictitious unit, or a physical entity, etc. However, in the most prevalent view, the phoneme was seen as a class of sounds that contrasts with all other sound classes in the language (see Fischer-Jørgensen, 1975, p. 77).

The descriptive linguists always began their analysis with the phonemic system of the language being studied. After finding the phoneme inventory, they attempted to describe the *morphological system*, which involves morphemes or "minimal meaningful units," and processes of word formation. *Morphophonemics* was a separate level dealing with the phonemic composition of morphemes and with morphemes that have phonologically conditioned variants, such as the plural morpheme in English. (This morpheme has three regular allomorphs or variants, /-s/, /-z/ and /-əz/, and the variant that is chosen depends on the final sound of the stem.) The grammar or syntax of the language was

dealt with last, after the other analyses were completed. The Bloomfieldians did not believe in "mixing levels." (Note that most Bloomfieldians,
in keeping with their behavioristic and antimentalist orientation, ignored
meaning.) In both their phonological and their grammatical analyses,
distribution was important. Zellig Harris (1951/1963) stated that
linguistic procedures involve two major steps: (1) setting up elements,
and (2) making statements regarding the distribution of those elements
(Robins, 1967, p. 210). Most Bloomfieldians avoided "process" terminology. That is, they simply described the distribution of the
allophones of each phoneme rather than trying to derive one from
another. However, Bloomfield did use an "item-and-process" approach
in his morphophonemic descriptions. One form (perhaps the one with
the widest distribution) was chosen as basic, and the others replaced it
under certain circumstances (Fischer-Jørgensen, 1975, p. 70). See Hockett (1955) for a discussion of item-and-arrangement and item-and-process
approaches.

The principles and the procedures used in phonemic analysis are explained below. These same basic procedures are still used whenever a
linguist wants to find the phoneme inventory of a language or of a child's
linguistic system. Phonemic analysis is based on phonetic transcriptions
of a large number of forms (a *corpus* or body of material).

Principles and Procedures for Phonemic Analysis. If two sounds
(*phones*) do not occur in any common phonetic environments, they are
said to be in *complementary distribution*. Such sounds may be allophones
or variants of one phoneme. Allophones, then, are variants of one sound
unit that occur in different environments. It is usually possible to predict
where each allophone will occur, unless they are in *free variation* in a
particular position. For example, aspirated /t/ ([tʰ]) and unreleased /t/
([t̚]) are allophones of the phoneme /t/ in English, but in word-final
position, either allophone can occur; they are in free variation in that
position. (For arguments against this view, see Hyman, 1975, p. 65.)

If two sounds are in complementary distribution, they may be allophones
of one phoneme, as stated above. However, another criterion that was important to the descriptive linguists is the requirement of *phonetic similarity*.
To be grouped together as allophones of one phoneme, two sounds must be
"phonetically similar" (a concept which, unfortunately, has never been well
defined). To illustrate, although /ŋ/ and /h/ are in complementary distribution in English, we would not want to group them together as one distinctive
sound unit (phoneme) because they are not phonetically similar, sharing very
few phonetic properties.

Minimal pairs are also used in finding contrasting sound units. If pairs of words can be found that differ in just one sound and also differ in meaning, then the sounds that distinguish the words from one another are said to belong to separate phonemes. For example, English has many pairs of words such as *pill/Bill, pole/bowl, pit/bit*, etc. The members of each pair differ in meaning and differ in just one phonetic element—the initial stop. Such minimal pairs clearly indicate that /p/ and /b/ are separate phonemes in English. English has many *minimal sets* such as *pill/Bill/dill/fill/kill*, etc., which are also useful in determining phonemic contrasts. (This set shows us that /p/, /b/, /d/, /f/ and /k/ all contrast in initial position and thus are separate phonemes.) Although the Bloomfieldians were not generally interested in meaning, they did have to pay attention to meaning differences in order to use this minimal pair approach.

In discovering the phoneme inventory of a language, it was sometimes necessary for the Bloomfieldians to refer to another principle, that of *pattern congruity* (although some of them did not accept this principle). They used pattern congruity to decide between two alternatives or to modify tentative solutions. Pattern congruity refers to the simplicity or the symmetrical nature of phonemic systems. Languages often have symmetrical phonemic systems. For instance, consider a language that has three voiceless stops and three voiced stops produced at the same points of articulation—labial, alveolar, and velar. If it also has three *homorganic* voiced fricatives (i.e., fricatives produced at the same points of articulation), we expect that in addition, the language will have three voiceless fricatives—labial, alveolar, and velar. (See Fischer-Jørgensen, 1975, pp. 86–87 for a more detailed discussion.)

Example of Bloomfieldian principle of pattern congruity

Many linguists (although not all) classify /ŋ/ as a separate phoneme of English. Others consider it to be an allophone of /n/. The velar nasal in English is clearly different from the other nasals in that it has a more limited distribution; it does not occur in syllable initial position. However, English has pairs of voiceless and voiced stops produced at the labial, alveolar, and velar places of articulation. Thus, the phonemic system of English is more symmetrical if /ŋ/ is considered as a separate phoneme:

	Labial	*Alveolar*	*Velar*
Stops	/p, b/	/t, d/	/k, g/
Nasals	/m/	/n/	/ŋ/

(See Hyman, 1975, pp. 93–94 for arguments against this solution.)

Although the Bloomfieldians were not in agreement on all issues, they had enough in common to be grouped together. For example, most wanted to make synchronic linguistics an exact science, and most believed in the separation of levels. That is, phonemic analysis had to precede morphemic analysis, and morphological (grammatical) information could not be used in phonemic analysis (Fischer-Jørgensen, 1975, p. 112).

Most Bloomfieldians considered the phoneme, rather than the feature, to be the smallest unit of sound, and one of their main goals was to establish phoneme inventories. Bloomfield's followers adhered to the *biuniqueness condition*. According to this requirement, every unique sequence of phones must have a unique phonemic transcription (Chomsky, 1964, p. 94). Given a phonemic transcription, it must be possible to figure out the actual sounds (except for cases of free variation among allophones). Conversely, given any utterance, it must be possible to determine the phonemes. In other words, we must be able to go from phonetic transcription to phonemic transcription and vice versa in a completely unambiguous way (Robins, 1967, p. 211).[3]

Another Bloomfieldian condition was *linearity*. According to this condition, a phoneme can be made up of a sequence of phones (as is the case with affricates like /tʃ, dʒ/), but a sequence of phonemes cannot be realized as one phone. So, for example, [kʰæt], which is a common rendition of *can't* could not be analyzed phonemically as /kænt/ because in that case a sequence of two phonemes (/æn/) would be realized as one phone ([æ̃]). According to the linarity condition, if one phoneme follows another in the phonemic representation, then the phones associated with those phonemes must occur in the same order in the surface phonetic representation (Fischer-Jørgensen, 1975, p. 282).

A pervasive principle of the Bloomfieldians was "once a phoneme, always a phoneme." This means that if two sounds contrast in any one position, they have to belong to separate phonemes. Most descriptive linguists subscribed to the *invariance* condition and did not allow *neutralization* of contrasts or *phonemic overlapping*.

According to the invariance condition, each phoneme has certain characteristic properties that are present wherever that phoneme occurs, and in all its allophones (Fischer-Jørgensen, 1975, p. 282). Neutralization refers to the loss of a contrast in certain positions or contexts. Phonemic overlapping (Bloch, 1941) refers to cases in which one sound (phone) in some contexts "belongs" to one phoneme and in some contexts to another.

One area of controversy among the Bloomfieldians concerned the *nonuniqueness* of phonemic solutions. Harris, for example, believed that sounds can be grouped in different ways and that solutions may differ depending on their purpose. (See also Chao, 1934.) Others, such as Pike and Hockett, believed there could be only one correct solution because the structure of the language was already there and simply had to be discovered (Fischer-Jørgensen, 1975, p. 78).

Later in the development of descriptive linguistics, the post-Bloomfieldians, especially Pike and Trager and Bloch, also dealt with suprasegmentals and talked about phonemic stress, pitch, and length (*suprasegmental phonemes*). For example, in the 1940s Trager and Bloch distinguished four phonemic degrees of stress, and Pike presented a new way of analyzing intonation. *Juncture*, a concept introduced by Trager and Bloch (1941) was also very important to some post-Bloomfieldians. Juncture has to do with the features that characterize the phonemes at the beginning and the end of an utterance. Several types of juncture were distinguished. For example, *open juncture* is the type found at the start and end of an isolated utterance. The difference between pairs of words such as *nitrate* and *night rate* was considered to be a difference in juncture (Fischer-Jørgensen, 1975, pp. 94–95).

Most of Bloomfield's followers were not interested in language history and language change, but a few, such as Archibald Hill and Henry Hoenigswald, were (as was Bloomfield himself, as shown in his 1933 book titled *Language*). Hill, in 1936, distinguished *phonetic change* from *phonemic change*, and Hoenigswald discussed different types of phonemic change, such as *phonemic split* (one phoneme splits to become two in the history of a language) and *phonemic merger* (two or more phonemes merge to become one phoneme) (Fischer-Jørgensen, 1975, p. 103).

Middle 20th Century:
Distinctive Feature Theory

As mentioned earlier, the work of the Prague School phonologists and their analysis of phonemes into distinctive phonetic properties paved the way for distinctive feature theory. The person whom we associate most with distinctive feature theory is Roman Jakobson, one of the original members of the Prague circle. The aim of distinctive feature theory is to find the minimal set of features that will account for the significant oppositions in any specific language, and that will also account for differences between languages (Schane, 1973, p. 33). Jakobson wanted to find a small number of features (12 to 15) that would be the "ultimate distinctive entities of language," "subphonemic particles" that could not be broken down further (Jakobson, 1949). He wanted these features to be universal (applicable to all languages) and binary, involving selection between two alternatives. That is, a linguistic property would either be present (+) or absent (−). In Jakobson's view, having one "correct" set of distinctive features would reduce the number of entities and relations in phonology and would therefore promote economical descriptions and would limit the number of possible correct solutions, solving the non-uniqueness problem referred to earlier (C. A. Ferguson, personal communication).

In 1952, a set of 12 distinctive features, defined in acoustic terms, was proposed by Jakobson, Fant, and Halle in *Preliminaries to Speech Analysis*. These features were challenged, and some were rejected. A revised set was put forward in 1956 by Jakobson and Halle in *Fundamentals of Language*. Today there is no one system of distinctive features that is totally accepted. There are many competing theories, and many distinctive oppositions have been proposed by various linguists. Some features are defined in acoustic terms, some in articulatory terms, and some in perceptual terms. The set of features that is most widely used at the present time in describing phonetic segments and in writing phonological rules is the set put forth by Noam Chomsky and Morris Halle in 1968 in *The Sound Pattern of English (SPE)* or a slightly modified version of that set. Some distinctive features from *The Sound Pattern of English* are discussed below. The definitions are basically those presented by Chomsky and Halle. Note that distinctive features are enclosed in square brackets.

Chomsky and Halle's (1968) Distinctive Features. Chomsky and Halle present three *major class features* (±sonorant, ±consonantal, and ±vocalic). These three features differentiate the major classes of sounds.

Sonorant. Sounds that are [+ sonorant] have a vocal tract configuration that allows spontaneous voicing. This category includes English vowels, semivowels (glides), nasals, and liquids. Obstruents or "true consonants" (stops, fricatives, and affricates) are [− sonorant]. They are characterized by a constriction that is greater than the constriction for glides.

Consonantal. Sounds that are [+ consonantal] are produced with a "radical obstruction" in the oral cavity. Liquids, nasals, and obstruents are [+ consonantal]. Vowels, glides and also /h/ and [ʔ] (glottal stop) are [− consonantal].

Vocalic. Sounds are said to be [+ vocalic] if the oral cavity is not more obstructed than it is during the production of the high vowels /i/ and /u/, and the vocal folds are positioned in such a way that spontaneous voicing is possible. In other words, there is fairly free passage of air through the vocal tract. Only vowels and liquids are [+vocalic]. Nasals, glides, and obstruents are [-vocalic]. In a later section of *SPE*, Chomsky and Halle give evidence to show that the feature *vocalic* could be replaced by the feature *syllabic*. Sounds that form the peak of a syllable are [+syllabic]. This includes vowels and syllabic sonorants (liquids and nasals). Obstruents, glides, and nonsyllabic liquids and nasals are [-syllabic]. Thus the crucial difference between these features involves nasals and liquids. Whereas nonsyllabic liquids are [-syllabic], they are [+vocalic] and syllabic nasals are [+syllabic], but [-vocalic].

Chomsky and Halle propose several *cavity features*. Most of these features specify the place of articulation of a sound.

Coronal. Sounds that are produced with the blade of the tongue elevated from the "neutral position" (of [ɛ], as in *met*) are [+coronal].[4] Dental, alveolar, and palato-alveolar consonants are [+coronal], as are the English liquids /l/ and /r/, which are produced with the tongue blade. Vowels, glides, labials, and velars are [-coronal].

Anterior. Sounds that are produced with an obstruction located in the front part of the oral cavity, farther front than the palato-alveolar region (at which /ʃ/ is produced) are [+anterior]. This includes labial, dental, and alveolar consonants. Vowels, and palato-alveolar, palatal, and velar consonants are [-anterior]. The English liquid /r/ is also classified as [-anterior].

Distributed. Sounds that are [+distributed] are produced with a constriction that extends for a fairly long distance in the direction of the flow of air. In [-distributed] sounds, the constriction extends for only a short distance (Chomsky & Halle, 1968, p. 312). This feature is used primarily for fricative distinctions. For example, bilabial fricatives /ɸ, β/ (which do not occur in adult English) are [+distributed], while labio-dental fricatives /f, v/ are [-distributed]. Both alveolar and palato-alveolar fricatives are [+distributed], involving a relatively long articulatory constriction, but /θ, ð/ are [-distributed].

In Chomsky and Halle's system, *high, low,* and *back* are *tongue body features*, as well as being cavity features.

High. Sounds are [+high] if they are produced with the tongue body raised from the neutral position. High vowels are [+high], as are palatal and velar consonants, as well as palatalized or velarized sounds. Nonhigh vowels and labial, dental, and alveolar consonants are [-high]. Uvulars and pharyngeals, which do not occur in English, are also [-high].

Low. Sounds that are [+low] are produced with the body of the tongue lowered from the neutral position. Low vowels are [+low], as are glottals such as /h/ and [ʔ], and pharyngeals. The two features *high* and *low* are used to differentiate three vowel heights. *High vowels* are [+high], [−low]; *low vowels* are [+low], [−high], and *mid vowels* are [−low], [−high]. (The other possible feature combination, [+high], [+low], is not physically possible, as the body of the tongue can not be raised and lowered at the same time.)

Back. The feature [+back] is used for sounds that are produced with the body of the tongue retracted from the neutral position. Back vowels and velar consonants (as well as velarized sounds) are [+back]. Pharyngeals and uvulars are also [+back]. Nonback vowels, dentals, labials, and palatals are [−back].

Round. Rounded sounds [+round] are produced with narrowing at the lips. Rounded vowels and labialized sounds are [+round], and all other sounds are [−round].

Three of the features put forward by Chomsky and Halle are classified as *manner of articulation features: continuant, delayed release,* and *tense.*

Continuant. Sounds that are [+continuant] do not involve complete blockage of the vocal tract. That is, the flow of air is not totally blocked by the main constriction. Vowels, glides, English liquids, and fricatives are [+continuant]. Only stops, nasals, and affricates are [−continuant]. The feature *interrupted* is sometimes used in place of continuant, although it has the opposite value. Only stops and affricates are [+interrupted].

Delayed release. This feature concerns only sounds produced with a closure. Sounds that are [+delayed release], affricates like /tʃ, dʒ/, are characterized by a gradual and turbulent release of the closure, while plosives, such as English /p, t, k/ are produced with an abrupt release. This feature is not necessary in English because English affricates are "strident stops" and can thus be classified as [−continuant], [+strident]. If English had a contrast between, for example, /ts/ and /tθ/, the latter being a nonstrident affricate, this feature would be necessary, as [−continuant], [−strident] would not differentiate /tθ/ from /t/ (see Hyman, 1975, p. 52).

Tense. [+Tense] sounds are said to involve greater effort on the part of supraglottal musculature or greater tension in the muscles of the vocal cavity. They are produced with a more deliberate articulatory gesture that is maintained for a longer period. In English, voiceless obstruents are classified as [+tense] and voiced obstruents are [−tense]. The feature *tense* also is used for vowel differences. Tense vowels are more distinct and involve greater movement from rest position than [−tense] or lax vowels, which are more centralized. The vowels /i, u, e, o, ɑ/ are generally classified as [+tense], and /ɪ, ʊ, ɛ, ɔ, æ, ə/ as [−tense] (Sloat, et al., 1978, p. 88).

The features *nasal* and *lateral* (and even *distributed*) are also classified as manner features in some systems, although in *SPE* they are called *cavity features*:

Nasal. Sounds that are [+nasal] are produced without velo-pharyngeal closure. That is, the velum is lowered, allowing air to escape through the nose. Only the nasal consonants /m, n, ŋ/ and nasalized vowels are [+nasal]. Nasal sounds are generally voiced because the open nasal passage does not allow the buildup of air pressure in the mouth that would inhibit spontaneous voicing.

Lateral. In [+lateral] sounds, the middle part of the tongue is lowered at one or both sides so that the airstream is channeled laterally and escapes by the molars. In English, only /l/ is [+lateral]; all other sounds are [−lateral].

The features *strident* and *voice*, which are classified as manner features in some systems, are classified as *source features* by Chomsky and Halle, along with a feature called *heightened subglottal pressure*.

Strident. The feature strident applies only to obstruent continuants and affricates; [+strident] obstruents are characterized acoustically by greater noisiness or aperiodic sound than are the corresponding nonstrident obstruents. In English, the interdental fricatives are [−strident], while all other fricatives and the affricates /tʃ, dʒ/ are [+strident).

Voice. [+Voice] sounds are produced with the vocal folds positioned so that they can vibrate. In the production of voiceless or [−voice] sounds, the opening between the vocal folds is so great that they can not vibrate. All sonorants (vowels, glides, liquids, and nasals) in English and many other languages are [+voice], as are the obstruents /b, d, g, ð, v, z, ʒ, dʒ/. All other obstruents (and [ʔ] and /h/) are [−voice].

Heightened subglottal pressure. Sounds that are [+HSP] are produced with a relatively great amount of subglottal pressure (i.e., pressure below the vocal folds). Heightened subglottal pressure is necessary for aspiration, but aspiration also requires that there be no constriction at the glottis. Only voiceless aspirated stops in English are [+HSP].

Prosodic features such as [±stress] and [±long] and tone features are also sometimes discussed, though not by Chomsky and Halle (1968).

Table 3-1 contains the feature specifications for English consonants and selected English vowels. Only the most commonly used features are included. As can be seen from a careful inspection of this table, each English sound is characterized by a unique "bundle of features." That is, no two English sounds have exactly the same feature specifications. For example, the English phoneme /s/ is [−sonorant], [+consonantal],

TABLE 3-1
The feature specifications for English consonants and selected English vowels

	p	b	t	d	k	g	θ	ð	f	v	s	z	ʃ	ʒ	tʃ	dʒ	m	n	ŋ	l	r	w	j	h	i	ɪ	e	ɛ	æ	u	ʊ	o	ɔ	ʌ	ɑ
Sonorant	−	−	−	−	−	−	−	−	−	−	−	−	−	−	−	−	+	+	+	+	+	+	+	−	+	+	+	+	+	+	+	+	+	+	+
Consonantal	+	+	+	+	+	+	+	+	+	+	+	+	+	+	+	+	+	+	+	+	+	−	−	−	−	−	−	−	−	−	−	−	−	−	−
Vocalic	−	−	−	−	−	−	−	−	−	−	−	−	−	−	−	−	−	−	−	+	+	−	−	−	+	+	+	+	+	+	+	+	+	+	+
Coronal	−	−	+	+	−	−	+	+	−	−	+	+	+	+	+	+	−	+	−	+	+	−	−	−	−	−	−	−	−	−	−	−	−	−	−
Anterior	+	+	+	+	−	−	+	+	+	+	+	+	−	−	−	−	+	+	−	+	−	−	−	−	−	−	−	−	−	−	−	−	−	−	−
High	−	−	−	−	+	+	−	−	−	−	−	−	+	+	+	+	−	−	+	−	−	+	+	−	+	+	−	−	−	+	+	−	−	−	−
Low	−	−	−	−	−	−	−	−	−	−	−	−	−	−	−	−	−	−	−	−	−	−	−	+	−	−	−	−	+	−	−	−	+	−	+
Back	−	−	−	−	+	+	−	−	−	−	−	−	−	−	−	−	−	−	+	−	−	+	−	−	−	−	−	−	−	+	+	+	+	+	+
Round	−	−	−	−	−	−	−	−	−	−	−	−	−	−	−	−	−	−	−	−	−	+	−	−	−	−	−	−	−	+	+	+	+	−	−
Continuant	−	−	−	−	−	−	+	+	+	+	+	+	+	+	−	−	−	−	−	+	+	+	+	+	+	+	+	+	+	+	+	+	+	+	+
Tense	+	−	+	−	+	−	+	−	+	−	+	−	+	−	+	−	−	−	−	−	−	−	−	−	+	−	+	−	−	+	−	+	+	−	+
Nasal	−	−	−	−	−	−	−	−	−	−	−	−	−	−	−	−	+	+	+	−	−	−	−	−	−	−	−	−	−	−	−	−	−	−	−
Lateral	−	−	−	−	−	−	−	−	−	−	−	−	−	−	−	−	−	−	−	+	−	−	−	−	−	−	−	−	−	−	−	−	−	−	−
Strident	−	−	−	−	−	−	−	−	+	+	+	+	+	+	+	+	−	−	−	−	−	−	−	−	−	−	−	−	−	−	−	−	−	−	−
Voice	−	+	−	+	−	+	−	+	−	+	−	+	−	+	−	+	+	+	+	+	+	+	+	−	+	+	+	+	+	+	+	+	+	+	+

[-vocalic], [+coronal], [+anterior], [-high], [-low], [-back], [-round], [+continuant], [+tense], [-nasal], [-lateral], [+strident], [-voice]. The only feature that differentiates /s/ from /z/ is *voice*. Whereas /s/ is [-voice], /z/ is [+voice]. Similarly, /s/ differs from /θ/ only in the feature *strident*; /s/ is [+strident], but /θ/ is [-strident].

Generally, it is not necessary to specify all the features that characterize a sound.[5] Some of the information that is specified when the entire feature composition of a sound is given is *redundant*. For example, if an English sound is [+vocalic] and [-consonantal], it is necessarily a vowel. Therefore, it is also [+continuant], [-nasal], [+sonorant], [-anterior], [-coronal], [+voice], and [-strident] (MacKay, 1978, p. 232). It is unnecessary to state these redundancies; they can be inferred or predicted from the features [+vocalic] and [-consonantal]. Similarly, the feature [+nasal] characterizes just three English phonemes /m, n, ŋ/. When we wish to refer to these three sounds, we can do so by using the feature [+nasal]. All of the other features shared by these three sounds [+sonorant], [+consonantal], [-vocalic], [-continuant], etc., can be inferred from or predicted by the feature [+nasal]. (Nasal vowels are also [+nasal] but they are not phonemes in English.)

Implicational formulas or *rules* may be used to express redundancies (Sloat, et al., 1978, p. 94). To illustrate, the fact that sounds cannot be both [+high] and [+low] (a *universal redundancy*) is captured by a rule that may be written in either of the following ways:

$$[+high]$$
$$\downarrow$$
$$[-low]\qquad\text{(Schane, 1973, p. 36)}$$

or [+high] ⇒ [-low] (Sloat, et al., 1978, p. 94).

Predictable feature information may be "filled in" by means of *redundancy rules* (MacKay, 1978, p. 232). For example, English liquids (/l/ and /r/) are [+consonantal] and [+vocalic]. These are the only two features that need to be specified when we discuss /l/ and /r/. The other features can be filled in by a redundancy rule as follows:

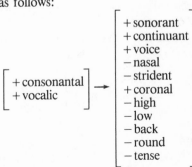

When discussing a sound or several sounds that share many features (a *natural class* such as liquids, nasals, or vowels) it is customary to specify only the minimal features that are necessary to differentiate that particular sound or class of sounds from all other English sounds, as illustrated above. To give a few more examples, the velar nasal /ŋ/ is uniquely specified by the two features [+nasal] and [−anterior] because it is the only [−anterior] nasal in English. If we wish to talk about the true consonants, we need to mention only one feature, [−sonorant], as all other English sounds are [+sonorant] with the possible exception of /h/, the classification of which has always been problematic and controversial.

As these examples show, a natural class can be specified with fewer features than any member of that class (Hyman, 1975, p. 139). The two features [+continuant] and [−sonorant] define the natural class of fricatives. If we want to talk about any subgroup of fricatives, we have to add at least one more feature. For instance, if we add the feature [+voice], we are limiting our discussion to /ð, v, z, ʒ/, or if we add the feature [+strident], we are specifying /f, v, s, z, ʃ, ʒ/ and are excluding /θ, ð/.

Distinctive features have several uses. One of the primary uses is to specify and define natural classes of sounds, as the examples above illustrate. As just noted, natural classes of sounds share many features. It is important to be able to specify natural classes of sounds because they frequently undergo the same changes or act together in phonological processes (Schane, 1973, p. 33). Distinctive features often allow us to capture significant generalizations in phonological rules relatively simply. Usually only the relevant features or those that change are stated. For example:

$$
\begin{bmatrix} +\text{vocalic} \\ -\text{consonantal} \end{bmatrix} \rightarrow [+\text{nasal}] \ /\_\_\_ \ [+\text{nasal}]
$$

is a shorthand way of representing a common assimilation process. It indicates that a vowel is nasalized (becomes [+nasal]) when it precedes a nasal sound. Similarly, the palatalization of /s/ when it precedes a palatal glide in casual speech, as in "I miss you" [aɪ mɪʃju] can be shown (rather informally) by the following rule:

$$
/s/ \rightarrow [+\text{high}] \ /\_\_\_ \begin{bmatrix} -\text{cons} \\ +\text{high} \end{bmatrix}
$$

The fact that people tend to confuse sounds that are close in terms of distinctive features (such as /f/ - /θ/ and /d/ - /ð/) indicates that features do have some "psychological reality." For example, in their 1972 study of the substitution errors of a large group of standard English speaking children, Cairns and Williams found that most of the errors made by these children involved changes in just one distinctive feature. To illustrate, the common [d] for /ð/ substitution involves a change from [+continuant] to [−continuant]. Since the late 1960s, several researchers have attempted to use distinctive features in analyzing the substitution errors of children with articulation disorders. This application of distinctive feature theory will be discussed in more detail later in this book.

One of the aspects of distinctive feature theory that has been criticized is the requirement of binarity, i.e., the requirement that features must be either plus (+) or minus (−). Binarity is particularly unsatisfactory where vowel height is concerned. In order to handle languages that have four vowel heights, it is necessary to differentiate two mid ([−high], [−low]) vowels by means of the feature *tense*. For example, in English [e] would be [+tense] and [ɛ] would be [−tense] (Hyman, 1975, pp. 55–56).

Linguists such as Foley (1970), Ladefoged (1971), and Vennemann (1972a) have argued for *multivalued* or *scalar features*, which specify a continuous scale and have more than two possibilities (Hyman, 1975, p. 57). For instance, English would have five feature specifications for the height feature because English has consonants that are "maximally" high, in addition to four degrees of vowel height. To illustrate, the low vowels [æ] and [ɑ] would be [1 height], and the high vowels [i, u] would be [4 height], along with the glides [w, j] (Ladefoged, 1975, p. 239). Similarly, Ladefoged (1975, pp. 238–239) argues for [place] as a multivalued feature with five values for English because English has phonemic contrasts involving five places of articulation: labial, dental, alveolar, palatal, and velar.

CONCLUSION

Phonological inquiry dates back to the ancients, who were interested in issues such as describing and preserving languages and devising alphabetic writing systems. Where our account resumes in the 19th century, linguists focused on comparative and historical linguistics. A number of distinguished scholars concerned themselves with understanding how languages shared common origins and features, particularly the Indo-European languages. During this same period, descriptive phoneticians were interested in formulating careful symbolic descriptions of speech sounds, symbol systems that are currently used by linguists, speech-language pathologists and others concerned with phonology.

The first half of the 20th century included phonological inquiry by two groups that have continued to influence theory and practice. The work of The Prague School (e.g. Roman Jakobson) and the American Structuralists (e.g. Bloomfield) has had a marked influence on the conduct of research and clinical practice in communicative disorders and in other applied disciplines.

There are many additional approaches to phonology that have been of interest during the 20th century, such as stratificational theory, prosodic theory, glossematics, and autosegmental phonology. Due to space limitations, these approaches could not be discussed in this chapter. The interested reader is referred to discussions in Fischer-Jørgensen (1975) and to readings in Dinnsen (1979).

FOOTNOTES

[1]de Saussure was influenced by Jan Baudouin de Courtenay, a Polish linguist who believed that the sounds which are psychologically important are the ones used to differentiate meaning (Fischer-Jørgensen 1975, p. 9).

[2]Phonemics is actually narrower than phonology; it concerns how sounds function to distinguish meaning.

[3]N. Chomsky (1964) later referred to this principle as "local determinacy"—it is possible to determine the phoneme a phone belongs to by looking at the neighbors (phonetic environment) of the phone.

[4]Chomsky and Halle (1968, p. 300) follow Daniel Jones, a famous phonetician, in defining the blade of the tongue as the part that usually lies opposite the alveolar ridge. The blade includes the point or tip of the tongue.

[5]Not all features apply to all sounds. Thus in a feature matrix, blank spaces may be left to indicate that the features in question are not applicable. For example, vowel sounds cannot be strident and they must be voiced, so these features may be left blank.

4

Generative Phonology

OVERVIEW

The major theory of phonology since the late 1950s or early 1960s has been *generative phonology*. In 1957, Noam Chomsky presented his theory of *transformational-generative grammar* in a book called *Syntactic Structures*. As the name of the book indicates, Chomsky's main concern was *syntax*, which involves "the principles and processes by which sentences are constructed in particular languages" (1957, p. 11).

According to Chomsky's (1957) model, there are three sets of rules: *phrase structure rules, transformational rules,* and *morphophonemic rules*. When all of these rules apply, the result is a "string of phonemes" of the language (p. 114). Phrase structure rules, such as Sentence → Noun Phrase + Verb Phrase (S→NP + VP) plus the lexicon form the *base*. The deep structures generated by the base component then undergo transformational rules, such as the passive transformation. The sequences of morphemes or surface syntactic structures derived in this way (by the phrase structure rules and the transformational rules) are then subject to morphophonemic rules which generate sequences of phonemes from them. So, Chomsky viewed phonology and morphology as "two distinct but interdependent levels of representation, related by morphophonemic rules," such as: *take* + past→ /tuk/ (1957, p. 58). In

FIGURE 4-1

A simplified sketch contrasting (a) the Bloomfieldian view of the phonemic level of analysis (i.e., grammar) with (b) Chomsky's (1957) view of the phonological component of grammar. The area within the dotted lines corresponds to the *phonological component,* as depicted more generally in Figure 1-1 and Figure 2-4. Note that whereas American structuralists usually worked from the phoneme level up to larger units, Bloomfield (1933) introduced Immediate Constituent (IC) analysis, which started at the level of the sentence and broke down sentences into ICs.

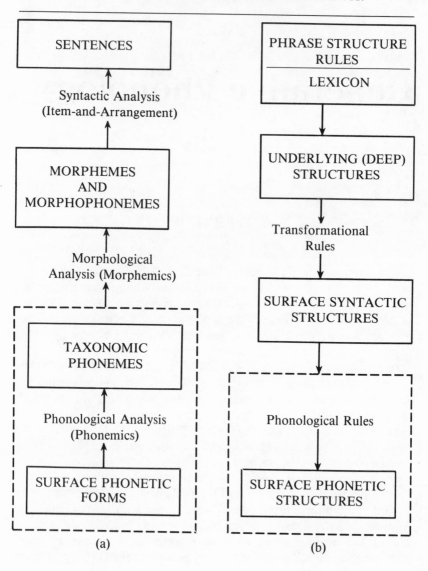

other words, Chomsky did not object to mixing levels as the Bloomfieldians did; he disagreed with the Bloomfieldian idea that phonological and morphological problems have to be solved before syntactic problems can be handled. The phonological component of transformational-generative grammar is viewed as *interpretive*. That is, it interprets surface syntactic structures and converts them into surface phonetic structures. Figure 4-1 illustrates schematically how Chomsky's (1957) view differed from that of the Bloomfieldians, to whom "grammar" was nothing more than analysis, and phonemic analysis was basic.

Chomsky's (1957, 1958) generative-transformational grammar was a reaction against the structuralism and behaviorism and had been predominant in the United States for over 20 years. Chomsky's model is much more theoretical, abstract, and mentalistic than that of the descriptive linguists. Contrary to the Bloomfieldians, Chomsky is concerned with what goes on in the speaker-hearer's mind. In many ways, he is closer to the Prague phonologists than to the Bloomfieldians. For example, he and other generative phonologists prefer distinctive features to the Bloomfieldian concept of the phoneme. As Fischer-Jørgensen (1975, p. 113) points out, they have also criticized the narrow descriptive approach of the Bloomfieldians and their "biuniqueness condition," as well as their "separation of levels." However, the generative phonologists have been influenced by Bloomfield's "item-and-process" type of morphophonemic description, which consists of base forms and derivations, e.g., the /z/ of the plural morpheme is replaced by [s] after voiceless sounds (Fischer-Jørgensen, 1975, p. 70).

In the view of generative phonologists, there is no need for (what they call) a *taxonomic* or *autonomous* phonemic level, the level of primary interest to most descriptive linguists. In fact, Chomsky believes that generalizations are missed if such a level is posited. Rather, Chomsky and his followers are concerned with what they call the *systematic phonemic level*. This resembles the traditional morphophonemic level (Hyman, 1975, p. 82). As mentioned earlier, one of the main concerns of generative phonology is accounting for phonemic alternations that occur in pairs of related words (or in allomorphs of one morpheme), such as the /k/ ~ /s/ alternation that occurs in *electric* and *electricity*. In order to account for such alternations, generative phonologists posit an abstract *underlying* or *lexical representation (a systematic phonemic representation)* from which all of the related (systematic) phonetic forms can be derived by the application of phonological rules such as *velar softening*, which changes /k/ to [s] before the suffix *-ity*, as in *electricity*. This is illustrated schematically in Figure 4-2.

FIGURE 4-2
An expanded schematic representation of the phonological component of generative-transformational grammar. The level designated as the systematic phonemic level is said to be similar to the Bloomfieldian morphophonemic level (see Figure 4-1)

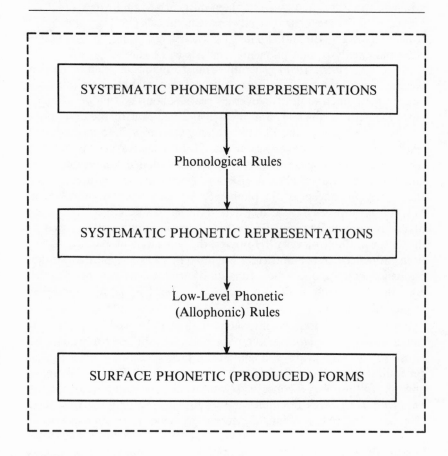

Generative phonology was most fully elaborated in *The Sound Pattern of English (SPE)* by Noam Chomsky and Morris Halle (1968). In this book, Chomsky and Halle put forward their views, developed over a period of several years, of the phonological component of the grammar. (See also Halle, 1959, 1962, 1964, and Chomsky, 1964). Generative phonological theory, as presented in *SPE*, is sometimes called *standard theory*. The following sections discuss in turn major elements of generative phonology: phonological rules and underlying representations.

PHONOLOGICAL RULES

The concept of sound change was introduced in Chapter 1. Phonologists are interested in how sounds may change over time within a language, within a child, and so forth. In generative phonology, phonological rules, as stated above, convert underlying representations in a language (systematic phonemic representations) to derived or surface representations (called systematic phonetic representations). Phonological rules, according to Schane (1973, p. 62) state the exact conditions under which sound changes takes place. That is, they "capture linguistically significant generalizations." These rules can be stated formally or informally. In order to formulate a phonological rule, we need to know which segments change and how they change and under what conditions (Schane, 1973, p. 62). The general form of phonological rules is as follows:

$$A \rightarrow B \;/\; C\_D$$

The underlying form (A), which is the *input* to the rule, is written on the left of the arrow. The arrow means "becomes" or "is replaced by" or "is realized as." The derived form (B) (or *output*) is written directly to the right of the arrow. The diagonal line or slash means "in the environment of," and C and D represent the phonetic context or environment. The segment that undergoes the change belongs in the blank (__). C and D may be sounds (e.g., /t/, /i/), features, (e.g., [+ anterior]) or boundaries between words, syllables, or morphemes.

In some cases, only the preceding or following element needs to be specified, as in A→B / C__ or A→B / __D. A rule in which the environment must be specified is called a *context-sensitive* rule. Sound changes that take place in all phonetic contexts are called *context-free*. Phonological rules may be *obligatory*, affecting all appropriate segments consistently, or *optional*, applying less than 100% of the time.

When phonological rules are written formally, distinctive features are used to specify the input, the output, and the environment. The input is identified by the minimal set of features needed to specify the sounds that are changed (Schane, 1973, p. 62). For example, a rule by which an obstruent [– sonorant] becomes voiceless [– voice] when following a voiceless sound (a voicing assimilation rule) would be written as follows:

$$[-\text{sonorant}] \rightarrow [-\text{voice}] \ / \ [-\text{voice}] \ \_\_$$

To give another example, a rule stating that obstruents [– sonorant] are devoiced in word-final position (preceding a word boundary) would be written as:

$$[-\text{sonorant}] \rightarrow [-\text{voice}] \ / \ \_\_ \ \# \ (\text{where} \ \# \ \text{is a word boundary})$$

As noted earlier, nasalization of vowels preceding a nasal consonant, a process that is common in English, may be represented as:

$$[+\text{syllabic}] \rightarrow [+\text{nasal}] \ /\_\_ \ [+\text{nasal}]$$

Rules may be optional. An example of an optional rule (which may apply but does not have to) is palatal assimilation (or assimilatory palatalization), mentioned earlier. This rule, which often applies in casual speech, states that alveolar sounds are palatalized preceding an [i] vowel or [j] glide, as in [wi mɪʃ ju] for *we miss you* (Hyman, 1975, p. 13). It may be formalized as follows:

$$
\begin{bmatrix} -\text{sonorant} \\ +\text{coronal} \end{bmatrix}
\rightarrow
\begin{bmatrix} +\text{high} \\ -\text{back} \end{bmatrix}
\ /\_\_
\begin{bmatrix} -\text{consonantal} \\ +\text{high} \\ -\text{back} \end{bmatrix}
\quad (\text{optional})
$$

Optional rules produce alternations, for example between [mɪs] and [mɪʃ] for *miss*.

Sometimes informal devices or notational conventions are used in writing rules. For example, V may be used to represent vowels and C to represent consonants. These capital letters are used as a shorthand notation for the features that specify these classes of sounds. Occasionally, capital letters also are used for other classes of sounds, e.g., N for nasals, L for liquids, G for glides, etc.

Phonetic symbols may be used to simplify rule writing. For example, if a sound change affects only /f/ and /v/, these phonetic symbols may be used in place of the features [+ strident], [– coronal]. To make it easier to interpret rules, phonetic symbols are sometimes written in parentheses under the appropriate set of features (e.g. see Sloat et al., 1978, p. 143), as in

$$\begin{bmatrix} +\text{strident} \\ -\text{coronal} \end{bmatrix}$$

(f, v)

Instead of writing out the features that specify a sound class, phonologists, in informal rules, sometimes use the name of the class of sounds, such as *stop*, *fricative*, etc. To illustrate, in English, voiceless stops are aspirated (become [+HSP]) at the beginning of a word preceding a stressed vowel. This rule can be written informally as:

$$\begin{bmatrix} +\text{stop} \\ -\text{voice} \end{bmatrix} \rightarrow [+\text{HSP}] \;/\; \# \underline{\quad} \; \acute{V}$$

Note that $\acute{V}$ represents a vowel with primary stress. Secondary stress is indicated by $\grave{V}$ in informal rules. A somewhat more formal way to represent a stressed vowel would be to use the feature specification

$$\begin{bmatrix} +\text{syllabic} \\ +\text{stress} \end{bmatrix}$$

Occasionally, phonological rules are written in a *structural description* or *transformational format*. The structural description of the rule (the input) appears on the left of the arrow, and the *structural change* the (output) appears on the right of the arrow. Numerals are used to represent each element in the input and the output. For example, Schane (1973, p. 118) discusses the following rule (from French), written in the structural description format:

$$\underset{1}{V} \quad \underset{2}{\begin{bmatrix} C \\ +\text{nasal} \end{bmatrix}} \underset{3}{\begin{Bmatrix} C \\ \# \end{Bmatrix}} \rightarrow \begin{bmatrix} 1 \\ +\text{nasal} \end{bmatrix} \phi\, 3$$

This rule says that a sequence of a vowel plus a nasal consonant is replaced by a nasalized vowel preceeding a consonant or a word boundary. The nasal consonant is deleted (replaced by null ϕ). The structural description format is especially useful for capturing coalescence and metathesis processes, in which more than one segment is affected at once (Schane, 1973, p. 67).

Types of Phonological Rules

Phonological rules have several functions. For example, they may add, delete or change the order of segments or features. They also may change features or segments or collapse features from two adjacent segments. Keep in mind again that phonological rules serve as a type of formal shorthand to describe sound changes. Later in this book we will see how clinicians and researchers have used phonological rules in applied problems.

Segment Addition and Deletion Rules

In segment addition and deletion the *null sign* (ϕ) is used. In addition or insertion rules, the null sign is on the left of the arrow and the segment that is added is on the right of the arrow. For instance, $\phi \rightarrow \partial / \# C\_C$ is a rule that inserts [ə] between two elements of a consonant cluster in word-initial position. This rule is read as follows: [ə] is inserted (or ϕ becomes [ə]) between two consonants in word-initial position. This is a *vowel epenthesis* rule. For example, if a child said [tᵊrʌk] for *truck* and [kᵊlɔk] for *clock* and produced other liquid clusters in a similar way, we might describe his or her phonology as having a vowel epenthesis rule.

In deletion rules, the null sign is on the right of the arrow, and the segment or feature that is deleted is on the left of the arrow. For example, $C \rightarrow \phi / \#\_C$ is read as follows: a consonant is deleted (or replaced by zero) when it precedes another consonant in word-initial position. Children often exhibit some variation of this cluster reduction rule, as in [pun] for *spoon* and [tɑp] for *stop*.

Metathesis Rules

Rules that permute or change the order of segments are called metathesis rules. Such rules may be written in various ways. Informally, they may be written as follows: $C_1 C_2 \rightarrow C_2 C_1$. Both segments appear in both the input and the output, but their order is reversed. To illustrate, a common metathesis rule reverses the order of /s/ and /k/ in /sk/ clusters in final position, as in [æks] for *ask* in some English dialects. This rule may be written informally as: $sk \rightarrow ks / \_\#$. When such rules are written formally, the transformational format is often used, as mentioned above.

Feature Change
Rules

An example of a feature change rule is the following:
[– sonorant]→[– voice] /__#. This rule says that obstruents (which are
[– sonorant]) are devoiced (become [– voice]) in word-final position
(__#), as in [nos] for *nose*. Because the voicing feature is not mentioned
in the input of this rule, it is understood that the rule applies to both
voiced and voiceless obstruents. However, voiceless segments are already
[– voice], and thus they are not changed by this rule. We say that the rule
applies *vacuously* in such cases. The only segments that are actually
changed by this rule are those that are both [+ voice] and [– sonorant].
(This rule is sometimes considered to be an assimilation rule.)

Assimilation Rules

In assimilation rules, a sound segment takes on features of a nearby
sound. Thus, the environment and the output share features that are not
part of the input (Sloat et al., 1978, p. 145). If the sound that conditions
the assimilation precedes the sound that is changed, the assimilation is
progressive or *perseverative*, and if the conditioning sound follows the
sound that is changed, the assimilation is *regressive* or *anticipatory*. A
common assimilation rule of English involves nasalization of a vowel
preceding a nasal consonant, as in [kʰǣn] for *can*. This regressive
assimilation rule may be written as: [+ syllabic]→[+ nasal] /__[+ nasal],
as mentioned above. Another example of a regressive assimilation rule is
the rule described earlier that palatalizes alveolar consonants preceding a
palatal glide ([j]) or high front vowel ([i]), as in [āɪvgɑtʃə] for *I've got
you*.

Coalescence Rules

Some rules *collapse* or *coalesce* features from two adjacent segments.
For example, children sometimes replace /sp/ clusters by [f]. In this case,
the output shares features of both segments in the input. This rule may
be written informally as: sp→f /#__. Similarly, children may replace initial /sn/ clusters by a voiceless nasal (symbolized as [n̥]). This rule may
be written as: sn→n̥ /#__. When coalescence rules are written formally,
the transformational format is used. Coalescence may be treated as
assimilation followed by deletion (Schane, 1973, p. 68).

Alternation Rules

Some phonological rules produce alternations, as mentioned earlier.
For example, the palatalization rule discussed above is optional, taking

place more frequently in casual speech. It therefore results in alternate forms, such as [mɪs] and [mɪʃ]. These alternate forms are called allomorphs of one morpheme (meaningful unit), in this case *miss*. Allomorphs such as these are *phonologically conditioned*—their occurrence depends on neighboring sounds. Allomorphs are not always phonologically conditioned, however. In some cases, the "grammatical" environment is the crucial factor. For example, the plural form of *goose* is *geese*, and the past tense of *see* is *saw*. This type of situation, in which allomorphs are not derived by regular phonological rules, is called *suppletion* (Hyman, 1975, pp. 13-14).

Derivations

As noted above, phonological rules relate or connect two levels of representation—the underlying or phonological representation and the surface or phonetic representation. The underlying form is written in slashes or diagonal lines (virgules / /), and the surface form is placed in square brackets ([ ]). Very often, several rules apply in getting from the underlying representation to the surface or derived representation of a word. Thus there may be several intermediate representations, all of which are written in virgules (Schane, 1973, p. 91). A *derivation* shows all the steps that are involved and all the intermediate representations. In a derivation, it is generally understood that the output of one rule serves as input to the next applicable rule. Appendix B is a detailed discussion of rule application issues.

In child phonology, the child's underlying representation is usually taken to be roughly equivalent to the adult surface form, minus the phonetic detail. (This point will be illustrated in somewhat more depth in Part III of this book.) An example of a derivation from child phonology is given below. The adult word is *stop*:

Child's underlying representation	/stɑp/
/s/-cluster reduction	/ tɑp/
Initial voicing	/ dɑp/
Final consonant deletion	/ dɑ /
Child's surface form	[dɑ]

Functional Unity of Phonological Rules

Often several phonological rules have the same function or purpose. That is, they are *functionally related* or exhibit *functional unity*. Kisseberth (1970) used the term *conspiracy* in this connection. He stated that languages often have rules that conspire to produce (or avoid) the same output. For example, several functionally similar rules may conspire to produce CVCV sequences in a language. Kisseberth argued that there ought to be a way to express functional relatedness. Thus he introduced the concept of *derivational constraint* (Hyman, 1975, p. 136).

Derivational constraints are constraints on rules that prevent a particular output from being produced. To illustrate, a language may have a constraint that no rule can produce a sequence of three consonants. Stating this constraint once allows us to simplify certain rules. As long as the derivational constraint is understood, some elements can be omitted from the environments of rules. Thus the rules can be more general. For example, if a language had a rule deleting [ə] after a stressed syllable and also had a derivational constraint such that sequences of three consonants could not be produced, the [ə] deletion rule could be written as follows:

$$[\text{ə}] \rightarrow \phi \ / \ \acute{\text{V}}\text{C}\_\_\text{C}$$

The derivational constraint would prevent this rule from applying when a sequence of three consonants would result, i.e., in sequences such as $\acute{\text{V}}$CəCC.

Derivational constraints may even be able to "trigger" rules, such as the insertion of a vowel when an unallowable sequence of consonants might arise. Although Kisseberth (1970) wanted to find a formal way to express functional relatedness, many other linguists believe that functionally related rules should not be collapsed because they are separate and different rules, even though they happen to serve the same purpose. When rules are collapsed, it generally implies that they are really one rule (Hyman, 1975, p. 137).

There is some controversy as to whether phonological rules reflect rules that are actually used by speakers in producing utterances. Many linguists would say that at least some rules do. However, what is most important to linguists is that it is possible to find regularities in data from real languages and to represent these regularities by means of phonological rules (Sloat et al., 1978, p. 159).

UNDERLYING REPRESENTATIONS

As discussed above, phonological rules relate or connect two levels of representation, the *underlying phonological representation* and the *surface phonetic* or *derived representation*. That is, phonological rules apply to underlying representations and derive surface representations. Generative phonologists are interested primarily in the nature of underlying representations. The more the underlying representation differs from the surface representation, the more abstract it is, and the more rules are needed to relate the two levels (Sloat et al., 1978, p. 13). As noted earlier, generative phonologists are also interested in morphemes that have variant forms (or allomorphs), and they want to derive such pairs of related forms (e.g., *electric/electricity*, and *sane/sanity*) from the same underlying representation by means of phonological rules. In fact, this is one of the main characteristics of generative phonology. Thus their underlying representations are often quite abstract. For example, the underlying form postulated for *electricity* is /elektrik + iti/ and the underlying form of *serenity* is /serēn + iti/. To repeat, these abstract underlying forms, from which several related forms are derived by phonological rules, are called *systematic phonemic representations*, and the derived forms are called *surface* or *systematic phonetic representations*.

Systematic phonemic representations contain no redundant phonetic information. Only distinctive sound contrasts are represented. These underlying or lexical representations are said to approximate the *mental representations* that speakers have of words. The idea is that speakers "know" (though not necessarily consciously) that certain forms are related, and this must be accounted for in the grammar (Hyman, 1975, pp. 9, 80).[1]

In generative phonology, there is no level of representation that is the same as the taxonomic or autonomous phonemic level (although derived representations may be similar). In fact, generative phonologists reject that level (e.g., see Halle, 1959). However, Schane (1973, p. 97) states that a systematic phonemic representation should be equivalent to a traditional taxonomic phonemic representation unless there is a "good reason" (e.g., alternations among allomorphs) for it to be more abstract. So, for a word with no alternate forms (e.g., *cat, walk*), the systematic phonemic representation would be the same as a taxonomic phonemic representation. When there are alternate forms (such as *sane/sanity*), the underlying representation has to be abstract enough to allow us to derive all surface variants from it by means of phonological rules. In this way, surface irregularities can be accounted for at a deeper level (Hyman, 1975). Similarly, the underlying form of the plural morpheme is generally taken to be /-z/ and the other allomorphs are derived from /-z/ by phonetically motivated phonological rules.

Alternate forms (allomorphs) that are not phonologically conditioned are handled in a different way. For example, several allomorphs of the plural morpheme in English are *morphologically conditioned*—we cannot account for their distribution by general phonological rules, and they are not *productive*, i.e., they are not added to new words. Such allomorphs include the *-en* of *oxen*, the *-i* of *fungi*, the *-a* of *criteria*, etc. Nouns that take these "irregular" plural allomorphs have to be marked in the lexicon as exceptional. For some of these words, such as *fungus*, the form of the irregular singular is specified in the lexicon, and the plural form can be predicted by means of *lexical redundancy rules* (Sloat et al., 1978, p. 134). In the case of irregular nouns and verbs such as *man/men* and *was/were*, both forms have to be listed in the lexicon. *Suppletion* is the term for such alternations that cannot be accounted for by rules, as mentioned earlier (Schane, 1973, p. 82).

Determination of Underlying Representations

How are underlying representations determined? In analyzing a new language or language variety (or a child's language), it is necessary to discover the underlying representations and the rules that will derive the surface phonetic forms from them. Although there is no absolute way to determine underlying representations, there are some considerations that should be kept in mind. One of these, which is discussed by Hyman (1975, p. 91), is *predictability*. In generative phonology, underlying representations must be abstract enough to allow us to predict all related surface forms by means of phonological rules. In addition, both the underlying representations and the necessary rules must be *motivated* (e.g., the rules should capture processes in the language) and must promote simplicity or economy in the grammar, e.g., the lexicon is simpler when several variants can be derived from one underlying representation (Schane, 1973, p. 82).

Schane (1973, pp. 75-76) gives an example. In French, many adjectives have two forms when they appear before masculine nouns; one form ends in a consonant and one in a vowel. If the noun following the adjective begins with a vowel, the form of the adjective that has a final consonant appears, but if the noun begins with a consonant, the form of the adjective that ends with a vowel appears. So, for instance, we find [pətit ɑmi] "small friend" but [pəti gɑrsɔ̃] "small boy." Thus, it is necessary to postulate the underlying representation of these adjectives with a final consonant and also to postulate a rule deleting the final consonant when the following noun begins with a consonant. If the underlying representation of the adjective did not have a final consonant, we would have to posit a rule inserting a consonant before vowel-initial nouns, but, as Schane points out, we would have no way of predicting which consonant to insert ([t, z, k], etc.). (There is also additional evidence that the crucial rule is not one of consonant insertion.)

Another example (discussed by Schane, 1973, p. 77) comes from German. German has alternations between voiceless and voiced obstruents in related forms such as [tɑk] "day," [tɑgə] "days." In order to derive both allomorphs from the same underlying form, it is necessary to posit the underlying form with a final voiced obstruent and to postulate a final devoicing rule (e.g., g→k/__#). Before a vowel, the voiced obstruent is not devoiced (e.g., /tɑg+ə/→[tɑgə]). It would be equally plausible to posit underlying voiceless obstruents and an obstruent voicing rule. However, German does have medial voiceless obstruents, and thus if we postulated a voicing rule, we could not predict which forms would undergo voicing and which would not. Another possible solution, discussed by Hyman (1975, p. 92) would be to posit final voiceless obstruents in the underlying forms and to mark with a *diacritic* (e.g., [+D]) those morphemes undergoing the voicing change. However, diacritics are usually used for exceptions, and, as Hyman notes, the use of a diacritic here would make the misleading claim that these alternations are not phonologically conditioned.[2]

The plural morpheme in English has three regular (phonologically conditioned) allomorphs, [-s], [-z], [-əz]. Generative phonologists usually choose /-z/ as the underlying form because all the surface variants can be derived from it by means of phonetically motivated rules. The [-əz] ending is derived by an epenthesis rule that inserts [ə] between sibilant sounds and /-z/, as in *roses, dishes,* and *judges*. A voicing assimilation rule changes /-z/ to [-s] when the preceding sound is voiceless. The allomorph [-z] occurs after all other regular nouns.

Similarly, the underlying form of the regular past tense morpheme in English is generally taken to be /-d/ rather than [-t] or [-əd] because choosing /-d/ as the basic allomorph allows us to derive the other allomorphs from it by means of phonetically plausible rules, again epenthesis and voicing assimilation. As these examples show, the allomorph that is chosen as basic is usually the one with the widest distribution (e.g., in these cases the basic allomorphs also occur after vowels, as in *toes* and *owed*).

The negative prefix *in-* in English is realized as [ɪm-], [ɪn-], or [ɪŋ-] as in *immovable, indescribable, inconsistent,* etc. Generative phonologists usually consider /ɪn-/ to be the basic underlying form. One reason for choosing this variant is that it occurs before vowels where assimilation cannot occur, as in *inaccurate.* In addition, the other variants can be derived from this basic form by a natural rule of nasal assimilation by which /n/ assimilates in place of articulation to the following consonant. (However, Hyman (1975, p. 91) points out some difficulties with this analysis.)

Another criterion to keep in mind when positing underlying forms is economy or simplicity, as mentioned above. Solutions are more economical if they have fewer phonemes, although they may also require more complicated rules (Hyman, 1975, p. 93). To illustrate, Chomsky and Halle (1968) analyze the English velar nasal [ŋ] as being made up of two underlying phonemes /ng/. This solution is said to be more economical than the alternative (which would posit /ŋ/ as a separate phoneme) because one less phoneme is postulated for English. The nasal assimilation rule which converts /n/ to [ŋ] preceding /g/ is already needed in English to account for other forms, so no new rule is necessary. According to Hyman (1975, p. 94), the solution in which [ŋ] is analyzed as underlying /ng/ would also be chosen on the basis of *pattern congruity* (another criterion used in positing underlying forms) because /ng/, like the parallel clusters /mb/ and /nd/, does not occur in initial position. (However, remember our earlier example in which /ŋ/ was postulated as a separate phoneme of English, also based on pattern congruity.)

A major criterion to be considered in setting up underlying representations is *plausibility*, which has to do with phonetic naturalness (Hyman, 1975, pp. 97–98). If one solution is more natural than another, that is the solution that should be chosen. As indicated earlier, the aim is to set up underlying forms from which all surface forms can be derived by phonetically plausible rules, such as voicing assimilation.

In generative phonology, the underlying form of a morpheme is not necessarily like any of the surface derived forms, but is usually more abstract. To illustrate, Chomsky and Halle (1968) set up very abstract underlying forms to account for surface variants (allomorphs). These underlying forms are similar to historical forms and in many cases resemble orthographic representations. For example, the underlying forms /divīn/, /serēn/, and /profǽn/ are proposed to account, respectively, for *divine/divinity*, *serene/serenity* and *profane/profanity*. Notice that these surface forms have alternations between the stressed tense and lax vowels, i.e., [āɪ] and [ɪ], [i] and [ɛ], [eī] and [æ]. Chomsky and Halle (1968) claim that the stem-final vowel of the abstract underlying form must be a tense vowel if we are to predict stress placement correctly. According to their rules, stress is placed on the tense vowel that is farthest to the right, and the antepenultimate tense vowel is laxed by the *trisyllabic laxing rule* before the *-ity* suffix in forms such as *divinity*, *serenity*, and *profanity*. In forms like *serene, divine, profane*, etc. the underlying tense vowel first undergoes vowel shift (e.g. ī→ æ), then is diphthongized (e.g. æ → æy). Additional changes may also take place. In this type of analysis, the underlying vowels are not like the vowels in the surface forms. For example, underlying /ī/ is ultimately realized as [ɪ] in *divinity* and as [āɪ] in *divine*. However, as Schane (1973, p. 81) points out, the choice of underlying vowel is not arbitrary. The vowel is chosen that will lead to the correct vowels in the surface variants by means of plausible phonological rules. In approaches that do not allow such abstract underlying representations, such as natural generative phonology, all variants have to be listed separately in the lexicon, with statements about their distribution.

An example of a very abstract underlying representation postulated by Chomsky and Halle (1968) and reported by Hyman (1975, pp. 81–82) is the systematic phonemic representation of *resign*, which is said to be /rē = sign/ (= is a special morpheme boundary that allows for the voicing of the /s/). This abstract base form is postulated so that related forms such as *resignation* can also be derived from it. To derive the surface form of *resign* [rɪzāɪn] they posit a rule that voices the /s/ after the = boundary, a rule that deletes /g/ before /n/ in syllable-final position and tenses the preceding vowel, a vowel-shift rule (ē→ī and ī→æ), a diphthongization rule (ī→iy and æ→æy) and a vowel modification rule (æy→ay). In other words, several rules are needed to get from the abstract underlying base form to the derived (surface) form of this word.

Abstractness of Underlying Representations

One of the major controversies in phonological theory has centered on the issue of abstractness. How abstract are underlying representations?

Virtually all generative phonologists accept the idea of having one underlying form from which all related surface forms are derived; and nearly all generative phonologists reject the traditional taxonomic or autonomous phonemic level as not being abstract enough (Hyman, 1975, p. 91). (For example, see Halle, 1959.) However, they do not agree as to how abstract underlying representations should be.

As shown above, the underlying forms postulated by Chomsky and Halle (1968) are generally quite abstract, but there has been a more recent trend toward somewhat less abstract underlying representations. (See, for example, Stampe, 1972a, and Hooper, 1976.) Hyman (1975, p. 84) states that there seem to be no constraints on the degree of abstractness allowed in generative phonology. However, he suggests looking at the rules that are needed if extremely abstract underlying representations are posited. It has been argued (by Kiparsky, 1968a) that rules which result in *context-free (absolute) neutralization* should not be allowed. Such rules merge or collapse all instances of two or more underlying segments. To illustrate, if a child had [t] for both adult /t/ and /k/, in most analyses the child would be said to have a context-free neutralization rule (k→t) resulting in the "merger" of adult /t/ and /k/.

In Hyman's view (1975, pp. 85–86), however, what is objectionable is not the rules but the "imaginary" underlying segments that never show up on the surface, such as Chomsky and Halle's /œ/ which is posited as the underlying form of English [ɔ̄ɪ], as in *boy* (see Crothers, 1971). On the other hand, it has been argued that setting up such abstract underlying forms allows phonologists to account for surface irregularities and to simplify the lexicon, as well as to set up more symmetrical phonological inventories (Hyman, 1975). Clearly, abstractness is a controversial issue. (See for example, Schane, 1973, pp. 82–83; Kisseberth, 1969; Hyman, 1970).

CONCLUSION

Since its introduction in the late 1950s by Noam Chomsky and Morris Halle, generative phonology has been the central theory of phonology. In contrast to the descriptive linguists, Chomsky was concerned with mentalistic aspects of phonology and with relationships between underlying and surface forms. Consequently, generative phonology includes a rather complex set of abstract elements, along with various types of phonological rules. By means of notational devices and rule writing conventions, such phonological phenomena as alternations among allo-morphs are accounted for. The abstractness employed in generative phonology has been criticized for a number of reasons, essentially because the psychological reality of such descriptions is seen as difficult to test. Perhaps because of such issues, few speech-language pathologists have an extensive background in generative phonology. However, there have been a number of studies, several of which are reviewed in Chapters 7 and 8, that have used a generative phonological approach in attempting to describe the sound errors of children with phonological disorders. As we will see in the next chapter, a more thorough grounding in another approach to phonology called natural phonology may become common, partly because the main elements of the theory are more accessible (i.e., less abstract) than those of generative phonology and partly because the concerns of natural phonology are more consistent with those of speech-language pathologists.

FOOTNOTES

[1]Speakers have stored in their minds information regarding the meaning and pronunciation of each morpheme (minimal unit of meaning). The lexical entry for each morpheme contains all of the information that is mentally stored for that morpheme. This includes all of the information regarding its pronunciation that is not predictable from general rules (Sloat et al., 1978, p. 130).

[2]When a form either does not undergo a rule that it should undergo, or vice versa, the lexical entry of that form is marked with a diacritic or rule feature indicating that it is exceptional, e.g., [+ Velar Softening] (Sloat, et al., 1978, p. 159).

5

Naturalness in Generative Phonology and Natural Phonology

OVERVIEW

Since generative phonology, a number of approaches to phonology have been proposed. These include: atomic phonology, autosegmental phonology, upside-down phonology, natural generative phonology, and natural phonology. Each of these approaches is discussed by its major proponent(s) in *Current Approaches to Phonological Theory* (1979), edited by D. A. Dinnsen. The focus in the following discussion is on naturalness issues. Naturalness issues form a bridge between generative phonology and many of the newer theories and approaches. Discussion will first center on a variety of naturalness issues, followed by a close look at one particular post-generative approach—David Stampe's model of Natural Phonology.

NATURALNESS

Some segments, sound classes, consonant and vowel systems, types of syllables, and rules and processes are more natural than others. The more natural ones occur more often than the others—they are more widespread in languages of the world, are less likely to be lost historically, and are acquired earlier by children. For example, the more natural member of a pair of sounds can occur in a sound system without the less natural or more "marked" one (cf., Jakobson's implicational laws) and may be more widely distributed in one language. While some possible sounds never occur or occur rarely (e.g., /θ/) in human languages, others are very widespread and appear to be "preferred" (e.g., /n/). Many of the statements about natural classes, syllables, and rules in the following sections are derived from detailed discussions in Sloat, et al. (1978, pp. 99–107) and Schane (1973, pp. 111–120).

Natural Segments and Classes

Concerning sound segments and sound classes, anterior consonants are more natural than nonanterior consonants and consonants without a secondary articulation such as labialization are more natural than consonants with a secondary articulation. Obstruents are more natural (or less marked) than sonorants. (Although all languages have several obstruents, many have just one liquid or nasal.) Of the obstruent class, stops are the most natural, and affricates are the least natural. However, at the palato-alveolar point of articulation, affricates are apparently more natural than stops. Voiceless obstruents are more natural than voiced obstruents (e.g., /t/ is more natural than /d/ and /s/ is more natural than /z/). A language is not likely to have voiced obstruents without also having the corresponding voiceless obstruents. Unaspirated stops are more natural than aspirated stops. For example, Spanish and French, unlike English, have unaspirated stops but not aspirated stops. The most natural fricatives are said to be /s/ and /h/ (Sloat, et al. 1978, p. 105).

For resonants (vowels, nasals, liquids, and glides), voicing is natural. For instance, all languages have voiced vowels, but only a few (e.g., Japanese) have voiceless vowels. A few languages also have voiceless nasals, liquids, or glides. (Welsh, for instance, has a voiceless lateral [ɬ].) The most common nasal is said to be /n/.

The most natural vowels appear to be nonfront low vowels, such as /a/ or /ɑ/, one of which is present in all languages of the world. The high vowels /i/ and /u/ are also quite widespread; /i/ occurs in nearly all languages, but /u/ is somewhat less common. Oral vowels are more natural than nasal vowels, which involve a secondary articulation, and tense vowels are more natural than the corresponding lax vowels; for instance, /i/ and /u/ are more natural than /ɪ/ and /ʊ/ (Sloat, et al. 1978, p. 106). For nonlow back vowels, rounding is natural (e.g., /u/, /o/), but front vowels (e.g., /i/, /e/) and nonfront low vowels (e.g., /ɑ/, /a/) are naturally unrounded.

In some cases, there is a physiological explanation for the naturalness of segments. For example, the constriction in the vocal tract that is characteristic of obstruents hinders the flow or air through the glottis, and thus the vocal folds do not normally vibrate (Schane, 1973, p. 115). This is apparently why voiceless obstruents are more natural than voiced ones. However, there is less obstruction in the vocal tract during the production of sonorants, and therefore the vocal folds can vibrate naturally; this is why voiced sonorants are said to be more natural than voiceless ones. There is some physiological evidence (from experimental phonetics) which suggests that it is difficult to make complete closure in the palato-alveolar region. This corresponds to the fact that affricates are more natural in that position than stops (Schane, 1973, p. 115).

As discussed earlier under distinctive features, *natural classes* are classes of sounds that share common properties and behave together in phonological rules.[1] A natural class can be specified by fewer features than any member of that class (Hyman, 1975, p. 139). For example:

$$\begin{bmatrix} + \text{syllabic} \\ - \text{consonantal} \end{bmatrix}$$

represents the natural class of vowels, and any subset of that class would have to be specified with more features. Similarly, [– sonorant] specifies the natural class of obstruents (stops, fricatives, and affricates). To represent any subclass of obstruents, other features would have to be listed.

Natural Sound Systems

Regarding sound systems, the most natural (frequently occurring) three-vowel system is /i, a, u/ and the most natural five-vowel system is said to be /i, u, e, o, a/. Chomsky and Halle (1968, p. 409) have proposed principles for "feature counting" to account for natural vowel systems.[2] However, feature counting does not always lead to the correct conclusions concerning natural systems. This is partly because systems are not always comparable. Hyman (1975, p. 151) points out that although some segments are more natural than others, this does not lead to a simple way of evaluating the naturalness of systems because the complexity of a system (or class) is not directly related to the complexity of the segments that make it up but is a function of the relationships among the segments. The segments in two systems may be equally natural, but not the systems, and conversely, two systems that involve segments of differing naturalness may still be equally natural systems.

The most natural stop system is said to be /p, t, k/, and the minimal or least marked consonant system is /p, t, k, s, n/, according to Chomsky and Halle, but some phonologists disagree, because languages may lack one or more of these consonants. According to Sloat et al. (1978, p. 105) it is too early to try to decide what is the most natural consonant system.

Natural Syllables

Types of syllables, like segments and sound systems, also differ in naturalness. The following observations about natural syllables are based on a detailed discussion of the issue in Sloat et al., 1978, pp. 102–105. Syllables starting with a consonant are more natural than syllables starting with a vowel, e.g., CV is more natural than VC. The most natural syllable structure is CV, which is present in all languages of the world and is acquired earliest by children. CVC is less natural than CV, and syllables with initial or final clusters (such as CCVC or CVCC) are even less natural. Syllables containing long clusters, such as CCCVCCCC are quite uncommon.

Some clusters are more natural than others. For instance, in syllable-final position, resonant plus obstruent clusters (as in *belt*, *part*) are more natural than obstruent plus resonant clusters. In syllable-initial clusters, the opposite order is more natural (e.g., *play, train, swing, few*). In each case, the resonant is closer to the vowel than the obstruent is (Sloat et al., 1978, p. 103). Clusters with voiceless obstruents are more natural than clusters with voiced obstruents. In syllable onsets, fricatives usually precede stops, as in /sp, st, sk/, although stop plus fricative clusters (e.g., /ts/) also occur (but not in English). Clusters of two stops (e.g., /gd/) in syllable onsets are less common than fricative plus stop clusters, although they do occur in some languages.

In syllable-final position, fricative plus stop clusters are more natural than stop plus fricative clusters; but, if the fricative is /s/, both types are common. Clusters of two stops (particularly voiceless stops) are also relatively common in syllable-final position, as in *pact* or *lagged*. For clusters made up of resonants, nasal-liquid clusters and liquid-nasal clusters are apparently most natural, with the liquid being next to the vowel, as in *barn* and *film* (Sloat, et al., 1978, p. 104).

NATURAL PHONOLOGICAL PROCESSES

A *phonological process* is a systematic sound change affecting an entire class of sounds or sound sequence. As used here, *process* will refer to a sound change, and *rule* will refer to the (more or less formal) statement of a process. There are some phonological processes (and rules formalizing them) that are more natural than others. *Natural processes* are generally said to be phonetically motivated—due to articulatory, perceptual, or acoustic factors, and to involve the simplification of a more complex articulation. In addition to being phonetically plausible, these processes are well-attested in languages of the world. In other words, they are very widespread; they show up in historical sound change, in language acquisition by children, and synchronically in slips of the tongue, nativization of loan words, etc. (Stampe, 1969, 1972a). Many of the rules/processes in the phonological description of a language will be natural, and some will be more natural than others, as naturalness is not a "binary (+ or −) property" (Hyman, 1975, p. 161).

Physiological (articulatory) or psychological (perceptual) considerations may explain why some processes are more natural than others. For instance, assimilation processes are said to be motivated by "ease of articulation" which has to do with coarticulation and the coordination of tongue muscles (Schane, 1973, p. 119). On the other hand, perceptual considerations may explain certain processes, such as processes that result in CV syllable shapes, since the optimal perceptual contrast is between a consonant and a vowel.

As Schane (1973, p. 117) noted, we expect to find rules (processes) that make segments less marked. For example, *neutralization rules* (such as final obstruent devoicing) usually have as their output the less marked of the segments being neutralized. Natural processes should also result in simpler syllable structures, for instance CV rather than CCV. In fact, many processes, such as cluster reduction and vowel insertion, do give rise to CV syllable shapes.

In some cases, the notation that is used captures the naturalness of a process. For instance, this is true of assimilation processes, in which a sound takes on features from a nearby segment, e.g.,

$$V \rightarrow [+\text{nasal}] \ / \underline{\quad} \ [+\text{nasal}]$$

For many other types of processes, however, the notation does not reflect their naturalness (Schane, 1973, p. 118). For example final devoicing, formalized as

$$[-\text{sonorant}] \rightarrow [-\text{voice}] \ / \underline{\quad} \ \#$$

does not look any more natural than the opposite process (final voicing of obstruents).

Some natural processes are said to be automatic or *low-level phonetic rules*. Such processes, in English, include the assimilatory nasalization of vowels preceding nasal consonants and the lengthening of vowels preceding voiced obstruents. However, such low-level phonetic processes may become nonautomatic or phonologized (Hyman, 1975). For instance, a process may be exaggerated or may take on a phonological role in a particular language. Hyman (1975, p. 173) gives a clear example from English. In English, the lengthening of vowels before voiced obstruents has taken on a phonological role because English speakers tend to devoice final voiced obstruents. Thus vowel length has become a more important perceptual cue than the voicing of final obstruents. In Hyman's view, English is losing its voicing contrast in word-final position.[3]

In the following sections, several categories of natural processes are discussed: processes that change syllable structure, assimilation processes, dissimilation processes, weakening and strengthening processes, and others. It should be pointed out that processes may be classified in many ways, for example, into changes in place of articulation, manner of articulation, and voicing; and the same process often can be put into two or three categories. Most of the processes that are described here are not stated formally. Whenever possible, examples come from English or from other familiar languages or phonological acquisition. This is not intended to be an exhaustive list of natural phonological processes.

Syllable Structure
Processes

Some natural phonological processes change the number or the order of segments in a word. These processes add, delete or rearrange segments or syllables, or collapse (coalesce) features of adjacent segments or syllables. Usually they produce more natural syllable shapes.

Insertion or
Addition Processes

Prothesis. Prothesis is a process by which a vowel is added to the beginning of a word, especially when there is an initial cluster. This process was common in the history of the Romance languages. For instance, in Spanish an [ɛ] vowel was added to the beginning of words that had initial /s/ plus stop clusters, causing the syllable boundary to be placed between the /s/ and the stop. So, Latin *schola*, "lecture" or "school," became *escuela* "school." Similarly, *state* in English corresponds to *estado* in Spanish (from Latin *status*). Because initial /s/ plus stop clusters are not allowed in Spanish, native Spanish speakers frequently add a prothetic [ɛ] vowel to such words as *school* and *store* when speaking English.

Epenthesis. Epenthesis is a process whereby a segment is inserted within a word or at the end of a word. For example, a vowel may be inserted between two elements of a cluster to give a more "natural" CVCV structure. As noted previously, English speakers often insert an epenthetic vowel in words such as *elm* and *athlete*, and children may exhibit the same process, inserting [ə] in words like *blue* [bᵊlú], *green* [gᵊrin], etc. If the base form of the regular plural morpheme in English is taken to be /z/, then an epenthesis rule inserts [ə] in words such as *dishes* and *horses*, which have a stem-final sibilant. Children sometimes add a final reduced vowel to words ending in voiced consonants, as in [gʌ́mə] for *gum*.

An *epenthetic consonant*, particularly a glide, may be inserted to separate two adjacent vowels, thus making two more natural syllables. For instance, Hooper (1973, p. 182) shows that in some dialects of Spanish a palatal glide is inserted between the vowels in words like *creo* and *veo*, giving [kréjo], [véjo], etc. (Hyman, 1975, p. 164). Children who delete postvocalic obstruents may also exhibit an addition process, inserting a glide (or a glottal stop) to separate a sequence of two vowels, as in [déíjɪ] for *daisy*, [díwʊ] for *zipper*, and [hʌ́ʔɪ] for *honey*.

Another natural type of consonant *epenthesis* involves the insertion of an intrusive homorganic segment after a nasal to facilitate the transition from the nasal to another oral consonant, as in *tense* and *warmth*, which phonetically are [tenᵗs] and [wɔrmᵖθ] (Sloat et al., 1978, p. 119).

Diphthongization. Diphthongization is not actually an insertion process, but it is included here because the end result is an extra segment. *Diphthongization*, also called *breaking*, is a process whereby stressed or tense vowels break and become diphthongs—two vowels together in the same syllable (see Miller, 1972, 1973; Stampe, 1972b, 1973b). Diphthongization has been an important process in the history of the English language. In late Middle English, probably beginning in the 15th century, the *great vowel shift* took place. This shift involved vowel raising and diphthongization. Stressed tense (long) vowels changed their positions in the "vowel space." Basically, these vowels were raised, so that [ɑ:] → [e:], [e:] → [i:], [ɔ:] → [o:], [o:] → [u:] etc., and the highest vowels were diphthongized. So, [i:] became [a͡ɪ] as in *wife*, and [u:] became [a͡ʊ], as in *house*. In Chaucer's time, *feet* was pronounced as [fe:t], *stone* as [stɔ:n], and *fool* as [fo:l], etc. (Myers, 1966, p. 169).

The diphthongization or breaking of long vowels is also an active process in some dialects of modern English. The tense vowels /i, e, u, o/ are often produced as diphthongs, and in some dialects [æ] is produced as a diphthong before fricatives, as in [mæɪs] or [meəs] for *mass*. Long vowels preceding voiced velars are also likely to be produced as diphthongs, as in [ɛɪg] for *egg* (Sloat, et al., 1978, p. 118).

Deletion Processes

Cluster Reduction Processes. There are several processes that reduce or simplify clusters, usually by deletion of one element. Often, the segment that is left is identical to one of the underlying segments (usually the least marked one), but in some cases the remaining element shares features of both underlying segments. In such cases, the process that is postulated is one of coalescence or the collapsing of features of adjacent segments. The term *syncope* is sometimes used for the loss of an element of a consonant cluster in the history of a language. For example, in modern English, we do not pronounce the *t* in *hasten* or *fasten*. In some dialects of present day English, word-final clusters are simplified by deletion of one element, as in [tʰɛs] for *test* and [dɛs] for *desk*.

Several types of cluster reduction have been noted for children acquiring the phonological system of English. Some of the following sound changes are also attested in historical language change.

/s/-cluster reduction or */s/-loss* is a process whereby /s/ is deleted in word-initial and/or word-final combinations with other consonants (although the other element of the cluster may occasionally be lost instead). Some children delete /s/ only when the other element is an obstruent, as in [pun] for *spoon*, [bɔk] for *box*, and [kēɪt] for *skate*. Other children may also delete /s/ from /s/ plus nasal clusters, as in [nōū] for *snow*. In clusters of /s/ plus liquid or glide, as in *slide* and *swim*, either the /s/ or the other element may be deleted. Most children exhibit some form of /s/-cluster reduction during their phonological development.

Nasal cluster reduction is another common process in phonological acquisition. Interestingly, the element that is deleted often depends on the voicing of the obstruent. So, we may find [pɪk] for *pink*, with deletion of the nasal before a voiceless stop, but [hæn] for *hand*, with deletion of the voiced stop following the nasal. Some children delete the nasal after it has caused nasalization of the preceding vowel, as in [tɛ̃t] for *tent*. This can be considered as a type of coalescense (e.g., see Schane, 1973, p. 55).

Liquid cluster reduction generally deletes the liquid in stop plus liquid clusters during early stages of phonological acquisition. So we find [tēɪn] for *train*, [pēɪ] for *play*, [dɛt] for *dress*, [mɑk] for *Mark*, [mɪk] for *milk*, etc. In fricative plus liquid or glide clusters such as /fr/, /fl/, /sl/, and /sw/, the liquid or glide is likely to be lost, as in [fɑg] for *frog*, [sāɪd] for *slide*, and [fāūwə] for *flower*. However, occasionally it is the fricative that is lost, as in [wɑg̣] for *frog*, and [lɑ̄ɪ̣t] for *slide* (e.g., see Ingram, 1976, p. 33).

In some cases, presumably later in the acquisition period (see Greenlee, 1974) the liquid in obstruent plus liquid clusters is replaced by a glide. Then we find *play*→ [pwēɪ], *dress*→[dwɛt], *frog*→[fwɑg], *flower*→[fwāūwə], *slide*→[swāɪd], and so forth. Researchers differ as to whether or not they consider this to be a form of cluster simplification.

Coalescence, as mentioned earlier, is a process whereby features of two adjacent segments are collapsed or combined. The resulting segment shares features of both of the underlying elements. Such changes can be looked upon as cases of assimilation followed by deletion (e.g. see Schane, 1973, p. 56).

During acquisition, children may replace /sw/ sequences by [f], saying [fɪm] for *swim*, [fɪŋ] for *swing*, etc. The [f] that is pronounced has the sibilance and voicelessness of the underlying /s/, but the labial quality of the /w/. Similarly, [f] for underlying /θr/ sequences or /tr/ sequences, as in [fɛd] for *thread* and [fēɪn] for *train* may be said to be due to coalescence or assimilation plus deletion. (This assumes the substitution of [w] for /r/ before coalescence applies.) Occasionally children may replace an /sl/ sequence by a voiceless /l/ ([ļ]) or /sn/ by a voiceless /n/ ([ņ]). There is a historical parallel to this change in Burmese where /sm/→[m̥] and /sn/→[ņ] (H. Clumeck, personal communication). See Schane (1973, pp. 54–55) for additional examples. Such productions may be said to result from a coalescence of the voicelessness of /s/ and the other features of the sonorant.

Intervocalic Deletion. Of course, not all cases of deletion involve clusters. *Intervocalic consonants,* especially voiced fricatives, may be lost historically as the last step in series of weakening processes. For example, voiceless stops may be voiced intervocalically and then may become continuants, due to the continuancy of the neighboring vowels, and eventually may be lost altogether (e.g., see Hyman, 1975, pp. 164-166 and Sloat, et al., 1978, pp. 114-115). The voiced velar fricative [ɣ] is particularly weak and therefore prone to deletion. So, in the history of a language, we may find the following changes:

$$k \rightarrow g \rightarrow \gamma \rightarrow \phi.$$

To illustrate part of this sequence, in the development of Spanish from Latin, intervocalic /g/ was deleted. So for Latin *lego* "I read" we find the Spanish *leo* (Hyman, 1975, p. 166). In intervocalic position /d/ is usually pronounced as [ð] in present day Spanish, as in [deðo] for *dedo* "finger." However, in some dialects, the /d/ in this position may not pronounced at all, as in [deo] for *dedo* (e.g., see Ferguson, 1978b).

During phonological acquisition, children may also delete intervocalic consonants of various types, producing, for example, [dɑːɪ] for *daddy,* [bʌɪ] for *bunny,* etc. Later in the developmental period, children may continue to delete intervocalic consonants in longer words, such as *telephone,* which may be said as [tʰɛ́əfon].

Final Consonant Deletion. *Final consonant deletion* is a process that deletes one or more consonants at the end of a word. *Apocope* is the term that is used by historical linguists when a segment (particularly a vowel) is lost from the end of a word. This term has not been used by child phonologists, however. Several dialects of English drop /r/ at the end of a word (or preceding another consonant). These dialects can be said to exhibit apocope.

Child phonologists generally use the term final consonant deletion rather than apocope for the common childhood process that deletes one or more word-final consonants. In the early stages of phonological development we often find forms such as [kæ] for *cat,* [dɑ] for *dog,* and [no͞u] for *nose.* Children may exhibit a more limited form of this process, deleting only final voiced obstruents, or only fricatives, etc. (See Ingram, 1976, for a more detailed discussion of final consonant deletion.)

Vowel Deletion Processes. There are several *vowel deletion processes* by which unstressed vowels in various word-positions are deleted.

Syncope may involve the deletion of an unstressed medial vowel, usually one directly following the main stress in a word and preceding another unstressed vowel. For example, *family, frightening,* and *interest* often are pronounced without the *posttonic* vowel (i.e., the vowel following the stressed vowel). Note that syncope may give rise to more complicated syllable structures.

Apocope is a process that deletes word-final segments, including unstressed (reduced) vowels. In Middle English, many words, such as *sweet, root,* etc. were pronounced with a final [ə], but by the time of modern English, these final reduced vowels had been lost. We still see signs of final reduced vowels in the archaic spelling of words like *olde, shoppe,* etc. Schane (1973, pp. 57–58) notes that in colloquial French final [ə] may be dropped, as in [fi:] for /fijə/ "fille" *girl.*

Aphaeresis is the term sometimes used for the loss of a word-initial vowel after a word-final vowel (I. Lehiste, personal communication).[4] When two words appear in sequence, and the first ends in a vowel and the second begins with a vowel, the initial vowel of the second word may be lost. For example, in English, *I am* may be contracted to *I'm, you are* to *you're,* etc.

Aphesis may be used for the simple loss of an initial vowel without the influence of another vowel (I. Lehiste, personal communication). In English, there are examples of this process, as in *opossum,* which is pronounced without the initial vowel, or *around,* which may be shortened to *round.* Children often delete initial unstressed vowels, as in [baʊt] for *about,* but such examples usually are included under *weak syllable deletion,* discussed below.

Elision often refers to the loss of a final vowel preceding a word with an initial vowel (I. Lehiste, personal communication). Elision is a common process in French, where we find deletion of the vowel of the definite article *le* preceding vowel-initial nouns, as in *l'école* for "the school" (*le + école*). In English, we find deletion of stem-final vowels when a suffix with an initial vowel is added, as in *pianist* from *piano + ist* (see Schane, 1973, p. 53). This process results in the preferred CV syllable structure, as noted earlier.

Weak Syllable Deletion. Another type of syllable-structure process that is common in phonological acquisition is called *weak syllable deletion.* Very often, young children delete unstressed (weak) syllables, particularly posttonic weak syllables. For instance, we may find [tɛfoͣn] for *telephone*, with deletion of /lə/, and [tʰɛbɪzən] for *television*, also with deletion of the posttonic /lə/. Pretonic unstressed syllables are also frequently deleted, as in [nǽnə] for *banana*, [sɛp] for *except*, [bʌlə] for *umbrella*, etc. (See Ingram, 1976, for a more detailed discussion.)

Reduplication

Reduplication is a syllable structure process that is common in the speech of some very young children, but is uncommon in languages of the world. In reduplication, a syllable, usually the stressed syllable in a word, is repeated, either exactly or sometimes partially. By means of reduplication, children can produce two-syllable words before they have the ability to produce sequences of two completely different syllables. For instance, a child who does not yet have the ability to produce a word such as *blanket* with two different syllables may reduplicate a simplified form ([bɑ]) of the stressed syllable, producing something like [bɑ́bɑ]. (See Ingram, 1974b.)

Permutation Processes

Some syllable structure processes involve the permutation or reversal of segments or syllables. In metathesis, two segments are reversed or transposed. The segments that are interchanged are often contiguous. For instance, in some dialects of English, *ask* is pronounced as [æks]. Similarly, children may pronounce *mask* as [mæks], or *animals* as [ǽmənl̩z].

When parts of words in an utterance are interchanged by adults, we talk about *spoonerisms*, which are a type of speech error. For example, "mall walker" may be said as "wall mocker" or "May I show you to a seat?" may be rendered as "May I sew you to a sheet?" (See Fromkin, 1973a, 1973b for a variety of speech errors and discussion of their linguistic significance.)

Migration involves the movement of a sound from one position in a word to another. For example, a child may say [noͣs] for *snow* with the /s/ transposed to the end of the word, or [bul̩] for *blue* or [pəsgɛ́ti] for *spaghetti*. Permutation and transposition processes may provide one way for children to handle consonant clusters that they are not yet able to produce correctly (Greenlee, 1974).

Assimilation Processes

In *assimilation* processes, also called *harmony* processes, two segments become more alike; one "takes on" features from another. Assimilation may affect two adjacent segments, in which case it is *contiguous*. In *distant* or *noncontiguous* assimilation, the sounds that are involved are not adjacent. If assimilation is *complete*, one sound takes on all the features of (and becomes identical to) another sound, which may be called the *conditioning factor*. If assimilation is *partial*, one sound becomes more like another, taking on some of its features. If a later sound affects an earlier sound (‾‾), assimilation is *regressive* or *anticipatory*. When an earlier sound affects a later sound (⌒), assimilation is *progressive* or *perseverative*. Regressive assimilation is more common than progressive. In assimilation, a consonant may affect another consonant or a vowel, or a vowel may affect a consonant or another vowel. Thus many different types of assimilation can be distinguished.

Processes Affecting
Voicing

Prevocalic Voicing. In *prevocalic voicing* a vowel affects an obstruent that precedes it and causes it to become voiced. (The obstruent takes on the voicing feature of the vowel.) This process is very common in young children, who may say, for instance, [gæ] for *cat*, [dɑ] for *top*, etc. (This may be due to the child's difficulty in coordinating the timing of two phonetic events: the release of a stop and the onset of voicing.)

In some cases, only *intervocalic* obstruents (or obstruents between sonorants) are voiced. This natural process is sometimes considered a *weakening process*, as voiced obstruents are "weaker" than voiceless obstruents. To illustrate, the voiceless alveolar stop /t/ is often voiced in intervocalic position in English, as in *pretty* [prídɪ], *little* [lídl], *better* [bédɚ]. In fact, it may be replaced by a voiced flap [ɾ] rather than a stop.

Intervocalic stops, particularly voiced stops, may weaken further to fricatives, taking on the continuancy feature of the adjacent sonorants, e.g., b→β, d→ð, etc. In the development of the Romance languages from Latin, such a process took place. For example, Latin *ripa*, "*shore*," with a voiceless plosive, gave rise to Spanish *ribera*, pronounced with a [β], as well as English *river*. Weakening and strengthening processes are discussed in more detail in a later section.

Word Final Devoicing. *Word final devoicing*, a process evident in many languages (e.g., German, Russian, and English to some extent), is sometimes described as the assimilation of a voiced obstruent to the following silence, which functions like a voiceless consonant. A phonetic explanation for the devoicing of final stops is that the closure in the oral cavity results in an equalization of air pressure above and below the glottis so that voicing automatically stops (H. Clumeck, personal communication). The final devoicing rule that is part of the phonology of German has been discussed in an earlier section; in final position the contrast between voiced and voiceless obstruents is neutralized. Children often exhibit a similar process, replacing word-final voiced obstruents by voiceless obstruents, as in [pɪk] for *pig* and [bɔp] for *Bob*. (This also may be considered a weakening process as described later.)[5]

Voicing Assimilation. In many languages, two obstruents that occur together in a cluster must have the same voicing quality; either both become voiced or voiceless. Most commonly, voiced obstruents assimilate to voiceless ones. Recall that voicelessness is more natural for clusters (Sloat, et al., 1978, p. 104). As noted earlier, many phonologists take the basic (underlying) form of the regular plural suffix in English to be /-z/. The [-s] allomorph, as in *cats*, is then derived by a natural voicing assimilation rule:

$$/z/ \rightarrow [-\text{voice}]/ \ [-\text{voice}]\_\_\#$$

Processes Affecting
Place of Articulation

The terms discussed in this section may be confusing because the suffix *-ization* added to a place or manner feature (e.g., labial*ization*) has been used in two ways in linguistics. One use of terms like *labialization, palatalization,* or *velarization* refers to a type of secondary articulation that occurs during production of a sound. For example, if the back of the tongue is raised toward the soft palate during production of /l/ (normally an alveolar sound before vowels), the /l/ is said to be *velarized.* A second use of the *-ization* suffix refers to the influence of one sound on another. The following definitions involve situations in which the place or manner feature of one sound influences the place or manner feature of another nearby sound.

Labialization and Labial Assimilation. In assimilatory *labialization,* a round vowel or the labial glide /w/ causes a consonant, usually one preceding it, to be labialized or rounded due to coarticulation. For instance, the /s/s in *sweet* and *Sue* are pronounced with labialization or lip rounding, and in a narrow transcription would be transcribed as [š̫]. The segmental symbol itself would not change. Children often replace /r/ by [w]. Segments in clusters with /r/ then sometimes assimilate to the labial quality of the [w] substitute, so we may find [fwi] for *three*, and so forth. In some cases, the other element in the /r/ cluster also takes on the continuancy of [w], and we find, for example, [fwi] for *tree*, [fwēīn] for *train*, etc. (If only continuancy is assimilated, we may find, for instance, [swʌk] for *truck*.)

In *labial assimilation* a consonant anywhere in a word becomes a labial, due to the influence of another labial consonant elsewhere in the word. For example, in [bēību] for *table*, the /b/ later in the word affects the place of articulation of the earlier stop, /t/.

Palatalization and Palatal Assimilation. In assimilatory *palatalization* a nonpalatal consonant is palatalized when it precedes a high front vowel (/i/) or palatal glide (/j/) due to coarticulation. For example, in casual speech, *I'll get you* might be pronounced as [ɑl gɪtʃə] with a palatal affricate replacing the /t/. Velars may be fronted (palatalized) in the environment of palatal vowels or glides. For instance, the /k/ in *key* is produced quite far forward because of the following /i/ vowel. (Compare the /k/s in *key* vs. *cool* and the /g/s in *geese* vs. *goose*.) Other front vowels may occasionally cause palatalization, but most often the conditioning factor is /i/ (or /j/).

In *palatal assimilation* a nonpalatal consonant anywhere in a word becomes a palatal due to the influence of another palatal sound (e.g., [ʃuʃ] *shoes*, [ʃɪʃ] *fish*).

Velarization and Velar Assimilation. In assimilatory *velarization* a velar vowel (e.g., [u]) causes an alveolar consonant to be replaced by a velar. For example, a child may have [migu] for *middle* and [pʌgu] for *puddle* (Smith, 1973). *Velar assimilation*, a common process in young children, occurs when a sound in a word assimilates to a velar sound elsewhere in the word. The assimilation may be complete (e.g., [gɔg] *dog*, [kɪkən] *chicken*) or partial, involving only a change in place (e.g., [ŋēīk] *snake*.

Processes Affecting
Manner of Articulation

Manner assimilations include all changes in manner due to adjacent sounds or sounds anywhere in the same word. A common example of regressive *liquid assimilation* from child phonology is the production of *yellow* as [lɛ́lo]. For another example, a child may say [næm] for *lamb*, with regressive assimilation of the initial /l/ to the nasal quality of the final sound. Similarly, in [mɛn] for *smell*, there is partial progressive *nasal assimilation*. (The /l/ assimilates to the nasal quality of /m/, but the place of articulation does not change.) In [nʌ́no] for *candle*, there is complete regressive nasal assimilation.

Nasal assimilation should not be confused with what we call *assimilatory nasalization*, which refers to the nasalization of a vowel in the environment of a nasal consonant (e.g. [mæ̃n]).

Vowel Assimilation

Vowels may also undergo assimilation processes. For example, *umlaut* is a type of regressive assimilation affecting back vowels (Sloat, et al., 1973, p. 117). To illustrate, in German, back vowels are fronted before certain endings containing high front vowels. So, we find forms such as *Gott* "god" and *Göttin* "goddess" (Schane, 1973, p. 152). (Two dots over a vowel symbol indicate that it is fronted or umlauted.) In German there are also many plural forms that underwent umlaut historically when a plural /-i/ suffix was added. This vowel later changed to [ə], so the phonetic motivation for the umlauted plurals is no longer apparent, e.g., *der Hut* "the hat," plural *Hüte* [hy:tə] and *der fall* "the fall," plural *Fälle* [fɛ:lə]. In modern English, irregular plurals such as *mice* and *geese* show the effects of an earlier umlauting process.

In *vowel harmony*, the vowels in a word must agree in certain features, such as roundness and backness. For example, in Turkish if a suffix contains a high vowel, that vowel must agree in backness and rounding with the vowel of the stem. So, we find *ev* "house" and *evim* "my house," but *gul* "rose," *gulum* "my rose" (Schane, 1973, p. 52). Similarly, the plural in Turkish is formed by adding either *-lar* or *-ler*, and the allomorph that is chosen depends on the quality of the vowel in the preceding syllable. To illustrate, "bells" is *ziller*, but "arms" is *kollar*. The *-ler* allomorph is used when the preceding vowel is a front vowel, and *-lar* is used after nonfront vowels (Sloat et al., 1978, p. 116).

Dissimilation Processes

In *dissimilation*, like assimilation, one sound has an effect on another, but in contrast to assimilation, the two sounds become less similar. There is evidence of dissimilation in historical sound change, but it is rarely evidenced in phonological acquisition. An exception is found in Ingram (1974b, p. 62). One of the processes Ingram postulates to account for

A. Smith's [wibə] for *zebra* is "front dissimilation," which applies to the intermediate form /bibə/, causing dissimilation of the initial /b/ preceding another /b/.

Dissimilation affects primarily liquids and nasals (resonants). When two nasals or /l/s appear in the same word, one of them is likely to be replaced by another resonant. For example, Latin *marmor* (French *marbre*) corresponds to English *marble*, with an [l] in place of the second /r/. Similarly, Latin *peregrinus* corresponds to English *pilgrim*, with an [l] replacing the first /r/. *Chimney*, which has two adjacent nasals, is often pronounced by children as "chim(b)ly," with the second nasal being replaced by a liquid, and sometimes with an intrusive stop.

Syllabic dissimilation is called *haplology*. This is the process by which *interpretetive* has given way to *interpretive*. Two syllables are very similar, so one is dropped. Similarly, *syllabification* may be replaced by *syllabication* (I. Lehiste, personal communication).

Weakening and Strengthening Processes

Several of the processes already discussed may also be classified as weakening or strengthening processes, e.g., deletion processes, voicing changes, and the spirantization of intervocalic stops. The terms *weakening* and *strengthening* are used somewhat differently by different linguists. Often these terms refer specifically to modifications that depend on the position of a sound in a word or syllable. Weakening processes usually affect intervocalic or final segments, while strengthening processes are more likely to affect initial or postconsonantal segments (Hyman, 1975, pp. 168–169). According to *strength scales* put forth by Foley (1970, p. 90), labials are stronger than alveolars, and alveolars are stronger than velars. Regarding manner of articulation, voiceless aspirated or geminate (double) stops are stronger than voiceless unaspirated stops. Voiced stops are still weaker, and voiced fricatives are the weakest obstruents. Sonorants are even weaker. However, Hyman (1975, pp. 166–167) points out that in some languages, alveolars appear to be stronger than labials, and strength scales also differ for different positions. For example, in final position, voiceless stops are weaker than voiced stops, so that final devoicing is a weakening process. Any process that takes a segment one step (or more) closer to zero (deletion) can be considered a weakening process. A strengthening process is one that reinforces a segment, making it less likely to be weakened and lost (Hyman, 1975).

Weakening
Processes: Vowels

Vowel Reduction. As mentioned earlier, unstressed vowels often are weakened or reduced to schwa [ə] (or to [ɨ]) in English. (In fact, many unstressed vowels merge to [ə], and vowel contrasts are neutralized.) To illustrate, in *photograph* [fótəgræf] the second vowel is reduced to [ə]. However, the underlying representation of this word must have a full vowel because there are related forms such as *photography* and *photographer* in which the second vowel is not reduced, but in fact is stressed. In *photography* and *photographer*, different vowels (the first and third) are reduced to [ə]. (See Schane, 1973, p. 58 for other examples.) Similarly, *conflict*, as a verb, with stress on the second syllable, is pronounced with a reduced vowel in the first syllable, but the underlying form must be posited with a full vowel in the first syllable because of the related form *cónflict*, a noun with initial stress.

Reduced vowels, particularly in final position, are likely to be deleted, as happened in the history of English. Some vowels are more likely than others to weaken and be lost. For instance, Hooper (1973, p. 170) proposed a *strength scale* for Spanish vowels, with /e/ being the weakest vowel and /a/ being the strongest. Hyman (1975, p. 170) notes that such strength scales are language-specific and also depend on phonetic environment.

Weakening
Processes: Consonants

Spirantization of Stops. As mentioned above, stops, especially voiced stops, may weaken to fricatives in postvocalic or intervocalic position. This process, which was discussed under assimilation, is also a weakening process. Examples can be found in Spanish, for instance in the production of *nada* "nothing" as [náðə] or *pagar* "to pay" as [payár]. In some cases, affricates may become fricatives, losing their stop component. This also is a weakening process. For instance, children may weaken /tʃ/ to [ʃ], saying [ʃéɪə] for *chair*, and so forth.

Grimm's law (discussed in Chapter 2) involved, among other things, the spirantization of voiceless stops, with Proto Indo-European *p becoming [f], etc. This is illustrated by correspondences such as Latin *pater*, English *father*.

Gliding of Liquids. The gliding of liquids, also sometimes called *liquidation* (e.g., by Oller, Jensen & Lafayette, 1978) or *liquid simplification* is a process whereby liquids (/l, r/) are replaced by glides ([w] or [j]).

This process is well-attested in historical sound change and is also common in phonological acquisition. For instance, children often say [wɛd] for *red*, [jɑ̄ɪt] for *light*, etc. (Compare Italian *pieno* from *plenu*.) Word-final or preconsonantal liquids, if not deleted altogether, are frequently replaced by vocalic substitutes. So we may find [mɪʊk] for *milk*, [bɔʊ] for *ball* (in some regional dialects of English, as well as in children's speech), [kɑə] for *car*, etc. *Vocalization* is the term that is sometimes used for cases in which a syllabic liquid (/l̩/ or /r̩/) is replaced by a vowel, i.e., loses its *l* or *r*-coloring, as in [wɪdʊ] for *little*, [fɛdʊ] or [fɛdə] for *feather*, etc. (See Edwards, 1973.)

Gliding of Fricatives. Occasionally, fricatives are replaced by liquids or glides. For example, in phonological acquisition we may find [wʊt] for *foot*, [lʌm] for *thumb*, [djɛt] for *jet*, [lu] for *shoe*, [jʊt] for *shirt*, etc. Because sonorants are weaker than spirants, this is a weakening process. When a strident fricative, generally /z/, is replaced by [r], the process is called *rhotacism*. In English, there are forms that show the effects of this process. For instance, [z] and [r] alternate in forms of the verb *to be* (*was/were* and *is/are*). There are also pairs of related words such as *coherent/cohesion* that have alternations resulting from this process.

A fricative may weaken and lose all of its consonantal features, being replaced by [h], which is sometimes considered to be a glide (or, alternately, a voiceless version of the following vowel). For example, a child may have [hɪŋ] for *sing* (or *thing*), [hu] for *shoe*, etc. In historical language change, /s/ is sometimes weakened to [h], and the [h] may eventually be deleted.

Glottal Replacement. One of the weakening processes mentioned by Hyman (1975, p. 168) is the replacement of word-final voiceless velar stops by a glottal stop ([ʔ]). The glottal stop may then be lost. When children substitute a glottal stop for word- (or syllable-) final consonants, the process is called *glottal replacement*. For instance, a child may say [dɑʔ] for *dog*, [hæʔ] for *hat*, [bɑ́ʔɪ] for *bottle*, etc.

Strengthening
Processes: Consonants

Stopping. Stopping (also called *despirantization*) is a process whereby fricatives are strengthened to the corresponding stops or affricates, or affricates are replaced by stops.[6] (*Affrication* is sometimes used for the process replacing fricatives by affricates, as in [tʃu] for *shoe*, [pfɔʊ] for *fall*, etc.) Stopping is a very common process in phonological acquisition, affecting especially word-initial fricatives (Edwards, 1979). We typically find forms such as [ti] for *see*, [du] for *zoo*, [pɑ͡ʊwə] for *flower*, [dʌp] for *jump*, [bɛrɪ] for *very*, and so forth. Occasionally liquids or glides are replaced by stops, as in [jɛdo] for *yellow*. Such changes also may be included under stopping. All of these changes involve strengthening.

Aspiration. The aspiration of voiceless stops is a strengthening process because voiceless aspirated stops are stronger than voiceless unaspirated stops, as mentioned above. In English, voiceless stops in word-initial position preceding a (stressed) vowel are quite heavily aspirated, as in *top* [tʰɑp], *pay* [pʰeɪ], etc. Final voiceless stops are sometimes aspirated. Children learning English may produce voiceless unaspirated stops in place of aspirated stops early in their phonological development.

Assibilation. *Assibilation* is a process that may follow palatalization, changing the [ʲ] release of palatalized stops (e.g., /tʲ/) to a palatal fricative (e.g., giving [tʃ]). The resulting affricate may then be weakened to a fricative and eventually fronted to [s]. The [t] ~ [s] and [k] ~ [s] alternations in modern English (as in *democrat/democracy* and *medical/medicine*) may have arisen through this series of sound changes (Sloat, et al., 1978, p. 114).

Spirantization of Sonorants. A palatal glide /j/ occasionally may be spirantized, becoming a palatal fricative [ʒ], as in Argentine Spanish [kɑbɑʒo] for *caballo* "horse" (H. Clumeck, personal communication). Spirantization also may affect /j/ arising from an underlying /l/. If the resulting palatal fricative is then fronted, we end up with [z] for both /l/ and /j/ (see Stampe, 1972a). These substitutes have been noted in phonological acquisition, where forms such as [zɑːd] for *yard* and [zɑːb] for *lamb* may arise (Velten, 1943).

Obstruent Devoicing. Because voiceless obstruents are generally considered to be stronger than voiced obstruents, context-free obstruent devoicing can be categorized as a strengthening process. However, as Hyman (1975, p. 168) points out, in final position voiced obstruents are stronger. One part of Grimm's Law, the Germanic sound shift referred to previously, involved the change of voiced stops to voiceless stops (b→p, d→t, and g→k). This resulted in correspondences such as Latin *duo*, English *two*. The common [s] for /z/ substitution found in phonological acquisition (as in [sɪpə] for *zipper*) also would fall under the heading of obstruent devoicing.

Other Types
of Processes

There are many other natural phonological processes that have not yet been mentioned. Some of these involve changes in place of articulation not caused by assimilation. Most of these processes involve fronting; sounds produced in the back of the mouth are replaced by sounds produced further forward. (Remember that anterior sounds were said to be more natural than nonanterior sounds.) Some linguists (e.g., Foley, 1970) might consider these changes to involve strengthing, as labials and alveolars are said to be stronger than velars. However, Hyman (1975, p. 166) notes that strength hierarchies are language specific, i.e., they hold only for certain languages.

Depalatalization
Depalatalization or *palatal fronting* is a process whereby palatal sounds are replaced by sounds produced farther forward in the mouth, usually alveolars. This is a common process in phonological acquisition. Children frequently replace /ʃ/ by [s] (or [t], if stopping also applies). Similarly, /tʃ/ and dʒ/ may be replaced by [ts] and [dz], respectively, and /ʒ/ may be replaced by [z]. To illustrate, we often find [su] for *shoe*, [tseɪə] for *chair*, [bædz] for *badge*, etc. The fronted affricates may also be weakened to fricatives; so it is not unusual to find [seɪə] for *chair*, [pez] for *page*, etc.

Velar Fronting
Velar fronting, or the *fronting of velars*, is a common process in early phonological acquisition. Velars often are replaced by the corresponding alveolar consonants. So we may find [tutɪ] for *cookie*, [doʊ] for *go*, [sɪn] for *sing*, etc.

LOSS OF NATURALNESS

There are various ways in which natural phonological rules may lose their naturalness (i.e., their original phonetic motivation) over a period of time. These include *telescoping, morphologization*, and *rule inversion* (discussed by Hyman, 1975).

Telescoping (Wang, 1968, p. 708) involves "the loss of an intermediate stage in a phonological derivation" (Hyman, 1975, p. 173). To illustrate, the palatalization of /k/ preceding /i/ is a phonetically motivated natural process, as discussed earlier. However, the resulting segment, a palatalized /k/, may change further, becoming an affricate ([tʃ]), and these two processes (k→kʲ/__ i, and kʲ→tʃ) may then be collapsed or "telescoped" into one rule: k→tʃ/__ i. This telescoped rule "bypasses" the intermediate (historical) form /kʲ/ (Hyman, 1975, p. 174).

Telescoping may lead to *crazy rules*—rules with no apparent phonetically plausible explanation (Bach & Harms, 1972). Hyman (1975, p. 175) discusses such a rule in Bantu: p→s/__ i. This unlikely rule actually represents the telescoping of several plausible historical changes: pi ⟩ pʰi ⟩ pⁱi ⟩ tⁱi ⟩ si. However, a synchronic description usually does not include all of the diachronic stages.

Children may also exhibit odd-looking phonological rules that can be broken down into several phonetically motivated natural processes. However, in the analysis of a child's phonological system, it is generally thought to be important to find independent evidence for the intermediate steps. To give an example, a child may have [du] for *shoe*. This "complex" [d] for /ʃ/ substitution can be broken down into several natural *constituent processes* (Stampe, 1972a): ʃ→s (depalatalization), s→t (stopping), and t→d (voicing). In such an analysis, we hope to find other evidence for each individual process.

In *morphologization*, which is quite common, a phonetically motivated rule loses its phonetic plausibility and becomes morphologically conditioned (Kiparsky, 1972; Hyman, 1975, p. 175). A well-known example is the case of German umlaut. Originally, the [i] of the plural morpheme in German fronted the preceding stem vowel. However, the [i] suffix was later reduced to [ə]. Thus the rule lost its phonetic plausibility and had to be restated with morphological information in the environment. e.g., a→ɛ/__ [+plural]. Words that undergo this rule have to be marked in the lexicon with a diacritic feature because other very similar words (with different historical derivations) do not undergo this umlaut rule (Hyman, 1975, p. 176).

A third way in which a rule can lose its phonetic motivation is by *rule inversion* (Vennemann, 1972b). In rule inversion, an "unnatural" rule that has to be postulated in a synchronic description of a language is actually an inverted form of a phonetically motivated rule that applied in the history of the language. What was once the underlying segment has become the derived segment, and vice versa. According to Vennemann, the primary factor in rule inversion is semantic; categories that are "semantically basic," such as singular nouns and present tense verbs, tend to be considered as phonologically basic forms from which the others are derived. For example, if speakers have to "work backwards" from plural noun forms to derive the singular forms, this creates problems for language learners, and thus the crucial rules tend to be inverted so that the singular forms are basic. Again, lexical representations have to be marked with diacritic features so that the inverted rules will apply to the correct forms (Hyman 1975, pp. 183-184).

Because phonological rules may lose their naturalness over time, there is some question about whether or not naturalness should be used as a criterion in evaluating phonological systems (Hyman, 1975, p. 178). Skousen (1972), giving evidence from Finnish, argued that speakers prefer morphologized rules to phonetically conditioned rules. That is, speakers are more likely to interpret a rule as being morphologically conditioned than phonologically conditioned. Similarly, Hyman (1975, p. 181) argued that if naturalness is a valid criterion, there should be cases in which a sound change is prevented from taking place specifically where it would "destroy the naturalness" of another rule. However, he claims that no such tendency to preserve the naturalness of rules has been discovered. Instead, rules tend to lose their phonetic motivation and become morphologically conditioned, as shown, for example, by the German umlaut rule.

NATURAL PHONOLOGY (STAMPE)

David Stampe's model of *natural phonology* has had a great deal of influence on studies of phonological acquisition and phonological disorders. Stampe's (1969, 1972a, 1973) model of natural phonology focuses on phonetically motivated natural phonological processes. (Also see Donegan & Stampe, 1979.)

Description

According to Stampe's (1969, 1972a) model, humans are born with an innate system of natural phonological processes, such as the devoicing of obstruents and despirantization (stopping). These processes at first apply in an "unordered and unlimited" fashion to the child's mental or underlying representation of adult speech, which is roughly equivalent to the adult surface form. As a result, the child's first productions are very simple forms such as [mama], [dada], etc. The child's task in acquiring the phonological system of his or her native language is to revise this innate system of processes until it is congruent with the phonological system of the adult language (Stampe, 1969, p. 444). If the child succeeds, the resulting system is identical to that of adult speakers; if the child fails, a phonetic change takes place.

Mechanisms of Revision

There are three mechanisms by which the innate phonological system is revised: *limitation*, *ordering*, and *suppression*.[7] Stampe (1969, p. 445) believes that the regularity found in language acquisition can be explained by the properties of the innate system and by these three mechanisms of revision.

Limitation. Limitation means that the child may limit his or her processes to apply in fewer environments or to fewer segments. For instance, a child may at first produce stops for all fricatives but may later limit this process so that it applies only to word-initial fricatives or only to nonsibilant fricatives.

Ordering. In revising the innate system, a child may also impose an *order* of application on his or her processes. At early stages of development, processes are unordered. That is, they apply whenever they can. So, if a child has a process depalatalizing /ʃ/ and also a process weakening affricates to fricatives, *shoe* will be produced as [su] (ʃ→s), and *chair* as [seɪə] (tʃ→ʃ→s). However, at a later stage, the child may impose an ordering on these processes so that depalatalization cannot apply to the output of weakening. At this stage, the child will produce [ʃeɪə] for *chair* (tʃ → ʃ) but [su] for *shoe* (ʃ → s). In Stampe's (1972a) terms, the child has imposed an *antisequential constraint*. To give another example, Joan Velten (Velten, 1943) exhibited unordered application of denasalization and devoicing before she was 22 months old. So, for example, *lamb* was produced as [bɑp] (m→b→p). At the age of 22 months, Joan imposed an antisequential constraint such that devoicing could not apply to the output of denasalization. At this stage, Joan had [bɑt] for *bad* (final d → t), but [bud] for *spoon* (final n→d) (Stampe, 1972a, p. 61).

Suppression. In *suppression*, which Stampe says is quite rare, a process is prevented from applying altogether. To illustrate, Stampe claims that in English there is a context-free process of vowel denasalization (V→[– nasal]) that governs underlying representations. It has to apply before the context-sensitive (allophonic) process that nasalizes vowels preceding nasal consonants. However, in languages such as Portuguese, which have phonemic nasalized vowels, the natural vowel denasalization process must be totally suppressed, because it does not even govern underlying representations.

Context-Free and
Context-Sensitive Processes

In Stampe's view, the phonological system of an adult language is primarily what remains of the innate system of processes after limiting, ordering, and suppression. Processes that cause substitutions during phonological acquisition are later ordered so that they show up only as restrictions or conditions on underlying representations, although they also may appear in fast speech, slips of the tongue, secret languages, nativization of loan words, and other phonological phenomena.

Stampe (1969, p. 443) states that a phonological process "merges a potential phonological opposition into the member of the opposition which least tries the restrictions of the human speech capacity." He goes on to say that phonological processes often fall into contradictory sets that reflect "conflicting phonetic restrictions." One member of a pair is *context-free* or *paradigmatic* and the other is *context-sensitive* or *syntagmatic*. To illustrate, there is a context-free process that devoices obstruents regardless of environment ([– sonorant]→[– voice]). As noted earlier, the oral constriction that occurs during the production of obstruents interferes with spontaneous voicing, and thus is it natural for obstruents to be voiceless. Therefore, this context-free natural process is motivated by production constraints that have to do with the nature of the vocal tract. In Stampe's terms, such context-free or paradigmatic processes "respond to the inner complexities of a single segment" (1972a, p. 20). When obstruents occur between sonorants, however, they are very likely to take on the voicing feature of the surrounding sounds. This assimilatory voicing process ([– sonorant]→[+ voice] / V__V) is context-sensitive or syntagmatic and is motivated by ease of articulation factors that have to do with sounds in sequence. As Stampe notes (1972a, p. 21), context-sensitive processes "respond to the complexities of sequences of segments."[8]

The two processes just discussed are contradictory; one devoices obstruents, and one voices obstruents. Such contradictions are resolved, according to Stampe, by the same three mechanisms discussed above: suppression, limitation, and ordering. That is, one of the contradictory processes, usually the context-free one, may be *suppressed*. Or, one the processes may be *limited*. For example, the obstruent devoicing process may be limited to apply only in voiceless contexts, such as word-final position. Finally, the processes may be *ordered*. For instance, in languages that do not have an obstruent voicing distinction but do have voiced obstruents in certain environments, the context-sensitive voicing process must apply after the context-free obstruent devoicing process. In adult phonological systems, this is the typical state of affairs for pairs of conflicting processes. A context-free (or paradigmatic) process applies before the contradictory context-sensitive (or syntagmatic) process. The context-free process restricts underlying representations, and the context-sensitive process produces surface phonetic variants or allophones (Stampe, 1972a, p. 25).

Process vs. Rule

Phonological processes are the primitives of natural phonology (1969, p. 446), and an important aspect of Stampe's model is his distinction between *process* and *rule*. Natural phonological processes are phonetically motivated and innate. They have no exceptions. The languages learner "comes equipped" with these processes. A process is defined by Stampe (1972a, p. 1) as "a mental operation that applies in speech to substitute, for a class of sounds or sound sequences presenting a specific common difficulty to the speech capacity . . . an alternative class identical but lacking the difficult property." Stampe (1972a, p. 6) argues that although the substitutions are mental (i.e., not just motor), they are motivated by the physical character of speech. That is, their purpose is "to maximize the perceptual characteristics of speech and minimize its articulatory difficulties" (1972a, p. 9).

Rules, in contrast to processes, are arbitrary principles imposed by the language. They are not innate but are "acquired constraints" (i.e., they have to be learned), and they do not govern phonetic behavior (Stampe, 1972a, p. 43). Such rules include morphophonemic rules, for example the rules for the formation of regular noun plurals in English.

In making the process/rule distinction, Stampe often contrasts palatalization, which is a natural process, with velar softening, which is a phonological rule in English. According to Stampe, it is natural for alveolar consonants to be palatalized preceding the palatal glide [j], as in "I've got ya," pronounced in casual speech as [aɪv gɑtʃə]. The fact that palatalization is a natural process is also illustrated by examples from pig Latin. When sounds are reversed in pig Latin so that an alveolar consonant is placed before a palatal glide, palatalization is very likely to take place as in [ɛʃjeɪ] for *yes*. In fact, Stampe (1972a, p. 44) says that it is difficult to prevent natural processes from applying in cases like this.

Velar softening, unlike palatalization, is a phonological rule, in Stampe's view. It accounts for the alternations between [k] and [s] in forms like *electric/electricity* and between [g] and [dʒ] in forms like *pedagog/pedagogy*. He argues that if velar softening were a process, it would have to be suppressed in order for us to say words such as *kitty cat* and *persnickity* (not **persnisity*). Velar softening does not apply in pig Latin forms such as [o͞ok͟je͞i] for *yoke* or in slips of the tongue, such as [gɪnɪkʲ sa͞ɪz] for *cynical guys* (Stampe, 1972a, pp. 43–44). Context-sensitive natural processes, but not phonological rules, are said to show up in the nativization of loan words and in rapid speech, as well as in slips of the tongue and in secret languages. Because Stampe is primarily concerned with phonetic behavior, he has little to say about morphophonemic rules such as velar softening (which are major concerns in generative phonology).

Application
of Processes

Stampe (1972a) also discusses *sequenced substitutions* and *constituent processes*, or separate processes with different functions that have "cumulative results." In addition, he shows that these processes are not dependent on motor constraints. To illustrate, as mentioned earlier, Joan Velten (Velten, 1943) had a substitution of [z] for /l/, and also for /j/, which at first seems very odd. However, Stampe postulates three natural phonological processes to account for these substitutions: delateralization (l→j), spirantization (j→ʒ), and depalatalization (ʒ→z). All three processes apply to give [z] for /l/, as in [zɑb] for *lamb*, and the last two processes apply to give [z] for /j/, as in [zɑd] for *yard*. All of these processes are phonetically motivated and natural. *Delateralization* eliminates the difficult tongue shape of /l/. *Spirantization* is said to be perceptually motivated because it increases the audibility of /j/, and *depalatalization* changes the "fronted and raised" tongue position of /ʃ, ʒ/ to the more neutral position of [s, z] (Stampe, 1972a, p. 13). If all three of these changes were combined into one rule (l, j, ʒ→z), the functions of the individual processes would not be captured. So, Stampe argues for breaking down surface substitutions into their constituent processes whenever possible. (Complex surface substitutions may sometimes resemble the crazy rules discussed earlier in this chapter.)

Regarding the application of processes, Stampe argues that processes apply sequentially (rather than simultaneously) and that a process can apply more than once to any given form (i.e., application is *iterative*). If processes applied simultaneously, he claims that some processes would create the same configuration that others are eliminating (1972, p. 59). In his *divinity fudge* example (1972a, p. 55), he shows that three processes—syllabication, flapping, and flap deletion—each apply more than once to derive the fast speech form [də·vɪ̈ı·fʌdʒ]. Syllabication applies four times, and flapping and flap deletion each apply twice. In Stampe's view, sequences of process application and reapplication are "perfectly natural" and follow from the functions of the individual processes and their "mutual dependencies" (1972a, pp. 58, 59). According to Stampe, a process applies whenever the configuration that it would eliminate arises (1972a, p. 57).

Although Stampe discusses feeding and bleeding orders of application, first proposed by Kiparsky (1968b) (see Appendix B), he disregards the feeding/bleeding terminology. Feeding order, in which one process increases the application of another, is viewed as sequential application without order and is said to reflect phonetic motivation. In Stampe's view, it does not matter which process applies first; a derivation ends when all applicable processes have applied. If an order is imposed, "it is of the form B may not apply after A (i.e., to A's output)" (1972a, p. 60). That is, an antisequential constraint is imposed or the processes are put in a *counter-feeding order*. Stampe (1972a, p. 61) claims that children often constrain their processes in this way. For example, Hildegard Leopold (Leopold, 1939, 1947) at one stage had [ʒu] for *you* (j→ʒ), and [jaɪ] for *lie* (l→j). Spirantization (j→ʒ) was constrained so that it could not apply after (and thus to the output of) delateralization (l→j). This situation is not a natural one, because Stampe argues that it is unnatural "for a process to be prevented from applying when there is something for it to apply to" (1972a, pp. 63–64). However, as children progress in their phonological development, we often find this type of situation.

Underlying Representations

One way in which Stampe's model differs from standard generative theory is that Stampe does not allow such abstract underlying representations. In his view, underlying representations are composed of sounds that are pronounceable. All underlying segments are fully specified. Redundant features are not left unspecified as they are in systematic phonemic representations (Stampe, 1972a, p. 29). Conditions on underlying representations are not redundancy rules but innate processes, which often cause substitutions in phonological acquisition but then are ordered and show up only as restrictions on underlying representations.

Stampe (1972a, p. 28) claims that the "normal situation is for the underlying representation of a form to be identical to its surface representation." He says that there are just two constraints that cause the underlying representation to be "deeper." First, there is a general constraint barring allophonic features (e.g., nasalization on vowels in English, or aspiration on voiceless stops) from underlying representations. So, underlying representations have to be at least as deep as the traditional (taxonomic) phonemic level. Second, there is a more specific constraint: If a form has variants whose pronunciation "cannot be derived from the phonemic representation, its representation must be adjusted accordingly" (1972a, p. 28). That is, a morpheme is represented more deeply than the traditional phonemic level if its alternating forms require a deeper representation (1972a, p. 31). To use an example from German, words like *Tag* "day" ([tɑk]) must have final voiced obstruents on the underlying level because the corresponding plural forms (e.g., [tɑ́gə]) have voiced obstruents.

In discussing underlying representations, Stampe cites evidence from secret languages, fast speech, slips of the tongue, etc. To illustrate, he claims that on the underlying level, vowels are not nasalized in English. Underlying nasalized vowels are barred by the context-free process V→[– nasal], as mentioned earlier, but surface vowels are often nasalized by a context-sensitive nasalization process. However, if a word with a phonetically nasalized vowel is resyllabified in pig Latin, the vowel will lose its nasalization. So, for example, *own* is pronounced [õ͠ʊn] in English, but in pig Latin, it is [ō͞ʊ.nēɪ], with resyllabication. Since the [n] is no longer in the same syllable as [ō͞ʊ], that diphthong is not longer nasalized (Stampe, 1972a, p. 24). (Stampe uses a period to represent a syllable boundary.)

Stampe makes no distinction between processes that govern underlying representations (equivalent to phonotactic constraints or morpheme structure rules) and those that govern derived representations (morphophonemic or allophonic processes) because some processes may have both roles. However, processes that govern underlying representations are primarily context-free, while those that govern surface representations are context-sensitive. For example, the context-free process of vowel denasalization mentioned above is said to be a condition on underlying representations in English. On the other hand, the context-sensitive process nasalizing vowels preceding nasal consonants affects only surface representations (in English). The only distinction that exists (between processes that govern underlying representations and those that govern derived representations) is said to be determined by the "natural interrelationships of processes in the system" (Stampe, 1972a, p. 31). The only processes that can govern underlying representations are those whose output is not barred from the lexicon by an earlier process. Thus the inventory of underlying segments in a language is made up of those segments that are not prohibited by the context-free processes of the language (1972a, p. 37). Figure 5-1 is a schematic representation of Stampe's view of phonology.

This appears to be an accurate representation of Stampe's view of the child's phonological system. However, it is somewhat of a simplification of the adult phonological system because it does not show that natural phonological processes may have different functions. As just discussed, underlying representations, in Stampe's model, are governed mainly by context-free or paradigmatically motivated processes, while surface representations are governed mainly by context-sensitive or syntagmatically motivated processes. This is not shown in Figure 5-1.

FIGURE 5-1
A schematic representation of Stampe's (1972a) view of the phonological component, showing the relationship between (nonabstract) underlying representations and surface forms. (See text for additional description.)

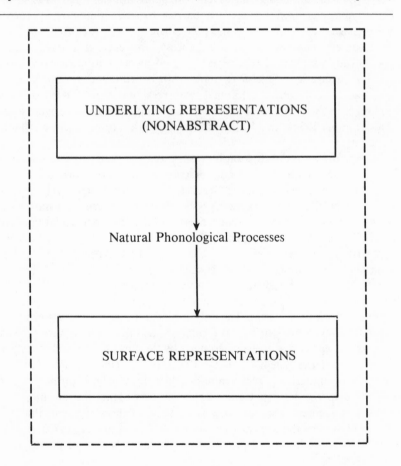

Diachronic
Phonetic Change

Stampe is concerned with accounting for historical phonetic change as well as language acquisition. In his view, language change originates from children, and therefore natural phonetically motivated processes should show up in diachronic change as they do in acquisition. Stampe sees the relaxation of antisequential constraints as a major source of phonetic change (1972a, p. 61). That is, rules go from ordered to unordered application, or the "conservative" order is relaxed. If children fail to master a certain sound (i.e., fail to suppress an innate process that does not apply in the adult language), it will look as though a process has been added to the language. If children fail to order processes correctly, it will look as though reordering of processes has taken place. Finally, if children fail to limit a process appropriately, it will look as though the process has been generalized.[9] In other words, changes originate when children fail to impose constraints that are found in the adult language. The standard language rejects most of these innovations, Stampe (1969, p. 449) claims, but some may be "gradually admitted," beginning as optional pronunciations in less formal styles.

Redundancy rules or conditions (see Appendix B) have no place in Stampe's model, which focuses on natural processes, nor do marking conventions. Stampe sees no need for Jakobson's implicational laws. To the extent that they are valid, he believes that they can be explained by the properties of the innate system (1969, p. 446).

CONCLUSION

Naturalness issues in phonological theory have been of continued interest to phonologists. The perceptual and articulatory aspects of sound classes have particular relevance for speech-language pathologists, for speech sound errors often seem to follow a certain phonetic logic. To capture sound change phenomena in languages or in an individual's idiolect, the term phonological process has been used in a number of theoretical contexts. Many such processes have been proposed to describe common features of individual sound changes. In David Stampe's natural phonology, which has been of considerable interest to child phonologists, this construct is primary. Stampe's theory, in which the natural phonological process is contrasted to the generative rule, argues for the psychological reality of phonetically motivated sound changes. As we will see in succeeding chapters, Stampe's notions have stimulated research in a number of applied areas of child phonology.

FOOTNOTES

[1]According to Hyman (1975, pp. 139-140), two segments belong to a natural class if one or more of the following criteria are met in several languages: (a) the segments undergo natural phonological processes together (to be described next), (b) they function together in the environment of natural processes, (c) one segment replaces the other in natural processes, and (d) one segment is derived in the environment of the other, as in assimilation.

[2]*Feature counting* is a procedure used by generative phonologists to evaluate naturalness. Feature counting is discussed in a later section; see Hyman (1975, p. 150) for a detailed discussion of Chomsky and Halle's two principles for feature counting.

[3]Voiced and voiceless stops often do not contrast between vowels (e.g., both /t/ and /d/ are frequently realized as a voiced flap), and in initial position, aspiration is the important perceptual cue, not voicing.

[4]*Sandhi* is a term that is used for processes that occur at the boundary of two words. For example, in French final consonants that are usually not pronounced (because they have been lost historically) may show up if the next word begins with a vowel. This is true of the definite article *les* "the" [lez], which is pronounced as [le] before words with initial consonants, but as [lez] before vowel-initial words. This is called *liaison* (MacKay, 1978, p. 174).

[5]Because the natural state of affairs is for obstruents to be voiceless, as discussed earlier, obstruents may be devoiced in any position. Stampe (1969, 1972a), in his theory of natural phonology discusses the fact that the context-free obstruent devoicing process and the context-sensitive obstruent voicing process are both natural.

[6]It is understood that the voicing and the place of articulation of the underlying sound generally remain unchanged. When these other features do change, additional processes have to be postulated to account for them.

[7]Innate processes do not have to be overcome if there is no counterevidence in the language. For example, if the language being learned has only voiceless obstruents in final position, the obstruent devoicing process does not have to be suppressed.

[8]According to Stampe (1972a), context-sensitive processes, which apply most often in casual rapid speech, may create allophones that are barred from underlying representations by more general context-free processes. For instance, in English, vowels preceding nasal consonants are nasalized. This context-sensitive process creates segments (nasalized vowels) that are barred from English underlying representations by a context-free process making all vowels oral.

[9]Rule addition, reordering, and generalization (as well as rule loss) are types of phonological change that have been discussed by generative phonologists. For example, see Kiparsky (1968b).

Part III

APPLICATIONS OF PHONOLOGY

6

Normal
Phonological
Development

This chapter is concerned with how children acquire the sound system of their native language. Of course it is somewhat unrealistic to separate phonological acquisition from syntactic and semantic acquisition and from the acquisition of pragmatics. Acquisition takes place in all areas concurrently. That is, children do not learn the sound system of their language first and then later learn how to put words together to form sentences and to interpret the meanings of words and sentences. Rather, as children are acquiring the phonological system of their language, they also are acquiring semantic and syntactic forms and learning language uses. Although development in all areas proceeds at the same time, development in any one area may be more noticeable at one time than at another and development in one or two areas may be ahead of development in the other areas. Appendix C provides a tentative overview of phonological stages (from Ingram, 1976, and others).

WHY STUDY NORMAL
PHONOLOGICAL
DEVELOPMENT?

As pointed out by Ingram (1974b, p. 49), the translation of Roman Jakobson's *Child Language, Aphasia and Phonological Universals* was undoubtedly an important factor in stimulating current interest in phonological theory, phonological acquisition, and in relationships between the two areas of study. Jakobson believed that the same principles that account for the properties of sound systems and how sound systems change over time also account for phonological acquisition by children. Others besides Jakobson (e.g. Stampe, 1969, 1972a; Smith, 1973; Ferguson, 1975b; Ingram, 1978; Menn, 1980) also believe that phonological acquisition is relevant to phonological theory.[1] Several of these linguists have argued strongly that data from children's acquisition of phonology can shed light on and help us understand important issues in phonological theory.[2] In fact, Smith (1973, pp. 206–207) in his study of his son Amahl's phonological development drew several conclusions that bear on phonological theory, for example, concerning rule ordering. Ferguson (1975b, p. 13) claimed that "phonological theory . . . is manifested . . . wherever and however language is used." He argued further that the study of phonological acquisition "should be recognized as a regular part of the general study of phonology."

Another reason for studying normal phonological acquisition is the hope that it will lead to an understanding of delayed or disordered phonological development and eventually to more efficient and effective ways of approaching management. As Ingram (1974b) suggests, research in child phonology has lagged behind research in other areas of child development. However, with new developments in linguistic theory and in techniques for analyzing children's speech, research in child phonology since the late 1960s has been more productive.

Books on language development and disorders often discuss several *stages of acquisition*. For example, Ingram (1976, p. 11) outlines six major *stages of prelinguistic and linguistic development*: I. Prelinguistic vocalization and perception (birth to 1 year), II. Phonology of the first 50 words (1 to 1½ years), III. Phonology of simple morphemes (1½ to 4 years), IV. Completion of the phonetic inventory (4 to 7 years), V. Morphophonemic development (7 to 12 years), and VI. Mastery of spelling (12 to 16 years), Dale (1976, p. 204) outlines four "broad stages" of early vocalizations (based on Kaplan & Kaplan, 1971), all of which would span the period covered by Ingram's first stage or first two stages. Dale's stages are: crying, other vocalizations and cooing, babbling, and patterned speech. These and other views are described in more detail in Appendix C of this book. (See also Shriberg & Kwiatkowski, 1980, Appendix A.)

STUDIES OF PHONOLOGICAL ACQUISITION

Of the many books and papers describing children's acquisition of the sound system of their native language, some have followed a particular theoretical orientation while others have been essentially atheoretical. That is, some studies describe the pertinent facts of speech sound acquisition, but not within any particular theoretical framework. What follows is a discussion of several widely referenced studies of normal phonological acquisition. It is not meant to be an exhaustive discussion, but rather a sampling to illustrate the types of studies that have been undertaken. Studies are discussed according to whether the basic phonological units of concern are (1) *segments* (phones or phonemes), (2) *features*, (3) *prosodic* or *suprasegmental elements*, or (4) *phonological rules* and/or *phonological processes*.

Segment-Based Acquisition Studies

Diary Studies
Many of the earlier descriptions of phonological acquisition were in the form of diaries or in-depth discussions of one child's development, usually over a period of months or years. Ingram (1976, p. 4) designates 1877-1929 as the "period of diary studies." Several aspects of the child's development were often covered in diary studies, not just phonology. The author was typically a linguist, psychologist, or educator and was a parent of the child being discussed. Such studies include those of Holmes (1927), Leopold (1939, 1947), Velten (1943), Grégoire (1947), and Smith (1973). Traditional diary studies, which tend not to follow a specific theory, usually consist of vocabulary lists, lists of sound substitutions, and discussions of the sounds used by the child.

Holmes (1927). In Table 6-1 we have reproduced some data presented by Holmes (1927, p. 220). Holmes gives a complete list of his daughter

TABLE 6-1
Examples from Holmes (1927, pp. 220, 221) of Mollie's productions at the age of 18 months (1;6).

Word	Mollie's Form(s)	Word	Mollie's Form(s)
bad	[bæ.dː]	dog	[dɔ]
bath	[bæ]	doll	[dɑ]
bed	[bɛ] ~ [bɛ.tː]	good	[gu] ~ [gu.d]
bird	[bo]	pick	[pi.kː]
coat	[ko]	pudding, spoon	[pu]
cracker	[kækæ]	shoe	[t.ʃu]
cry	[kɑi]	squirrel	[kœi]
Dick	[dɪ.k]	that	[dæ]

Mollie's words at 1;6 and draws several conclusions from them. For example, he states that she produced final [k], but not final [g] (e.g., see *Dick* and *dog*). Final [t] and [d] were sometimes present and sometimes absent (e.g., see *bad*, *bed*, and *coat*). Holmes lists all the new words and phrases produced by Mollie at 1;8 and 1;9, and he draws conclusions based on these new forms. To illustrate, at 1;8 she produced [pʰ.æ], [p.æ], or [bæ] for *fire*, *flower*, and *fall*, and she produced [pʰ.ʊ.tː] for *foot*. These forms show that at the age of 20 months she often produced initial /f/ as [p], usually with aspiration.

Because Mollie's vocabulary had grown so large by the age of 1;10, Holmes gives only a representative list of new words and phrases produced at that time. The conclusions that are drawn sometimes take the form of substitution statements. For instance, Holmes observes that at 1;10 initial /l/ was rendered as "zero," as in [ɛə] for *letter*. At the same time, intervocalic /l/ was produced as zero or [d], as in [mɑi] for *Mollie* and [dɑddi] for *dollie*. Final /l/ was produced as [ʊ], as in [pʊ.ʊ] for *pull*.

Holmes gives "typical" words and phrases produced by Mollie at 1;11 and 2;0, when her speech was "at a high point of development" (1927, p. 223). These productions are discussed and interpreted, and conclusions are again drawn. Forms produced at 1;11 show that Mollie consistently reduced multisyllabic words to two syllables, as in [måd.ʒi] for *Marjorie*. ([å] here represents the [ɔ] sound.)

Finally, Holmes makes additional statements about Mollie's speech at the age of 2;1 when his paper was written. At that time, she could produce nearly all English consonants, although she reduced long words and sometimes vacillated between two consonants. The most problematic sounds for her at that stage were /l/, medial and final /f/, and /s/ in clusters. Holmes reports (1927, p. 225) that at this stage, Mollie produced /sp/ as [f], /st/ as [t], and /sk/ as [k].

Leopold (1947). The most extensive diary study, made up of several volumes, is Leopold's study of his daughter Hildegard. One entire volume (Volume II) is devoted to Hildegard's learning of the sound systems of English and German up until the beginning of her third year. In this study, Leopold lists all of Hildegard's words in alphabetical order and gives the phonetic transcription for each, along with the date at which each appeared. Hildegard's renditions of every standard adult sound are discussed in detail, and her regular sound substitutions are summarized. Leopold also offers explanations for examples that do not fit into her regular patterns of substitution. In interpreting the facts, Leopold discusses consonant segments by place of articulation, manner of articulation, voicing, word-position, and presence in clusters. The sounds that Hildegard learned to produce are presented in order, from birth. In addition, all of her sounds are traced back to the adult sounds for which they substituted. Leopold also examines Hildegard's sound system as a separate entity, rather than with reference to the adult system. In this analysis, Hildegard's consonant system is discussed in terms of Jakobson's theory.

There is a wealth of information in Leopold's study. It is extremely thorough, and each sound is discussed in several places. Moreover, his interpretations do not obscure the facts, and some of his observations are of relevance to current investigations. For instance, he notes that until 1;7, Hildegard "resisted" using words containing labiodental fricatives (cf. our discussion of *avoidance*). He also comments that Hildegard handled fricatives more skillfully in final than in initial or medial positions. Both of these issues will come up again.

Although Leopold's survey of Hildegard's sound acquisition is very detailed and complete, there is no attempt to generalize or to integrate the data. Like most other diarists, Leopold limited himself to the task of recording rather than explaining.

Velten (1943). Velten's study of his daughter Joan's vocabulary growth and phonological development from 11 to 36 months is one of the best examples of a study based on Jakobson's theory of phonological acquisition, focusing on phonemic development. It consists primarily of statements about the child's successive phoneme inventories. Velten lists allophonic variations and describes how these allophones become separate phonemes. To illustrate, Velten (1943, pp. 289–290) states that in the 25th month [ı] appeared in Joan's speech as an allophone of /ʊ/ before dentals in accented syllables, first in [sıt] for *sit*, then [fıt] for *foot*, [dıd] for *good*, etc. (Earlier, these last two words were [fʊt] and [dʊd].) The phonemic opposition between [ʊ] and [ı] was not established until the 36th month, however.

As discussed in Chapter 3 of this book, Jakobson suggests that the child's phonemic system at any point may be noncongruent with the adult system. That is, the child may have phonemic distinctions that are not found in the adult system. For instance, at one stage before she could produce final voiced obstruents, Joan Velten had a vowel-length distinction not present in the adult language, as in [ba.t] *bad* vs. [bat] *back* and [bu.t] *bead* vs. [but] *beat* (p. 289).

Although a great deal of information is contained in Velten's study, it is not as useful as it might be because of the way the data are presented. For example, Velten (1943, p. 286) reports that at 22 months, Joan had a phoneme t/d for English /t, d, k, g/ and initial /tʃ, dʒ/, and he gives representative forms, such as [dut] for *coat* and [du] for *toe*. Because there is no complete list of Joan's vocabulary in phonetic transcription, reanalysis of the data from a different theoretical perspective is not possible.

Smith (1973). Smith's diary study of his son Amahl ("A") from the age of 2 to 4 years contains two types of analyses. One is based on Jakobson's theory. In this analysis, the child is seen as having a self-contained independent phonological system. Smith presents "A's" phoneme inventory, morpheme structure conditions, and sets of phonetic rules, for instance rules for the distribution of voiced and voiceless stops at a stage before the voicing distinction was acquired. After presenting longitudinal analyses from two points of view, Smith concluded that there was no evidence that "A" had his own phonemic system, and therefore Smith argued against the phonemic analysis and for the other type of analysis, to be discussed later.

Large Group Studies

Many studies of phonological development that could be called large group studies also focused on sound segments. These studies report on the articulatory proficiency of large groups of children. They include studies by Wellman, Case, Mengert, and Bradbury (1931), Poole (1934),

Templin (1957), Snow (1963), Bricker (1967), Olmsted (1971), and Prather, Hedrick, and Kern (1975). Ingram (1976) designates 1930 to 1957 as the period of large group studies. Generally, these studies are concerned with determining ages at which certain sounds are produced correctly by most children (e.g., by 75% of the children studied), or with discovering the most common production "errors."

These studies give a general picture of order of acquisition and of common substitutes, but there are several factors that limit their usefulness. For instance, there is frequently no way to tell which target words elicited each substitution, and thus possible effects of assimilation, metathesis, etc. are hidden. Also, substitutions are not always listed by word-position or phonetic context. Some studies use repetition of CV syllables (e.g., Bricker, 1967) or words (e.g., Templin, 1957). Moreover, in some cases (e.g., Templin, 1957), only one word is used to elicit each sound in each position. Data from all children of a given age usually are grouped together with no attempt to relate or explain the various substitutions. Finally, large group studies generally provide no information about how the surface substitutions of any particular child fit together into a phonological system.

Large group studies are generally atheoretical. They are concerned only with the phonetic production (or articulation) of specific sound segments of the adult language, such as /m, d, f, s/, etc. They do not attempt to explain, but rather to provide normative data, which is, of course, important in the field of speech pathology. Let us examine selected normative information from several of the more widely referenced studies.

Some Composite Norms. Age norms found in four widely referenced large group studies are summarized in Table 6-2. Just a glance at this table shows that there is considerable lack of agreement regarding the age at which particular sounds are acquired by children. It is instructive to consider some of the reasons behind this lack of agreement. First, investigators may define *acquired* differently. In the studies by Wellman et al. (1931), Templin (1957), and Prather et al. (1975), a sound was considered to be acquired when it was produced correctly by 75% of the subjects at any given age level. In the Poole (1934) study, however, 100% was the criterion. That is, a sound was considered to be acquired when it was produced correctly by 100% of the subjects at a particular age level. No doubt this accounts, in part, for the consistently higher ages reported in the Poole study (e.g., 5;6 for /f/, as opposed to 2:4 for Prather et al. and 3;0 for both Wellman et al. and Templin). Of course, any percentage could be chosen. For instance, a researcher could require 90% correct production. The results would be expected to differ accordingly.

TABLE 6-2

Age norms for all English consonant sounds, from four large group studies (based on Templin, 1957; Winitz, 1969; Prather et al., 1975).[a]

Sound	Age of Acquisition			
	Wellman et al. (1931)	*Poole (1934)*	*Templin (1957)*	*Prather et al. (1975)*
/m/	3	3;6	3	2
/n/	3	4;6	3	2
/ŋ/	—	4;6	3	2
/p/	4	3;6	3	2
/f/	3	5;6	3	2;4
/h/	3	3;6	3	2
/w/	3	3;6	3	2;8
/j/	4	4;6	3;6	2;4
/k/	4	4;6	4	2;4
/b/	3	3;6	4	2;8
/d/	5	4;6	4	2;4
/g/	4	4;6	4	3
/r/	5	7;6	4	3;4[b]
/s/	5	7;6[b]	4;6	3[b]
/ʃ/		6;6	4;6	3;8
/tʃ/	5		4;6	3;8
/t/	5	4;6	6	2;8
/θ/	—	7;6[b]	6	4 +
/v/	5	6;6[b]	6	4 +
/l/	4	6;6	6	3;4[b]
/ð/	—	6;6	7	4
/z/	5	7;6[b]	7	4 +
/ʒ/	5	6;6	7	4
/dʒ/	6		7	4 +[b]
/hw/	—	7;6	—	4 +

[a]A blank indicates that the sound was not tested or was not reported. A dash (—) indicates that the sound in question did not meet the criterion of correct production at the oldest age level tested. In Prather et al. (1975) a 4 + indicates that the sound was not produced correctly by 75% of the subjects at the highest age level (4) tested. In the Wellman et al. data, /hw/ reached criterion at 5 but not 6. Medial /ŋ/ reached it at 3, initial /θ/ at 5 and initial and medial /ð/ at 5.

[b]These sounds exhibited "shifts" or "reversals," appearing at an earlier age, then disappearing and later reappearing. The ages of reappearance are noted here except for Prather et al. /r, s, l/, which dropped only slightly at one age level and then again reached criterion.

Another potentially important factor is word-position. Each word-position may be considered separately, or all positions may be combined, or an investigation may be limited to one or two positions. Wellman et al. (1931), Poole (1934), and Templin (1957) required correct production in all three positions, initial (I), medial (M), and final (F). In Prather et al. (1975), the percentage is required in just two positions, initial and final. As Prather et al. (1975, p. 184) point out, this procedural difference may account for the lower age levels obtained in their study and for some of the large discrepancies. For instance, Templin places /t/ at age 6;0, while Prather et al. place it at 2 years and 8 months (2;8). This is because medial /t/ is acquired late (Prather et al. 1975, p. 184).

As indicated in the notes to Table 6-2, in the Wellman et al. study, medial /ŋ/ reached the percentage criterion (75%) at 3;0, and initial /θ/ and initial and medial /ð/ reached it at 5;0. But these later sounds are listed as not being acquired at the oldest age level tested because the 75% correct production criterion was not reached in all three positions. Clearly, the relative difficulty of a sound in one particular position can lower the age of acquisition considerably.

As Sander (1972) points out, the results of studies such as these also differ depending upon whether the researchers are concerned with the earliest age of acquisition or with the upper age limit (or complete mastery). This influences the way in which they treat reversals or shifts. In the case of a reversal or shift, a sound appears at one age and then disappears at a later age level. To illustrate, in Poole's (1934) study, /s/ and /z/ appeared at 5½ years, then disappeared, and reappeared at 7;6 or above. Similarly, /θ/ appeared at 6;6 and reappeared at 7;6, and /v/ appeared at 5;6 then reappeared at 6;6 (Winitz, 1969, p. 59). In each case the age listed by Poole is the older age at which the sound reappeared. Prather et al. treated reversals in the following way. If the percentage of correct production reached 75% at one age level, then dropped slightly (not below 70%) at just one age level, returning to at least 75% at the next age level, the earlier age level was reported. This was true of /s, l, r/ (Prather et al. 1975, p. 184). Otherwise, the later age was indicated, as in the case of /dʒ/, listed at 4;0 +.

Another factor to consider is how strict the researchers are in requiring complete phonetic accuracy. As Ingram (1978) pointed out in his study of fricative acquisition, /s/ may be considered an early acquisition if phonetic accuracy is not required, but if phonetic accuracy is required, /s/ may be considered a late acquisition. Note the different ages (from 3;0 to 7;6) listed for /s/ in Table 6-2.

Other potentially important factors include the following: the conditions under which the data were collected, whether judgments of production accuracy were made live or from tape recordings, whether spontaneous or imitated utterances were used, whether isolated words or connected speech was analyzed, what types of words were elicited (length of words, stress patterns, phonetic context, familiarity of words, etc.), the socioeconomic and dialectical characteristics of the subjects, and their ages.

In some studies, such as Templin's (1957), the youngest children tested were 3;0. Thus sounds acquired before that age would be listed as being acquired at 3;0. The oldest children tested by Prather et al. (1975) were 4 years of age. Sounds not reaching 75% correct production by that age are listed as being acquired at 4;0 + .

Although age norm charts may be useful because of their convenience and simplicity, they have many limitations and should therefore be used cautiously, if at all.

Age-Range Norms. In his analysis of Wellman et al.'s (1931) and Templin's (1957) data, Sander (1972) made a significant improvement on the concept of age norms. Instead of giving one particular age at which each sound is acquired, he gives age ranges. This approach is much more realistic and comes closer to capturing the variability that is found in sound acquisition. The age range for the acquisition of a sound begins at what Sander calls the "average age of customary production." This is defined as the age at which "the combined test average at the various word positions exceeds 50 percent correct production." The age range for a sound ends at the "upper age limit of customary production." This is defined as the age at which "the combined test average [at the various positions] reaches 90% correct production" (p. 61). Figure 6-1 is Sander's graphic presentation of age-range norms for segment acquisition. Sander's figure has been used here because it represents the first attempt to show both the "average age of customary production" and the "upper age limit" for sound acquisition. Prather et al. (1975) present a very similar figure that summarizes newer data from younger children.

Error Analyses. Several large group studies have been expressly concerned with children's errors, rather than establishing norms for segment acquisition. For example, Snow (1963) reported the results of a study of 438 first-grade children who were given a picture-naming task. Some of the most frequent segment substitutes (occurring more than 20 times each) in initial position and final position are given in Table 6-3, along with the total number of times each was found in each position across the 438 children. Omission and distortion errors are not included here. Omissions errors were quite rare, but distortions (particularly involving fricatives and /r/) were common.

FIGURE 6-1
Average age estimates and upper age limits of customary consonant production. The solid bar corresponding to each sound starts at the median age of customary articulation; it stops at an age level at which 90% of all children are customarily producing the sound. (From Templin, 1957; Wellman, Case, Mengert, & Bradbury, 1931.) Reproduced from E. Sander. When Are Speech Sounds Learned? *Journal of Speech and Hearing Disorders*, 1972, *37*, 55-63.

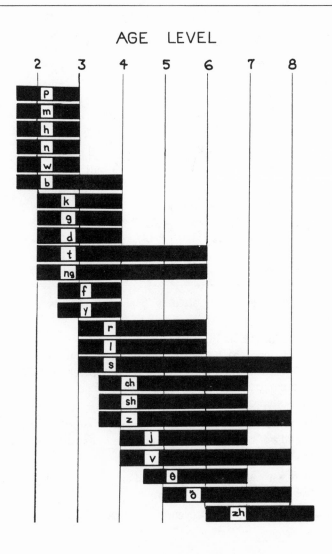

TABLE 6-3
The most frequent sound substitutions for initial and final positions produced by 438 first grade children (Snow, 1963).

Adult Sound	Child Sound	Position	Number of Occurrences	Adult Sound	Child Sound	Position	Number of Occurrences
ᵃ/ʒ/ ⁻ᵇ	[dʒ]	Final	625ᶜ	/z/ →	[s]	Initial	48
ᵃ/ʍ/ →	[w]	Initial	499ᵈ	/ʃ/ →	[s]	Initial	42
ᵃ/ð/ →	[v]	Final	212	/ð/ →	[d]	Final	37
ᵃ/ŋ/ →	[n]	Final	151ᵉ	/dʒ/ →	[tʃ]	Final	35
/θ/ →	[f]	Initial	145	/v/ →	[b]	Final	32
/v/ →	[b]	Initial	144	ᵃ/dʒ/ →	[dz]	Initial	29
/θ/ →	[f]	Final	130	ᵃ/ʒ/ →	[z]	Final	28
ᵃ/tʃ/ →	[ts]	Final	106	ᵃ/tʃ/ →	[ts]	Initial	28
/ʃ/ →	[s]	Final	98	/tʃ/ →	[ʃ]	Initial	25
/z/ →	[s]	Final	81	/ð/ →	[d]	Initial	24
/r/ →	[w]	Initial	76	/l/ →	[w]	Initial	24
ᵃ/z/ →	[dz]	Initial	64	ᵃ/z/ →	[ð]	Final	22
ᵃ/ʒ/ →	[dz]	Final	54	ᵃ/g/ →	[d]	Initial	21
ᵃ/ð/ →	[θ]	Final	53	ᵃ/t/ →	[k]	Final	21
ᵃ/dʒ/ →	[dz]	Final	53	/θ/ →	[s]	Final	21
ᵃ/v/ →	[f]	Final	50				

ᵃThese substitutions are not reported as "stable" by Cairns and Williams (1972).

ᵇFollowing the usual phonological convention, the target sound (i.e., the adult sound in question) is on the left of the arrow, and the child's substitute is on the right, as in /θ/ → [f]. In speech pathology, such substitutions are represented by writing the substitute on the left of a slash, and the adult sound on the right, as in f/θ.

ᶜSnow (1963, p. 287) notes that the frequent dʒ/ʒ substitution in *garage* probably should not be considered an error due to its frequent occurrence in adult speech.

ᵈIt is unlikely that w/ʍ should be considered an error, given the infrequent occurrence of /ʍ/ in adult English.

ᵉMost of these n/ŋ substitutions occurred in the word *swimming*.

In their study of 384 "standard English-speaking" school-aged children, Cairns and Williams (1972) list the "stable" substitutes, or those that occurred more than twice in the sample. The substitutes, elicited by the *Goldman-Fristoe Test of Articulation* (Goldman & Fristoe, 1972) are not given by word-position. The stable substitutes reported by Cairns and Williams are listed in Table 6-4, in decreasing order of frequency. Omission and distortion errors reported by Cairns and Williams (1972) are not included here. The sound most frequently omitted (10 times) was /r/, followed by /l/ (8 times), /θ/ (5 times), and /s/ (3 times). The sound most frequently distorted was /s/.

It is clear that there are several points of disagreement between the Snow (1963) data (Table 6-3) and those reported by Cairns and Williams (Table 6-4). Common substitutes reported by Snow but not by Cairns and Williams are preceded by a superscript[a] in Table 6-3. Substitutions

TABLE 6-4
The most frequent sound substitutions for 384 school-age children (Cairns & Williams, 1972).

Adult Sound		Child Sound	Number of Occurrences
/z/	→	[s]	42
/r/	→	[w]	31
/v/	→	[b]	29
/θ/	→	[f]	21
/ð/	→	[d]	18
/ʃ/	→	[tʃ]	8
[a]/p/	→	[b]	7
[a]/f/	→	[b]	6
/l/	→	[w]	6
[a]/tʃ/	→	[t]	6
/dʒ/	→	[tʃ]	6
/tʃ/	→	[ʃ]	5
/θ/	→	[t]	5
/θ/	→	[s]	4
/ʃ/	→	[s]	3
[a]/dʒ/	→	[d]	3

[a]These are not among the most frequent substitutions reported by Snow (1963).

reported by Cairns and Williams that Snow did not find to be common substitutes are preceded by an ˮ in Table 6-4. The differences between the results of these two studies may be partly due to the fact that substitutes were listed by word-position in the Snow study but not in the study by Cairns and Williams. In addition, the subjects differed in age. All of the children in Snow's study were first graders, while Cairns and Williams' subjects were in grades 1 through 12. The words were also elicited by different instruments in the two studies. Snow apparently made up her own picture-naming task to elicit two attempts at each sound in each position, while Cairns and Williams used the Goldman-Fristoe Test of Articulation. Therefore, many of the target words were probably different. We would expect that the results of other similar studies would differ somewhat, as do the results of the two studies discussed here.

In spite of the differences between these two studies, there are also many similarities in results. Several of the stable segment substitutes listed by Cairns and Williams, including the five most frequent, are also listed by Snow: /z/→[s], /r/→[w], /v/→[b], /θ/→[f], /ð/→[d]. These are apparently among the most common substitutes observed in children, at least children of school age.

Lists of common sound errors, such as those just discussed, give clinicians an idea of what types of substitutes to expect. However, when separate substitutes are listed in this way, important generalizations are missed. Many child phonologists and speech pathologists now believe that this is not the most revealing way to look at children's sound errors because there is no attempt to combine or relate similar substitutions. Presently, we will discuss how phonological processes are used to combine related substitutions and thus capture generalizations.

Small Group Studies

Some studies of normal phonological development could be called small group synchronic studies. In such studies, the acquisition of a small group of children at one particular time (or synchronic period) is discussed. Some of these small group studies are concerned mainly with sound segments—either phonetic elements or phonemes.

Moskowitz (1970). One example of a small group study is provided by Moskowitz (1970). Moskowitz presents data from three 2-year-old children in order to demonstrate that children's phonology is structured. The children in this study are Mackie (Albright & Albright, 1956), Hildegard (Leopold, 1939) and Erica (Moskowitz' own subject). Moskowitz gives a detailed discussion of each child's substitutions and presents a phonological analysis for two of the children. Commenting on the lack of a suitable theory that could be applied in writing phonologies for these children, Moskowitz argues that the abstract underlying forms and complex rules of generative phonology probably are not relevant, and the model of descriptive linguistics is not adequate because of its requirements (e.g., biuniqueness). Therefore, new procedures and criteria are needed for analyzing children's speech.

Moskowitz summarizes Mackie's consonant substitutions for each position at 2;2, along with the frequency of each. His consonants were found to be more stable in initial and medial positions than in final position. For example, stops were most often correct in initial position and least often correct in final position, and omissions were fairly frequent in final position.

Mackie had acquired 19 English consonant phonemes and was in the process of acquiring three more. Only /θ/ and /ʒ/ were totally missing (and /ʒ/ was never attempted). Stop consonants were relatively accurate, as were nasals, glides, and affricates. Fricatives were the most problematic sounds for Mackie. Only /s/ was completely mastered in all positions, but Mackie also had learned /f/ and /ʃ/ and was in the process of acquiring /ð, v, z/. These facts are said to argue against the importance in phonological acquisition of frequency of occurrence, as /ð, v, z/ are more frequent in adult English than /f, ʃ/. Only in the case of interdentals was the voiced member of a cognate pair of fricatives more advanced than its voiceless counterpart. Although /ð/ was often replaced by [d], it was produced correctly several times.

From a distinctive feature view, Moskowitz states that Mackie had mastered [± high] and [± anterior], which are the features differentiating velar stops from labials and dentals. The feature [± coronal] was also learned, and the [± voice] feature was correct for all stop consonants and for some fricatives, although /z/ was often replaced by [s]. [± continuant] was learned for several stop/fricative pairs, but stops often replaced /v, θ, ð/. Although Mackie had learned all the distinctive features needed for correct production of /f, s, θ, v, z, ð/, some of these phonemes were not yet a stable part of his system. This indicates, according to Moskowitz, that learning distinctive features was not a goal for Mackie, and it also suggests that when a feature is learned, it does not spread rapidly through a child's system (Ferguson & Slobin, 1973, p. 58).

Hildegard's sample was characterized by a large variety of long vowels and diphthongs. She had 12 vowel phonemes, which sometimes occurred in unique combinations. In Moskowitz' view, she was "experimenting" and was producing complex vowels (such as [ʊɪ] and [ɛa]) that are not found in adult English. Hildegard had 15 consonant phonemes. Most contrasts occurred in initial position, but more experimentation occurred in final position, and the voicing contrast was represented as a contrast between aspiration and lack of aspiration. Hildegard also had a phonetic rule inserting a glottal stop before an initial vowel or between sequences of two vowels.

Regarding the third child in this study, Moskowitz reports that Erica's mastery of English vowels and intonation patterns made her speech sound quite correct. Except for some details of consonant production, her system was very close to the adult system. Nasals and stops were almost completely mastered at this time (at the age of 2 years and 12 days), although the voicing of stops was not always correct. Erica seemed to have a tense/lax distinction rather than one of voicing.

Like Mackie, Erica had trouble with fricatives. /s/ and /ʃ/ were too "loose" and were produced as blade rather than groove fricatives (Ferguson & Slobin, 1973, p. 65). The place for /ʃ/ was correct, but /s/ varied from dental to palato-alveolar. Erica had similar problems with /z/, with the additional problem of voicing. Although /f/ was established, /v/ was not, being replaced by [b] in initial position and by a voiceless fricative finally. /θ/ and /ð/ were reportedly the most "interesting" fricatives. Initial /ð/ was produced as [d] or was omitted, but medial /ð/ was correct after a dental stop, a nasal consonant, or a nasalized vowel. In Moskowitz' view, this is important because it shows that in child phonology unusual situations may arise that do not occur in natural languages.

Moskowitz argues that a theory which includes only oppositions or features or phonemes or rules cannot adequately account for the diverse patterns found in phonological acquisition. The data that she presents show some cases of feature learning (e.g., learning place features for stop consonants) and some cases of the acquisition of individual phonemes. The data from Hildegard are said to provide evidence of the child's ability to deal with phonology in a rule-based way, and Erica's unique rules are seen as exemplifying the lack of uniformity among children. Moskowitz emphasizes the fact that phonological acquisition is a creative process, and she states that this creativity must be considered in any theory of acquisition. She also stresses that both phonetic and phonological acquisition must be accounted for, and she argues that the traditional focus on phonetic acquisition has obscured some of the patterns that are present in phonological acquisition. This differentiation between phonetic and phonological acquisition forms the basis of a later (1975) paper by Moskowitz that concerns the acquisition of fricatives.

Moskowitz (1975). In a later article, Moskowitz (1975) discusses the acquisition of fricatives. As was the case earlier, she uses data from published studies (by Leopold, 1939, 1947; Albright & Albright, 1956; and Weir, 1962) as well as data from her own subjects. For each child, Moskowitz formulated a list of fricative substitutes. These fricative systems were then organized in a pseudo-longitudinal fashion, from simplest to most complex (1975, p. 143). This is supposed to represent the process of fricative acquisition.

As shown in the first set of these data, one child (Withe, age 2;2) attempted /f, s, z, ʃ, θ, ð/, but only [f] was ever produced correctly (in addition to being rendered as [p]). For the last child (Steven, age 3;5), on the other hand, all fricatives were produced correctly except /θ/, which was replaced by [f]. Moskowitz' discussion of fricative acquisition is based on the eight sets of data presented in addition to her observations of other children.

In this paper, Moskowitz argues for a clear distinction between phonetic and phonological acquisition, which she says often conflict in the acquisition of fricatives. Phonetic acquisition involves learning to recognize and to produce the sounds of the adult language, while phonological (phonemic) acquisition involves learning the contrasts between sounds (Moskowitz, 1975, p. 141). Phonetic acquisition is said to be less regular than phonological acquisition.

In Moskowitz' view, children may be said to have a functional phonological opposition if they can perceive a distinction between two contrasting sounds and know which one they intended to produce, even if adults do not perceive the productions as being distinct (1975, p. 142). For instance, if a child shows on perceptual tests that he or she can distinguish between /ð/ and /d/, but produces only [d], the child can be said to have a phonological (but not a phonetic) /d/ – /ð/ distinction. In this case, the child's articulatory inabilities limit the production of sounds that are acquired phonologically.

On the other hand, phonological restrictions may interfere with phonetic abilities. For example, "idiomatic" utterances of young children may involve more advanced phonetic productions than their normal (i.e., phonologically regular) utterances. To illustrate, a child might first produce *dog* correctly at the age of 1 year and might continue to do so for several weeks (or even months). However, later on, the word could become phonologically regular, undergoing the child's systematic processes. At that point, it would be produced in a more infantile form, such as [dɑ] or [gɑ] (cf. Hildegard Leopold's production of *pretty*). In such cases the restrictions of the child's phonological system interfere with his or her phonetic abilities.

Concerning phonological acquisition, Moskowitz (1975, p. 146) argued that a phoneme can be said to be acquired when its pattern of phonetic realization is "consistently distinct from the pattern of phonetic realization of any other phoneme." She argued further that voiceless fricatives are learned before voiced fricatives phonologically, but phonetically the picture is less clear.

Moskowitz poses several questions about the phonetic acquisition of fricatives. For instance, why do the voiced fricatives have different acquisition patterns than their voiceless counterparts; and why is [v] sometimes used as a substitute for /ð/ in imitation, while [d] is found in spontaneous speech? In seeking answers to these questions, she discusses two sources of phonetic information, *perceptual*, which provides acoustic information, and *physiological* (or articulatory), which provides motor information (p. 147). Although these two sources of information eventually reinforce one another, she states that they may conflict temporarily. Information from these two sources provides an explanation for the second question above. For a child who has not mastered [ð] (and who does not produce [θ] or [z]), the closest substitute in articulation is [d]. In spontaneous speech, the child seems to be trying to learn to change [d] to [ð], but in the imitation situation, there is an attempt to match the acoustic characteristics of the model, and therefore [v] is more satisfactory (Moskowitz, 1975, p. 147).

Both acoustic and articulatory facts play a role in the phenomenon of *suppression*, which Moskowitz claims is important in phonetic acquisition. Suppression is explained as follows: For each major allophone, a speaker has a "prototypical specification," which is "a single point in phonetic space" (1975, p. 148). Around that point, there are many possible phonetic productions that are acceptable renditions of the target sound. Beyond that is a second layer that consists of the productions that are not acceptable (but may be tried). Beyond that is a third layer that includes the rest of phonetic space. Moskowitz hypothesizes that in learning any specific allophone, the child will try many renditions of it until he or she learns where the boundary is between the acceptable phones and the unacceptable ones (the second layer). In doing this, the child has to suppress any phonetic realizations that fall in the second layer. Moskowitz claims that a conflict may arise when sounds in a particular range are acceptable for one phoneme but not for another.

In Moskowitz' view, the problems that children have with [θ] are related to suppression, for [θ] falls into the suppressed layer of phonetic realizations of /t/, /s/, and /f/, all of which are learned before /θ/. Therefore, as /θ/ emerges, [θ] conflicts with the phonetic realizations of the other phonemes and is suppressed by all three (1975, p. 148). So, the child settles on [f], which is the best "temporary solution" (acoustically). The parallel situation does not hold for /ð/ because [v] and [z] are being acquired along with [ð] and are thus not available to suppress it.

Moskowitz states that the development of /z/ is related to the learning of morphology. The child is exposed to many morphemes (e.g., plurals and possessives) that exhibit an alternation between [s] and [z]. The child's productions indicate that [s] and [z] seem to be in "free variation" in final position.[3]

Finally, Moskowitz gives an example to show that "functional load" may be an important factor in fricative acquisition. For one child, [b] and [v] were nearly always in alternation for /v/. However, /v/ was correct in *very*, which contrasted minimally with *berry* (produced with correct [b]).

Ferguson and Farwell (1975). Ferguson and Farwell (1975) investigated the early production of word-initial consonants by three children (T, K, and H) from the age of about 1 year until their productive vocabularies reached 50 words. Two of the children (T and K) were part of a larger study of consonant acquisition, and the other (H) was Hildegard Leopold (Leopold, 1939, 1947).

In this study, two linguistic units were of importance—*words* and *word-initial consonants*. The word was used as "the framework for phone identification and classification" (p. 424). In their analysis, Ferguson and Farwell grouped together all productions of each specific word at each session, and they noted all the variants of the initial consonants. Next, all the words with the same initial phones (or the same set of variant phones) were grouped together. *Phone classes* were then set up consisting of "the set of initial-consonant variants of each of these groups of words" (p. 424). Phone classes were represented by the use of phonetic symbols within boxes or between vertical lines. To illustrate, a phone class $\boxed{\text{m} \sim \text{n}}$ or |m ~ n| is made up of the initial consonants of all words whose initial consonant sound varies between [m] and [n].

All of the phone classes for one child at one session were placed in a horizontal row, arranged more or less by place of articulation, with labials on the left, etc. Vertical lines were then drawn between successive phone classes containing the same word. Dotted lines were used to connect successive phone classes if they did not contain the same word but were related to phone classes that did (p. 424). Dotted lines were also used to connect phone classes that were identical (or very similar) but did not have any words in common. Diagrams of this type that connect corresponding phone classes at successive sessions are called *phone trees*

(p. 425). The number of words in a phone class is indicated by a small number to the right of that class.

The following diagram from Ferguson and Farwell (1975, p. 427) illustrates part of a phone tree for K, including just one set of related phone classes at sessions I through VI:

Session	*Phone Classes*
I	$\boxed{d \sim d\eth \sim t}_{(4)}$
II	$\boxed{d}_{(1)}$
III	$\boxed{d \sim {}^{\eth}d \sim g}_{(3)}$
IV	$\boxed{d \sim \phi}_{(2)}$
V	$\boxed{d}_{(3)}$
VI	$\boxed{d \sim \eth}_{(1)}$

Ferguson and Farwell present phone trees for all three of their subjects. Some of the phone classes that are included are quite complicated. One such example is from T (session VI): $|b \sim \beta \sim bw \sim p^h \sim \phi \sim \phi|$. This phone class encompasses several words and initial-consonant variations.

In this study, Ferguson and Farwell found more variation in word forms than they expected, based on previous reports of phonological acquisition. Other unexpected findings included the "selectivity" of the child in deciding which words to produce and the fact that early forms ("progressive phonological idioms") were sometimes later replaced by less accurate forms. According to Ferguson and Farwell, such findings emphasize the importance of the "lexical parameter" in phonological acquisition—a parameter that has generally not been considered because of the focus on finding generalizations.

Implications for various issues in linguistics are derived from the results of this study. For instance, Ferguson and Farwell report that, although their subjects exhibited some similarities in acquisition (e.g., [m] was the first nasal for all three), Jakobson's idea of a universal order was not supported. In addition, several aspects of acquisition observed in this study were not predicted by Jakobson (e.g., preferences for certain sounds). According to Ferguson and Farwell (1975, p. 435), children differ in their "paths of development," perhaps partly because of differences in input and differences in strategies (e.g., the avoidance of certain sounds). The authors urge child phonologists to focus on the idiosyncratic paths that individual children follow in acquiring the sound system of their language.

Ferguson and Farwell (1975, p. 437) claim that their data suggest a model of phonological development (and thus of phonology in general) that stresses the importance of individual variation and of the lexical parameter in phonological acquisition. This model "would assert that children learn words from others, construct their own phonologies, and gradually develop phonological awareness" (p. 437). Although they do not elaborate this model, they do list four "key assumptions" involving: (1) "the primacy of lexical learning in [early] phonological development" (p. 437); (2) the gradual building of phonological organization (i.e. abstractions and generalizations); (3) the "gradual development of phonological awareness" (p. 438); and (4) the existence of an adult "stage" of phonological development with the same type of structure that is exhibited in children's phonological development.

Summary of Current
Information on
Phonetic Acquisition

Overview. In this last subsection let us attempt to summarize current information on phonetic acquisition. That is, what is known about children's acquisition of the surface phonetic elements of English?

Phonetic acquisition is generally said to begin between the ages of 10 and 14 months, with a child's first identifiable words (although some phonologists would argue that it begins even earlier), and it continues into kindergarten or first grade. Normally developing children are said to exhibit articulatory proficiency by the age of 7 or 8 years (see Figure 6-1), but for many the upper age is much lower. We now realize that there is no universal order of acquisition of sounds, as claimed by Roman Jakobson (1941/1968).[4] Rather, there is considerable variation among children. However, there do appear to be general tendencies. For example, nasals (/m, n, ŋ/), glides (/w, j/) and stops (/p, k, t, b, d, g/) tend to be acquired relatively early. Liquids (/l, r/), fricatives (/θ, ð, f, v, s, z, ʃ, ʒ/), and affricates (tʃ, dʒ/) tend to be acquired later. In general, sounds produced in the front of the mouth are acquired earlier than sounds produced in the back of the mouth. For instance, /n/ is acquired before /ŋ/, /t/ is acquired before /k/, and /s/ is acquired before /ʃ/. Before back sounds are learned, they may be replaced by similar front sounds. For instance, [s] may replace /ʃ/ and [t] may replace /k/.

It is often said that sounds are acquired first in initial position, then medial position, and then final position. However, while initial position does seem to be favored for stops, there is evidence that fricatives may be acquired first in postvocalic or final position (Ferguson, 1975a; Farwell, 1977; Edwards, 1979).

It also has been argued that voiceless consonants are acquired before the corresponding voiced consonants. For example, Macken (1980) makes this claim for stop consonants, and Moskowitz (1975) makes this claim for fricatives. However, other researchers (e.g., Edwards, 1979) have found that the position of a sound within a word may be a crucial factor. For instance, voiced sounds may precede voiceless sounds in prevocalic position (preceding a vowel), while voiceless sounds are likely to be earlier in word-final position.

In the following pages, we will make some generalizations about the acquisition of various types of consonant sounds in English. As vowels are acquired early (with /ɑ/ being the earliest, followed by /i/ and /u/) and are usually not problematic for children, we will focus on the acquisition of consonants. (See Lieberman, 1980, for an acoustic study of the development of vowel production in preschool-aged children.) Similarly, glides will not be discussed further, as they are generally learned early and are seldom problematic for children.

Nasals. The front nasals, /m/ and /n/ are usually among the first sounds to be learned by English-speaking children. The velar nasal /ŋ/ is learned somewhat later. It is frequently replaced by [n], as in [swɪn] for *swing* or [wɪn] for *ring*. Occasionally nasals may be denasalized or replaced by homorganic stops, as in [bud] for *moon* (Velten, 1943), but this type of substitution is not common. Other sounds may assimilate to nasals in early development, as in [nʌm] for *thumb*.

Stops. Stops also tend to be acquired early, as noted above. Several studies on the acquisition of stops have concerned themselves with the acquisition of the voicing contrast or the acquisition of adult *voice onset time* (VOT) values.[5] Macken and Barton (1980) studied the acquisition of the voicing contrast in word-initial stops by four monolingual English-learning children whc were between 1;4 and 1;7 at the beginning of the study. Macken and Barton found evidence for three general developmental stages in the acquisition of the voicing contrast. At the first stage, the child shows no evidence of having a voicing contrast. Both adult voiced and voiceless stops are produced with "short lag voicing." That is, they are produced as voiceless unaspirated stops. For example, [t] would be used for both /t/ and /d/. At the second stage, the child has a voicing contrast, but it is not adult-like, and in fact, it is not perceptible by adults. Both sounds in a cognate pair fall into the same adult phoneme category, usually the voiced member of the pair. Although most of the child's stops are short lag, the VOT values for the voiceless member of a cognate pair are consistently longer than the VOT values for the voiced member, and the differences between the mean values for the voiceless and voiced pairs are significant. At the third stage, the child has a contrast that resembles the adult voicing contrast, even though the VOT values are not yet exactly correct.

Macken and Barton (1980) found a considerable amount of variation in the age of acquisition of the voicing contrast. In their view, it is acquired gradually between the ages of about 1;3 and 2;8. Their data also show the development of the voicing contrast across places of articulation, generally from alveolar to labial to velar. Although they found no invariant order of acquisition, they predict that the voicing contrast usually will be acquired first in a front cognate pair.

Macken (1980) also reports that there is no universal or invariant order of acquisition for stops, although there are general patterns. One of the "statistical probabilities" or "universal tendencies" mentioned by Macken is that children rarely acquire a velar stop first or acquire the voicing contrast first at the velar point of articulation.

In their study of the acquisition of word-initial consonants (discussed earlier), Ferguson and Farwell (1975) found that two children "strongly preferred" [k] over [g], while for the labials and alveolars, the voiced cognates ([b] and [d], respectively) were preferred in initial position. A similar pattern showed up in Olmsted's (1971) study of the sound errors of 100 children. Using these data, along with data concerning universals of human languages and information in Gamkrelidze (1974), Ferguson (1975b) proposed the following "stability scale" for stops, from most to least stable:

$$t \rangle k \rangle b \rangle d \rangle p \rangle g$$

Support for this stability scale was found in data from four Spanish-learning children between the ages of 1;4 and 1;10. As predicted, these children preferred [b] over [p] and [k] over [g] across word positions (Ferguson, 1975b, p. 5). They frequently substituted [b] for /p/ and also tended to substitute [k] for /g/. Futher support was found in data from seven English-learning children studied by Johnson and Bush (1972). These results led Ferguson to hypothesize that children may select to produce more *b* than *p* words, which indicates their awareness of the voicing contrast.

Fricatives and Affricates. The acquisition of fricatives and affricates is more complicated than the acquisition of stops. Like stops, fricatives are acquired gradually, and correct production often fluctuates with various types of substitutes (Ferguson, 1975a; Edwards, 1979). There is no universal order of acquisition for fricatives, but in general front fricatives are said to be acquired before back fricatives (e.g., [s] before [ʃ], and voiceless fricatives are generally acquired before voiced fricatives. An apparent exception is /θ/, which is acquired late.

In a large group study of word-initial fricative acquisition, Ingram, Christensen, Veach, and Webster (1980) found the following order of acquisition, based on percentage of correct production, across 73 subjects: /f-/, /tʃ-/, /dʒ-/, /ʃ-/, /s-/, /v-/, /z-/, /θ-/. These results differ from those reported in earlier studies, perhaps partly because Ingram et al. used four words to test each sound, and these words differed systematically in number of syllables and in stress patterns. Moreover, three elicitation methods were used: sentence completion, sentence recall, and direct imitation. (Spontaneous productions were not used.)

According to Moskowitz (1975), phonemic acquisition is ahead of phonetic acquisition for fricatives, as pointed out above. For instance, a child may know that /s/ and /z/ contrast and may keep them apart in production without producing either sound accurately.

According to Farwell (1977), Ferguson (1975a), and others, fricatives tend to be slightly easier to produce in postvocalic or final position; thus they may be acquired earlier in those positions than in initial position. (Some supporting evidence is found in Edwards, 1979.)

Ferguson (1975a) noted that before fricatives are acquired, they may be replaced by sounds of tighter closure (stops and affricates), sounds of looser closure (liquids and glides), or similar fricatives (e.g., [f] for /θ/). Fricatives may also be omitted, especially in clusters or in word-final position. Common substitutes for word-initial fricatives are reported by Ingram et al. (1980).

Ingram (1978) hypothesized an order of appearance for fricative substitutes, as well as several stages of acquisition for fricatives. (See also Ingram et al. 1980.) However, Edwards (1979), in her longitudinal study of fricative acquisition, did not find support for either Ingram's proposed order of fricative substitutes or his stages of acquisition. Rather, Edwards (1979) found that the type of substitute that occurs often varies among different lexical items or varies with the position of the fricative in the word. For instance, substitutions of tighter closure are more likely to occur in word-initial position, while similar fricative substitutes are more likely to occur in final position. Ingram et al. (1980, p. 189) found the production of initial fricatives to vary in simple and familiar words vs. complex and unfamiliar words.

Liquids. As noted earlier, liquids tend to be acquired late by children. This is particularly true of /r/. Generally, liquids are replaced by glides. So, for example, we find [jaɪt] or [waɪt] for *light*, [jέwo] for *yellow*, [bwu] for *blue*, [wɛd] for *red*, [twi] for *tree*, [ówɪn] for *orange*, and so forth, with consonantal glides replacing prevocalic liquids. Preconsonantal or word-final liquids are generally deleted or replaced by vocalic glides, as in [mɪk] or [mɪʊk] for *milk*, [bɛʊ] for *bell*, and [kʰɑ] or [kʰɑə] for *car*. Ingram (1976, p. 41) claims that very early on, liquids may be replaced by stops, as in [daʊn] for *round*. In his view, the last possible stage before correct production involves the interchange of liquids, as in [laɪt] for *right* and [raɪk] for *like*. However, these stages are very uncommon in children acquiring English as their native language. Liquids, especially /l/, may also be replaced by nasals occasionally, as in [neɪg] for *leg* (Edwards, 1973). Syllabic liquids tend to be replaced by vowels, as in [báwo] for *bottle*, or [fέdə] for *feather*. It has been claimed that liquids may be first produced correctly in clusters, as in *train* or *dress*. (See Greenlee, 1974, p. 86.)

Clusters. Clusters of two or more consonants tend to be acquired rather late. Most often, the more "marked" or difficult element of the cluster is omitted. For example, in clusters of /s/ plus voiceless stop, the /s/ is generally deleted, as in [pun] for *spoon*. In liquid clusters, the liquid is often deleted or replaced by a glide, as just mentioned.

Greenlee (1974, p. 86) outlined three major stages in the production of initial stop + liquid clusters, based on data from six languages: deletion of the liquid, replacement of the liquid, and correct production of the cluster. In addition, she also discussed (p. 88) several subprocesses, such as: deletion of the entire cluster, velar-dental interchanges, deletion of the stop component (with retention of the liquid), weakening of the stop (by assimilation) to a continuant (fricative), insertion of an epenthetic vowel, and metathesis or migration of the liquid element.

It has been noted that /tr/ and /dr/ clusters may be treated as single segments (e.g., see Menyuk, 1971). So, a child may say [dʒɛs] for *dress* or [tʃʌk] for *truck*. Kornfeld (1971b) observed that even when the /s/ of an /s/ plus stop cluster appears to be deleted, the other consonant may be marked for stridency and gradual release. Similarly, using spectrographic analysis, Menyuk (1971) found underlying clusters to be distinguished from underlying single stops (e.g., by duration) even when they sounded the same to adults. See also Kornfeld, 1971a.

Occasionally, a cluster is replaced by a sound that is unlike either of the underlying segments but has features of both (e.g., see Greenlee, 1973: Kornfeld, 1971a). For example, a child may have [fɪm] for *swim*, with [f] for /sw/ or [n̥oʊ] for *snow*, with a voiceless nasal replacing the /sn/ cluster. These examples illustrate coalescence or assimilation plus deletion. We will have more to say about clusters and singleton (single segment) errors in later sections.

Feature-Based
Acquisition Studies

Menyuk (1968)

Relatively few studies have approached normal phonological development from the point of view of distinctive features. One such study is reported in Menyuk's (1968) article on the role of distinctive features in sound acquisition. Menyuk noted that children's acquisition of phonology is presumably based on their ability to differentiate sounds by means of distinctive features. For instance, a child may be able to distinguish nasal from nonnasal sounds (e.g., /m/ from /b/) but not be able to distinguish sounds in terms of place of articulation (e.g., velars from labials). However, Menyuk pointed out that we do not yet know the specific order in which distinctive features are acquired, if there is such an order.

In an attempt to define an order of acquisition of features and to obtain information concerning cues in the perception and production of consonants by children, Menyuk (1968) reanalyzed, from a distinctive feature viewpoint, some available data on the correct production of consonants by children and on consonant substitutes (as well as data on the consonant errors of children with articulation problems to be discussed in Chapter 7). She also looked at the productions of Japanese children and perceptual confusions of adults.

Menuyk investigated the following six distinctive features (Jakobson, Fant, & Halle, 1963): [grave], [diffuse], [strident], [nasal], [continuant], [voice] (see feature definitions in Chapter 2).[6] The children's data were obtained from an analysis of consonant substitutions made while children spontaneously produced sentences. The percentage of correct usage of each feature was calculated. For example, if 4 out of 10 [+ continuant] sounds were correct at a certain age, the percentage of correct usage would be 40% for [+ continuant] at that age. (It is important to keep in mind in interpreting these data that the methodological limitations of this approach are similar to those discussed in the previous sections.)

Menyuk found a "striking" similarity between the Japanese and American children in the order of feature acquisition for the ages observed—2½ to 5 for the American children and 1 to 3 for the Japanese. Both the American and Japanese children correctly used consonants that were [+ nasal], [+ grave] and [+ voice] "earlier and more frequently" than consonants that were [+ diffuse], [+ continuant], and [+ strident]. According to Menyuk, this might indicate that a "hierarchy of feature distinctions may be a linguistic universal" (1968, p. 142).

In order to investigate the role of distinctive features in consonant substitutions, Menyuk analyzed all substitutes in terms of feature maintenance. To illustrate, in a substitution of [t] for [θ], all of the features under investigation were maintained except the [+ continuant] feature; [θ] is [+ continuant], but [t] is [− continuant]. A rank order of maintenance of features in substitutes was then obtained. The rank order of feature maintenance in consonant substitutes for the normally developing group is shown below (from Menyuk, 1968).

Rank Order	Normally Developing
1	voice
2	nasal
3	strident
4	continuant
5	grave
6	diffuse

In Menyuk's view, these results support the idea that the features [± nasal] and [± voice] are easiest to "perceive, recall, and produce" (1968, p. 143). Both the normally developing group and the articulation disordered group (discussed in Chapter 7) tended to maintain [+ voice] and [+ nasal] most often. For the normally developing children in this study, the tendency was to maintain all but a single feature in consonant substitutes. In other words, a target sound usually differed from its substitute by just one feature, such as stridency.

Crocker (1969)

In 1969, Crocker proposed a model of children's developing phonological competence (for consonants). This model was based partly on Chomsky and Halle's phonological competence model and partly on distinctive feature theory (e.g, Jakobson et al.).[7] The data underlying Crocker's model were taken from studies reviewed previously (Templin, 1957; Snow, 1963; Menyuk, 1968) and from the recorded speech of 15 kindergarten and first grade children.

Crocker assembled his normative feature data in the form of a phonological model made up of three general rules. The three rules are "hypothesized to underlie all feature combinations and separations" involved in the development of the phonological system (p. 205).[8] In Crocker's view, children develop the phonology of American English by applying these rules to combine phonological features. Children do not acquire sounds or features as such, but "rules for the manipulation of . . . features" to form new feature sets (p. 206). The model is illustrated in Figure 6-2. According to Crocker's model, a child adds or combines a new feature with a set of features that he or she already has. For instance, a child may combine the [+strident] feature with the "prime feature set" /p/ to form the new set /f/. Similarly, "the [-grave] feature is combined with the prime base feature set /p/ to form the new set /t/ (Crocker, 1969, p. 208).

Crocker also attempts to account for some of the common sound substitutions found in the speech of children acquiring English. He claims that each substitution can be predicted from observing "the sounds that appeared earlier in the same line of development" (p. 210). Because some feature sets develop earlier than others, a substitution generally involves a similar sound represented by an earlier feature set. For instance, in the line of development from the prime set /p/, one expected substitution would be [p] for /f/.

While noting that his model needs to be specified further and tested with larger groups of children, Crocker also claims that it adequately represents the development of the child's phonological system. His model also supports the idea that there is a definite and systematic pattern in sound acquisition.

Cairns and Williams (1972)

Cairns and Williams, whose study was reviewed previously, also analyzed their data by features, using a slightly modified version of Chomsky and Halle's (1968) feature system. For instance, a substitution of [s] for /z/ would involve a change from [+voice] to [-voice]. This procedure was followed in an attempt to gain insight into the aspects of speech sounds that are likely to change and those that are more stable.

Out of a total of 200 substitution errors across grades 1 through 12, 148 involved just one feature value change. To illustrate, a substitution of [t] for /θ/ involves just a change from [+continuant] to [-continuant]. Fifteen substitution errors involved a change of two features. So, in most cases, only one or two features were changed. The major exceptions were the substitution of [w] for /l/, which involves a change of five

FIGURE 6-2

Diagram of the Phonological Model of children's articulation competence as it develops from prime feature sets, through the formation of base sets, to terminal feature sets. Reproduced from J. Crocker. A Phonological Model of Children's Articulation Competence. *Journal of Speech and Hearing Disorders, 1969, 34, 203–213.*

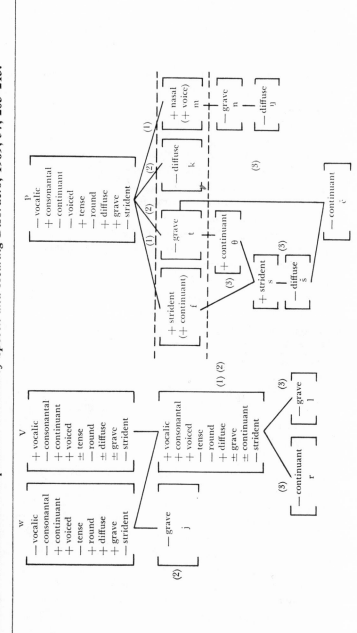

features, and [w] for /r/, which involves a change in four feature values. It was found that substitutes and target sounds were always members of the same major class of sounds. For example, children never substituted a glide for an obstruent.

Regarding place of articulation features, [coronal] was the most likely to change. For instance [f] for /θ/ and [w] for /l/ both involve a change from [+coronal] to [−coronal]. (In fact, no substitution errors involved a change from [−coronal] to [+coronal].) Cairns and Williams hypothesize that this is due to the fact that lingual sounds are more difficult to produce than nonlingual sounds. The [anterior] feature was also likely to be changed, but errors involved both [+anterior] to [−anterior], as in [w] for /l/, and [−anterior] to [+anterior], as in [s] for /ʃ/.

Regarding manner of articulation features, the [continuant] feature was found to be the most vulnerable. Out of 70 errors involving this feature, 65 were from [+continuant] to [−continuant], as in [t] for /θ/. This is explained as being due to "ease of articulation"; [+continuant] sounds presumably require more "fine muscle control" (Cairns & Williams, 1972, p. 818).

Out of 61 errors involving voicing, 48 were from [+voice] to [−voice], and 13 were from [−voice] to [+voice], as in [b] for /f/. The authors state (p. 818) that voicing changes cannot be due to ease of articulation, but at least some may be due to the "perceptual cues" of the targets that are preserved in the substitute. (However, see Stampe, 1972a.) For example, a change from [+voice] to [−voice], as in [s] for /z/ preserves the stridency of the target, and in fact stridency is "enhanced" by the devoicing (Jakobson, 1962).

The least vulnerable feature of all, according to Cairns and Williams (1972, p. 818) was [strident], which was preserved in all but 13 errors. Nine of these 13 errors involved the substitution of a stop for an affricate. In the view of the authors, the only real counterevidence to the stability of the strident feature was the substitution of [s], a strident fricative, for /θ/, a nonstrident fricative.[9] Cairns and Williams claim that their results indicate that individual substitutions can be explained by ease of articulation and perceptual distinctiveness. They also note (p. 819) that in many cases, "phonetic features are not independent." That is, a value change for one feature may necessitate or imply a value change for another in the same bundle of features. This may help explain why some common substitutions, such as [w] for /l/ and for /r/, involve a change of several features. Cairns and Williams also discuss markedness theory briefly and note (p. 819) that, as it is supposed to capture generalizations about the "interdependence of features within . . . phonemes," it may provide explanations for some of the substitutions observed in their study.

Prosody- or Suprasegmental-Based Studies

Few studies of normal development have had prosodies or suprasegmentals as their basic element. However, the early acquisition of adult-like intonation patterns has been noted frequently.

Ferguson and Macken (1980) in their discussion of babbling and early speech, state that the increase in speech-like behavior that is exhibited as young children progress shows that prosodic features may "take precedence over" segments (p. 144). They also point out that recent studies of the acquisition of tone languages (especially Chinese) have shown that lexical tone is acquired early and is not subject to many mistakes in comparison with segments. (See Clumeck, 1980, for a review of research on the acquisition of tone.)

Ferguson and Macken (1980, p. 144) view the early acquisition of prosody as being related to the importance of words as phonetic units in the early stages of language acquisition. See, for example, Ferguson and Farwell (1975), discussed earlier in this chapter.

For a discussion of research on the development of "phonological rhythm" in children see Allen and Hawkins (1980), which is in the same volume as Clumeck's chapter on the acquisition of tone. Other articles of relevance here include those of Pike (1949), Tonkova-Yampol'skaya (1968/1973), Naeser (1970), Atkinson-King (1973), Cruttenden (1974), Eilers (1975), Allen and Hawkins (1978), and Allen, Hawkins, and Morris (1979a, 1979b).

Crystal (1979)

In his 1979 chapter titled "Prosodic Development," David Crystal discusses prosody in general and its importance in adult language before discussing prosodic acquisition. Crystal first contrasts the segmental component of phonology with the nonsegmental component. The segmental component includes consonants, vowels and syllables. He defines (p. 33) nonsegmental phonology as "any linguistically contrastive sound effect which cannot be described by reference to a single segment (phoneme), but which either (i) continues over a stretch of utterance . . . or (ii) requires reference to several segments in different parts of the utterance." The units of nonsegmental phonology are called *prosodic features*. Crystal notes that traditionally prosody has been used to refer just to the features of pitch, loudness, speed, and rhythm, although much more can be included (e.g., nasality and whispered voice). He also emphasizes that prosody is not a "single homogeneous phenomenon," as it is often discussed in the language acquisition literature (p. 34). In this paper, he limits his discussion to three aspects of prosody that generally are considered to be of importance: (1) *intonation*, or the linguistic use of pitch, (2) *prominence*, the prominent or tonic syllable of an utterance being characterized by pitch movement, extra loudness, and sometimes also duration and pause, and (3) *tone units*, which Crystal defines (p. 35) as "prosodic configurations" made up of pitch direction and change, along with rhythm and pause. Tone units, in Crystal's view, provide "the most general level of organization that can be imposed upon prosodic data" (p. 35). To illustrate, the slash in the following sentence indicates the tone-unit segmentation: "When he arrives/we'll leave."

In Crystal's chapter, five functions that are served by prosodic patterns are distinguished: (1) *grammatical*, e.g., to signal a singular/plural contrast, (2) *semantic*, e.g., to signal the most important parts of a discourse, (3) *attitudinal*, to signal personal emotions regarding the subject matter or context, (4) *psychological*, e.g., to facilitate recall, and (5) *social*, to convey information regarding the sociolinguistic characteristics of the speaker.

Crystal also discusses five "stages of prosodic development," although he notes that it may be too early to outline clear stages because little empirical research is available:

Stage I: This stage, which could be called the "prelinguistic antecedents of prosodic features," begins at birth and includes the period of "biologically determined" vocalizations and also the period of "differentiated vocalizations" (p. 37). It is said to be similar across languages.

Stage II: This stage, which begins at about 2 or 3 months, is characterized by an awareness of adult prosodic contrasts in speech directed to the child (p. 38).

Stage III: From the age of about 6 months, nonsegmental features, such as pitch and loudness, are evident in infant vocalizations and begin to resemble prosodic patterns of the adult language.[10]

Stage IV: During the second half of the first year, infants' output contains "learned patterns of prosodic behavior" involving pitch, rhythm, and pause (p. 39). Recognizable intonation contours occur, even though the segments may not resemble those of the adult language.[11] Crystal (p. 40) notes that these early prosodic units have been variously interpreted as serving a semantic, syntactic, pragmatic, or social function, with the last view being most prevalent.[12] Another approach is to consider them as having mainly a formal role, e.g., as "place holders" (Bruner, 1975).

Crystal also proposes an analysis of early tonal development consisting of eight substages and covering the period from about 1;0 to 1;6, and he notes that research on the acquisition of tone languages indicates that the acquisition of lexical tone is similar to the acquisition of intonation and that the tone system of such languages is learned before the segmental system (cf. Ferguson & Macken, 1980).

Stage V: What Crystal calls "tonic contrastivity" appears at about 1;6 (p. 45). Lexical items are at first juxtaposed, retaining their "prosodic autonomy." Then the pause between them is reduced. Finally, there is "prosodic integration" of sequences of items into one tonal unit. So at about 1;6, children use two-element sentences with single prosodic contours and "nonrandom tonic prominence" (p. 46).

Crystal stresses that we need to be careful in interpreting information concerning children's use of prosodic features.[13] The fact that adults can differentiate and interpret children's prosodic patterns does not necessarily mean that the children are using them that way. Thus we need a detailed analysis of phonetic form along with accompanying context. Crystal points out that children may use contrasts that are not part of the adult language, and they may use a familiar form with an unfamiliar function (and vice versa). For example, at the age of about 1 year, children may contrast loud vs. soft, or rhythmic vs. arhythmic. Crystal claims that prosodic learning probably continues until puberty.

Waterson (1970, 1971a)

The person most associated with a "prosodic view" of phonological development (but not necessarily a "suprasegmental view") is Natalie Waterson. In fact, Waterson's (1970, 1971a, 1971b, 1971c, 1978) model of phonological acquisition is called "prosodic theory." Waterson's prosodic theory has its background in the prosodic analysis of Firthian linguists (Firth, 1935, 1948). Her theory is based primarily on a small amount of data from one very young child, her son "P" at about the age of 1½.

Waterson's theory is not concerned with phonemes nor is it concerned with distinctive features. According to Waterson, the child pays attention to "salient" (e.g., "strongly articulated") adult forms that tend to occur in certain situations. In addition, the child perceives utterances as units having certain features, such as nasality or friction, but he or she is not necessarily aware of their location.[14] For example, a child perceives stridency in a word without being aware of its exact location. We will defer further description of Waterson's theory to a later discussion on theories of phonological acquisition.

Phonological Rule- and Phonological Process- Based Studies

Since the early 1970s, there have been many studies of normal phonological acquisition in which phonological rules or phonological processes are the basic elements. These studies are based either on generative phonology or natural phonology, two modern theories of phonology discussed earlier in this book. It will be remembered that in generative phonology, phonological rules (and underlying representations) are basic, while in natural phonology, phonological processes are of major importance. However in studies of phonological development, the terms *rule* and *process* are sometimes used interchangeably, making it difficult to separate rule-oriented from process-oriented studies. Therefore, no such separation is made here. Instead, selected studies are discussed in their approximate chronological sequence.

Smith (1973)

Smith's diary study of his son Amahl ("A") from the age of 2 to about 4 contains a generative phonological analysis (as well as the phonemic analysis discussed earlier). Although Smith's book on "A" was published in 1973, the unpublished manuscript (1970) was widely circulated, making it one of the earliest acquisition studies based on generative phonology. Smith postulates a set of ordered "realization rules," written in distinctive feature notation. These rules map the adult forms onto the child's surface forms as discussed in Chapter 4.[15] To illustrate, Smith's (1973, p. 25) "realization rule 7" (R 7) is as follows:

$$
\begin{bmatrix}
+\text{coronal} \\
+\text{anterior} \\
+\text{continuant} \\
+\text{strident} \\
-\text{voice}
\end{bmatrix}
\longrightarrow \phi \ / \ \underline{\quad} \ [-\text{syllabic}]
$$

This rule says simply that /s/ is deleted ($\rightarrow \phi$) preceding a consonant (i.e., a [−syllabic] element), as in [wi] for *swing*, [bun] for *spoon*, and [mɪt] for *Smith*.

Changes that occur in the child's output over time are represented by changes in the sets of rules. For instance, R 7 was modified at a later stage as represented below:

$$
\begin{bmatrix}
+\,\text{coronal} \\
+\,\text{anterior} \\
+\,\text{continuant} \\
+\,\text{strident} \\
-\,\text{voice}
\end{bmatrix}
\rightarrow \phi\ /\ \underline{\hspace{2em}}\
\begin{bmatrix}
+\,\text{consonantal} \\
-\,\text{voice}
\end{bmatrix}
$$

At this stage, "A" deleted /s/ only before voiceless consonants, such as /p/, but not before /m, w/, etc.

Smith gives sample derivations of words, and he shows that it is necessary for certain rules to apply in a specific sequence. For example, R 7, as originally given, has to precede R 16 because /s/ plus sonorant clusters are treated differently by "A" than other consonant plus sonorant clusters (Smith, 1973, pp. 25, 28).

$$
\text{R 16} \qquad [+\,\text{sonorant}] \rightarrow \phi\ /\ [+\,\text{consonantal}]\ \underline{\hspace{2em}}
$$

R 16 says that a sonorant is deleted following a consonant. However, it does not apply to /s/ plus sonorant clusters because /s/ is deleted preceding all consonants by the earlier rule (R 7). Smith devotes a considerable amount of space to discussions of which feature system to use in writing rules and precisely how to formulate specific rules. Whenever possible, Smith combines rules in order to "save features" and to make his description as "economical" as possible. This is in keeping with the principles of generative phonology.

Edwards (1973)

The earliest study of normal acquisition based on Stampe's (1969, 1972a) model of natural phonology is Edwards' study on the acquisition of liquids, written as a master's thesis in 1970 and published in 1973. Edwards reported on six children she studied who were learning English as their native language. In addition, she reanalyzed data from four published studies, including one of a child learning English and German (Leopold, 1947) and one of two boys learning French (Grégoire,

1947). Edwards postulated several "natural" phonetically plausible phonological processes that would account for all the liquid substitutions
and omissions in the speech of her subjects. As hypothesized, a few basic
processes were evident in the speech of these children. In keeping with
Stampe's theory, surface substitutions, such as [w] for /r/, were broken
down into their constituent processes, in this case: labialization (r→r̈),
deretroflexion (r̈→o), raising (o→u), and strengthening (u→w). (The
diacritic [̦] under a vowel symbol indicates that the vowel is nonsyllabic.)

Edwards also showed how the processes that she postulated were gradually limited and suppressed by the children in her study as they progressed. For
example, for her subject Daniel at the age of 1;6 to 1;7, glide loss applied
quite regularly to preconsonantal glides, as in [mʌk] for *milk*, and glides
after noncoronal consonants, as in [kɑkɑ] for *glasses*. However, it was later
limited so that it applied only to round glides following a high back vowel.
At this stage, Daniel had [mɛʊk] for *milk*, but [wuf] for *wolf*.

As predicted by Stampe's theory, Edwards found that the processes
operating for the French and German children were somewhat different
because the types of liquids used in those languages differ from English liquids. For instance, Charles and Edmund Grégoire, two French-speaking
children (Grégoire, 1947), never substituted [w] or [u] for /l/, as most of the
English-speaking children did. Instead, /l/ was represented by [y] (IPA [j])
or was lost entirely. Presumably, labiovelarization of /l/ did not apply
because French /l/ is "light." Then loss of coronality (light /l/ →i¹),
delateralization (i¹→i), and strengthening (i→y) give the correct forms
for these children. (Edwards used [i¹] to symbolize a nonsyllabic [i] with
"l-coloring.")

In this paper, Edwards also presented evidence from various language
families to show that the processes operating for the children in her study
appear in historical language change and dialectal variation, as well as in acquisition. For example, Passy (1890, p. 156) discussed the labiovelarization
of French *r*, which eventually results in [w] in some dialects, and Bailey
(1969, pp. 250–253) notes that in "r-less" dialects of English, [ɝ] before
consonants and word boundaries often loses its retroflexion and becomes
[ə], as it did for most of Edwards' subjects. Similarly, loss of intervocalic *r*,
as evidenced in some children, is reported by Castro (1924, p. 12) in Vulgar
Castilian Spanish, as in quió for *quiero*. Thus all of the natural processes
postulated to account for the acquisition of liquids also show up in other
sound change phenomena.

Ingram (1974b)

Ingram (1974b) discusses several "general" phonological rules that are
found to operate in normal language acquisition, and he argues against the

view that phonological development consists mainly of sound substitutions. Ingram first describes what phonological rules are and how they capture the relation between adult and child forms. In his view (p. 63), "The operation of phonological rules shows the organizational and generalizing capacities" of the child. Discrepancies between adult production and the child's production can be shown to result from the application of a series of rules. Ingram gives supporting evidence from French and Czech, as well as English.

Ingram differentiates what he calls substitution rules from phonotactic rules. Substitution rules are said to be segment-specific and place-specific, but also context-free. They state that one sound is replaced by another in a particular position or set of positions, but they do not include neighboring sounds as part of the condition for the change. In contrast, phonotactic rules state that a segment does not appear because of a neighboring sound.[16] They are context-sensitive, but usually not place-specific.

According to Ingram, many earlier studies (e.g., Compton, 1970; Poole, 1934; Templin, 1957) were concerned with substitution rules rather than phonotactic rules, and he argues that this emphasis on substitution rules has "missed a significant part of the complex process of phonological development" (p. 53). The general phonological rules discussed by Ingram (1974b) are: reduplication, diminutive, weak syllable deletion, cluster reduction, voicing, and assimilation.[17]

Regarding the nature of the child's underlying representation on which processes operate, Ingram makes the assumption that in early development, the child's perception of the adult system is not complete. Thus at that time, the child's underlying system is a "mental representation" of the adult model. This underlying representation results from the child's inadequate perception along with what Ingram calls "organizational principles" used by the child to systematize the data. Ingram argues (p. 52) that the child represents adult models as "basic syllabic and canonical shapes" on which the rules operate. Thus, in Ingram's view, several different components contribute to the child's phonological system, as shown below (1974b, p. 52):

1. Adult pronounced form = APF
2. Child's perceived form = CPF
3. Child's underlying form = CUF
4. Phonotactic rules = PR
5. Substitution rules = SR
6. Child's spoken form = CSF

Ingram gives evidence to support the idea that 2 and 3 above are actually different. For example, the CUF may have additional information to qualify it for the application of a particular rule (i.e., process) (p. 52). To illustrate, Holmes' (1927) daughter Mollie produced (waki) for *walk* and [bɪbi] for *bib*. Ingram argues that in this case, the underlying forms of *walk* and *bib* must contain information that allows them to undergo the diminutive rule.

If a child produced *bed* as both [bɛ] and [bɛ.t:] (Holmes, 1927), the CUF, in Ingram's view, would be /bɛt/. However, if the same child produced *bird* as [bo], the CUF would be /boC/, with C representing a consonant that is perceived but not produced. By comparing the child's production of *bird* with her production of a similar word (*bed*), Ingram determines that the child perceived a final consonant in *bird*. The final C in the CUF (/boC/) then qualifies *bird* for the application of a process of final consonant deletion.

Ingram uses the term noise for any part of the adult word that is never represented in the child's production. To indicate noise in the child's perception, he uses X for sounds and X̠ for syllables. To illustrate, if a child never represents final consonants in production, as in [bo] for *bird* and [ke] for *cake*, etc., Ingram assumes that the final consonants are perceived only as noise. Thus the CPF for these words would be [boX], and [keX], etc. Noise is not counted in canonical shapes, and therefore the underlying syllable structure of these words would be CV rather than CVC. Ingram argues that this approach enables him to distinguish, in underlying forms, among homonyms (words that sound alike but differ in meaning). For example, if a child produced both *spoon* and *pudding* as [pu], Ingram would represent them differently in the CUF: /XpuC/ and /puCX̠/, respectively. This claims that the child hears the two words as being distinct, even though they are produced the same. Ingram states that this allows him to "grossly approximate" the child's perception.[18]

Reduplication, according to Ingram, is a common phenomenon in early phonological development. The child cannot produce the second syllable of a word, and so the initial syllable is repeated. In the *diminutive* process an [i] vowel is added to the end of a word, often with reduplication of the initial consonant, as in [bɑbi] for *blanket*. Ingram claims that reduplication and diminutive are simply "attempts to represent syllabic noise" (p. 54). The following example (from Holmes, 1927) illustrates this:

cracker	APF [krækɹ̩]	
	CPF [kXæX̠]	
	CUF /kæS/	(S = syllable)
	reduplication /kækæ/	
	CSF [kækæ]	

According to Ingram, reduplication and diminutive qualify as rules because they are sometimes overgeneralized. That is, they are sometimes applied to adult monosyllables, as in [dɑti] for *dot*, and [a͞υti] for *out*. The fact that these rules are sometimes overgeneralized to one-syllable words supports the idea, in Ingram's view, that the child's underlying forms are unique from his or her perceptual forms. For example, the underlying canonical form (or "whole word shape") of *dot*, for the child who produced [dɑti], would be CVC(S), with S representing a syllable.

In his discussion of *weak syllable deletion*, Ingram claims that weak (unstressed) syllables, especially in word-initial position or in three-syllable words, are likely to be deleted in children's productions. For instance, Smith's (Smith, 1973) son said [weː] for *away*, and [nisən] for *ignition*, and Roussey's (1899) daughter (learning French) produced [kɔ] for *école*.

Another general process discussed by Ingram is *cluster reduction*, which involves the simplification of consonant clusters to a single element. The specific types of cluster reduction discussed (p. 57) are:

1. S-reduction, simplifying sC or Cs sequences.

2. Liquid reduction, simplifying consonant-liquid or liquid-consonant sequences.

3. Nasal cluster reduction, simplifying nasal-consonant sequences.

According to Ingram, when stops occur in /s/ clusters and liquid clusters, the stop is retained, as in [pun] for *spoon*, [apè] for *asperge* "asparagus" (French), and [pontɑ] for *sponka* "buckle" (Czech). Similar examples of *liquid reduction* include: [bis] for *please*, [gɑk] for *truck*, [pɑ] for *place* "seat" (French) and [totɑn] for *krocan* "turkey" (Czech).

Regarding nasal clusters, Ingram points out, following Smith (1973), that the voicing of the stop in a nasal + stop cluster will often determine which element is deleted. When the stop is voiceless, the nasal is deleted, as in [bʌp] for *bump*, but when the stop is voiced, it tends to be deleted, as in [mɛn] for *mend* (from Smith, 1970 version of 1973).

Voicing, as Ingram uses the term, is a process by which initial consonants are voiced and final consonants are devoiced, as in Joan Velten's (Velten, 1943) [du] for *toe*, but [mɑt] for *mud* at 1;9. Ingram points out that this version of voicing probably lasts a relatively short time, while certain aspects of voicing are quite common in children learning English. He claims (p. 59) that in the earliest stages of phonological development, when the child has only about a dozen words, voicing does not necessarily appear. For instance, a child may have [pɑ] as an early word. Later on, when the child has more CVC forms, voicing will be evident. In Ingram's view (p. 59), devoicing of final consonants, especially stops, is "a very common aspect of voicing" that occurs in phonological development. He states that the voicing distinction usually is acquired first in initial consonants. Ingram also notes that voiceless stops are typically voiced after cluster reduction, as in [dɑp] for *stop* (although transcribers may sometimes hear voiceless unaspirated stops, as in adult *stop*, as though they were voiced stops, i.e., [t=] is heard as [d]).

Ingram also discusses one form of assimilation, called *back assimilation* (or *velar assimilation*), that is well documented in phonological acquisition. In this form of assimilation, the front stops /t, d/ assimilate to back stops /k, g/, as in [gɔgi] for *doggie* or [gʌk] for *truck* or *duck*.

Ingram points out that a number of other rules, in addition to the general ones he discusses, will be needed to characterize any child's phonological system. Some of these may be quite common, while others may be idiosyncratic, capturing variations among children. According to Ingram (p. 61), such individual rules "represent different strategies that children use." To illustrate, Smith's (Smith, 1973) son had [wibə] for *zebra*. Ingram (1974b, p. 52) derives this form as follows:

Adult form	/zibrə/
Liquid cluster reduction	/zibə/
Substitution rule (z→d)	/dibə/
Front assimilation	/bibə/
Front dissimilation	[wibə]

All of the processes except the last are quite widely used. While pointing out that other solutions are possible, Ingram argues for his analysis, which is based on other forms produced by the particular child in question, rather than on what others "normally" do.

The rules discussed in this paper are called, in Ingram's terms, *statement rules*. (See Ingram, 1973, for a more detailed discussion.) He says that these rules "refer to an apparent generalization without making claims concerning the steps involved" (p. 61). He contrasts these statement rules to what he calls *natural rules* (see Stampe, 1969). Natural rules are said to be more explantory because they make claims about natural intervening processes in a change. To illustrate, he notes that bl→b is a statement rule of cluster reduction, whereas bl→bw→b is a corresponding natural rule.[19] Determining statement rules, he argues, is a necessary and important first step toward characterizing the natural rules involved in phonological development (Ingram, 1974b, p. 61).

In his 1976 book, Ingram discussed numerous phonological processes that have been observed in normal and or disordered phonological development, summarizing the information available at that time. Shriberg and Kwiatkowski (1980) integrated Ingram's information with other normative data, and discussed 16 processes that have been identified in the speech of normal and/or deviant phonological development. See also Khan (1982). Normative studies in child phonology very likely will continue to explore and expand the concept of phonological processes, as illustrated next.

Schwartz, Leonard, Wilcox, and Folger (1980)

Schwartz, Leonard, Wilcox and Folger (1980) investigated the role of one particular process, reduplication, in normal phonological acquisition. The subjects in their study were six children between the ages of 1;3 and 1;9 who were classified as reduplicators and six children between 1;5 and 2;0 who were classified as nonreduplicators. Schwartz et al. compared the phonologies of the children in these two groups in order to determine if the adoption of a "strategy" of reduplication was related to the production of final consonants and nonreduplicated multisyllabic forms and to discover "the role of the process of reduplication in production constraints" (p. 75).

The results of this study indicate that the adoption of a strategy of reduplication is related to constraints on the production of adult non-reduplicated multisyllabic words and constraints on the production of final consonants. The six reduplicators exhibited more constraints on the production of multisyllabic words and final consonants than did the six nonreduplicators. Constraints on the production of final consonants were found to be at least partially due to the frequent occurrence of final consonant deletion. Although reduplication functioned mainly to constrain the production of multisyllabic words, it also apparently "conspired" with final consonant deletion and syllable deletion to constrain the production of final consonants.[20] It is hypothesized (p. 86) that for children who reduplicate, the strategy of reduplication may "play a transitional role in the acquisition of multisyllabic words."

THEORIES OF
PHONOLOGICAL ACQUISITION

We have to this point touched on theories of phonological acquisition in review of the empirical data. As we begin a detailed inspection of theories, it is important to point out that no one theory of phonological acquisition is well accepted by all—or even most—child phonologists. There are at least three theories that are of special importance because of the impact that they have had in the past or are having at the present time. Others are of importance because of the different view of child phonology that they present. The theories discussed here are those put forward by O. H. Mowrer (1952), Olmsted (1966), Jakobson (1941/1968), Stampe (1969, 1972a), Waterson (1970, 1971a), and Kiparsky and Menn (1977; Menn, 1976). This is not intended to be an exhaustive list. Rather, it is an overview of those theories that in our view have had the greatest impact on or offer unique and valuable insights into the study of phonological acquisition.

What Should a Theory of Phonological Acquisition Account for?

Ferguson and Garnica (1975), in their detailed discussion of several theories of phonological acquisition, address the following question: What are the requirements of a theory of child phonology? Or, stated differently: What should a theory of phonological acquisition account for? Several of the questions they raise are included in the list that follows, along with issues discussed by Smith (1973). (See also Menn, 1978, 1980):

1. A theory must account for all the facts of phonological acquisition, as we understand them (consider the many empirical findings we have just reviewed).

2. A theory must relate to and be consistent with more general theories of development (e.g., cognitive development and general linguistic development).

3. A theory must account for the development of all aspects of the adult phonological system and must not conflict with facts about adult phonology, (e.g., concerning universals of human language).

4. A theory should build on earlier theories of phonological development or should at least take them into consideration.

5. A theory should make testable predictions regarding phonological development.

6. A theory should address some of the unresolved issues in phonological development, for example, the relationship between babbling and true speech, the existence of phonological idioms, the notion of one phonological system for bilinguals, the role of input, individual variation (as well as similarities among children), and the nature of the child's underlying form or lexical representation.

7. A theory should explain the regularity that is found in phonological acquisition, but it should also account for what Smith (1973, p. 1) calls the "nonrandom nature of exceptions."

8. A theory should account for how the child's phonological system changes over time.

9. A theory should account for the fact that there is often not a one-to-one correspondence between adult and child segments. For example, a child may neutralize several adult sounds to [d] in a certain environment or may represent one adult sound in several ways, as in [l, d, g] for /l/ (Smith, 1973, pp. 2–3).

10. A theory should account for the fact that a child may produce sounds or sound sequences that do not occur in the adult language or may produce English sounds in environments where they are not allowed in the adult language (Smith, 1973, p. 4). For example, a child learning English may produce velar fricatives or [fw] or [tl] sequences or may produce [ŋ] or [ʒ] in initial position, as in [ʒu] for *shoe.*

11. A theory should account for the fact that a child may produce a problematic sound as a substitute for another sound but not for itself. Smith (1973, p. 4) refers to such cases as puzzles. For example, a child may product [ʃ] for /tʃ/, as in [ʃeɪr] for *chair,* but may at the same time substitute [s] for /ʃ/, as in [su] for *shoe.* In these cases, there is a displaced contrast (Kiparsky & Menn, 1977).

12. A theory should account for the loss of an earlier acquired contrast, or what Smith (1973, p. 4) calls recidivism. To illustrate, Smith's son Amahl had [daɪt] for both *side* and *light* at an early stage. However, he later produced [daɪt] for *side* but produced *light* with an /l/. He then overgeneralized the /l/, using it for both words. Thus he failed to make a contrast that was made at an earlier stage.

13. A theory should account for perception and the relationship between perception and production. For example, it has been claimed

(e.g., by Smith, 1973) that a child can understand tape recordings of his or her own speech, but only if they represent the child's present stage of development. The "fis" phenomenon (Berko & Brown, 1960) must also be taken into consideration, as pointed out by Ferguson and Garnica (1975). This refers to a well-known observation of a child who said [fɪs] for *fish*, but rejected an adult's pronunciation of "fis," saying, "not *fis*, *fis*!" Such examples are quite common. See, for example, Locke (1979a).

14. A complete theory of language, according to Kornfeld and Goehl (1974, p. 216), should also include many extralinguistic factors such as what they term the "cuteness hypothesis." That is, why should a child change his or her early hypotheses if they are considered cute and bring the child attention? Kornfeld and Goehl claim that such extralinguistic factors may help us understand how rules are acquired and how they change.

In the following sections we will see how several theorists have selectively accounted for certain of these issues in their theories of phonological acquisition.

Mowrer's Autism Theory (1952)

O. H. Mowrer's (1952, 1960) autism theory of speech acquisition was never followed by linguists, but it did have considerable influence in the field of speech pathology (e.g., see Winitz, 1969). Mowrer, a psychologist, presented his theory within the framework of learning theory and also psychoanalysis, as it stressed the emotional relationship between caregiver and learner (Ferguson & Garnica, 1975). It was intended to account for the acquisition of speech sounds (not phonological rules), and it was based on evidence from talking birds rather than children.

According to Mowrer's theory, there are four basic steps in the learning of speech sounds:

1. The learner first attends to the caregiver and identifies with him or her (Ferguson & Garnica, 1975).

2. The caregiver's vocalizations become reinforcing because of their association with "basic satisfactions" (e.g., feeding).

3. The learner's vocalizations become reinforcing to the extent that they resemble the caregiver's vocalizations.

4. The sounds that are similar to those of the caregiver are "selectively reinforced" by extrinsic reinforcement and also because of the reinforcement inherent in matching the caregiver's vocalizations (Ferguson & Garnica, 1975). That is, words etc. are perfected on this autistic or self-satisfaction basis (Mowrer, 1952, p. 264). It is presumed that the caregiver selectively reinforces those utterances that are recognized as attempts at adult forms, and, consequently, the learner (child) gradually changes his or her production to make it more like the caregiver's.

Behaviorists such as Mowrer stressed the continuity of prelinguistic behavior and linguistic behavior (i.e., Ingram's (1976) Phonological Stage I and Stage II, see Appendix C). In this view, babbled sounds that resemble those in the adult language are reinforced (either by external reinforcement or secondarily). Sounds that are not part of the adult language drop out because they are not reinforced. Mowrer (1960) claimed that babbling starts only when secondary reinforcement of the child's vocalizations has been established (Ferguson & Garnica, 1975). However, this claim has little support, and in fact there is a considerable amount of counterevidence. For example, hearing children of deaf parents appear to babble normally even though there is little or no secondary reinforcement of their vocalizations.

Other problems with the continuity view include the following: Children do not necessarily produce all of the sounds used in the adult language during the babbling period. Thus not all sounds are available to be reinforced. Moreover, children's earliest words generally contain only a limited number of sounds—not all the sounds that were babbled. In addition, caregivers have not been found to selectively reinforce those sounds that are closest to adult speech (see Rees, 1972).

Olmsted's Ease of Perception Theory (1966)

Olmsted was one of several people who attempted to extend Mowrer's theory (Ferguson & Garnica, 1975). Like Mowrer, Olmsted believed that there is continuity between prelinguistic and linguistic vocalizations, with the child's productions becoming gradually more like those of the adults. Olmsted's theory, which was supported by a research study involving 100 children (Olmsted, 1971) and also by one study of the acquisition of

Russian phonology (Timm, 1977), includes 21 postulates (cf. Bloch, 1948) along with corollaries, definitions, and theorems. For example, Olmsted's (1966) Postulate 6 (in Bar-Adon & Leopold, 1971, p. 361) says that stretches of adult speech become secondarily reinforcing "in proportion to their frequency." According to Postulate 13, "some phones are more discriminable than others," and Postulate 18 states that "easily discriminable" phones are likely to be learned earliest (Bar-Adon & Leopold, 1971, p. 362). As these postulates show, Olmsted's theory stresses the importance of input and ease of perception. In fact, phonological acquisition is seen as depending primarily on ease of perception.

In making his predictions concerning ease of perception, Olmsted used the findings of Miller and Nicely (1955), who studied adults' perceptual confusions. His "order of discriminability" (Postulate 19) is as follows, from most easily discriminable to least (Bar-Adon & Leopold, 1971, p. 362):

(a) voicing and nasality
(b) friction and duration
(c) place of articulation

This "hierarchy" predicts that voicing and nasality features are learned earliest (and therefore are least likely to be in error), that friction and duration are more likely to be in error, and that still more errors will involve place of articulation. However, children learning English appear to offer counterevidence to this hierarchy in that the oral/nasal distinction is learned before the voiced/voiceless distinction (see Ferguson & Garnica, 1975). In addition, Locke (1969) suggests that children may differ as to whether they preserve place features or manner features in learning new sounds.

Jakobson's Universal Order Theory (1941/1968)

Jakobson's (1941/1968, 1971) theory of phonological acquisition, as noted in Chapter 3, was not available in English until 1968. (However, see also Jakobson & Halle, 1956.) Jakobson's theory is probably the most widely known theory of phonological acquisition. It has had a great influence in linguistics, and in fact, most studies of phonological acquisition that were done by linguists from the 1940s through the 1960s were based on Jakobson's model.

Jakobson's theory, as introduced in Chapter 3, is concerned primarily with the child's developing system of phonemic contrasts. In this view, the child's task during acquisition is to master the system of phonemic contrasts or oppositions of the adult language. According to Jakobson, the "principle of maximal contrast" and the "laws of irreversible solidarity" (also called implicational universals) determine the order in which the phonemic contrasts of the adult language are learned. These same principles are also said to account for universals of human language, as well as for the order in which phonemic contrasts are lost in aphasia.

According to the *principle of maximal contrast*, the first phonological opposition learned by a child is between a maximally open sound, such as /ɑ/, and a maximally closed sound, such as /p/ (i.e., between a vowel and a consonant). There is then a split resulting in the first consonantal opposition, the opposition between an oral stop and a nasal stop (e.g., between /p/ and /m/). This is followed by a labial/dental split, for example between /p/ and /t/. In Jakobson's view, the order of development of these contrasts is quite uniform across children and also across languages. Thus his theory is referred to as the universal order theory.

Order of acquisition is also said to be uniform because it agrees with the general *laws of irreversible solidarity*. An example of such an implicational law is the following: fricatives ⊃ stops ("fricatives presuppose or imply stops"). According to this "law," fricatives are less common than stops in languages of the world, and fricatives will be lost earlier in aphasia. In addition, fricatives are acquired after stops by children (or, more precisely, a fricative at a certain point of articulation is acquired only after a stop produced at the same point of articulation).[21] Before fricatives are acquired, children substitute the corresponding stops for them, e.g., [t] replaces /s/. (See Ferguson & Garnica, 1975 for a more in-depth discussion of Jakobson's laws of irreversible solidarity.)

Some specific claims made by Jakobson or derived from his theory include the following:

(a) Dental stops ⊃ labial stops (e.g., /p/ precedes /t/).

(b) Back sounds ⊃ front sounds (e.g., the child should acquire /t/ and /p/ before /k/ and should contrast /p/ – /t/ before contrasting /p/ – /k/ or /t/ – /k/, Macken, 1980).

(c) Before back sounds are acquired, front sounds should substitute for them; for example, [t] should replace /k/, [d] should replace /g/, [s] should replace /ʃ/, etc.

(d) Back fricatives ⊃ both front fricatives and other back consonants (e.g., /ʃ/ follows /f/, /s/, and also /k/).

(e) Voiced consonants ⊃ voiceless consonants (e.g., /p/ precedes /b/).

(f) Before children produce a phonemic contrast between voiced and voiceless stops, voiceless unaspirated stops will be used for both.

(g) The first fricative to be acquired will be /s/, and if a child has only one fricative, it will generally be /s/, although phonetically it may not be distinct from [ʃ].

(h) Mellow fricatives ⊃ (corresponding) strident fricatives (e.g., /s/ is learned before /θ/, and before /θ/ is acquired, [s] should replace it.

In Jakobson's view, the child has his or her own system of phonemic contrasts. In other words, the child's system is treated as a separate entity, without reference to the adult system. What this means is that the child's system may, at any point, differ from the adult system. So, the child may have phonemic distinctions that are not found in the adult system. For instance, a child learning English could have a vowel length distinction, even though adult English does not. Joan Velten (Velten, 1943) was such a child, distinguishing, for example [bɑt] "back" from [bɑ·t] "bad" at the age of two by means of vowel length alone.

In addition, sounds may be allophones of one phoneme in the child's system before they become phonemic. For instance, Jakobson claims that a narrow and more front vowel such as [ɛ] often appears simply as a variant of the "more fundamental" vowel /ɑ/ in certain positions. To illustrate, [pɑpɑ] might vary freely with [pɛpɛ], or [ɑ] might occur after labials and [ɛ] after dentals, as in [pɑpɑ], but [dɛdɛ]. According to Jakobson, as soon as both become separate phonemes, [ɛ] is narrowed to [i] to maximize the difference between the two sounds.

Jakobson contends that babbling bears no connection to true or meaningful speech. In fact, he claims that there may be an actual break between prelinguistic and linguistic activity. This could be called a "strict discontinuity" view (Ferguson and Garnica, 1975). During babbling, the child is said to produce all the sounds used in all the languages of the world. Once true speech starts, however, the child loses this ability.

Two studies discussed previously that follow Jakobson's model closely include Velten's (1943) report of his daughter Joan and Leopold's (1947) account of his daughter Hildegard's phonological development. Several of Jakobson's claims have been supported to some extent in these accounts and in the accounts of other linguists. For instance, Jakobson's claim that voiceless unaspirated stops are produced before children have acquired the voicing distinction has been confirmed by Macken and Barton (1980). According to Macken (1980, p. 163), children probably do acquire front stops before back stops and substitute dental (or alveolar) stops for velars, as Jakobson claimed, but some children learn dental stops before labials. Research also has shown that stops generally are acquired earlier than fricatives and often substitute for them.[22] Front fricatives often substitute for back fricatives (e.g., [s] for /ʃ/), as claimed by Jakobson, and /θ/ is usually a late acquisition, following /s/. In addition, /s/ occasionally occurs as a substitute for /θ/, although other substitutes are more common, especially [f] (Edwards, 1979).

Some of Jakobson's claims have not been supported in recent research. For instance, it is not clear that /s/ is the earliest fricative acquired by children; some learn /f/ first.[23] For some children, /ʃ/ is an early acquisition, while Jakobson claimed it should be learned late. (For example, see Moskowitz, 1975, and Farwell, 1977.)

Most important, research has not strongly supported Jakobson's idea of a universal order of acquisition. It is now generally viewed as overly simple. Although certain types of sounds, such as nasals and stops, tend to be acquired early, while other types of sounds tend to be acquired late, there is a great deal of variation among children in order of acquisition, e.g., for fricatives (Edwards, 1979), and for stops (Macken, 1980).

It is also important that Jakobson paid no attention to factors such as word-position, which more recent research (e.g., Edwards, 1979) has shown to be significant in phonological acquisition, at least for certain types of sounds. As Menn (1976a, p. 172) observed, a theory that is concerned only with phonemic contrasts is very limited and cannot deal with other important aspects of language such as those listed at the beginning of this section. Besides word-position, other omissions noted by Macken (1980, p. 145) in her discussion of the acquisition of stops include the role of phonological processes in acquisition and the role of perception. In addition, it has been pointed out (e.g., by Kiparsky & Menn, 1977) that it may be difficult to tell if a child does or does not have a phonemic contrast unless he or she clearly merges two phonemes.

Jakobson's view of babbling was accepted for many years. However, research that has been undertaken in recent years (e.g., by Oller, Wieman, Doyle, & Ross, 1976) has shed serious doubt on his view of "strict discontinuity" between babbling and true speech as well as certain other aspects of his theory.

In his famous diary study discussed previously, Smith (1973) first presents a Jakobsonian-type analysis of his son's speech. In this analysis, the child is seen as having a self-contained independent phonological system. However, later in his book, Smith rejects this analysis, concluding that there is no evidence that the child has his own phonemic system.

Stampe's Natural Phonology Theory (1969, 1972a)

According to Stampe's theory of natural phonology as introduced in Chapter 5, the child's pronunciation is derived from his or her "mental representation" of adult speech (e.g., his or her underlying representation). This corresponds roughly to the adult surface pronunciation. An innate system of natural phonological processes (such as depalatalization and devoicing) operates on the child's underlying representations.

In Stampe's view, these natural phonological processes are changes that are phonetically motivated and therefore show up in historical sound change, language acquisition, nativization of loan words, slips of the tongue, and other sound change phenomena. Stampe (1972a, p. 1) defined them as innate "mental operations" that apply in speech to "substitute for a class of sounds or sound sequences presenting a specific common difficulty to the speech capacity . . . an alternative class, identical, but lacking the difficult property." For instance, Stampe (1972a, p. 13) stated that the process of depalatalization "eliminates the fronted and raised tongue posture of [ʃ, ʒ] etc. in favor of the more neutral posture of the alveolars [s, z], etc."

Many of these processes occur in pairs that have contradictory results because one member of the pair is a context-free or paradigmatic process, while the other is context-sensitive or syntagmatic. As discussed in Chapter 5, for example, there is a general tendency for obstruents to be devoiced because the obstruction in the mouth, which is necessary for the production of obstruents, impedes the airstream on which voicing depends. However, between vowels, obstruents tend to be voiced by an assimilatory (context-sensitive) process.

The child's innate phonological system is said to express the full set of restrictions on speech, i.e., a full set of unlimited and unordered phonological processes (Stampe, 1969). Thus in early stages when all of these processes are applying in an unordered fashion, simple sequences such as *dadada* and *mamama* appear. Each phonetic opposition that the child learns to produce involves a modification of the innate phonological system. Changes in the child's phoneme inventory are seen simply as secondary effects of changes in the system of processes.

You will recall (Chapter 5) that there are three mechanisms by which the innate system is revised: limitation, ordering, and suppression of processes. Stampe (1969, p. 444) states that the child's task in acquiring the adult pronunciation is to modify those aspects of the innate system that separate his or her pronunciation from the "standard." If the child succeeds, the resulting system will be identical to that of adult speakers. The child's "closer approximations" of adult pronunciation are seen as reflecting his or her limitation or suppression of those processes that are not part of the adult system.

According to Stampe, there is no need to refer to implicational laws such as those proposed by Jakobson. Stampe (1969, p. 445) claims that the regularities in the order in which phonetic representations are mastered can be explained by the characteristics of the innate system ("its processes, their inner hierarchies, and their interrelations") and by the three mechanisms of revision. Moreover, there may be contradictions to the order of acquisition predicted by Jakobson's implicational laws. As Jakobson was only interested in the child's phonemic system, Stampe (1969) notes that he could ignore such problems by interpreting the implicational laws in terms of phonemic representation. Jakobson did not have to account for contextual variation; thus he could disregard context-sensitive processes that might contradict his implicational laws.

Stampe argues that Jakobson's universals, to the extent that they are correct, are really just innate universal phonological processes that govern phonetic (not phonemic) representations and that have to be ordered for acquisition. The child has to "unlearn" those processes that are not appropriate to the language being acquired.

According to Stampe, the child cannot create an opposition that does not exist in the adult language because the child's underlying system is the adult system. Stampe (1969) argues that there is no evidence that the child has a phonemic system of his or her own, and in fact, he says that there is counterevidence. In his view, there is evidence indicating that the child has internalized a representation that "transcends" his or her own production and forms the base on which the innate system of processes operates.

In a Stampian analysis, a child's surface substitutions are broken down into their constituent phonological processes, as noted earlier. For instance, a surface substitution of [z] for initial /ʃ/ would be seen as resulting from the operation of two natural processes, depalatalization and word-initial voicing.

Edwards (1973), in her study of the acquisition of liquids, found evidence to support Stampe's view. That is, the substitutions made by her normal subjects could be accounted for by a set of phonetically motivated natural processes, for instance labiovelarization and delateralization of /l/, and labialization and deretroflexion of /r/. Moreover, the changes in their substitutions over time could be accounted for by the limitation and suppression of those processes.

One of the major objections to Stampe's model has been directed toward his view of the child's underlying representation. Stampe apparently assumes that the child's perception is intact at the onset of language development (or at least language production). However, several experimental studies (e.g., Garnica, 1973; Barton, 1976) have indicated that children's phonemic perception, although generally ahead of their productive abilities, is not adult-like at the beginning of language acquisition. Instead, it develops over time. In addition, there is some evidence (e.g., in Macken 1979) that children may occasionally misperceive words or sounds. Consequently, more recent models of phonological acquisition (e.g., Kiparsky & Menn, 1977) have attempted to account for children's developing perceptual abilities as well as their productive abilities. However, as Kiparsky and Menn point out, it would be possible to modify Stampe's view to include perception.

Waterson's Prosodic
Theory (1970, 1971a)

Waterson's (1970, 1971a, 1971b, 1971c, 1976, 1978) nonsegmental or prosodic theory, which has its background in Firthian linguistics or prosodic analysis (Firth 1935, 1948) was briefly introduced earlier because of its novel basic unit of analysis. The main points of Waterson's theory, particularly as described in Waterson 1970 and 1971a, are that it emphasizes the importance of perception and input (cf. Olmsted). Because each child's input is different, each child may exhibit his or her own patterns of acquisition (Ferguson & Garnica, 1975). In fact, each child's speech is treated as an "independent language." Individual differences in phonological acquisition can therefore be accounted for in this theory (cf. Jakobson, 1941/1968). Phonemes are not seen as being important. Rather, entire words are treated as units.

As described previously, Waterson states that the child perceives adult words or utterances as units having certain features such as nasality or frication, but the child is not necessarily aware of their sequence or location. The child pays attention to and reproduces noticeable (e.g., strongly articulated) features that are not too difficult and that are recognized as being functional. Features that occur in more than one place in an utterance are also likely to be perceived and reproduced. To illustrate, for a word like *pudding* the child may at first perceive only [pʊ] because that is the stressed part. This syllable may then be reduplicated, so that the child's form is [pʊpʊ]. According to Waterson (1970), the child may be aware of the number of syllables in an adult utterance but will not have a clear impression of the unstressed syllables. Thus we find reduplicated forms. In Waterson's view, the child observes patterns of features in adult forms and uses them to construct his or her own structural patterns. These structural patterns are then used in producing the child's own forms (cf. Menn, 1976a).

The structural patterns discussed by Waterson (1971a) include a labial structure, a continuant structure, a sibilant structure, a stop structure, and a nasal structure. To illustrate, Waterson's son "P" had a sibilant structure that he used for several adult words containing sibilants. These words were pronounced as follows:

fish   [ɪʃ] ~ [ʊʃ]

vest   [ʊʃ]

fetch [ɪʃ]

dish   [dɪʃ]

brush [bʌʃ]

According to Waterson (1971a, p. 185) the basic features shared by all of these child forms are: a monosyllabic structure; a high or close vowel; a voiced onset; a syllable ending with features of "voicelessness, sibilance, continuance, frontness, labiality, and palato-alveolarity." The "differential" features include: rounding vs. nonrounding ([ʊʃ] vs. [ɪʃ]), backness vs. frontness on onset ([ʊʃ] vs. [ɪʃ]), bilabiality ([b]) vs. alveolarity ([d]), and VC vs. CVC word structure.

Another structure pattern, called a nasal structure was exemplified by the adult words *finger, window, another,* and *Randall,* all of which share features of continuance, voiced syllable endings, voiced onset to the second syllable, penultimate stress, and a "strongly articulated" nasal (i.e., a nasal next to a stressed vowel). All were produced by "P" in the general form [ɲVɲV]. That is, they were produced as either wholly or partially reduplicated syllables consisting of a palatal nasal plus a vowel, with initial stress (1971a, p. 181):

finger   [ɲẽːɲẽ] ~ [ɲiːɲɪ]

window   [ɲeːɲeː]

another   [ɲaɲa]

Randall   [ɲaɲɸ̞]

Using her son's forms for *pudding* and *fly*, Waterson (1970) illustrates how these forms develop gradually over a period of time. As the child's perception improves, finer and finer differentiations are made, and structural patterns are revised. Eventually, all the features of the adult forms are acquired and appear in the same sequences and combinations as in the corresponding adult forms.

Waterson's theory has several strong points, some of which are discussed by Ferguson and Garnica (1975). For instance, it can account for the fact that children may use different substitutes for the same sound in different words, because different words may be involved in different structural patterns. Similarly, it can account for situations in which a sound is used in place of another sound but not for itself. It also takes perception and input into consideration and can account for individual differences. Thus it does try to explain phenomena that are not of concern in certain other theories (Ferguson & Garnica, 1975). In addition, it may be very useful in analyzing the speech of young children who do not yet have a real phonological system or children with very delayed phonological development.

Some of the weak points in Waterson's theory include the following: It does not take phonemes into consideration; it is based primarily on a very small "corpus" (about 21 words) from one child; and it refers only to early stages of development, up to the age of about two years. Waterson does not attempt to come up with a sequence of sound acquisition or to predict general types of errors, although her model may allow us to predict what a particular child will do with a certain type of word (Ferguson & Garnica, 1975).

Menn and Kiparsky's Interactionist-Discovery Theory (Menn 1976a; Kiparsky and Menn, 1977)

The interactionist-discovery theory of phonological acquisition proposed by Menn (1976a) and Kiparsky (Kiparsky & Menn, 1977) is said to be antiabstract and to exemplify a "real-world" approach to phonological acquisition. (See also Menn, 1977, 1978, 1980.) It is a "discovery-oriented" approach which holds that phonological acquisition is a problem-solving activity. The child is said to be an "active organizer" who organizes the distinctions she or he can perceive into manageable pieces and discovers the structure of the adult language.

One of the tenets of this theory is that phonetic mastery and the acquisition of phonemic contrasts are not necessarily "in step." Menn (1976a, p. 172) hypothesizes that the child starts by learning sets of phonetic targets in a word-by-word manner. Later these are reorganized into phones and phonemes.

According to the interactionist-discovery theory, children invent their own phonological rules by active experimentation and the use of "strategies." Rules are not seen as being innate, and there is no process/rule dichotomy. All rules are said to be learned. The child takes the adult language as his or her starting point and imposes structure on the adult form when "taking it in" (Menn 1976a, p. 170). Eventually, children construct abstract representations connecting related morphemes, but for very young children, underlying forms are not distinct from their perception of adult forms.

In this view, acquisition is seen as typically involving mastery of "special cases" (Menn 1976a, p. 169). The child then generalizes and tries to find patterns to relate the separate pieces. The successes that the child encounters in matching the sounds of some adult words are said to form the basis for general strategies that lead to new successes. Successes that are never generalized are called *phonological idioms* or *progressive idioms* (Moskowitz, 1973, 1980). The best known example of a progressive idiom is Hildegard Leopold's correct production of *pretty* at 10 months. Later, it regressed to [pɪti] and then to [bɪdi].

Menn (1976a, p. 176) argues that beginning speakers limit their output to a few types of forms. That is, children use a few set patterns or grooves or "articulatory subroutines" for most of their words. One goal of strategies and rule formation, in Menn's view, is to reduce output variety.

Two means of rule formation or invention discussed by Menn (1976a, p. 171) are the following:

(1) *Consolidation* or *coalescence.* The child may collapse two different but similar outputs. For example, a child discussed by Menn (1976a) at first produced both *tape* and *tea* as [teɪ] ~ [ti]. He then collapsed the two outputs to [ti], and when he learned a new word, *cake* (similar to *tape*) he produced it only as [ki]. In Menn's terms, he had "invented" the rule eɪ→i.

(2) *Generalization* of existing patterns. Menn claims that articulatory habits are transferred or carried over from one or two established words to new words. Moreover, children add new words that resemble those already present in their lexicon. In this way, their existing capabilities are "exploited."

Strategies that are said to contribute to limited output variety are selective avoidance of difficult sounds, and the use of "favorite sounds" (cf. Farwell, 1977). In Menn's opinion, selective avoidance lends support to the idea that phonetic and phonemic learning are separable. One of the children Menn discusses could produce initial /d/, but not /b/. She claims that he "honored" the /b/ – /d/ contrast by avoiding words with initial /b/ (1976a, p. 173).

Menn notes that it is possible to state the rules of child phonology formally in order to capture the strategies any given child has adopted to produce adult words. These rules can be written, for convenience, as though they "map" the adult surface form directly onto the child's output, but in Menn's view, this is not accurate; rules refer only to the connection between the child's perception and his or her production of the adult form.

The claims made by the interactionist-discovery theory are said to be very different from those made by Jakobson (1941/1968) and Stampe (1969, 1972a), especially with regard to "natural unfoldings" (Menn 1976a, p. 169). As noted earlier, Menn and Kiparsky contend that rules are "invented." Menn argues that a theory (like Jakobson's) that deals only with contrasts misses many important aspects of development.

Support for the interactionist-discovery model comes mainly from Menn's case study of a child named Jacob (1976b), although Menn also cites evidence from Ferguson and Farwell (1975), Vihman (1976), and Drachman (1973a). More recently, Leonard, Newhoff, and Mesalam (1980) present data that are also consistent with the interactionist-discovery theory. This model appears to be gaining in popularity as child phonologists (such as Ferguson & Macken, 1980; Macken & Ferguson, 1982; Fey & Gandour, 1979, 1982; and Klein, 1977, 1981) take a more cognitive view of phonological development.

THE CREATIVITY
OF THE CHILD:
THE USE OF STRATEGIES

In this final section, we look at a central controversy in the child phonology literature. This discussion is intended to amplify and consolidate views developed earlier in this chapter. A major area of controversy in child phonology involves the child's role in phonological acquisition. As reviewed previously, theorists and researchers differ as to whether or not they stress the creativity of the child. One part of this controversy has to do with whether the child's rules or processes are innate or invented. The theories of Jakobson (1941/1968) and Stampe (1969, 1972a) stress universal laws and innate natural processes, respectively. They do not see the child as an "active organizer." One the other hand, we have seen that the theories of Waterson (1970, 1971a, 1971b, etc.) and also Kiparsky and Menn (1977; Menn, 1976a) view the child as a "creator" and "active participant." In Waterson's view, children derive "structural patterns" from recurring adult forms and use these patterns to form their own words. In the view of Kiparsky and Menn, children organize language into "manageable pieces" and invent their own rules.

Since about 1976, there has been more of a tendency to view the child as an active participant or creator as child phonologists have gotten further away from Jakobson's theory. For example, Leonard et al. (1978) in their study of imitation see the child as an active organizer, and Ferguson and Macken (1980) argue for a more cognitive model of phonological acquisition. As early as 1973, Drachman (1973b, p. 146) noted that generative phonology ignores some of the "creative efforts" that the child engages in to "undo" the results of his or her maturational or articulatory incompetence. A year later, Ingram (1974b, pp. 63, 64) stated that "the operation of phonological rules shows the organizational and generalizing capacities that the child brings to the language learning process."

There are several types of evidence that bear on the issue of creativity (e.g., see Macken & Ferguson, 1982). One of these is the overgeneralization of a rule, i.e., the application of a rule to forms that it should not apply to. For example, Ingram (1974b) claims that children may overgeneralize the diminutive rule (which adds $/-i/$ to nouns, as in *doggie*), applying it to new (and inappropriate) forms. For instance, he reports that at 1;4 Jennika added a diminutive ending to *dot*, *out*, and even to *hi* and *no*, producing [dɑti], [ɑ͞ʊti], [hɑ͞ɪdi] and [nodi]. He also notes that Holmes' (1927) daughter overgeneralized the diminutive rule, as in [bɪbi] for *bib* and [wɑki] for *walk*. In addition, Ingram reports overgeneralization of reduplication to monosyllabic words, as in [pɔpɔ] for *pot* "pot" (French) (Roussey, 1899), and reduplication together with the diminutive, as in [bɪki] for *brick*, and [wɔ:kɔ] for *walk* (Ross, 1937).

Macken (personal communication; see also Ferguson & Macken, 1980) discusses a child who produced stop plus /r/ clusters by deleting the /r/ (as in [pɪti] for *pretty*) from the age of about 1;6 to 1;10. However, at the age of 1;11, she began producing /tr/ and /dr/ clusters as [f], presumably because of the rounding and frication of /r/ following these stops. A little later on, she overgeneralized her cluster rule so that it also applied to /pr/ and /kr/. Thus her production of these clusters got worse, because [f] is "further" from /pr/ and /kr/, from an adult view, than the stops alone are.

Another type of evidence concerning the child's creativity is the use of strategies. There is no agreed upon definition of the term strategy. According to Farwell (1977, p. 97), strategies are ways in which children take an "active organizational role" in determining the structure of their language. They also have been called operating principles, or particular ways in which individual children approach the problem of sound learning (Menn, 1973; Ferguson & Farwell, 1975). Drachman (1973b) stated that strategies help the child "get closer to" the adult model. In Farwell's (1977) view, strategies may provide a way for the child to "concentrate" on a certain class of sounds, such as fricatives. According to Kiparsky and Menn (1977), the child uses strategies to invent rules.

Since the mid-1970s, there has been increasing interest in the child's use of strategies (e.g., see Ferguson & Farwell, 1975; Farwell, 1977, Kiparsky & Menn, 1977; Menyuk & Menn, 1979; Ferguson, 1979b; Klein, 1977, 1981; Vihman, 1981; Fee & Ingram, 1982; Schwartz & Leonard, 1982). This goes along with the current trend toward seeing the child as an active participant and organizer. However, even in 1973, Menn stated that we should search for evidence regarding children's use of strategies instead of concentrating on general patterns, and in 1974 Ingram (1974a, p. 233) noted that there is a "growing interest in the possibility that developmental differences among children may be due to the selection of distinct strategies."

Many strategies have been proposed since the early 1970s. At this point, there is no general agreement as to what should be considered a strategy, and in fact, it sometimes seems as though anything can be a strategy. For example, several of the phonological processes that have been discussed earlier in this book have also been proposed as strategies. In some cases, there is no clear dividing line between processes and strategies. In this section we will discuss the proposed strategies listed in Table 6-5. This is not necessarily a complete list, and the studies cited under each heading are only meant to be representative, as the literature in this area is expanding rapidly. The studies that are listed contain relevant examples and/or discussion.

It should be noted that there is considerable overlap among some of the categories to be discussed. For example, Menn (1978, p. 161), who introduced the terms *relative position constraint* and *absolute position constraint*, listed examples of metathesis under each category. Similarly, *unique reduction devices* may be considered as one type of *limited output pattern* rather than as a separate category.

Selection/Avoidance

The phenomenon of avoidance has been noted for many years. For instance, Holmes (1927) reported that his daughter Mollie tended to avoid difficult sounds. Similarly, Leopold (1947) mentioned that his daughter Hildegard avoided labiodentals until the age of 1;7, and Velten's (1943) daughter Joan appeared to avoid final voiced stops until she was 2 years old. Ferguson (1975a) noted that early on, children may avoid producing fricative words, and Ingram (1978) said that children may avoid initial fricatives until they have a small inventory of stops and nasals. Farwell (1977) discussed the avoidance of fricatives and reported that some of her subjects even "refused" to learn adult words containing fricatives. Menn (1976b) reported that her subject Jacob avoided words with initial /g/ and /p/ at one stage. In her discussion of cluster acquisition, Greenlee (1974) stated that children may at first avoid clusters, and she discussed metathesis (as in [bul] for *blue*) and migration (as in [nos] for *snow*) as "cluster-avoiding strategies."

Ferguson, Peizer, and Weeks (1973) argued for a "selectivity of production" model. Similarly, Branigan (1976) claimed that children choose to represent those adult forms that most nearly correspond to their productive abilities. Vihman (1981, p. 261) argues that children may select words to learn based on their phonological characteristics. In other words, "early lexical choices are at least partly phonologically governed." This shows that children are aware, at some level, of the phonotactic and inventory constraints of their language. Vihman (1976) found "clear evidence" of a selection (or avoidance) strategy. During the 50-word stage (see Appendix C) her daughter Virve, who was learning Estonian as her first language, would attempt to repeat only words "within her range;" adult

TABLE 6-5
Proposed "strategies," or ways in which children actively organize the structure of their language (Farwell, 1977)

Strategy	Author(s)
Selection/avoidance	Drachman, 1973a; Greenlee, 1974; Ferguson and Farwell, 1975; Ferguson, 1975a, 1978a, 1979b; Ingram, 1975; Menn, 1976a, 1976b; Vihman, 1976, 1981; Farwell, 1977; Kiparsky and Menn, 1977; Schwartz and Leonard, 1982
Avoidance of homonymy	Drachman, 1973b; Ingram, 1975
Homonymy	Menn, 1978; Vihman, 1979, 1981; Locke, 1979b; Smith and Brunette, 1981
Limited output patterns	Braine, 1971; Ferguson, 1979a, 1979b; Menn, 1976a, 1978; Priestly, 1977; Waterson, 1970, 1971a
Absolute position constraints	Branigan, 1976; Farwell, 1977; Macken, 1977; Menn, 1978
Relative position constraints	Ingram, 1974a; Vihman, 1976; Menn, 1978
Assimilation/harmony	Drachman, 1973a; Menn, 1975; Vihman, 1978
Reduplication	Drachman, 1973a; Moskowitz, 1973; Ingram, 1974b; Ferguson, 1978a, 1979a, 1979b; Schwartz, Leonard, Wilcox, and Folger, 1980; Fee and Ingram, 1982
Metathesis/migration	Vihman, 1976; Drachman, 1973a, Greenlee, 1974; Menn, 1978
Unique reduction devices	Menn, 1972; Smith, 1973; Ferguson, 1978a, 1979a; Vihman, 1981
Vowel lengthening	Drachman, 1973b; Ingram, 1975
Syllabic fricatives	Farwell, 1977
Favorite sounds	Menn, 1971; Farwell, 1977; Ferguson, 1978a; Ingram, 1979
Rule ordering	Kiparsky and Menn, 1977
Coalescence or consolidation	Menn, 1976a, Vihman, 1981

words that did not fit into her system were rarely attempted. Consequently, over half of her first 50 words had no sound substitutions or distortions, although there were some omissions. New phonological structures were added very gradually. Vihman notes that there may be a personality factor involved, however. She hypothesizes (1976, p. 234) that the pattern exhibited by Virve may be that of a cautious child who tries only things that are within (or close to) her range.

Vihman (1976) also indicated that children may find clever ways to use words that violate their constraints. To illustrate, Virve had a constraint that required the first vowel in a word to be more open than the second. So, for a while she did not even attempt the Estonian words for *mother* (*ema*) and *father* (*isa*), which violated her constraint. However, she later metathesized the vowels, producing *ami* (or *ani*) and *asi*. Thus other strategies (in this case metathesis) may allow the child to expand his or her productive repertoire. Vihman (1976, p. 233) discusses two specific cognitive tools or strategies that allow expansion of the repertoire. These are assimilation and accommodation. That is, the child can assimilate new words to existing patterns (as in the vowel metathesis example) or accommodate (expand) old patterns. Vihman (1976, p. 238) notes that Virve gradually and systematically expanded her old patterns, relaxing her phonotactic constraints.

Avoidance may be viewed (e.g., by Vihman, 1976) as a temporary "holding pattern" to keep phonological acquisition manageable. In Menn's (1976a) view, mentioned earlier, the phenomenon of avoidance supports the idea that phonetic and phonemic acquisition are separate. Menn claims that a child may honor a phonemic contrast by avoiding one of the sounds involved in the contrast. This shows that the child is aware of his or her difficulty with one of the sounds and avoids it rather than merge it with the other sound.

Substitution is sometimes cited as a strategy exemplifying avoidance. For instance, Drachman (1973b, p. 156) noted that children may avoid sounds either by substitution or deletion, which he calls "local avoidance." Similarly, Vihman (1976) stated that for her daughter, /k/ was at first avoided altogether and was later replaced by [t].

It is well known that some children, particularly older children, may skillfully avoid words or sounds that they are not able to produce correctly. For example, a child who produces *queen* as [krin] may avoid that word by saying "lady" when presented with a picture of a queen. Other children may simply refuse to say problematic words, or words containing difficult sounds.

There is a considerable amount of anecdotal evidence indicating that children may avoid certain sounds and select words containing only sounds that are relatively easy for them. However, much more experimental evidence is needed before we can be certain that children actually choose not to produce particular sounds, and other factors that could contribute to the absence of those sounds (e.g., input) must be ruled out. Drachman (1973a) pointed out that we need to be able to show which forms the child comprehends (as well as those he or she produces) in order to sharpen our concept of avoidance. More recent experimental studies that have found support for selection and avoidance include those of Leonard, Schwartz, Morris, and Chapman (1981) and Schwartz and Leonard (1982).

Avoidance of Homonymy

Avoidance of homonymy has also been proposed as a strategy (e.g., by Drachman, 1973b, and Ingram, 1975).[24] Drachman (1973b, p. 150) claimed that children devise strategies to diminish homonymy. In fact, he stated that this is "the whole aim of their linguistic being." One strategy that he mentioned is avoidance. That is, children may avoid one sound or word in order not to merge it with another. To illustrate, he noted that Joan Velten (Velten, 1943) produced word-final nasals as voiced stops. So, she avoided producing words containing final voiced stops until the age of 22 months, when adult voiced stops were devoiced in final position. Drachman (1973b, p. 154) also claimed that children may use a "nonhomologous articulation" for one of the sounds that would otherwise be merged. What this apparently means is that the child may use an alternate production mechanism (position or structure) for one of the sounds, producing it differently even though it may sound just like the other (cf. Kornfeld, 1971a, and Macken & Barton, 1980).

Avoidance of homonymy was discussed at length by Ingram (1975) in a report of five young children learning different languages. Ingram claimed that children are concerned with relations among their words and that they compare their forms and change them when necessary in order to maintain distinct surface forms. In Ingram's view, children may have alternate pronunciations for one or both members of a potential homonym pair, or they may make up unusual processes to keep the words apart (or to "resolve" their potential homonym pairs). Odd or unique processes that Ingram cites include metathesis (as in [me] for *plane* to maintain a contrast with *plate* [pe]), stress assignment (as in *papa* for *father*, but *papá* for *grandfather*), and vowel lengthening before voiced consonants, as in Joan Velten's [bu·t] for *bead* vs. [but] for *beat*. He also mentions a specific t→k rule that Jennika applied only in *hat* ([ak]) in order to keep it distinct from *hot*, which she produced as [at]. In Ingram's opinion, children use fewer homonyms than would be expected. He sees this as evidence for avoidance of homonymy as a strategy.

Homonymy

The situation regarding homonymy is not as simple as it might at first appear. Vihman, in an unpublished paper (1979) and also later (1981) challenged Ingram's claims, and moreover, she argued that early in acquisition, children may use a "homonym strategy." This is, they may deliberately make use of or "collect" homonyms, and they may even utilize an "unmotivated" process in order to merge two or more adult words (1981, p. 24). In Vihman's view, children may use homonyms to reduce the number of different sound patterns in their productive lexicon. She sees this as evidence of early phonological organization. For some children, homonymy is said to be a "strategy for vocabulary building." Vihman notes that her son Raivo ("R"), who was learning Estonian as his native language, had a "production strategy" by which he used a single sound pattern for two or more phonologically (and sometimes semantically) similar adult words. For example, he produced *kana* "chicken" and *kala* "fish" as [tã]. He sometimes even collapsed words that were at first pronounced differently. For instance, Raivo collapsed or merged four adult (Estonian) words *lind* "bird," *rind* "breast," *king* "shoe," and *kinni* "closed" into one form [nǝn], even though they were at first produced slightly differently, e.g., *king* was [næniŋ] ~ [næn] and *rind* was [nǝnǝn]. Vihman also presents data from several additional children who collected homonyms. In Vihman's view, "R" and the other children she discusses exhibited a desire for efficiency rather than clarity (1981, p. 241).

Locke (1979b) also discusses homonymy, which he views as a basic feature of language. He argues that children do not "feel pressured" to keep words apart, and in fact, they may not even notice that they are collapsing two or more adult words. To illustrate, he notes that Joan Velten (Velten, 1943), between the ages of 22 and 27 months, used three forms [bat], [but], and [bu] to represent 29 adult words. A. Smith (Smith, 1973) also produced many homonyms and apparently was not bothered by this homonymy. According to Locke (1979b), research does not support the notion that children keep their homonyms apart in subtle ways, as some child phonologists (e.g., Ingram, 1975) have argued. In a "communicative failure" experiment, Locke found that children did not apply strategies in order to keep homonymous forms separate, although they did fidget and apparently knew that they were collapsing different adult words (such as *rake* and *lake*, merged as *wake*).

As Menn (1978, p. 160) points out, children probably vary in their tolerance for homonymy, and as Drachman (1973b) pointed out much earlier, we need to clarify where or under what conditions it is tolerated.

It may be the case that an age factor is involved. That is, a child who might tolerate (or even use) homonyms at one stage might go out of his or her way to avoid homonyms at a later stage. Much more research is needed if we are to fully understand the child's use of or avoidance of homonymy. See Smith and Brunette (1981) for a review of this controversy, along with some additional data.

Limited Output Patterns

The fact that children may use one sound pattern or whole word shape to represent several words, presumably to get the most out of their limited repertoire, has been noted by Menn (1976a, 1978) and by Waterson (1970, 1971a) among others. As discussed earlier, Waterson (1970, 1971a) states that children abstract salient features from recurring adult words that are phonologically similar. These features form a structural pattern that is then used by the child in producing several adult words. Waterson discusses five such patterns used by her son "P." For instance, he used the nasal structure [ɲVɲV] to produce several words sharing features of nasality, penultimate stress, etc., including *Randall* and *another*. Similarly, Menn (1978) claimed that children use "articulatory subroutines." That is, they use a limited number of output patterns to represent numerous words. By doing this, they "maximize their existing skills."

As pointed out earlier, Menn (1976a) claims that children, by experimentation and the use of strategies, invent rules in order to limit their output. Specifically, they may (1) avoid difficult sounds, (2) use favorite sounds, (3) consolidate or collapse two or more output forms, (4) generalize existing patterns to new words, and (5) add new words that are similar to words already in their repertoire.

Priestly's (1977) report of his son's phonology also falls under the heading of limited output patterns. Priestly notes that his son Christopher, between the ages of 22 and 26 months, used the general phonological pattern or *canonical form* (whole-word shape) [CVjVC] to represent many multisyllabic words. The child's general strategy was to use [j] plus a neutral vowel to represent the second syllable of a word. (He also had several substrategies that will not be discussed here.) To illustrate, Christopher produced *hanger* as [hajan], *carrot* as [kajat], *basket* and *blanket* as [bajak], and both *fountain* and *flannel* as [fajan]. Ferguson (1979b, p. 196) calls this a "word-shaping strategy." Although Christopher's idiosyncratic word shape could have grown out of a regular substitute (e.g., [j] for intervocalic liquids), it could not be considered a straightforward substitution at the stage discussed by Priestly.

Ferguson (1979a, p. 15) discusses what he calls an "early phonotactic strategy" reported by Braine (1971) that would fit under the heading of limited output patterns, (and also under selection and favorite sounds). The child discussed by Braine (1971) had the following strategy very early on: Select monosyllables with front consonants, and produce them as [d] plus vowel. In other words, the child produced several monosyllabic adult words containing front consonants as dV.

Absolute Position Constraints

Children sometimes exhibit strategies that could be considered absolute position constraints (Menn, 1978, p. 162). In other words, certain sounds or features can occur only in particular word or syllable positions.[25] For instance, Farwell (1977, p. 102) discusses a strategy, observed in her study of fricative acquisition, which she calls word position. This strategy involves producing a sound or type of sound in a position or context in which it should be easiest. For instance, one of her subjects produced his "first regular fricative" in word-final position, where fricatives are said to be relatively easy to produce, and he tried out fricatives in that position before using them in initial position. Another child required a fricative, if produced at all, to go at the end of the word, (as in [nos] for *snow*, [ɪʃ] for *fish*, etc.). A third child did not add fricative words to her vocabulary until she was able to produce final sounds. Similarly, Daniel Menn (Kiparsky & Menn, 1977, p. 60) used new phonemes first in word-final position. In contrast, Branigan (1976) reports that his subject, Shaun, tried out all new sounds in initial position first.

Macken's (1977) report of the phonological acquisition of a young Spanish-speaking child named Si also contains evidence of an absolute position constraint. At one stage in Si's development, between 1;7 and 2;1, her "preferred form" was: labial C + V + dental C + V.[26] For instance, she produced the word *manzana* "apple" as [mana] (with deletion of /anz/). *Soupa* become [pota], by metathesis and stopping. Thus both forms obeyed her absolute position constraint.

Relative Position Constraints

Some strategies, which could be called relative position constraints (Menn, 1978, p. 162), have the effect of constraining the order in which sounds can appear in the child's output form. For example, Ingram (1974a) discussed a strategy that he called fronting. According to this strategy, if there are two or more consonants in a word, the first must be produced either at the same point or farther forward in the mouth than the second, and the second must be produced either at the same point or farther forward than the third, etc. In other words, front sounds precede back sounds in a child's words. So, in a word with three consonants, the first could be a labial, the second an alveolar, and the third a velar, but the first could not be a velar (unless all three were velars). Ingram (1974a, p. 238) claims that children will more easily acquire words in which the consonants are in the unmarked order, i.e. those that obey this relative position constraint. Words that do not obey this constraint in the adult form are modified so that they do obey it in the child's output. To illustrate, *cup* was produced by one child as [pʰʌk], and *coffee* was produced as [baki]. In both cases, the consonants were metathesized. (In *coffee*, stopping (f→p) and voicing (p→b) also applied.) According to Ingram (1974a, p. 235) groups of processes may conspire to achieve this type of output. Ingram also mentions a fronting strategy for vowels: If a word has more than one high vowel, the first must be either the same as or produced farther forward in the mouth than the second. So, i – u, i – i, u – u are allowed, but not u – i (p. 236).

A relative position constraint involving vowels is also discussed by Vihman (1976) in her report of her daughter's phonological development. As noted above, Virve's constraint required that, if a word had more than one vowel, the first had to be more open than the second. She at first would not even attempt words that did not obey this constraint, including *isa* "father" and *ema* "mother" (Estonian). Later on, however, she metathesized the vowels to make these words fit her pattern, producing [asi] for *father* and [ami] or [ani] for *mother*.

Assimilation/Harmony

Assimilation or harmony has also been discussed as a strategy.[27] For example, Drachman (1973a) discussed the use of what he called "long-domain processes," some of which produce assimilation across syllables. These include, among others, *syllable harmony*, in which two syllables become alike (e.g., Greek *filipáki* "Philipaki" (a name) may become *papáki*), *vowel harmony*, in which vowels in adjacent syllables become more alike (e.g., *lemóni* "lemon" may become *mamoni*), and *consonant harmony*, in which consonants in adjacent syllables become more alike (e.g., *kapélo* "hat" may become *papélo*). According to Drachman (1973a) such long-domain processes are particularly likely to occur in the period just after the babbling stage.

Children (like languages of the world) sometimes have output constraints as that the consonants in a word must agree in place or manner of articulation or that the vowels have to agree in backness or rounding. The use of assimilation or harmony is somewhat similar to the use of a limited number of output patterns or the use of one particular word shape. Like these other strategies, it increases redundancy and therefore makes production more manageable. Presumably, it is easier to produce a word that has two similar or identical consonants, vowels, or syllables than to produce one containing two or three different consonants, vowels, or syllables. For instance, [gɑg] or [dɑd] for *dog* should be easier to produce than [dɔg]. Similarly, [mɑmɑ] should be easier than [mɑmi]. The use of assimilation or harmony allows children to produce two- or three-syllable words without producing a sequence of consonants and vowels that differ. See Vihman (1978) for a report on the extent and function of consonant harmony in phonological acquisition. Also, see Leonard, Miller, and Brown (1980) for a study of the function of consonant assimilation (and reduplication) in the speech of language disordered children.

Reduplication

Reduplication (discussed by Ingram, 1974b, and Schwartz, Leonard, Wilcox & Folger, 1980, among others), fits in well with the strategies that have just been discussed. As mentioned above, Drachman (1973a) included syllable harmony among his long-domain processes. Reduplication (or syllable harmony) results in two syllables being either more alike or identical. In *complete reduplication*, one syllable (usually the stressed syllable) of a word is produced as a CV and is repeated. For instance, Waterson's (1970) son said [pupu] for *pudding*. Similarly, a child may say [bɑbɑ] for *blanket* or *bottle* and [wɑwɑ] for *water*. In *partial reduplication*, the first CV is repeated, but with a change in the vowel or consonant (Ingram, 1981, p. 25). For example, a child may say [bɑbi] for *blanket* or *bottle* or [wɑwi] for *water* or [pudu] for *pudding*. By reduplicating, the child is able to produce two syllables without producing two completely different CV sequences (Ingram, 1974b). In other words, reduplication may be used to constrain or limit the structure of multisyllabic words. To illustrate, Leslie, a child discussed by Ferguson (1979a, p. 15) had the following strategy: "Select for production a two-syllable word ending in -i and make it a reduplicative CVCV," as in [gɑgɑ] for *doggie*.

Moskowitz (1973) claimed that reduplication is universal, but Ferguson (1979b) argued that it varies from child to child. It has been said that some children are reduplicators, while others are not.

Schwartz, Leonard, Wilcox and Folger (1980) investigated the role of reduplication in phonological acquisition. Both reduplicators (children whose speech sample consisted of at least 20% fully and or partially reduplicated forms) and nonreduplicators were studied. When attempting nonreduplicated multisyllabic adult words, the reduplicators failed to produce nonreduplicated multisyllabic forms. They also produced final consonants less frequently than the nonreduplicators. The authors concluded that some children appear to adopt a reduplication strategy in order to cope with the production of multisyllabic words, as suggested by Ingram (1974b) and, to a smaller extent, to constrain the production of final consonants.

In another study concerned with the role of reduplication in phonological acquisition, Fee and Ingram (1982) concluded that reduplication is not a "unique alternative" for specific children, but is rather a "general feature" available to children in their earliest attempts at multisyllabic productions. See Leonard et al. (1980) for a study on the role of both syllable and consonant harmony in the speech of language-disordered children.

Metathesis/Migration

As pointed out previously, metathesis, which involves the reversal of two sounds, and migration, in which one sound is moved to another position in the word, are processes that have been proposed as strategies. Greenlee (1974) cited them as "cluster-avoiding strategies." For instance, a child may avoid producing the /bl/ cluster of *blue* by metathesizing the /l/ and /u/ as in [bul] or a child may avoid the /sn/ cluster of *snow* by moving the fricative into final position where it should be easier to produce, as in [nos].

Metathesis was also cited as a strategy by Vihman (1976), as previously mentioned. Vihman noted that her daughter Virve metathesized the vowels in *isa* "father" and *ema* "mother" (in Estonian) so that the words would obey her output constraint, which required the first vowel of a word to be more open than the second vowel. Thus she produced these words as [asi] and [ami], respectively. Metathesis is also discussed by Drachman (1973a) and Menn (1978).

Unique Reduction Devices

Unique reduction devices (Ferguson, 1978a, p. 293), which also are called "dummy syllables" (e.g., Kiparsky & Menn, 1977, p. 59) have been mentioned by several researchers, including Menn, 1972, Smith, 1973, Vihman, 1978, 1981, and Ferguson, 1978a, 1979a. If a child consistently uses a particular vowel or CV combination to represent an unstressed syllable of a two- or three-syllable word, this is called a unique reduction device or URD. According to Ferguson (1978a, p. 293), URD's allow children to cope with complex words. (However, it should be noted that Ferguson uses the term with a somewhat broader meaning, encompassing some of the examples that we discussed earlier under limited output patterns.) Like some of the other strategies discussed above, the use of a URD allows a child to maintain the correct syllable structure of a word without producing all of the segments in that word. To illustrate, for a time, Smith's (1973, p. 172) son "A" used the syllable [ri] or [ri:] to represent initial unstressed syllables. So, he produced [ri:tǽk] for *attack*, [ri:dzɔ̄ɪ] for *enjoy*, etc. Similarly, Stephen Menn (Menn, 1972) used [tɨ] as a dummy syllable, producing, for instance [tɨbɛ́t] for *barrette* and [tɨdǽf] for *giraffe*. Some children use just a schwa vowel ([ə]) to represent initial unstressed syllables, as in [əzɝ́t] for *dessert*. Virve (Vihman, 1981, p. 256) at 1;8 and 1;9 generalized the sounds of one of the unstressed syllables of several three-syllable Estonian words, as in [tázizi] for *tágasi* "go/put back" and [má:nunu] for *ráamatut* "book" (objective).[28]

Vowel Lengthening

Drachman (1973b) noted that children may lengthen the vowel before an underlying (adult) word-final voiced obstruent, thereby maintaining the contrast between voiced and voiceless obstruents in final position while devoicing the voiced cognate. For instance, as mentioned earlier, Joan Velten (Velten, 1943) differentiated words on the basis of vowel length alone at one stage, as in [bu·t] for *bead*, vs. [but] for *beat*. Ingram (1975) also mentions this phenomenon in his article on the avoidance of homonymy.

Syllabic Fricatives

One of the strategies proposed by Farwell (1977) in her study of fricative acquisition in seven young children was the use of syllabic fricatives. This strategy involves the production of fricative words as elongated fricatives without accompanying vowels, as in [ʃ:] for *shoe* or *sheep*. This phenomenon was also mentioned by Leopold (1947) in his diary study of his daughter Hildegard, although it was not called a strategy. According to Farwell, the use of syllabic fricatives allowed one of her subjects to begin producing fricative words such as *sheep*, *shoe*, *chicken*, and *juice*. Only later did she learn to produce these words with vowels.

Favorite Sounds

The use of favorite sounds is another strategy proposed by Farwell (1977). It involves the extensive use of one particular sound or a few familiar sounds that the child has mastered. For example, one of Farwell's subjects seemed to be "focusing on" mid to back fricatives and affricates. Farwell (1977, p. 100) notes that the child seemed to enjoy saying words containing these sounds and that she played with different ways of saying them. The extensive use of one sound or class of sounds has also been noted by other child phonologists. For instance, Hildegard Leopold (Leopold, 1947) seemed to prefer the voiced bilabial stop [b] at one stage, and Menn (1971) noted that her subject Jacob preferred velars. Jonathan Braine (Braine, 1971), who produced monosyllabic words with front consonants as dV, could be said to have [d] as a favorite sound. However, as noted earlier, Ferguson (1979a, p. 15) calls this an example of an early phonotactic strategy: "Select for production a monosyllable with a front consonant, . . . and produce d̠V," where V is the vowel (of the set /a, i, o, u/) that is most similar to the vowel in the adult model. Ferguson (1979a) reports that at the age of 1;11 Karlyn Geis used [ç] (a voiceless palatal fricative) in place of word-final /t, d, n, p, f/ after a high vowel to "show the shortness of syllables." This is another example of the overuse of one particular sound, although perhaps for a somewhat different reason.[29]

The use of sound preferences by phonologically disordered children has been mentioned by several researchers, including Edwards and Bernhardt (1973a), Ingram (1976), and Hodson (1980). These preferences are discussed in much more detail by Weiner (1981) and Edwards (1980b). For example, Edwards (1980b) discusses 14 phonologically disordered children, each of whom neutralized many adult contrasts to one particular sound, such as /g, j, d, k, l, h/, etc. Weiner (1981) discusses eight unintelligible children who exhibited what he calls a "sound preference process."

Rule Ordering

Rule ordering has been proposed (by Kiparsky & Menn, 1977, p. 73) as a strategy that allows children to represent adult contrasts in spite of their "limited phonetic resources." If two rules are put into "nonfeeding" order, so that the output of one rule cannot undergo the other, then contrasts can be preserved, although they are altered (see Appendix B). To illustrate, if the rules (a) tʃ→ʃ and (b) ʃ→s are in a feeding relationship, so that the output of (a) feeds into (b), then both adult /tʃ/ and /ʃ/ end up as [s] (tʃ→ʃ→s). That is, the contrasts are reduced. However, if the rules are put into nonfeeding order (b, a), then adult /ʃ/ is produced as [s], and adult /tʃ/ is produced as [ʃ]. The output of (a) cannot undergo rule (b) because (b) applies first. The adult contrast between /tʃ/ and /ʃ/ is therefore preserved, but it is realized as a contrast between [ʃ] and [s]. This is what Kiparsky and Menn (1977, p. 73) call a *displaced contrast*.[30] (In Stampe's [1972a] terms, an *antisequential constraint* has been imposed.)

Coalescence or Consolidation

Coalescence or consolidation involves the collapsing of several different forms into one output form. Menn (1976a) cites coalescence or consolidation as a strategy by which children invent rules to limit their output. For instance, her subject Jacob at first produced both *tape* and *tea* with either an [eī] or an [i] vowel. Later he used [ti] for both words. In Menn's view he had invented a rule eī→i. As noted previously, Vihman's son "R" (Vihman, 1981) at first produced four phonetically similar (Estonian) words (*lind*, *rind*, *king*, and *kinni*) somewhat differently. However, fairly soon he consolidated or collapsed all of these forms into the stable form [nən]. In this way, he was able to limit his variety of output patterns.

Summary

There has been a considerable amount of speculation about the role of strategies in phonological acquisition. Ingram (1974a, p. 234) pointed out that one big question concerns how strategies are related to each other and to a general theory of processes. In his view, several processes may conspire toward a strategy, such as avoidance of clusters or fronting. Some of the phonological processes that are typically included in discussions of phonological development (e.g., assimilation, metathesis, and reduplication) also have been discussed as strategies, as shown above. Other processes that could perhaps be called strategies because they make words more manageable include: weak syllable deletion, final consonant deletion, and glottal replacement.

Apparently, strategies may be realized as (or carried out by means of) rules or processes. For example, if a child has a fronting strategy (Ingram, 1974a), then metathesis may apply to the underlying form so that the consonants appear in the right order in the child's output form. Similarly, metathesis and migration may apply in the realization of a cluster-avoiding strategy (Greenlee, 1974). Absolute position constraints and relative position constraints also "motivate" rules, as argued by Menn (1978, p. 162). That is, many rules (or processes) satisfy output constraints.

Ingram (1974b, p. 49) suggests that identifying general rules that operate in phonological acquisition "can ultimately lead to more insightful information concerning separate strategies that individual children [may] follow."

In this view, individual rules (as opposed to common or general rules) "represent different strategies that children use" (Ingram, 1974b, p. 61). In the view of some child phonologists (e.g., Kiparsky & Menn, 1977, Menn 1976a), rules "capture" strategies. It also has been said that children use strategies to invent rules. Farwell (1977, p. 103) argues that children who use strategies to produce fricatives may "never learn [fricative] rules." However, Farwell herself points out that the relationship between strategies and phonological development is unclear. There remains a need for research on the relationship of strategies to rules and processes and to phonological development in general.

CONCLUSION

Although we do not yet have a complete account of how children learn to speak their language, a great deal of information has been gathered on this question. In this chapter we have reviewed only selected aspects of this growing literature. We have limited coverage to studies that have used perceptual phonetics. An increasing focus in the child phonology literature is on acoustic and physiological phonetic descriptions of children from birth through the several stages of phonological development. Undoubtedly, the decade of the 1980s will yield a rich data base of children's speech perception and speech production development. These data should promote continued theoretical proposals for how children learn to talk.

FOOTNOTES

[1]Although some linguists believe that the study of child language is very important, it has not had an important place in generative phonology. As Ferguson (1975b, p. 2) points out, *The Sound Pattern of English* (Chomsky & Halle, 1968) makes claims about phonological development but does not report results of empirical research and does not appear "to take the study of child phonology very seriously."

[2]However, Ingram (1978, p. 153) also gives several reasons for being cautious in attempting to use data from children to substantiate more general claims about phonology. One of his reasons is that translating theoretical claims into issues that can be tested in phonological development poses serious methodological problems.

³ Although this is a plausible explanation, more data are needed so as to separate the possible effects of final devoicing, a phonological process, from the effects of morphological learning.

⁴ Roman Jakobson's (1941/1968) theory of phonological acquisition will be discussed in more detail in a later section, along with other major theories of phonological development.

⁵ Voice onset time (VOT) refers to the difference in time (in milliseconds) between the release of an articulation and the onset of vocal fold vibration (voicing). If voicing starts 20 milliseconds before the release of the articulation, the sound is said to have a voicing lead or VOT of − 20 milliseconds. If voicing starts 20 milliseconds after the release, there is voicing lag or VOT of + 20 milliseconds (see Ladefoged, 1975, pp. 124-127).

⁶ The feature [grave], which is no longer widely used (and thus was not discussed earlier) is an acoustically defined feature that refers primarily to stops and fricatives. Labials and velars, which have more acoustic energy in the lower frequencies, are [+ grave], while alveolars, which have higher frequency energy are [− grave].

⁷ Following Chomsky (1965, p. 4). Crocker defines competence as the hypothesized "underlying system of rules that has been mastered by the speaker-hearer."

⁸ Phonological development, as defined by Crocker, involves the "emerging consistent usage of the feature-combinations as language units in the phonological system of the child" (1969, p. 205).

⁹ Some of the statements discussed could be questioned because Cairns and Williams apparently treated /f/ as a nonstrident phoneme, while in the feature system of Chomsky and Halle (1968), labiodentals are classified as [+ strident].

¹⁰ Crystal notes (p. 38) that when a short babbled utterance is produced with a language-specific prosodic feature, parents are likely to see this as an attempt at a meaningful utterance. These early productions thus tend to be focused on and interpreted by parents.

¹¹ Early productions that are wordlike (i.e., have stable prosodic and segmental shapes) and that are used consistently but do not resemble specific adult words have been called *proto-words* (Menn, 1976b), *phonetically consistent forms* (Dore, 1975; Dore, Franklin, Miller, & Ramer, 1976), and *vocables* (Ferguson, 1978a).

¹² Regarding the social function view, Crystal (1979, p. 40) notes that prosody may be considered (e.g., by Bruner, 1975) as "one means of signaling joint participation in an action sequence shared by a parent and child." Concerning attempts to describe the "pragmatic"

functions of utterances such as these, Crystal points out that we should be cautious about ascribing "intention" to a child when we have no empirical verification. It is safer to talk about what is conveyed than what is intended on the part of the child.

[13]He also cautions that prosody should not be used to "discover" semantics or grammar, as it is just one important factor.

[14]"Features" here refer to characteristics such a sibilance, stress, and lip rounding, not distinctive features.

[15]In this study, Smith assumes that the child's underlying form on which the rules operate is basically equivalent to the adult surface form.

[16]The term phonotactic rule is used by Menn (1971) to mean phonological rule in Ingram's sense.

[17]These are now generally discussed as phonological processes, rather than rules. In fact, Ingram is one of the researchers who does not make a clear and consistent differentiation between the two terms.

[18]It is not clear why Ingram chooses to do this without attempting to show that children actually perceive such words differently.

[19]It will be remembered, however, that Edwards (1973), closely following Stampe's model, broke down these substitutions even further into their constituent steps, finding the natural processes that would account for them.

[20]The notion of "conspiracies" (as in Kisseberth, 1970) is discussed elsewhere in this book. Rules that have a similar function may be said to conspire to produce (or prevent) a particular output.

[21]The opposition between complete closure (a stop) and partial closure (a fricative) is seen as less basic than the opposition between complete closure (a stop) and complete opening (a vowel). Thus the phonemic opposition between stops and fricatives is a relatively late one.

[22]There are exceptions, however. For example, Joan Velten (Velten, 1943) learned /s/ before /d/.

[23]As pointed out earlier, whether /s/ is considered to be an early or late acquisition depends in part on how one defines acquired (Ingram, 1978). If we require phonetically correct production, then [s] is likely to be a late acquisition, but phonemically, /s/ may be acquired quite early, though it may not be produced accurately.

[24]Homonyms are words that are transcribed the same but have different meanings.

[25]It is questionable whether constraints should be discussed as strategies. (In Branigan's [1976] view, constraints supplement strategies.) However, certain constraints are included here in keeping with the way they are discussed by various child phonologists.

[26]This example could also be put under limited output patterns. In fact, several of the examples discussed in this section on strategies could easily be discussed under more than one general heading, as noted earlier.

[27]It should be noted that this type of assimilation, which involves the modification of one element to become more like another, is not the same phenomenon as the assimilation discussed by Vihman (1976); the latter is said to be a cognitive tool.

[28]These last examples are very similar to those discussed by Drachman (1973a) under syllable harmony.

[29]Schourup (1974, reported in Ferguson, 1979a, p. 12) calls this the "segmentalization of a strategy" to block final vowel length, i.e., to indicate the shortness of a closed syllable.

[30]It should be pointed out that Drachman (1973b) does not view examples such as ʃ→s, tʃ→ʃ as evidence for rule ordering. He suggests (1973b, p. 155) that most, if not all, such cases will prove to be "cases of strategic nonhomologous articulation"—cases not of rule ordering, but "the circumvention of rule ordering."

7

Developmental Phonological Disorders

The study of developmental phonological disorders is motivated by the goal of helping children whose speech is a handicap. Most of the approaches to phonological analysis that we will review have involved American English speaking children, although excellent literatures in articulation disorders exist in other countries. The format will be similar to that used in the previous chapter. We will review in turn, selected studies that base phonological analyses on differing units; segments, features, suprasegmentals, and phonological rules and processes.

Segment-Based Phonological Studies

The Articulation Test Approach

Most studies of the speech of individuals with articulation disorders have focused on the question: What sound segments (particularly consonants) are "correct"? If sounds are not produced correctly, are they omitted, distorted,

or replaced by other sounds? Most articulation tests (e.g., the *Photo Articulation Test*, the *Templin-Darley Tests of Articulation Competence*,
the *Arizona Articulation Proficiency Scale*, the *Goldman-Fristoe Test of
Articulation*, and others) follow this format. Individuals are generally
asked to name pictures designed to elicit each consonant sound in each
word-position in which it occurs in the language, in addition to selected
consonant clusters. Each consonant sound is typically tested once in each
possible position, as in *pig*, *zipper*, and *cup*, which might be used to elicit
initial, medial, and final /p/, respectively. The child's performance is
then compared to age norms that indicate the age at which each sound is
produced correctly by a certain percentage (usually 75%) of children
tested. Such tests frequently are used as a basis for deciding if a child
does or does not need articulation therapy. If a child performs considerably below his or her peers, the conclusion is likely to be that
therapy is needed.

Information about the types of errors that are made, (i.e., omissions,
distortions, or substitutions) may not play a part in the decision regarding the need for therapy. However, this information may be used in
deciding if the articulation problem is mild, moderate or severe.
Although views differ, omission errors are usually considered to be most
severe, followed by substitution errors. Distortions are said to be least
severe because they involve the production of a sound that is close to the
target sound. (This ignores the fact that distortions are sometimes very
unusual sounds that may call attention to a person's speech.)

Using developmental data, along with information about *stimulability*
(i.e., can the person produce the problem sounds with stimulation) and
frequency of the error sounds, the speech pathologist decides which
sounds to work on first in therapy. Error patterns are not necessarily
analyzed in this type of approach. To illustrate, even if it is observed that
a child replaces fricatives with stops, this information might not be used
in therapy in a traditional approach. Rather, an "early" and "visible"
fricative, such as /f/ would probably be trained, first in isolation, then in
nonsense CV, VC, and CVC syllables, then in real words, and eventually
in connected speech. When /f/ was produced with a certain percentage
of accuracy, another sound, such as /s/ might be chosen for remediation. The emphasis is generally on phonetic production (regardless of the
error pattern), and sounds are remediated one (or two) at a time, with
therapy focusing first on isolated sounds, and ending up with sounds in
sentences and spontaneous conversation.

An example of a segment-based study of the speech of a child with a
functional articulation disorder is provided by Cross (1950). The study

by Cross is discussed by Lorentz (1976, p. 31), who says that it is "insightful," though not "explicit or complete."

Very few studies of articulation disorders have analyzed the child's phonemic system as a separate entity apart from the adult system, as would be done if Jakobson's (1941/1968) model were followed closely. Let us look at three reports of this type. We begin with Haas' (1963) paper, which appeared just before generative phonology became popular.

Haas (1963)

Haas was one of the first researchers to suggest that speech pathologists could make use of linguistics. In an article titled "Phonological Analysis of a Case of Dyslalia" (1963), Haas reports an attempt to examine children's "defective speech" from the viewpoint of structuralist phonology or "functional phonetics." After a discussion of what functional phonetics has to offer concerning the organization and classification of speech sounds, Haas describes the application of the principles of functional phonetics to a particular case.

Haas presents his analysis of the speech of K.C., a 6½-year-old boy with a severe functional articulation disorder. The analysis was derived from a very short sample (about 2 minutes) of connected speech that was elicited by means of a series of pictures. K.C.'s idiolect is first analyzed from a phonological (structuralist) point of view. That is, the child is seen as having "a language of his own" (1963, p. 240). Then Haas relates K.C.'s productions to standard English, using the techniques of "comparative linguistics."

The phonological analysis of K.C.'s idiolect reveals that, although his diphthongs also tend to be incorrect, most of his errors involve consonants. Haas notes that some of the "distinctive articulatory features" of standard English (concerning place, manner, and voicing) are not present in K.C.'s system. For instance, the voiced/voiceless distinction is not maintained. Rather, voiced and voiceless sounds appear to be in "free variation" (p. 242). To illustrate, K.C. has [ti:n] for *green*, but [dʊd] for *good*. Instead of having six places of articulation, K.C. has three, which Haas calls bilabial, lingual, and glottal. Glottal, which is not distinctive for K.C., occurs either as a conditioned variant of the other two stop positions (as in [oʔm̩] for *opened*) or as a strong vocalic onset, as in [ʔɒp] for *up*. K.C. is said to have four obstruction features: plosive, sibilant, liquid, and nasal. However, instead of distinguishing the various fricatives, he has one sibilant that has a wide range of (phonetic) variation.

K.C.'s consonantal system consists of the following phonemes (p. 242): (1) a labial plosive [p], with a glottal variant [ʔ]; (2) a lingual plosive [ḍ(b)] ~ [t] with a glottal variant;[1] (3) a glottal plosive [ʔ]; (4) a lingual sibilant [θ] ~ [ʃ] ~ [s(ẕ)]; (5) a labial or lingual liquid or semivowel [w] ~ [ɭ ˮ]; (6) a labial nasal [m] and (7) a lingual nasal [n].

In comparing K.C.'s consonant system with that of standard English, Haas makes the following statements (1963, pp. 243–244): (a) K.C.'s [p] generally corresponds to English /p/ (except when it alternates with a glottal stop). (b) K.C.'s "lingual plosive" appears to correspond to other plosives (besides /p/) and to /f/. (/b/ varies with [d, ḍ], as in *bigger*, which appears both as [ḍiḍʌ] and as [biḍə].) (c) K.C.'s sibilant corresponds to standard English voiceless lingual fricatives ([θ, s, ʃ, ẕ]) and sometimes sounds like a combination of these fricatives. (d) K.C.'s labialized liquid corresponds to standard English /v, w, l/ (and probably also to /r/), as in [téḷɪn] for *Kevin*. (English /w/ may also correspond to K.C.'s [m], as in [mɪḍ] for *with* or may be omitted.) (e) English /m/ is usually represented by [m] in K.C.'s speech, as in [tāɪm] for *time*, and [méni] for *many*, although it is not always distinguished from /n/. (f) /ŋ/ may be represented simply as "final nasalization" (transcribed as ˜) in K.C.'s speech and may not be differentiated from final /n/. (g) Initial /h/ is absent, although it is sometimes represented by [ʔ], as in [ʔɪm] for *him* and [ʔāōh] for *hole*.

Regarding phonotactics, Haas notes that only one cluster (an incorrect one) is produced in the sample, and he hypothesizes that this absence of clusters might account in part for K.C.'s unintelligibility. K.C. also has a tendency to omit final consonants, as in [ḍɪ] for *big*, or to replace them with breath, as in *hole* above (with [h] representing the final breathiness).

Haas points out that a thorough analysis of K.C.'s speech would have to be based on a larger sample, but he shows that even a sample as small as the one used here allows him to make some predictions, and it also suggests other areas that need to be investigated further. His main purpose in this paper is simply to illustrate certain analysis and comparison techniques that he believes may be useful to speech therapists.

Concerning therapy, Haas (1963, p. 244) states that what has to be taught are "discriminations" among sounds rather than sounds themselves. That is, the child has to be taught to make distinctions that he or she is not making. To formulate an appropriate sequence of steps, it is necessary to take into account both the importance of various phonological distinctions in English, and the difficulty of the distinctions for the child. For K.C., Haas recommends (p. 245) extending the range of distinctive places of articulation, introducing nonlingual fricatives (to contrast with stops), and introducing a voicing distinction. Haas outlines six quite general steps that might be followed to achieve these goals. For instance, the first step involves teaching K.C. to discriminate /t/ vs. /k/ (as he already has a /p/ – /t/ distinction). Only much later, in step five, would the voicing distinction be worked on. Pairs of words with voiced vs. voiceless plosives would be used to train this distinction, e.g., *bear/pear, goat/coat.* Haas hypothesizes that successful completion of the steps would greatly improve K.C.'s intelligibility.

Finally, Haas (1963, p. 246) argues that speech therapy would be more efficient if it paid closer attention to the interfering idiolect of the child whose speech is to be treated. In his view, linguistic analysis and comparison can help the therapist determine what to teach and in what sequence for each individual case (just as linguistic analysis and comparison can help the foreign language teacher). In other words, linguistics can make an important contribution in the area of diagnosis and assessment.

Weber (1970)

Weber (1970) studied 18 children between 5 and 10 years of age who had moderate to severe articulation disorders. His goal was to discover "patterns of deviant articulation" that would lead to recommendations for therapy. Using concepts from linguistics, Weber derived phoneme classes and allophones for each subject. He then made up an individual auditory discrimination test for each child to test the sounds that were incorrectly produced. Using his transcriptions, along with the phonemic analyses and the results of the auditory discrimination testing, Weber compiled a description of each child's "phonologic principles" (p. 136).

According to Weber (1970, p. 137), "patterning of articulation" refers to the "the general principles or rules which seem to underlie deviant articulation." When the members of a certain category of phonemes are found to exhibit something in common, a "phonologic pattern" is said to occur.

Each subject was found to exhibit at least one "deviant articulatory pattern," and most subjects exhibited two or three such patterns. However, no two subjects had exactly the same patterns. If real patterns did not occur for a subject, Weber used generalizations (e.g., "a major auditory discrimination problem") to describe that child's phonologic behavior. Examples of Weber's patterns and generalizations include: "stops used for fricatives," "forwarding of place of articulation within the categories of stops, fricatives, and resonants," and "nasals and resonants often palatalized" (p. 138).

Each subject's patterns are listed separately. To illustrate, subject Q is said to have no expressive manner contrasts between semivowels and resonants. This child's manner of articulation for fricatives was also inconsistent, with stops being used for fricatives, and affricates for fricatives (and vice versa). Sometimes the place of articulation for fricatives, stops and nasals was fronted, but [g] was also used for /d/ and [ʒ] for /z/ (Weber, 1970, p. 139).

The patterns and generalizations discovered for the children in this study were used in planning therapy. For instance, for one child, M, therapy centered on establishing more complete manner contrasts, e.g., between stops and fricatives and between stops and semivowels. This child was first taught to discriminate the relevant contrasts auditorily (e.g., [t] vs. [s] and [t] vs. [w]) and then to produce them.

Weber (1970, p. 140) points out two important differences between traditional speech therapy techniques and his "patterning" approach. First, in his approach, entire patterns are worked on because all sounds in the relevant category are involved. That is, the focus is on patterns rather than individual sounds. Second, contrasting features are paired at all stages of therapy, e.g., the child is taught to contrast stops vs. fricatives.

Grunwell (1975)

Grunwell provides a set of "simple" procedures that she says should be useful in analyzing the speech of children with articulation disorders and in planning remediation, and in most of these procedures, sound segments are basic. In Grunwell's view (1975, p. 34), any analysis of an articulation disorder should answer the following questions:

(1) What kinds of articulations are used?

(2) How are they distributed?

(3) How do the child's phonetic and phonological systems compare with those of the adult language?

Following Cruttenden (1972), Grunwell assumes that the child is using a "reduced version" of the adult phonological system. This view leads to "contrastive analysis," which she considers to be very important in investigating severe articulation disorders. As Grunwell considers a severe articulation disorder to be "a language problem manifested only at the phonological level" (p. 34), she believes that techniques of phonological analysis are appropriate to investigate such disorders.

In this paper, Grunwell (1975) suggests analytical techniques that should answer the three questions posed above. First of all, the clinician has to discover the child's phonetic inventory. Next, the phonetic data can be analyzed further in terms of traditional articulatory features (e.g., regarding place and manner of articulation). This gives information about the range of contrasts available in the manner category and the number used at each point of articulation. A table can be constructed from these data that shows where phonetic contrasts are missing or are "overly abundant" (p. 36). This allows the clinician to infer an "articulatory setting" (Honikman, 1964), such as the predominance of palatals and the absence of fricatives. Therapy can then be aimed at changing the non-English "setting," for example, by focusing on front sounds and on fricative production (Grunwell, 1975, p. 37).

By formulating a table showing how each phonetic element is distributed, it is possible to see any gaps in the occurrence of sounds in different word-positions. For instance, there may be a lack of stops in final position. What comes next in Grunwell's analysis is what she calls a "comparative analysis," which shows how each adult phoneme is realized phonetically in each word-position. To illustrate, for the child discussed by Grunwell, adult /θ/ was realized as [ʃ~tʃ] in initial position, and as [k] in final position. Model-and-replica contrastive analysis charts (Ferguson, 1968) can be formulated to show which adult phonemic distinctions are maintained by the child and to show the variant forms of the child's contrasts. Such charts indicate the areas on which therapy should focus to "build up" the child's phonemic contrasts.

Next, Grunwell discusses a "phonology of substitution," which she says is based on generative phonology; however, she notes (p. 38) that this type of analysis may not be useful in all cases. This "process" part of her analysis procedure will be discussed later under processes and rules.

Feature-Based
Phonological Studies

During the late 1960s and early 1970s, many reported analyses of phonological disorders had features as their basic element.

Menyuk (1968)

In her 1968 article titled "The Role of Distinctive Features in Children's Acquisition of Phonology," Menyuk discussed both normally developing and articulation disordered children, as noted earlier, and she investigated just six distinctive features (from Jakobson et al., 1963): [grave], [diffuse], [strident], [nasal], [continuant], [voice].

To obtain data on children with articulation problems, Menyuk transcribed the consonant substitutions made by children in spontaneous production of sentences, as well as the results of the Templin-Darley articulation test (Templin and Darley, 1960). In order to investigate the role of distinctive features in children's consonant substitutions, she analyzed all substitutions in terms of which features were maintained. For instance, in a substitution of [t] for /θ/, all features under investigation are maintained except the [+continuant] feature. (/θ/ is [+continuant], but [t] is [−continuant].)

Menyuk found that the children in the articulation disordered group maintained the feature [±strident] least often, while the normally developing children maintained the [±strident] feature most often in their consonant productions after [±voice] and [±nasal]. Both normally developing and disordered children tended to maintain [±voice] and [±nasal] most often. The feature [±grave] was maintained more often by the articulation disordered children than by those developing normally. The rank order of feature maintenance in consonant substitutions for the articulation disordered group is shown below (p. 142):

Rank Order	Children with Articulation Problems
1	nasal
2	voice
3	grave
4	continuant
5	diffuse
6	strident

The children with articulation problems were reported to maintain all features significantly less in their substitutions than normally developing children, except for the [±nasal] feature, and the difference between the two groups was not as great for the [±grave] feature.

Whereas the normally developing children in this study generally failed to maintain only a single feature in their consonant substitutions, the children with articulation disorders often failed to maintain several features at once. For instance, a child with an articulation disorder might substitute [d] for /k/, changing both the [+grave] feature and the

[– voice] feature. Menyuk (1968, p. 145) hypothesizes that there may be differences in basic memory capacity to acquire the phonology of a language—memory for various features that distinguish speech sounds and memory for their use in phonological rules.

McReynolds and Huston (1971)

McReynolds and Huston analyzed, from a distinctive feature viewpoint, the articulation errors (substitutions only) of 10 children between the ages of 4;4 and 6;5 who were said to have "severe functional articulation problems." They used features proposed by Jakobson et al. (1952) and Chomsky and Halle (1968). The data utilized in this study consisted of phonetic transcriptions of responses to McDonald's Deep Test of Articulation (1964). In addition to analyzing the children's misarticulations from a traditional (phoneme) view, they compared each child's feature system with that of standard adult English.

McReynolds and Huston found that the feature errors of these 10 children were consistent across most phonemes containing the features in question. For instance, if a child had difficulty with the [+ strident] feature in one phoneme, that feature was also likely to be problematic in other phonemes containing it.

The authors found two patterns of feature errors in their study. In the first, one or more features are completely lacking from a child's repertoire. For example, for five of their subjects, the [+ strident] feature was completely lacking, and for one, the [+ continuant] feature was also lacking. In the view of McReynolds and Huston, the children in this group exhibit at least some errors involving the "motor production of features" (p. 163).

In the second pattern of feature errors, all features are present in the child's repertoire, but they are sometimes used inappropriately in particular contexts or combinations. These children are said to have inappropriate phonemic rules, or rules for feature usage that are unlike the phonological rules of English. To illustrate, one child in this study had both the [+] and the [–] aspects of the [voice] feature but he changed [+ voice] phonemes to [– voice] in the releasing position of words, and he changed [– voice] phonemes to [+ voice] in the arresting position.

McReynolds and Huston (1971, p. 165) hypothesize that distinctive feature analysis may provide a more efficient approach to articulation therapy by "decreasing the number of articulatory responses to be trained," and by providing a "basic unit" to train (i.e., features). They also note that efficiency will be increased if it can be shown that training on just one feature will decrease errors on several phonemes containing that feature. The authors make the following recommendations regarding therapy: If a feature is completely lacking from a child's repertoire, start at a basic level and attempt to establish that feature. However, if all features are present in the child's repertoire, the focus should be on training the child to use the features appropriately in various contexts.

Singh and Frank (1972)

According to Singh and Frank (1972), the development of the phonological system of a language is the development of a set of distinctive features in both speech perception and production. A child's phonological system grows from a few distinctive features to the number in the adult language. In a chart, Singh and Frank (1972, p. 210) show the presumed developmental sequence of distinctive features, following Jakobson's principle of maximal contrast and preceding from simple to highly differentiated. For instance, the first consonantal distinction is "oral" ([p]) vs. "nasal" ([m]).[2]

Singh and Frank analyze, from a feature viewpoint, the consonant substitution errors of 90 children "with consonant articulation problems" not due to a hearing deficit or organic problem. The children ranged in age from 3;4 years to 10 years, with a mean age of about 6 years. All children were given an articulation test to elicit all "true consonants" in three word positions (initial, medial, final). All errors were recorded as substitutions, omissions, or distortions, but only the substitution errors were analyzed.

Singh and Frank (1972, p. 212) present a table showing all the substitutions that occurred for each target phoneme and the number of times each occurred. For example, [t] replaced /θ/ 19 times and [t] replaced /s/ 33 times. The total number of times each target was replaced by any other sound also is listed, as is the total number of times each sound occurred as a substitute. To illustrate, /θ/ was replaced more than any other single sound (a total of 104 times) and [t] was the most frequent substitute across target sounds, occurring a total of 159 times (out of a total of 706 substitutes). All 16 of the target sounds in this study were replaced by other sounds at least a few times. (Labial stops were least often replaced.) However, not all of these phonemes appeared as substitutes for other sounds.

All the substitutions in this study are also restated in terms of features. A grid is given (p. 213) that has the substituting features on one axis and the replaced features on the other axis. It was found that most substitutes differed from the target sound by just one feature (as Menyuk, 1968, reported for her normally developing subjects). In other words, the substituting sound usually differed from the target only in place, manner, or voicing.

Singh and Frank also found that substitutions were usually "one-way on a given axis" (p. 212). For instance, regarding manner substitutes, stops replaced fricatives and nasals, but nasals and fricatives seldom appeared as substitutes. Out of a total of 311 manner replacements, 299 involved stops substituting for other sounds. In general, nasals and fricatives did not substitute for each other. In fact, fricatives never replaced nasals.

Regarding place substitutes, Singh and Frank found that a place feature was usually replaced by "the closest more fronted place feature" produced with the same manner (p. 214). For example, labial stops sometimes replaced alveolar stops and labial fricatives replaced interdental fricatives. One exception involved /f/, which was replaced by an alveolar stop twice as often as it was replaced by a labial stop. According to Singh and Frank, if a child does not yet have in his or her repertoire "the closest place feature" that would generally be used as a substitute, there is a change in manner, sometimes with an accompanying change in place. For example, /ʃ/ is usually replaced by [s], but if [s] is not available, the substitute is [t] (p. 215). Concerning voicing, Singh and Frank found that voiceless sounds are more likely to substitute for voiced than vice versa.

The principle underlying the substitution rules postulated by Singh and Frank is said to be a combination of "stability and similarity" (p. 216). Features that are acquired earlier are more "stable" and are more likely to replace less stable features. Relative stability (in terms of percentage of correct production) for features in their study is as follows: stop ⟩ nasal ⟩ voiceless ⟩ labial ⟩ voiced ⟩ alveolar ⟩ back ⟩ interdental.

Similarity is also important in that a phoneme tends to be replaced by a similar one, or one that shares most of its features. So, the rule (summarizing all earlier rules) that Singh and Frank (1972, p. 216) propose to account for the substitutions found in their study is the following: A phoneme is replaced by the most similar phoneme—the one that is closest and more fronted but is produced with the same manner of articulation. However, if this phoneme is not in the child's repertoire or is not used "with confidence," the change is to the most stable manner (stops) and the most stable place feature involving the same articulator. For example, /θ/ is generally replaced by [f] because [f] differs from /θ/ by just one feature, but if the child has no [f] available, the substitute is a stop produced at the alveolar region—the most stable place involving the same articulator (the tongue).

Singh and Frank (1972, p. 217) state that many of the children studied seem to have "a perfect phonemic system" but are simply not able to realize it in their production. Only 10 children in their study showed an "apparent lack of regularity" and thus could be said to have trouble with the underlying phonemic system.

Pollack and Rees (1972)

Pollack and Rees (1972) also discuss clinical applications of distinctive feature theory, that is, how distinctive features may be used in analyzing the speech of children with articulation disorders. Their goal is to show that distinctive features are useful "at every stage of the clinical management of a child with an articulatory disorder" (p. 452), i.e., in assessment, planning and conducting therapy, and evaluating progress in therapy.

Pollack and Rees argue that it is necessary to distinguish phonetic errors from phonemic errors. A child who has phonetic errors that result from structural anomalies may still have the adult phonological system while having "deviant" speech. In contrast, phonemic errors are said to be indicative of an inadequate or deviant phonological system. Thus in their view (p. 453), children with "functional" articulation disorders should be considered to have "a linguistic disorder of a phonological type" (cf. Grunwell, 1975). Such children have a regular and consistent rule system, but one that differs from the adult rule system. Therefore, the speech pathologist's task is to understand the rules that are operating for any given child.

Pollack and Rees give examples from two articulation disordered children who can be said to have phonemic errors. For both children, the features that are in error are part of their phonetic repertoire, but they are not incorporated appropriately. To illustrate, one child, aged 4 years, consistently produced a voiceless lateral fricative in place of /s/, but this same child used [s] consistently as a substitute for /f/, indicating that the phonetic production of [s] was not a problem, although [s] was not used correctly. Similarly, it is argued (p. 453) that good stimulability does not necessarily mean that the short-term prognosis for a child is good because stimulability may be indicative of a child's phonetic ability but not his or her "phonemic competence."

Pollack and Rees stress the importance of analyzing a child's errors before planning therapy, rather than just classifying them as substitutions, omissions, or distortions. As they point out, most articulation tests do not give importance to the types of errors a child makes, but simply consider the number of phonemes produced incorrectly. If substitution errors are analyzed into distinctive features, however, it is possible to discover which errors are most severe. For example, an error of [t] for /s/ violates two features ([+ continuant] and [+ strident]), while an error of [θ] for /s/ violates just one feature ([+ strident]). On an articulation test, each would be counted as one phoneme error. Moreover, subtle improvement, for instance from a [t] substitute for /s/ to a [θ] substitute, does not show up if only the number of phoneme errors is considered.

If errors are analyzed into distinctive features, it is said (p. 455) that this can aid the clinician in deciding whether speech therapy is necessary for a particular child at a particular time. For example, a child with a [θ] for /s/ substitute might not be recommended for therapy, while a child with [t] for /s/ might be considered for therapy. It is also argued that distinctive feature theory makes it possible to account, at least partially, for relative intelligibility. While intelligibility is not necessarily related to the number of phonemes produced incorrectly, it may be accounted for by a consideration of which features and how many features are in error, as well as which features and feature combinations are maintained.

To illustrate their approach, Pollack and Rees present their analysis of one articulation disordered child, BN, at three ages, 5;2, 5;8, and 6;3. The authors found BN's distinctive feature rules at each stage and compared them to the adult system. For instance, BN's [t] for /k/ substitution was accounted for by a rule changing:

$$
\begin{bmatrix} +\,\text{grave} \\ -\,\text{diffuse} \end{bmatrix} \quad \text{to} \quad \begin{bmatrix} -\,\text{grave} \\ +\,\text{diffuse} \end{bmatrix}
$$

They also compared his rules at each succeeding stage to see how they changed over time. For example, one rule postulated for the first test period (5;2) was:

$$
\begin{bmatrix} -\,\text{diffuse} \\ -\,\text{continuant} \end{bmatrix} \quad \rightarrow \quad \begin{bmatrix} +\,\text{diffuse} \\ +\,\text{continuant} \end{bmatrix}
$$

(as in tʃ→s and dʒ→z). By the time of the second test date, this rule had "split into two parts," with the position of the target sound in the test word being the important factor (p. 457). Similarly, by the time of the last test session (6;3), the first rule mentioned above was no longer operating. That is, BN had incorporated /k/ and /g/ into his phonemic system. Tables are given that summarize the distinctive feature rules (and corresponding sound omissions and substitutions) postulated for BN at each of the three periods investigated.

Pollack and Rees acknowledge that distinctive feature analysis of the type they describe takes more time than a traditional articulation test, but they argue (p. 461) that, at least for children who exhibit "clear substitutions or omissions" of sounds, this type of analysis has practical value because it leads to a greater understanding of the child's articulation problem as well as to more economical therapy.

Leonard (1973)

In his article titled "The Nature of Deviant Articulation," Leonard addressed the "delayed" vs. "deviant" issue from a distinctive feature viewpoint. He asked: Is the course of development of a child with articulation errors the same as for "normal" children but slower, or are there substantive differences? If it is not the same, how can we differentiate deviant phonological systems from normally developing systems?

The order of acquisition of distinctive features for consonants that Leonard assumes is basically equivalent to the order put forward by Menyuk (1968): [+nasal] ⟩ [−coronal] ⟩ [+voice] ⟩ [−anterior] ⟩ [+continuant] ⟩ [+strident]. Although he takes this to be the general order of development, Leonard (1973, p. 157) notes that when a feature is starting to emerge, it is not used in all appropriate speech sounds at once. For instance, the [−anterior] feature is relatively early in /k/, but not in /tʃ/. Crocker's (1969) model of phonological acquisition offers a possible explanation for this; according to this model, which was reviewed previously, children add or combine new features with sets of features that are already present, and some sets develop earlier than others. When substitutions occur, sounds are replaced by others that are represented by earlier feature sets.

According to Leonard, many children with articulatory problems appear to have "less mature" or "delayed" phonological systems. Like normally developing children, they tend to use substitutes that are only one or two features away from the target sounds. To illustrate, a child who has [d] for /ð/, [f] for /θ/, [b] for /v/, etc., may be following the normal developmental sequence, but perhaps more slowly. It is claimed (p. 158) that most of these children will probably acquire "standard usage" without therapy.

However, Leonard argues that some children with articulation problems apparently are not just using a less mature phonological system. Rather, they have their own phonological system with its own rules. These children may reach a certain "inadequate level," as noted by Menyuk (1972) and stay there for some time. Moreover, they may have unexpected errors that probably will not become standard without intervention. That is, their systems may be different, not just delayed. As pointed out by Menyuk (1968), children with deviant articulation tend to maintain some features significantly less often in their consonant substitutions, e.g., [+strident], [−anterior], and [+continuant]. McReynolds and Huston (1971) also reported that the [+strident] feature was missing in half of the children they studied. For instance, a child may be able to produce the later developing continuant /θ/, but not the earlier developing /f/, which is [+ strident]. This is an example of a "deviant distinctive feature rule," according to Leonard (p. 159). However, deviant rules also include cases in which a feature is not totally absent, but is used incorrectly.

Leonard argues that we must give "deviant speakers" first priority in scheduling therapy because they probably will not improve as they mature. Thus we need to find out more about "deviant" or nondevelopmental feature patterns that occur in children with articulation errors, and we also need to find out about the prevalence of such patterns.

In order to obtain information addressing these questions, Leonard analyzed, from a distinctive feature viewpoint, articulation test results from 200 children between the ages of 4 and 11 who were referred to a university clinic because of defective articulation. He found that about 70% of these children had "developmental" errors. However, he points out that this percentage may be misleading because children with more severe articulation problems may be treated earlier. In fact, the children in the 4- to 6-year-old group did have a higher percentage of deviant rules. The most frequent "deviant feature rules" found by Leonard for the 4-, 5-, and 6-year-olds are (p. 160):[3]

$$\begin{bmatrix} + \text{coronal} \\ + \text{strident} \end{bmatrix} \rightarrow \begin{Bmatrix} [-\text{strident}] \\ [\text{null}] \end{Bmatrix}$$

$$\begin{bmatrix} - \text{vocalic} \\ + \text{continuant} \end{bmatrix} \rightarrow \begin{Bmatrix} [-\text{continuant}] \\ [\text{null}] \end{Bmatrix}$$

$$\begin{bmatrix} + \text{strident} \end{bmatrix} \rightarrow \begin{Bmatrix} [-\text{strident}] \\ [\text{null}] \end{Bmatrix}$$

$$\begin{bmatrix} + \text{coronal} \\ + \text{continuant} \end{bmatrix} \rightarrow \begin{Bmatrix} [-\text{continuant}] \\ [\text{null}] \end{Bmatrix}$$

$$\begin{bmatrix} + \text{continuant} \end{bmatrix} \rightarrow \begin{Bmatrix} [-\text{continuant}] \\ [\text{null}] \end{Bmatrix}$$

These rules represent either the substitution of a feature (e.g., [+ strident] → [– strident]) or the omission of a sound containing a feature (e.g., [+ strident] → [null]). Leonard (1973, p. 160) also notes (following Menyuk, 1972) that deviant patterns may involve the inappropriate use of features, as in the use of [+ voice] for all [– voice] phonemes in releasing positions of syllables. Moreover, how features are used inappropriately may vary considerably among children. Thus Leonard argues that we need to carefully analyze the rules of children with deviant articulation, and he states that this can best be done through longitudinal studies.

More recent features-based studies of children with articulation disorders include those of Singh, Hayden, and Toombs (1981) and Toombs, Singh, and Hayden (1981).

Suprasegmental-Based Studies

There are few studies of articulation disorders that focus specifically on prosody or suprasegmentals. In fact, suprasegmentals are seldom mentioned in the clinical literature. (However, see Shelton, 1976.) Grunwell (1975) notes that her subject Philip, as well as other children she observed, had normal prosody and rhythm. That is, "they sounded as if they were speaking 'English' with a different sound system" (p. 34). However, some children with articulation disorders appear to have abnormal prosodic patterns and syllable-timed speech, as opposed to the stress-timed speech of normal adult English. Children with articulation disorders may also exhibit less variation in pitch and intensity than normally developing children (Shadden, Asp, Tonkovich, & Mason, 1980).

Shadden, Asp, Tonkovich, and Mason (1980)

Shadden, Asp, Tonkovich, and Mason (1980) investigated the imitation of suprasegmental patterns by 10 5-year-old children with normal articulatory development and 10 5-year-olds with inadequate articulation. All subjects were given the *Templin-Darley Test of Articulation* (1960) and the *Northwestern Syntax Screening Test* (Lee, 1971) as well as the *Test of Rhythm and Intonation Patterns* (TRIP), which assesses imitative suprasegmental skills (Koike, 1977, Koike & Asp, 1977).

The TRIP consists of 25 recorded test items made up of the syllable *ma* produced with varying rhythm and intonation patterns. The suprasegmental parameters that are tested include stress, intonation, tempo and/or number of syllables. A response is scored as correct if the suprasegmental aspect of the test item is imitated correctly on at least one of two presentations; the segments (/m/ plus /ɑ/) are not of concern.

Although the average TRIP scores were somewhat higher for the adequate articulation group, the difference in mean percentage correct between the two groups was not significant. In addition, the two groups were not found to perform differently on three TRIP subtests. Both groups scored highest on the rhythm subtest and lowest on the intonation subtest. On most test items, the group with inadequate articulation scored somewhat lower than the adequate articulation group. When the Templin-Darley scores were compared with the TRIP scores for each group, no significant correlations were found. The inadequate group exhibited more variability, however. The two groups did not differ significantly in their average scores on the *Northwestern Syntax Screening Test*, and significant correlations were not found between TRIP scores and scores on the NSST for either group.

Shadden et al. (1980) note that future research on the development of suprasegmentals is needed, partly because the performance of the inadequate group in this study may have been influenced by their enrollment in articulation therapy. Possibly techniques in articulation therapy (including use of exaggerated stress and intonation) may "indirectly influence suprasegmental skill development" (p. 398). It is suggested that future research compare children with adequate articulation to children with inadequate articulation who have had no previous therapy (as well as children who have been enrolled in therapy). The authors state that future research should also investigate the relationship between the perception, imitation, and spontaneous production of suprasegmentals, as the TRIP assesses only imitation. It is hypothesized (p. 399) that for children with inadequate articulation, improved suprasegmental skills might "facilitate segmental development" and might also serve to improve intelligibility and contribute to more natural sounding speech.

Phonological Rule- and Phonological Process- Based Studies

Many studies of functional articulation disorders that have been completed since 1970 have been based on either generative phonological rules or natural phonological processes. That is, they have been based on either Chomsky and Halle's (1968) theory of generative phonology or Stampe's (1969, 1972a) model of natural phonology. In keeping with the goals of this text, we have chosen to illustrate these approaches by reviewing only certain studies of historical interest. The following discussions demonstrate the clinical application of phonological principles reviewed in this text. Appendix D includes detailed descriptions of eight procedures for the phonological analysis of disordered speech.

Compton (1970, 1975, 1976)

Compton was apparently the first researcher to apply the principles of generative phonology to the analysis of articulation disorders. Compton (1970) formulated what he called "generative phonological rules" to describe the misarticulations of two boys, Jim and Tom, ages 4;6 and 6;0, who had "abnormal" articulation not due to hearing loss or physical anomalies. Compton's rules were derived from narrow phonetic transcriptions of the responses of these children to 100 pictures. First, Compton listed the substitutions, omissions, and distortions found for each phoneme. Then he attempted to organize the misarticulations to find the "underlying patterns." "Derivational rules" of the general form X → Y (e.g., r→ w) were constructed, and each rule was classified as obligatory (applying 100% of the time) or optional (applying only part of the time). These rules were organized into what Compton calls a "descriptive analysis" of the sound system of each child (p. 322), and the rules were then restated in distinctive feature notation. Compton considered only consonants in word-initial and word-final positions and did not try to generalize across positions. To illustrate, two rules formulated for Jim in initial position were m→φ, and n→φ. These substitutions rules were then combined into one rule using distinctive feature notation as follows:

$$
\begin{bmatrix} \text{nasal} + \\ \text{consonant} + \end{bmatrix} \longrightarrow \phi \quad \text{(optional)}
$$

To give another example, three of the phonological rules (actually substitution rules) formulated for Tom in initial position were tʃ→s (obligatory), dʒ→d (obligatory), and ʃ→s (optional). These three rules were later combined into one distinctive feature rule:[4]

$$
\begin{bmatrix} \text{place}_5 \\ \\ \text{voice} \pm \end{bmatrix} \longrightarrow \begin{bmatrix} \text{place}_4 \\ \text{voice } \alpha \\ \text{nasal} - \end{bmatrix} \quad \text{(obligatory)}
$$

Compton, who attempted to describe the entire phonological system of these two children rather than just selected rules, was one of the first to demonstrate that the defective sounds that characterize an articulation disorder are part of a "coherent" and "productive" system. In addition, he showed how diagnosis and therapy can take this into account.

Regarding therapy, Compton states that the elimination of any specific articulation error will be effected when the principle underlying the error is "revised, eliminated, or replaced." The correction of a misarticulation for any one sound in a class should result in the correction of the remaining members of the class (without specific training on them). He presents evidence to support this "generalization hypothesis" (p. 331).

Compton stresses that the first step is to determine what the child's system is, which has to be done separately for each child. He also notes that it is necessary to formulate a new analysis quite frequently, at least every few months, to monitor a child's progress. Compton concludes his early paper by arguing that clinicians should also act as researchers, formulating and testing hypotheses that are provided by the "systematic analysis" of the child's phonology.[5]

In later book chapters published in 1975 and 1976, Compton further explains his approach to phonological analysis and how it can be utilized in the diagnosis and treatment of articulation disorders. In his view, the purpose of phonological analysis is to characterize the "relational principles" that underlie a child's deviant productions. In other words, surface misarticulations are analyzed to discover the underlying regularities that should be the focus of therapy.

In his 1975 paper, Compton demonstrates his analysis procedures by presenting actual analyses of the speech of one 5-year-old child, Frank, at the initial evaluation and six re-evaluation periods. At each re-evaluation period, he shows the changes that have taken place in Frank's rule system. As in his earlier paper, Compton analyzes word-initial and word-final positions separately and does not consider medial position at all. For each optional rule, a percentage of application is given. Rules postulated for Frank (Compton, 1975, p. 70) include, in initial position:

$$[z] \rightarrow [s] \quad /\#\_\_ \quad \text{obligatory}$$

$$\begin{bmatrix} t \\ d \end{bmatrix} \rightarrow \begin{bmatrix} k \\ g \end{bmatrix} \quad /\#\_\_ \quad \text{optional 10\%}$$

$$[ʃ] \rightarrow [s] \quad /\#\_\_ \quad \text{optional 50\%}$$

The phonological principle underlying the second rule above is said to be that alveolar ($[place_4]$) stop consonants are replaced by velars ($[place_6]$);

all other features stay the same. The feature rule that captures this is (Compton, 1975, p. 71):

$$
\begin{bmatrix} \text{stop} + \\ \text{place}_4 \\ \text{voice} \pm \end{bmatrix} \longrightarrow \begin{bmatrix} \text{stop} + \\ \text{place}_6 \\ \text{voice } \alpha \end{bmatrix}
$$

Although he notes that all phonological rules should actually be specified in terms of features, Compton abbreviates all of Frank's rules, using traditional phonetic symbols. This is done to "simplify the presentation" (Compton, 1975, p. 72).

In his 1976 chapter, Compton talks more about therapy applications based on systematic phonological analysis. He argues (1976, p. 74) that the effects of therapy are maximized if specific "key sounds" are selected that will have the greatest influence on the child's system, and he also claims that there is more generalization from the voiced to the voiceless member of a cognate pair than vice versa. To illustrate his views, Compton follows the course of therapy for one 5-year-old child, Grace, showing how this child's phonological system evolved through the therapy period. Compton stresses that it is necessary to keep close track of the child's underlying principles, and he gives evidence of the "potentially sweeping results" that can be obtained if therapy is directed toward the principles underlying a child's misarticulations (p. 82). In his view, phonological analysis is a "map" to help choose the best route for therapy.

Compton also presents preliminary normative data from about 20 children, aged 5 to 6, with severe articulation problems, and he discusses their more common deviant phonological rules. Three of Compton's rules are given below, including their percentage of occurrence (pp. 89,90):

Initial Consonants:

$$
\begin{bmatrix} \text{stop} + \\ \text{fricative} - \\ \text{voice} - \end{bmatrix} \longrightarrow \begin{bmatrix} \text{stop} + \\ \text{fricative} - \\ \text{aspiration} - \end{bmatrix} = 65\%
$$

(i.e. initial stops are deaspirated)

$$
\begin{bmatrix} f \\ v \end{bmatrix} \longrightarrow \begin{bmatrix} p \\ b \end{bmatrix} = 25\%
$$

Initial Blends:

$$\begin{bmatrix} r \\ l \end{bmatrix} \longrightarrow \phi \;=\; 60\%$$

Compton notes (p. 92) that for the children that he studied, initial stops were seldom misarticulated (except for deaspiration and fronting of velars), and final consonants were more likely to be deleted than initial consonants. In addition, final stops were slightly more prone to deletion than final fricatives, and final voiced fricatives were deleted more than final voiceless fricatives. Compton states (p. 94) that the less common or idiosyncratic rules (which he calls "unique creations") affect intelligibility more and attract attention to a child's speech and he notes that the presence of such rules may be an important diagnostic sign for detecting potential phonological disorders. Examples include the substitution of [r] for /l/ and /w/ in /sl/ and /sw/ clusters and the use of [fw] for stop + liquid clusters.

Oller (1973)

Oller was one of the earliest researchers to show that there is more regularity in abnormal speech than often appears at first. Like Compton, he attempted to apply the principles of generative phonology in analyzing the sound substitutions of children with severe functional articulation disorders. However, his early (1973) analyses are more technical than Compton's, and his rules look more like actual generative phonological rules.

In his 1973 paper, Oller reports the conclusions from a study undertaken to determine the usefulness of applying the principles of generative phonology to the sound substitutions of five children with "delayed articulation." Oller gives evidence to show that, by using the conventions of generative phonology, it is possible to "capture generalizations" that could not be captured in more traditional treatments (p. 39).

In Oller's study, after speech samples were obtained, "substitution rules" were formulated to describe each child's sound errors, for instance dʒ → ʒ/#__ and tʃ → ʃ/#__. These rules were then formulated using distinctive feature notation, and related substitution rules (such as the two just listed) were combined. By following this procedure for all the substitution rules, Oller reduced the total number of rules needed from 223 to 76 and captured many "significant generalizations." For example, the generalization "affricates are replaced by the corresponding fricatives" can be drawn from the two substitution rules listed above.

Oller gives examples of the types of rules formulated and discusses several common rules, though not all. The rule written to capture the "general process" or sound change referred to above was (p. 38):

$$\begin{bmatrix} +\text{strident} \\ +\text{coronal} \end{bmatrix} \rightarrow [+\text{continuant}]/\# \underline{\hspace{1cm}}$$

Oller claims that this is a natural change that can be captured with just a few features. On the other hand, if a child had the following two rules tʃ→g/#__ and dʒ→m/#__, which do not look very different from the substitution rules given earlier, these rules could not be captured in one distinctive feature rule because they do not represent two natural and related changes. Using a generative phonological approach allows Oller to differentiate the pair of rules given earlier from the pair just discussed.

Oller gives several other examples, some of which are quite technical, to demonstrate the "collapsing" or "combining" of separate but related substitution rules. To illustrate, Oller formulates two separate distinctive feature rules in order to collapse the following five substitution rules:

$$\int \rightarrow t\int/\# \underline{\hspace{0.6cm}}$$

$$s \rightarrow t/\# \underline{\hspace{0.6cm}} \text{ optional}$$

$$s \rightarrow ts/\# \underline{\hspace{0.6cm}} \text{ optional}$$

$$\theta \rightarrow t/\# \underline{\hspace{0.6cm}}$$

$$\eth \rightarrow d/\# \underline{\hspace{0.6cm}}$$

These substitution rules, together, show that nonlabial fricatives become affricates or plosives. Oller's two distinctive feature rules are (p. 40):

$$\begin{bmatrix} -\text{vocalic} \\ +\text{coronal} \end{bmatrix} \longrightarrow [-\text{continuant}]/\#\underline{\quad}$$

$$\begin{bmatrix} -\text{vocalic} \\ +\text{coronal} \\ +\text{anterior} \end{bmatrix} \longrightarrow [-\text{strident}]/\#\underline{\quad}\text{ optional}$$

These rules are then combined, using the conventions of generative phonology. The final reformulation that Oller presents, in order to show the relatedness of these two rules is (p. 41):

$$\begin{bmatrix} -\text{vocalic} \\ +\text{coronal} \end{bmatrix} \longrightarrow \begin{bmatrix} -\text{continuant} \\ \langle -\text{strident} \rangle \end{bmatrix} \; /\#\underline{\quad} \; \begin{bmatrix} \overline{\langle +\text{anterior} \rangle} \end{bmatrix} \; \langle\text{optional}\rangle$$

What this rule says is that segments that are both [− vocalic] and [+ coronal], that is, coronal consonants (dentals, alveolars, and palatals) become [− continuant], i.e., become affricates. If the coronal consonant that is changed is also [+ anterior] (dental or alveolar, but not palatal), it may optionally become [− strident] as well. That is, it may become a true stop. This accounts for the fact that /s/ appears both as [ts] and as [t] for the child being discussed. (See Appendix A for a discussion of notational devices used in generative phonology.)

Although Oller formulates generative-type phonological rules, he is also influenced by Stampe's theory of natural phonology. However, he notes that it is not clear that Stampe's theory should be applicable to "abnormal" children. Nevertheless, he does make comparisons across the children in his study, pointing out processes that are similar for them and that are also similar to processes found in normal development. To illustrate, Oller reports that all five of his subjects exhibited cluster reduction processes (e.g., most /s/ plus stop clusters were reduced to the stop). In addition, all five subjects exhibited some fricative and/or affricate substitution processes. For instance, in the speech of one child, the voiceless fricatives /f, ʃ, θ/ were replaced by [h] in nonfinal positions.

Oller points out (1973, p. 44) that this same type of process also occurs in historical sound change (supporting Stampe's model), as in the change of Latin *facĕre* "to do, or to make" to Spanish *hacer*.

All five subjects also treated labiodental and/or interdental fricatives differently from other fricatives, and for most of the subjects, fricatives and affricates were treated differently in word-final position. (In two cases, fricatives appeared in final position first, as has been noted in normal development, e.g., by Ferguson, 1975a). Finally, all five children in this study had some sort of liquid change, which usually involved the liquid being replaced by a vowel-like sound (although one child had stops for liquids). These similarities caused Oller to conclude that the children in his study looked much like normal children at earlier ages. That is, they exhibited "delayed" phonological development.

Oller found it necessary, in some cases, to "order" rules. For instance, for one of his subjects, affricates were replaced by homorganic fricatives; but for this same child, fricatives were replaced by stops. So, for example, she had one rule (1) ʃ→t, but another rule (2) tʃ→ʃ. Oller claims that for this child these two rules have to apply in the order in which they are listed here (1, 2). Otherwise, the /ʃ/ produced by rule 2 would also undergo rule (1) and become [t], as adult /ʃ/ does.[6] This example shows that phonological rules cannot always be explained by what Oller (1973, p. 45) calls "peripheral motor constraints." If the child could not produce /ʃ/, and therefore replaced it with [t], how could [ʃ] occur as a replacement for /tʃ/? (Recall that Smith, 1973, refers to such examples as "puzzles.")

Although Oller does not discuss therapy in detail, he does point out that if, in therapy, a child eliminates an entire rule at once, this indicates that the rule is formulated correctly and that it captures a real generalization for the child.

Edwards and Bernhardt (1973a)

Edwards and Bernhardt (1973a) present phonological analyses of the speech of four language disordered children with low intelligibility. These children, who were under 6 years of age, were enrolled in a preschool language class at a clinic for children with severe language disorders.

Each child was tape-recorded individually two or three times over a 1-month period. Picture cards and objects were used to elicit all English consonant sounds in a variety of word positions. Following Stampe's (1969, 1972a) model, Edwards and Berhardt attempted to find the phonological processes underlying each child's substitutions, omissions, etc. Their analysis focused on obstruents and nasals, as liquids and glides were found to contribute little to the unintelligibility of these children. Several processes were exhibited by all four children, but the children often applied or limited these common processes differently. To illustrate, all four subjects exhibited two cluster reduction processes, /s/-loss and nasal cluster reduction. For "Matt," aged 3;3, any /s/ adjacent to an obstruent, liquid, or glide was deleted, as in [ɖɑəp] for *stop* and [wɛɪn] for *swing*. For "Jeanne," aged 4;4, an /s/ adjacent to a [– vocalic] segment usually was deleted. (This excludes liquids, which are [+ vocalic].) Thus she produced [pʊũ] for *spoon* and [wɪˀm] for *swim*. For "Billy", aged 3;3, and "Carolyn," aged 5;3 /s/-loss applied only to /s/ in word-initial position preceding a stop, as in Billy's [pʰʊⁿn] and Carolyn's [bⁱømˀ] for *spoon*.

Although all four children reduced nasal clusters, all applied this process somewhat differently. For Billy, a nasal was generally deleted before an oral stop. When Jeanne reduced nasal clusters, she usually deleted the nonnasal consonant. Her retention of nasals in clusters illustrates the fact that nasals were "prominent" sounds in her system (p. 23). For Matt, nasals were typically deleted preceding stops, especially voiceless stops. However, in some cases, the stop was deleted instead. For example, *candle* was produced both as [kǎdʌˀ] and as [ɖǎˀnʌ]. For Carolyn, the voicing of the obstruent was crucial in determining which element was lost (cf. Smith, 1973). In a cluster with a voiceless obstruent, the nasal was deleted, as in [pʰʌkʰ] for *pink*, but when a nasal preceded a voiced stop, the nasal was retained and the stop was deleted, as in [kɔ̌nɔʊ] for *candle* (p. 33).

Other processes that were shared by all four children were: stopping of fricatives and/or affricates, labial assimilation, labialization of obstruents in clusters, prevocalic voicing, final devoicing, and depalatalization. As noted for the cluster reduction processes, these processes were often limited differently by the four children in this study.

Additional processes were exhibited by just two children. These included: weakening of fricatives and glides, fronting of velars, loss of final segments, neutralization of labials, nasal intrusion (as in Jeanne's [wæ^ⁿt] for *red*), velar assimilation, nasal assimilation, and methathesis.

In addition to the processes that were shared by two or more children, there were also idiosyncratic processes. For instance, word initial /ʃ/ was optionally backed and stopped (and sometimes voiced) in Jeanne's speech, as in [g̃ĩũ] for *shoe*. Jeanne also exhibited a very limited substitution process replacing initial obstruents with nasals, as in [ʰnɪpʰ] for *crib*. (As mentioned earlier, nasals are said to be "important sounds" for Jeanne.) Carolyn labialized /θ/ in all positions and /v/ intervocalically. Initial /h/ was replaced by [s], as in [sǽnʊɛkˀ] for *hanger*. Word-final /s/ (including /s/ derived from adult /z, ʃ, ʒ, tʃ, dʒ/) was replaced by a "nasal snort," transcribed as [F̃]. Carolyn also exhibited very limited prevocalic devoicing. In addition, she had some alveolar assimilation and exhibited an unusual syllable structure change by which [ə] or even [wə] or [wɛ] was added to the end of a word, as in [ʃúwɛ] for *shoe* and [bɑᵘwə] for *ball*.

For Billy, word-final /θ/ was replaced by [s], and intervocalic obstruents were optionally replaced by a glottal stop, as in [kʰɔ́ʔʊɪ] for *coffee*. Occasionally, intervocalic voiced stops were weakened to fricatives, as in [mɑ̄ʊ̄vɛʔ] for *rabbit*. In addition, alveolar stops preceding /r/ were fricated, resulting in an [s] substitution, with loss of the liquid, as in [s̠ʌkʰ] for *truck*. Billy also produced [m] in place of initial /w/, including /w/ from adult /r/, as in the *rabbit* example.

For Matt, alveolars, including alveolars derived from adult palatals and velars, were dentalized. For example, he produced [t̪ǽ·ʊ] for *cow*, and [d̪ʊ·s] for *shoe*. The resulting dental stops were frequently produced with a fricated release, as in [t̪θɪ̪t̪θị̈] for *T.V.* Matt also neutralized all final fricatives to [s], or a palatalized variant.

In discussing the implications of their analysis, Edwards and Bernhardt note that most of the processes underlying their subjects' substitutions were "quite normal," in spite of the fact that these children exhibited low intelligibility. However, they also stress that the phonologies of these four children are "not entirely similar to those . . . [of] 'normal' children, even those who are much younger" (p. 48). They argue that children who exhibit "young" processes such as prevocalic voicing do so before they begin producing longer words. In contrast, these children, who have multisyllabic words, still exhibit prevocalic voicing. The authors (p. 48) state that there are other examples of this type which show that processes that are common in young children may coexist with characteristics that are typical of older children. For instance, Matt produced /l/ correctly and yet still exhibited velar fronting and prevocalic voicing. They claim that their subjects also differ from normally developing children in exhibiting a larger number of phonological processes and processes that are less consistent. These features are said to account for their low intelligibility. They hypothesize that if a child has 10 or 12 processes, including some optional or variable processes and one or two unusual processes, then that child's speech will be difficult to decode.

Edwards and Bernhardt note that Billy, who exhibited the smallest number of processes and no particularly unusual processes, was the easiest of their four subjects to understand. On the other hand, Matt, who carried fronting "to the extreme" and also labialized extensively, fricated dental stops, and neutralized final fricatives, was quite unintelligible. Jeanne was hard to understand partly because of her labialization, extra nasalization, and final consonant deletion. Carolyn is described as the least intelligible. Edwards and Bernhardt state (p. 49) that "her two idiosyncratic processes, one changing final /s/ to a nasal snort and one adding extra syllables, when combined with her 'normal' processes, simply put too much of a strain on the listener's ability to decode."

The authors argue for the importance of including articulation therapy in a language training program for children like the four described here and they make several suggestions regarding therapy. The first step, they say, is to decide what contributes most to the child's unintelligibility. This may be the child's least "normal" process (e.g., Carolyn's process replacing word-final /s/ with a nasal snort). In their opinion, it is necessary to "focus on the crucial process," training on the sound that is on the left of the arrow (p. 50). If there are two sounds on the left of the arrow, then both are trained at one time (i.e., in the same session). The important thing is that only one process is being trained, even though more than one sound is involved. For example, to eliminate Matt's velar fronting process, both /k/ and /g/ would be trained.

Another suggestion is to look for optional processes. For instance, Carolyn optionally fronts velars in final position, but they are sometimes produced correctly; so, training on final /k/ and /g/ should give immediate success. If no processes can be singled out as contributing most to the child's unintelligibility, and if there are no optional processes, "young" processes should be the focus of therapy. If a child exhibits several processes that are common only in early normal development, it is recommended that the clinician test the child's ability to discriminate phonemic contrasts in minimal pairs and to imitate individual sounds. The sounds that give the child the most success on these tasks should be considered first, and the clinician should focus on the early processes that change or eliminate these sounds in the child's spontaneous speech.

Lorentz (1974)

Lorentz (1974) reported on the "deviant phonological system" of a 4-year-old boy named David. Lorentz noted that David exhibited several regular phonological processes, including deletions, assimilations, simplifications, etc. that made his speech almost entirely unintelligible. Only vowels and nasals were usually produced in a normal way. The exact phonetic form of the other sounds was determined by the phonological environments in which they occurred.

In initial position, the voiced fricatives /v/ and /ð/ were realized as homorganic voiced stops ([b] and [d], respectively). For instance, David had [bɛri] for *very* and [dɛr] for *there*. This rule, which is very common in child phonology, is formalized by Lorentz (1974, p. 56) as follows:[7]

$$
\begin{bmatrix} + \text{fricative} \\ + \text{predental} \\ + \text{voice} \end{bmatrix} \longrightarrow [+ \text{stop}]/\#\underline{\hspace{1cm}}
$$

All other word–initial fricatives were replaced by a "relevant homorganic sonorant" (p. 56). The voiceless fricatives /f, θ/ were usually replaced by the glide [w], but in words such as *think* and *thing*, where /θ/ precedes a high front vowel, it was replaced by [l] in David's speech. So, *thumb* was [wʌm], but *thing* was [lɪŋ]. The fricatives /s, ʃ, ʒ/ were also systematically replaced by [l] in prevocalic position, as in [lɪŋ] for *sing*, [larp] for *sharp*, [tlɪn] for *chin*, and [dlɔ̄ɪ] for *joy*.[8]

In Lorentz' view, the fact that the voiced fricatives /v, ð/ did not become /l/, as did most other initial fricatives, suggests that the rule realizing /v/ and /ð/ as stops "was well established in David's phonology when the more general fricative ⟶ sonorant rule emerged" (1974, p. 56).

The following rules, as well as the one given above, were formulated by Lorentz to account for David's treatment of word-initial fricatives:

$$
(1) \ /\theta/ \longrightarrow [+ \text{postdental}]/\#\underline{\hspace{1cm}} \begin{bmatrix} \text{V} \\ + \text{high} \\ + \text{front} \end{bmatrix}
$$

This rule says that /θ/ is retracted to a postdental position when it precedes a high front vowel, as in *think*. In Lorentz' analysis, this rule must precede rule (2), below, which realizes postdental fricatives as [l] and predental voiceless fricatives as [w] after an optional initial consonant and before a syllabic nucleus (SN).[9]

(2)
$$
\left\{
\begin{array}{c}
\left[\begin{array}{c} +\text{fricative} \\ +\text{postdental} \end{array}\right] \longrightarrow \text{[l]} \\[2em]
\left[\begin{array}{c} +\text{fricative} \\ +\text{predental} \\ -\text{voice} \end{array}\right] \longrightarrow \text{[w]}
\end{array}
\right\} \Big/ \# \ (C) \ \underline{\quad\quad} \ SN
$$

The rule given earlier by which voiced predental fricatives are realized as the corresponding voiced stops is rule (3) for Lorentz. The fourth rule is the following (1974, p. 57):

$$(4) \ [+\text{fricative}] \longrightarrow \phi \, / \, \#\underline{\quad}C$$

This rule says simply that fricatives in word initial consonant clusters are deleted, as in [wɛn] for *friend*, [wiʰ] for *three*, and [nōū] for *snow*.

In David's speech, word-initial /y/ (or /j/) was replaced by [l], "falling together with" the postdental fricatives, as in [lu] for *you* and [lɛʰ] for *yes* (p. 57). This rule is stated as follows:

$$(5) \ /y/ \longrightarrow [l]/\# \ \underline{\quad}$$

Word-initial /r/, in contrast to /y/, was realized in various ways—as [r], as [w], as a sound between [r] and [w] (represented as [w/r]) and occasionally as [l]. There appear to be further restrictions on where each variant occurs, but because of the small number of examples, Lorentz does not make any general statements.

When /r/ and /w/ occur in initial clusters, they are usually realized as [l], and /l/ is always correct in initial clusters for David. So, for instance, we find [tlu] for *true*, [glōū] for *glow*, [tlɛl] for *twelve*, and [plēī] for *play*. Rule 6, which must apply after rule 4, captures the fact that all sonorants in this environment are neutralized to [l] (p. 57):

$$(6) \ [+\text{sonorant}] \longrightarrow [l]/\# \ \underline{\quad}$$

For David, fricatives and stops in final postconsonantal position were systematically deleted, as in [læm] for *lamp*, [tlɛl] for *twelve*, and [wat] for *watch*. This is captured in rule 7:

(7) C⟶ ɸ / C ___ #

After syllabic nuclei (SN), either word finally (___ #) or medially, David deleted voiced fricatives and realized voiceless fricatives as [ʰ], which actually represents a partial devoicing of the preceding vowel. (The only exception is that David deleted final /θ/.) So, we find [ɪʰ] for *if*, [lo͞uʰə] for *sofa*, [lə] for *love*, [dēιd] for *David*, [ti] for *teeth*, [nəʰɪŋ] for *nothing*, [bəɪŋ] for *buzzing*, [waʰ] for *wash*, and so forth. The rule formulated (p. 58) to capture this situation is rule 8.

(8)

$$
\left\{
\begin{array}{l}
\left[\begin{array}{l} +\text{fricative} \\ +\text{voice} \end{array}\right] \longrightarrow \phi \\[3em]
\left[\begin{array}{l} +\text{fricative} \\ -\text{voice} \end{array}\right] \longrightarrow [\text{h}]
\end{array}
\right\}
\Big/ \text{SN} \underline{\hspace{2em}} (\#)
$$

David exhibited more variation in his treatment of word final and medial stops between syllabic nuclei. Voiceless stops in these positions were generally reduced to glottal stops (when they were reduced at all), as in [hæʔi] for *happy* and [bæʔæt] for *back at*. When final and medial voiced stops between syllabic nuclei were reduced, they were completely deleted, as in [hæə] for *had a* and [bɪæn] for *big and* (compare [rāιdɪn] for *ride in*, and [tugeɹ] for *together*). Lorentz gives percentages that capture the variation for each stop in each of these positions (SN ___ # SN and SN ____ SN) and he notes (p. 59) that in both environments, voiced stops appear to be preserved better than voiceless stops.

When voiceless stops were reduced in word-final position before silence or before a word beginning with a consonant, they were reduced to a glottal stop, but when voiced stops were reduced in these positions they were completely deleted. Lorentz (1973, p. 60) notes that stops were reduced much less often by David in these environments. (That is, words were pronounced better in isolation or in phrase-final position than when they were within a phrase.) In addition, David usually assimilated velar stops to alveolar stops whenever both types of stops occurred in the same word, as in *duck* [dat] and *dog* [dad].

To summarize David's rendition of medial and final sounds: Voiceless consonants are generally reduced, and voiced consonants are generally deleted. In word initial environments, on the other hand, fricatives and sonorants are generally reduced to [l] or [w]. Lorentz sees these as the "major regularities" in David's "deviant phonological system" (1974, p. 60). However, a number of subregularities are also apparent. For instance, syllabic [l̩] is realized as a mid- or high-back vowel. Lorentz also notes that there are several interesting "morphological" (actually lexical) regularities. For example, [ʃ] is produced correctly in just one word, *she*, and *to see* is consistently produced with a phonetic [s], rather than [l]. This may reflect "the relative importance of certain vocabulary items" (1974, p. 61).

Lorentz ends his paper with several statements regarding the importance of the detailed study of deviant phonological systems (1974, pp. 61, 62). In a subsequent book chapter (Lorentz, 1976), Lorentz presents a detailed analysis of the deviant phonological system of a 4½-year-old boy named Joe. Lorentz makes considerable use of generative phonology formalisms (see Appendix A, Appendix B) particularly the notion of surface phonetic constraints (SPCs) (Shibatani, 1973) which he uses to account for general constraints on the child's phonetic output. He attempts to show that by using SPCs it is possible to pinpoint that aspect of a child's phonology that "initiates" the deviant development. See Gandour (1981) for a reanalysis of these data using a syllable-based model of generative phonology.

Grunwell (1975)

Grunwell (1975) outlines a set of procedures for use in analyzing the speech of children with articulation disorders and in planning remediation.[10] Her phonetic inventory analysis and contrastive analysis procedures already have been discussed in this book.

The last type of analysis that Grunwell (1975) describes, which is called a "phonology of substitutions," is said to be based on generative phonology and to be a simplification of the procedures described by Compton (1970). In Grunwell's view, stating the child's substitutions in terms of processes is valuable because "it emphasizes the confusion of normal contrasts," and it also suggests possible directions for therapy (pp. 39–40).

To give an example, one of the "processes" (for word-initial position) that Grunwell lists for her subject Philip is the following (p. 39):[11]

$$\begin{Bmatrix} /f/ \\ /\theta/ \end{Bmatrix} \rightarrow \begin{Bmatrix} [ʃ] \\ /ʃ/ \end{Bmatrix} \rightarrow \begin{Bmatrix} [tʃ] \\ /tʃ/ \end{Bmatrix} \rightarrow [j]$$

This is said to be a combination of three substitution rules:

(1) $\left\{\begin{array}{l}/f/\\/\theta/\end{array}\right\}$ ⟶ [ʃ], as in [ʃɪ] for *fish*

(2) $\left\{\begin{array}{l}/f/\\/\theta/\\/ʃ/\end{array}\right\}$ ⟶ [tʃ], as in [tʃɪʃ] for *fish*, [tʃɪ?] for *ship*, and [tʃʌm] for *thumb*, and

(3) $\left\{\begin{array}{l}/f/\\/ʃ/\end{array}\right\}$ ⟶ [j], as in [jɒk] for *fox*, and [jʊkə] for *sugar*.[12]

According to Grunwell, the "process" listed above indicates that anterior fricatives should be remediated first to "break the chain." This same recommendation was also derived from her phonetic analysis.

Ingram (1976)

Ingram (1976) provides a phonological analysis of the speech of a language-disordered child, Ethel, who was the subject of an early diary study (Hinckley, 1915). When first seen by Hinckley at the age of 5;6, Ethel had no spoken language. Hinckley began working with her in February of 1912, and speech samples were collected during March, April, and May as her speech developed. These samples are analyzed by Ingram.

During March and April, Ethel was found to be in the first 50 word stage. However, May marked the beginning of more rapid development. Thus Ingram examines data from March and April (Ethel I) separately from data for May (Ethel II). At each stage he discusses Ethel's perceptual, organizational, and production inventories, as well as her phonological processes. Only her processes are summarized here.

During the first stage, final consonant deletion was a prevalent process, affecting all final consonants. There were also a few cases of unstressed syllable deletion. Although there was no total reduplication, some partial reduplication occurred, as in [tudi] for *Susie*.[13] Nearly all clusters were reduced to the unmarked member, but *sweep* was produced as [nθwi]. According to Ingram, this may be an *advanced form*.[14]

Ethel optionally nasalized glides to [m], and the resulting nasal then caused assimilation of medial consonants, as in [mɛma] for *yellow*. Fricatives and affricates were typically replaced by stops, often with a change in place. In fact, alveolar stops replaced all fricatives, as in *four* [toə]. Alveolar stops were optionally "lisped" by Ethel, even when they replaced other sounds.

Ethel nearly always fronted velar stops to alveolars, and palatal affricates were also fronted (and stopped). Occasionally a glottal stop was used in place of intervocalic stops, as in [teʔʌ] for *table*. The liquid /l/ was usually replaced by [d], but it was sometimes modified further by nasal assimilation or glottal replacement.

In Ethel's speech, /r/ was generally glided, and the resulting /w/ was sometimes nasalized, as in *ruler* [muma]. The palatal glide /j/ was also replaced by /w/ and was then subject to the same processes affecting adult /w/, e.g., optional nasalization. Final syllabic liquids and nasals were vocalized, and unstressed final vowels were neutralized to [a].

To account for data at the second stage, Ingram revises Ethel's nasalization process to include cases in which a nasal onset is produced, as in [mbu] for *book*. It is assumed that nasalization occurs first, producing an optional nasal onset in words with initial consonants. Then a new process, ordered after nasalization, optionally deletes consonants following initial /m/, as in [mi] for *pig*.

At Ethel II, the process stopping /l/ was optional and final consonant deletion was optional for nasals and stops. There were a few examples of alveolar assimilation, as in *plate* [tet]. To account for the occurrence of medial [mt] sequences, as in *blanket* [bʌmptɛt], Ingram hypothesizes that Ethel had either an optional rule changing noninitial /n/ to [m] or a labial assimilation rule affecting nasals. Optional unstressed syllable deletion was still evident in some forms, but two-syllable words were usually attempted. Ethel's stopping rule had changed slightly at this stage so that [b] replaced /f/ and [d] replaced /dʒ/. Other fricatives were still replaced by [t].

In his conclusion, Ingram points out that linguistic analysis is an "active process." In his view, an analysis is "a hypothesis about what constitutes a real pattern in the child's speech" (Ingram, 1976, p. 75). Thus it should be revised as new insights are gained.

Dinnsen, Elbert, and Weismer (1979, 1980)

Most process-based studies of children with phonological disorders (as well as normally developing children) assume, whether or not this is stated explicitly, that the child's underlying form or lexical representation or mental representation on which processes operate is basically equivalent to the adult surface form, minus the predictable phonetic detail (as in Stampe, 1969, 1972a). In recent years, this view has been challenged, for example by Macken (1979), who claimed that some mispronunciations must be due to perceptual problems, resulting in the "storing" of incorrect forms.

Dinnsen, Elbert, and Weismer (1979, 1980) have argued that researchers should not assume that phonologically disordered children have adult surface forms as their underlying representations. Rather, this has to be established for each individual child. They discuss several types of evidence that may be used to determine the nature of a child's underlying forms, but they focus on *morphophonemic alternations*. In their 1979 paper, they discuss two children who, in most process analyses, would be said to exhibit a process of final consonant deletion. For one of the children, Matthew, final consonants never showed up, even when morphological endings were added. So, for example, he produced [dɔ] for *dog* and [dɑi] for *doggie*. For Jamie, however, final consonants did show up when endings were added. Thus he had alternations between [dɔ:] and [dɔgi], [dʌ] and [dʌki], etc. In the view of Dinnsen et al. (1979), Jamie would be said to have adult-like underlying forms, along with a final consonant deletion process. Matthew, in contrast, would be said to have a phonotactic constraint disallowing postvocalic obstruents at both the underlying level and at the phonetic level. His underlying forms would not have final consonants and he would not be said to exhibit a process of final consonant deletion.

Maxwell's (1979) paper, reviewed next, provides a detailed illustration of the view taken by Dinnsen et al. (1979, 1980).

Maxwell (1979)

In a 1979 article, Maxwell presents two detailed analyses of the phonological system of a 7½-year-old girl with a "functional speech disorder." In the substitution analysis (Analysis B), it is assumed that the child's underlying forms are basically equivalent to the adult surface forms, while in the other analysis (A), the child's underlying forms are said to be much less abstract; surface forms are taken as basic in the absence of alternations.

Maxwell's subject lacked morpheme internal obstruent clusters and also lacked the segments [s, z, θ, ð], as well as the alternations involving these segments. For example, she had [pāɪdə] for *spider*, [tɔə] for *store*, [næpɪn] for *napkin*, and [æfə] for *after*. Maxwell (1979, p. 182) claims that, as these morphemes never show consonantal alternations, there is no evidence for a deletion rule. Moreover, it is not possible to predict which obstruent will appear. Thus, in Maxwell's view, the only possible correct generalization is one referring to syllable structure, which is a surface-level concept: In one-syllable morphemes (such as *store*), the second obstruent of the sequence occurs, but in two-syllable morphemes (such as *napkin*), the most anterior obstruent appears (p. 182). In Analysis A, Maxwell takes the surface form of these morphemes to be basic and accounts for her subject's production by a morpheme structure condition that prohibits morphemes from containing obstruent clusters. (This has to be a statement about underlying structures because phonetic sequences of obstruents do occur across morpheme boundaries.)

For Maxwell's subject, [t, d] occur in place of /s, z/ before vowels and glides and in final position, as in [to] for *sew* and [tʃid] for *cheese*. Before stops (as in *spider*), /s, z/ are absent. The stops used in place of /s, z/ are, according to Maxwell (1979, p. 183), "perceptually . . . and apparently acoustically identical" to [t, d] (corresponding to adult [t, d]). Because [s, z] never occur for this speaker, words such as *sew* and *cheese* are said to have underlying dental (alveolar) stops.

Although these stops are phonetically identical to [t, d], Maxwell claims that they are not phonologically identical because they have a different effect on the cluster reduction rule. This cluster reduction rule is obligatory when the focus is a /t, d/ corresponding to adult [t, d], as in [dʒʌmp] for *jumped*, but when the input is a /t, d/ corresponding to adult [s, z], the rule is optional as in [tipɔb] ~ [tiptɔb] for "teepsob" (a nonsense word). This rule, which deletes dentals after labial and velar obstruents, (i.e., noncoronals) is stated as follows (p. 184):

$$
\begin{bmatrix} +\text{coronal} \\ +\text{anterior} \end{bmatrix} \longrightarrow \phi \ / \begin{bmatrix} -\text{coronal} \\ -\text{sonorant} \end{bmatrix} \underline{\hspace{2cm}}
$$

(A surface redundancy rule states that all anterior coronal consonants are stops; therefore it is not necessary to specify noncontinuancy in the input of this rule.)

As the two types of dental (i.e., alveolar) stops behave differently in the same environment (e.g., in clusters following noncoronals) they cannot be identical on the underlying level. However, there is no strong evidence, according to Maxwell (p. 185), for positing underlying fricatives for the dentals that correspond to adult [s, z]. Instead, Maxwell attaches an abstract diacritic feature ([+S]) to the /t, d/ corresponding to adult [s, z] (cf. Harris, 1969). This is said to allow for the difference in rule application and also to indicate that the child is making the same kinds of distinctions that are made in the adult language by phonetic features (p. 186).

The cluster reduction rule is therefore modified so that [+S] is added to the feature specifications of the input for the optional part of the rule, but not for the obligatory part. Maxwell refers to the principle of *Proper Inclusion Precedence* (Koutsoudas, Sanders, & Noll, 1974) to sequence the parts of this rule so that the more specific case (optional deletion) will apply before the more general case (obligatory deletion).

There is also an optional rule of final dental deletion or glottalization that affects both kinds of /t, d/ phonemes. Examples include [bʌ] for *but*, [gɔʔ] for *got*, and [hoəʔ] for *horse*.

Next, Maxwell presents evidence to show that there is need for two more dental phonemes that alternate with [f, v], as in [tuf] for *tooth* and [tutpɛɪt] for *toothpaste*. These dental stops are diacritically marked with [+ θ]. The final spirantization rule that accounts for these alternations is (p. 188):

$$[+\theta] \longrightarrow \begin{bmatrix} +\text{continuant} \\ -\text{coronal} \\ +\text{strident} \end{bmatrix} \ / \underline{\qquad} \# \ (\text{obligatory})$$

(As all diacritically marked phonemes are redundantly [– continuant], [+ coronal], and [+ anterior], only [+ θ] needs to be specified in the input.)

The fact that /t, d/θ never undergo final deletion or glottalization is explained by the principle of Proper Inclusion Precedence, which is said to be an "independently motivated principle of rule application" (p. 188). Final spirantization, which is the including rule or the more special case, takes precedence over final deletion or glottalization, the more general case.

Maxwell (1979, p. 189) rejects the view that children who misarticulate perceive the same cues or interpret them in the same way as do normal speakers. Because little is presently known about perception, Maxwell argues that her subject's underlying forms should be based on what she produces rather than what she hears. Nevertheless, Maxwell next presents her "substitution analysis" (B), which is based on the traditional assumption that misarticulating children have underlying representations that are identical to the adult surface forms (cf. Compton, 1976; Lorentz, 1976). In this type of analysis, the child's underlying forms are abstract in comparison with his or her produced forms and it is necessary to have rules which account for segments that never exhibit alternations (cf. Dinnsen et al., 1979, 1980).

Maxwell (1979, p. 190) notes that it is not possible to choose positively between the two analyses because of our lack of knowledge about perception. However, she attempts to show that Analysis A is preferable because it captures generalizations that are missed by Analysis B.

Analysis B assumes that the child has the phonemes /s, z, θ, ð/ (and also /l, r/). First, there is a cluster reduction rule that accounts for the deletion of the first of two adjacent consonants in a single one-syllable morpheme, as in [tɔə] for *store*. In its final formulation, this rule is stated as follows (p. 192):

$$[-\text{sonorant}] \longrightarrow \phi \;/\; + \;\$X \underline{\hspace{1cm}} \left\{ \begin{array}{c} [-\text{sonorant}] \\[1.5em] \begin{bmatrix} +\text{nasal} \\ +\text{consonantal} \end{bmatrix} \end{array} \right\} \quad Y\$\; +$$

Condition: X and Y do not include morpheme (+) or syllable ($) boundaries.

This rule says that an obstruent ([– sonorant]) is deleted preceding another obstruent or nasal in the same morpheme (tautomorphemically) and in the same syllable (tautosyllabically). The variables X and Y represent any other (irrelevant) segments.

An additional rule is needed to account for the deletion of the least anterior of two adjacent consonants when there is an intervening syllable boundary ($), as in [næpɪn] for *napkin*. This rule accounts for the deletion of a dental in the neighborhood of a labial in another syllable and for the deletion of a velar in the neighborhood of a dental or labial in another syllable.

Maxwell uses the mirror image device (%) and the angled bracket notation (⟨ ⟩) in her final formulation of this rule for least anterior deletion (p. 193):

$$\begin{bmatrix} -\text{sonorant} \\ \langle +\text{anterior} \rangle \end{bmatrix} \longrightarrow \phi \;\% \; + \; X \underline{\hspace{1cm}} \$ \begin{bmatrix} -\text{sonorant} \\ +\text{anterior} \\ \langle -\text{coronal} \rangle \end{bmatrix} \quad Y \; +$$

Condition: X and Y do not include morpheme boundaries.

Use of the mirror image device (%) allows Maxwell to show that the least anterior consonant is always deleted whether it precedes or follows the other consonant. This device and the angled bracket notation make it possible to collapse several rules (see Appendix A for relevant discussion of notational devices in generative phonology).

The rules for cluster reduction across morpheme boundaries (heteromorphemically) are similar to those in Analysis A except that they require more feature specifications (p. 193):

$$
\begin{bmatrix} - \text{continuant} \\ + \text{coronal} \\ + \text{anterior} \end{bmatrix} \longrightarrow \phi \Bigg/ \begin{bmatrix} - \text{sonorant} \\ - \text{coronal} \end{bmatrix} \quad + \underline{\hspace{2cm}} \quad \text{(obligatory)}
$$

This says that /t, d/ are deleted after labial and velar obstruents across morpheme (+) boundaries.

The rule deleting /s/ and /z/ after nondental obstruents across morpheme boundaries is (p. 194):

$$
\begin{bmatrix} + \text{anterior} \\ + \text{coronal} \\ + \text{continuant} \\ + \text{strident} \end{bmatrix} \longrightarrow \phi \Bigg/ \begin{bmatrix} - \text{sonorant} \\ - \text{coronal} \end{bmatrix} \quad + \underline{\hspace{2cm}} \quad \text{(optional)}
$$

Maxwell next presents the rules necessary to convert the child's underlying adult-like phonemes into their surface forms. For instance, /θ, ð/ conversion (p. 195) states that /θ, ð/ become labiodental fricatives before nonsyllabic sonorants and in final position and become dental (alveolar) stops elsewhere. This rule is necessarily complex because it derives two sets of surface forms from abstract underlying forms (/θ, ð/) that never occur phonetically:

$$
\begin{bmatrix} - \text{sonorant} \\ + \text{continuant} \\ - \text{anterior} \\ - \text{strident} \end{bmatrix} \longrightarrow \begin{cases} \begin{bmatrix} - \text{coronal} \\ + \text{strident} \end{bmatrix} \Big/ \underline{\hspace{1.5cm}} \begin{bmatrix} - \text{syllabic} \\ + \text{sonorant} \end{bmatrix} \\ [- \text{continuant}] \quad / \quad \text{elsewhere} \end{cases} \quad \text{(obligatory)}
$$

This rule must precede the optional glottalization or final dental deletion rule because /θ, ð/ are never deleted or replaced by glottal stops in word-final position.

There is another similarly complex rule of /r/ conversion that changes underlying /r/ to a vowel in word-final position and to a glide elsewhere (p. 197). As this rule potentially produces alternations (e.g., between [ə] and [w]), Maxwell argues that it has to be viewed as a phonological rule rather than a morpheme structure rule. Thus, it has to follow the morphophonological rules (i.e., the rules for morpheme internal cluster reduction), because these rules take precedence over strictly phonological rules (Walsh, 1977).

An additional rule of lateral gliding accounts for the fact that /l/ becomes a glide obligatorily after consonants and optionally after vowels. As this is strictly a phonological rule, it also must follow the morphophonological rules. Finally, there is an obligatory rule that converts underlying /s, z/ to stops.

Both analyses (A and B) are said to provide adequate accounts of this child's phonology. Thus Maxwell compares the two analyses in order to decide which is more adequate and expresses more generalizations.

Regarding the absence of morpheme internal consonant clusters, Maxwell (p. 201) concludes that Analysis A, which contains just one morpheme structure statement, "appears to generalize more concisely about the facts." The substitution analysis (B) needs more than one rule to capture this same generalization. Other problems with Analysis B include the fact that it has nonexistent alternations and that it necessitates specifying syllable structure at the abstract level.

The rules of Analysis A are said to be simpler than those of Analysis B with regard to the differential rule application corresponding to /t, d/ and /s, z/. For instance, in Analysis B, the feature [+continuant] is needed to replace the diacritic specification used in Analysis A. Analysis B also has to include the [+strident] feature to exclude /θ, ð/ from the input of the rule reducing clusters across morpheme boundaries. Additionally, a morpheme boundary apparently has to be included in the environment of the rules for heteromorphemic cluster reduction, thus increasing their complexity.

Analysis A is also said to be preferred in its handling of the alternation of [t, d] with [f, v]. In Analysis B, the glottalization or final deletion rule has to be ordered after the /θ, ð/ conversion rule to keep /θ,ð/ from being deleted in final position, but in Analysis A, this is handled by the universal principle of Proper Inclusion Precedence. In addition, the /θ, ð/ conversion rule of Analysis B is much more complex than the corresponding part of Analysis A because it derives surface forms from underlying forms that never occur phonetically.

Regarding the surface realization of liquids as [w] or [ə], Analysis A is again preferred because it states the facts in a more "general" and "concise" form, and the "unmotivated abstraction" of the substitution analysis does not occur (p. 203).

Analysis A is also preferred by Maxwell in its handling of the surface realization of /s, z/ as [t, d]. Where Analysis A has a redundancy rule stating that all dentals are stops, Analysis B requires a rule converting /s, z/ to [t, d]. This rule has to include the rule of Analysis A in addition to other specifications.

Maxwell (1979, p. 204) concludes that Analysis A is less complex and has more empirical support. It is preferable because it has fewer and more general rules, as well as fewer specifications and conditions. The rules and conditions of Analysis A are also said to be "independently motivated."

In Maxwell's view (p. 205), the results of this study are crucial if it is assumed that different therapy approaches will be of value depending on whether or not the child has "normal" underlying forms. According to Dinnsen, Elbert, and Weismer, children whose underlying forms are unlike those of the adult language have different therapy needs from those of children whose underlying representations are normal. For example, they might benefit from training on phoneme contrasts (Dinnsen et al., 1980).

Leonard, Miller, and Brown (1980)

Leonard, Miller, and Brown (1980) investigated the function of two "harmony" processes, consonant assimilation and reduplication, in the speech of eight children with language disorders. In assimilation (which may be progressive or regressive and contiguous or noncontiguous) one consonant is influenced by another and becomes more similar to it, as in [bop] for *boat* and [kok] for *coat*. In reduplication, two syllables are produced that are identical (full reduplication) or nearly identical (partial reduplication), as in [wɔwɔ] for *water* or [tɪtɪ] for *chicken*. Both of these processes have been observed in the speech of language disordered children, as well as normally developing children.

It has been claimed that these processes may serve important functions for normally developing children. For instance, Vihman (1978), in her cross-linguistic study, concluded that consonant assimilation may provide a source of substitutions for difficult sounds and may reduce the overall complexity of words (Leonard et al., 1980, p. 337). According to Ingram (1976), reduplication may compensate for a child's inability to produce nonreduplicated multisyllabic words. (See also Schwartz & Folger, 1977.) Leonard et al. (1980) sought to determine whether similar functions are served for children with language disorders.

The subjects in this study were eight male language disordered children between the ages of 3;8 and 4;10. None had received sound production training. A spontaneous language sample of at least 100 utterances was obtained from each subject. In addition to familiar toys and objects, special stimuli were used to elicit a variety of consonants, clusters, and syllable types. These spontaneous samples were analyzed for the occurrence of consonant assimilation and reduplication.

Twenty-five instances of consonant assimilation were observed, and 19 of the assimilated words contained target consonants (or clusters) that were never used by the child. There were also 24 words in which assimilation did not apply, even though they contained "assimilatory contexts." Nineteen of these contained consonants or clusters that were produced in other words. These results indicate that target consonants or clusters that underwent assimilation were usually not present in the "productive repertoires" of the children (Leonard, Miller, & Brown, 1980, p. 341). In contrast, target consonants and clusters that did not undergo assimilation were usually produced elsewhere. Another finding was that the assimilated sound was often an apical consonant. However, apicals in a large number of assimilatory contexts did not undergo assimilation, indicating that the presence of an apical consonant in an assimilatory context did not necessarily trigger assimilation (p. 341).

Concerning the results for reduplication (Leonard et al., 1980, p. 341), all of the words (30) that were reduplicated had multisyllabic targets, even though most attempted words had monosyllabic targets. Moreover, children who did not produce any nonreduplicated multisyllabic words exhibited more reduplication than children who produced some nonreduplicated multisyllabic words. For the two children who produced both reduplicated and (a few) nonreduplicated forms, the reduplicated syllables replaced consonants that did not appear elsewhere in their speech. The two children who did not exhibit any reduplication produced a total of nine nonreduplicated multisyllabic words.

The results of this study suggest that assimilation allowed the children to use words containing difficult target consonants without actually producing those consonants. This is similar to the hypothesis made by Vihman (1978) for normally developing children (Leonard et al., 1980, p. 343). Reduplication was found to be more frequent in the speech of children who produced few or no nonreduplicated multisyllabic words; therefore, it may have allowed them to produce multisyllabics. The results also indicate that reduplication may allow children to produce multisyllabic words containing difficult consonants (by enabling them to avoid the syllable containing the difficult sound). These findings, together with those of Vihman (1978), "suggest that consonant and syllable factors may . . . interact" (p. 343). That is, syllabic factors may motivate consonant assimilation, and consonant factors may motivate syllable harmony.

The authors draw several implications for therapy. For example, if a new lexical item is being taught that has a nonreduplicated multisyllabic form, the clinican might expect (and accept) reduplicated productions at the beginning. If therapy is directed toward giving the child a larger number of intelligible words, the clinician should choose words that are not likely to undergo reduplication or assimilation—for instance, words containing no difficult sounds or multisyllabic words that are already reduplicated. In sound production training, consonants should first be taught in words that are not likely to undergo assimilation. According to the authors (1980, p. 344), knowledge of the "functions of processes" may lead to therapy that requires more advanced planning but that is more effective and efficient.

Schwartz, Leonard, Folger, and Wilcox (1980)

Phonological processes were just one part of a study reported by Schwartz, Leonard, Folger, and Wilcox (1980). Schwartz et al. compared the phonological behavior of language disordered children with that of "normal" children at a comparable stage of language development. The subjects were three linguistically normal children between 1;7 and 1;9 and three language disordered children between 2;7 and 3;7. MLU's ranged from 1.01 to 1.40 for the normal subjects and from 1.01 to 1.31 for the language disordered subjects. The subjects in the two groups were matched on sex, MLU, and level of "sensorimotor intelligence" (p. 360).

All subjects were audio- and video-taped for two to four 90-minute sessions in an experimental playroom. Several tests were administered and spontaneous language samples were obtained. At each session, the experimenters presented a standard set of toys, books, and situations in order to provide all of the subjects with comparable stimuli. For each child, a total of at least 100 nonimitative utterances was obtained.

The following aspects of phonological development were analyzed in this study: (1) *selection constraints*, inferred from the consonants and syllable structures of the attempted adult words, (2) *production constraints*, derived from analyzing the consonants and syllable structures of the forms produced by each child, (3) *phonological processes* involving assimilation, syllable structure, and consonant substitutions, (4) *phonological variability*, examined from three perspectives: (a) analyses of word-initial phone classes (as described by Ferguson & Farwell, 1975)[15] (b) optional processes, and (c) variability in the production of lexical items.

The phonologies of the two groups of children in this study were found to be very similar. The selection constraints were nearly the same for each group. There were minor differences in the syllable structures of the adult words attempted, but for both groups, CVC was the most commonly attempted. There were also minor differences in the phonetic characteristics of the adult words that were produced by the two groups. For example, one language disordered child did not try any adult words containing word-initial nasal consonants. However, the similarities between the two groups "far outweighed the differences" (Schwartz et al., 1980, p. 366).

The two groups of subjects also exhibited "substantial similarities" regarding production constraints, although there were again some slight differences, for instance, in the number of children for whom certain types of syllable shapes were "productive" (Schwartz et al., 1980, p. 367). There were few differences between the two groups in the consonants that were produced in each position. Differences were greatest for intervocalic and postvocalic sounds. For example, the normal subjects produced a greater variety of stops in intervocalic position, while the language disordered children produced a greater variety of consonants in postvocalic position. Some of these differences may be related to the fact that the normally developing children exhibited more reduplication. (Reduplication results in the production of intervocalic but not word-final consonants.) The authors note that the differences observed between the two groups regarding production constraints may be indicative of individual variation rather than group differences, and they emphasize that there were more similarities than differences.

Concerning phonological processes, there were again more similarities than differences. In fact, the processes that were productive for the two groups were identical except that deaspiration, which was not productive for any of the language disordered children, was productive for two of the normal children.[16] The most frequent process for two of the normally developing children and for all three of the language disordered children was final consonant deletion. Differences in process application between the two groups include (Schwartz et al., 1980, p. 369): the number of children for whom certain processes (e.g., stopping) were productive, and the frequency of occurrence of particular processes (e.g., reduplication). The authors again note that differences between the two groups may indicate individual variation more than group differences.

Regarding phonological variability, Schwartz and his associates found no real differences between the two groups. There were no observable differences concerning word-initial phone classes. The two groups were also found to have "similar frequencies of optional processes" (p. 372). Finally, there were no differences concerning variable forms of words.

In their discussion, Schwartz et al. (1980) claim that the differences betweeen language disordered children and linguistically normal children that have been reported in the literature (e.g., by Ingram, 1976) do not show up when subjects are matched for linguistic development. For instance, they did not find that their language disordered subjects exhibited a larger number of processes than the normal subjects (cf. Edwards & Bernhardt, 1973a). Neither did they find that processes from different stages co-occurred more for the language disordered children. The language disordered children were not found to make "common use of uncommon processes" (Ingram, 1976) or to exhibit unusual processes. One language disordered subject was found to have a nasal preference, but this was also noted for one of the normal subjects. Although the language disordered children were not found to exhibit unique processes, the authors state that data from larger groups of children may show that unusual processes are more common for language disordered children. While Schwartz et al. did not find that certain processes were absent for the language disordered children, they did find that reduplication was more common for the linguistically normal children. Thus they suspect that there may be differences in the frequency of occurrence of certain processes (p. 373). In this study, the language disordered children were not found to exhibit more variability (cf. Edwards & Bernhardt, 1973a), and there were no significant differences concerning the contrastive use of sounds (cf. Ingram, 1976).

Schwartz and his associates (1980, p. 374) hypothesize that the lack of direct comparisons between normal and language disordered children in earlier studies may have resulted in misconceptions about differences between the two groups. However, they also state that the small number of subjects in their study might have affected their results, although they think that this is unlikely. Another possible explanation for the differences between the results of this study and earlier studies concerns the relationship between phonological acquisition and other aspects of linguistic development, according to Schwartz et al. (1980). They suggest that phonological development may be closely related to other aspects of language development (such as MLU) at the early stages. However, it may "lag behind" as syntactic complexity increases (p. 375). (For example, see Schmauch, Panagos, & Klich, 1978.) This relationship needs to be investigated with children at other stages of linguistic development.

Schwartz and his co-workers conclude that the phonological behavior of language disordered children is not different from that of normal children at a similar (early) stage of language development. Thus the results of this study are said to support the idea of a "synergy of linguistic disorders" (p. 375). In other words, there is a close relationship between phonological disorders and other linguistic disorders. Therefore, the authors argue for less of a separation between the two in both diagnosis and remediation. For instance, they advocate an integrated approach to training on syntactic rules and phonological rules.

Weiner (1981)

In an article published in 1981, Weiner describes what he calls "systematic sound preference" as a "common phonological process seen in young children with unintelligible speech" (1981, p. 281). According to Weiner, systematic sound preference, "in its classic form," involves replacement of a whole class of sounds by one specific sound. In his study, Weiner found that fricatives were affected more frequently than any other class of sounds, and word-initial sounds were most likely to be subject to this "process."[17] When only some members of a class of sounds were affected, voiceless and/or nonlabial sounds were most often affected. Weiner (1981, p. 281) points out that when the phonological processes that are commonly talked about do not account for a child's surface forms, an attempt should be made to find other possibilities, and systematic sound preference is one such possibility.

Weiner notes that Ingram (1976) first discussed sound preference as a characteristic of phonological disability. For instance, Ingram referred to the extensive use of nasalization where it would not be expected to occur as a "nasal preference," and he also talked about a "fricative preference." Ingram stated that children with disordered phonology may tend to overuse some articulation that has been developed, but he did not describe how to discover sound preferences or how to distinguish them from other processes.

Weiner (1981, p. 281) reports that a large number of children in a longitudinal study of unintelligible children were found to have sound errors that did not follow "typical phonological patterns." For example, one child replaced /s/, /θ/ /ʃ/, and /f/ by [t]. Although these substitutions at first looked like instances of stopping, Weiner notes that it was difficult to account for both ʃ → t (which involves fronting) and f → t (which involves backing). Thus, these data were reinterpreted in terms of a sound preference by which word initial voiceless fricatives were replaced by [t]. In Weiner's view, this interpretation more accurately represents the child's phonological system. As Weiner (p. 282) defines *systematic sound preference process*, a group of sounds within the same manner category (e.g., fricatives) are produced as one sound or a few similar sounds.

In his paper, Weiner presents data from eight children (out of 14 children involved in a longitudinal study) whose phonologies support the idea of a systematic sound preference process. Each child was unintelligible and was classified as having a severe articulation disorder, based on the results of the *Arizona Articulation Proficiency Scale* (Fudala, 1970). These children ranged in age from 3;5 to 5;10. The first samples obtained from each child (using Weiner's *Phonological Process Analysis*, 1979) were used for the analysis. A child was considered to have a sound preference if one or two similar sounds replaced the sounds in one manner category more than 70% of the time (p. 282). The results for each child are summarized here.

Nathan, aged 4;3, used [θ] or [ð] in place of word-initial fricatives, affricates, liquids, and glides. (Noninitial fricatives were replaced by stops.) The voicing quality was usually maintained when the interdentals replaced fricatives, as in [θi] for *cheese*, [θʌn] for *sun*, [ðu] for *zoo*, and [ðʌmi] for *jumping*. However, liquids and glides were consistently replaced by [θ], as in [θi] for *witch*, [θʌŋ] for *young*, [θi] for *leaf*, and [θɛd] for *red*.

Scott, aged 4;8, used [h] in place of word-initial voiceless fricatives and stops (except /p/), even when they occurred in clusters. So, for instance, he produced [hɑ̄ɪv] for *five*, [hɪŋk] for *sink*, [hu] for *shoe*, [hʌm] for *thumb*, [hɛnt] for *tent*, [hɪtən] for *kitten*, [hɑ̄ɪ] for *fly*, [hʌk] for *truck*, [hi] for *ski*, and [hin] for *queen* (but [dʒɛts] for *dress* and [bwɑk] for *block*).

Matthew, aged 3;11, exhibited a preference similar to Scott's. For Matthew, initial voiceless stops and fricatives were replaced by [h], even when they appeared in clusters. However, unlike Scott, Matthew also used [h] in place of /p/. Examples of Matthew's sound preference include: [hʌm] for *thumb*, [hup] for *soup*, [hʊdʌ] for *sugar*, [hɑ̄ɪjɪ] for *fire*, [hebo] for *table*, [hɪʔ] for *pig*, [hɪdn̩] for *kitten*, [hʌ] for *truck*, [hi] for *ski*, and [hɑ̄ɪ] for *fly*. Clusters made of of voiced stop + liquid were replaced by [b]. Weiner (1981, p. 284) notes that this may be another sound preference process, although there are not enough examples to be sure. For instance, Matthew said [bʌ] for *glove* and *brush*, and [bæ] for *glass*.

John, who was 5;1, used [l] in place of nonlabial fricatives and stops in word-initial position, as in [lɪs] for *this*, [lɔt] for *short*, [lʌm] for *thumb*, [lu] for *shoe*, [lɔ] for *car*, [lo͞u] for *toe*, [lots] for *ghost*, and [lʊdo] for *turtle*. (Compare Lorentz, 1974.) There were numerous exceptions to John's sound preference process, primarily due to a very "strong" tendency to assimilate. For example, regressive labial assimilation shows up in forms such as [vʌvo] for *shovel*, [bup] for *soup*, and [bebo] for *table*; and regressive nasal assimilation shows up in [nɪn] for *thin*. According to Weiner (p. 284), this is a good example of a stronger process (in this case assimilation) overriding another process (in this case a sound preference).

Joey, aged 5;4, replaced fricatives in all positions with the affricates [tʃ] and [dʒ]. Occasionally, he maintained the correct voicing feature, but more often he used [tʃ]. Examples include [witʃ] for *leaf*, [tʃwi] for *three*, [tʃu] for *shoe*, [titʃ] for *teeth*, [tʃɪtʃ] for *fish*, [dɪtʃ] for *dish*, [dotʃ] for *nose*, and [wʌtʃ] for *glove*.

Jonathan, who was 4;3, also exhibited a preference for palatal sibilants. In his sample, word-initial fricatives, fricative clusters, and stop + liquid clusters (or the stop elements of such clusters) were replaced by [ʃ], [ʒ], [tʃ], or [dʒ]. Examples of Jonathan's preference include [ʃaɪv] for *five*, [ʒɪs] for *this*, [ʃʌb] for *thumb*, [ʃʌd] for *sun*, and [ʒɪpə] for *zipper*. Examples involving clusters include [tʃwɛs] for *dress*, [ʃwɔd] for *frog*, [ʃwipi] for *sleeping*, [ʃwɛdə] for *sweater*, and [ʃwi] for *three*. Although Jonathan's preference differs from the others (in that four sounds were used), Weiner still considers it a preference process because the target sounds and clusters "converge on the palatal place of articulation" (p. 285).

Chuck, aged 5;10, exhibited two sound preference processes. Voiceless fricatives in word-initial position were replaced by [t], and voiceless sibilants in syllable-final position were replaced by a glottal stop [ʔ]. To illustrate, *five* was [taɪf], *sink* was [tɪŋk], *thin* was [tɪn], and *shovel* was [tʌvo]. Examples of Chuck's glottal stop preference include [vɪʔ] for *this*, [bʌʔ] for *bus*, and [dɪʔɪʔ] for *dishes*.

Dana, aged 4;10, used [d] in place of initial fricatives. Examples include [daɪv] for *five*, [dʌn] for *sun*, [dɪts] for *this*, [dɪŋk] for *sink*, and [du] for *zoo* and *shoe*. In discussing Dana's sound preference process, Weiner argues that this is a good example of a sound preference that could easily be misinterpreted as a regular process, in this case, stopping. The key point, in Weiner's view, is that /ʃ/ would need to be fronted (and stopped and voiced), while /f/ would need to be backed (and stopped and voiced).[18]

Although these eight children differed in the specific sounds they preferred, Weiner considers all of these examples as illustrating a "unitary phonological process" (p. 285). His reasons are as follows. First, in each case a class of sounds produced with the same manner was systematically replaced by one sound or a few similar sounds. Second, the preference was usually evident only in specific phonetic contexts, typically word-initial position. Third, voiceless and/or nonlabial sounds were most likely to be affected if the whole class was not affected. Fourth, fricatives, were more likely to be affected than any other manner class.

In Weiner's view, sound preference differs from processes such as stopping or fronting, which involve feature changes. Rather than a feature-changing process, it is a "collapsing process" by which a group of sounds with certain common features are represented by a "restricted feature arrangement" (1981, p. 286). Weiner argues that it is important to distinguish "the sound preference process" from feature-changing processes partly because training stimuli would differ for the two kinds of processes. For feature changing processes, stimuli having the crucial plus and minus feature values would be contrasted. For the sound preference process, however, he recommends contrasting the preferred sound(s) with each of the affected sounds.[19] Thus, accurate identification of sound preferences should lead to more effective therapy as well as to more revealing descriptions of the phonological patterns exhibited by children with disordered phonology.

Hodson and Paden (1981)

In a 1981 article, Hodson and Paden compare the phonological systems of 60 "essentially unintelligible" children between 3 and 8 years of age to the phonological systems of 60 normally developing 4-year-olds. The main purpose of this study was to determine which phonological processes, if any, were operating for the unintelligible children. The secondary purpose was to find the processes operating for the normally developing children and to compare the processes found for the two groups (p. 369).

Speech samples for each subject were obtained and analyzed in accordance with procedures outlined in *The Assessment of Phonological Processes* (Hodson, 1980). This procedure requires naming 55 common objects or simple concepts. Transcriptions of these single word responses are then examined for the occurrence of 42 phonological processes (see Appendix D).

All 60 of the unintelligible children in this study were found to exhibit the following five processes, though not necessarily 100% of the time (p. 370): (1) Cluster reduction, especially involving the loss of /s/ in clusters, as in [twɪŋ] for *string*; (2) Stridency deletion, involving either omission of the strident phoneme as in *string* (above), or substitution of a nonstrident phoneme, as in either [hoʊp] or [toʊp] for *soap*; (3) Stopping, involving the substitution of stops for continuants. (This may occur with stridency deletion.) Examples include [tʌm] for *thumb*, [dip] for *leaf*, and [toʊp] for *soap*; (4) Liquid deviations, including particularly "vowelization" of postvocalic or syllabic /l/, as in [kændo] for *candle*, or /ɚ/, as in [tʃɛʊ] for *chair*, and gliding of prevocalic liquids, as in [wʌg] for *rug* and [jif] or [wif] for *leaf*.[20] (5) Assimilation, especially labial assimilation, as in [pum] for *spoon*, and nasal assimilation as in [niŋ] for *string*. Hodson and Paden (1981, p. 372) note that all of these shared processes except liquid deviations are "heavily damaging to intelligibility." In their view, this group of processes may be a "key indicator" of a phonologically deviant system.

Other processes that were evidenced by the least intelligible children include (p. 371):[21] velar deviations, especially fronting, as in [dʌn] for *gun*, and omission; backing of anterior consonants to velars or glottals as in [hæʔəkwɔ] for *Santa Claus*; final consonant deletion, as in [bɛ] for *bed*; syllable reduction, involving weak syllables in multisyllabic words, e.g., [tɛbɪdʌn] for *television*; prevocalic voicing, as in [dʌ] for *tub*; glottal replacement, as in [hæʔ] for *hat*. Hodson and Paden report that several other processes also were exhibited by some of their unintelligible subjects. These included metathesis, coalescence, epenthesis, reduplication, and diminutive.

No two unintelligible children had identical phonological processes. In addition, nearly all of the very unintelligible children had one or two rather unusual "rules" (p. 371). For instance, three children used glides to begin word-final syllables, as in [bæwə] for *basket* (cf. Willbrand & Kleinschmidt, 1978). One 4-year-old child substituted [l] for all word-initial voiceless obstruents except when there was a nasal in the word. In that case, [n] was used for the initial obstruent. So *sore* and *tore* were [lɔɚ], but *some* and *come* were [nʌm].

The normal 4-year-olds in this study had just a few deviations from adult speech. These included (p. 371): devoicing of word-final obstruents, as in [peɪtʃ] for *page*; production of anterior strident phonemes in place of /θ, ð/, as in [fʌm] or [sʌm] for *thumb*; liquid deviations, including vowelization and gliding (especially of /r/); tongue protrusions, or frontal lisps, usually for /t, d, n, l/; depalatalization of /ʃ, ʒ, tʃ, dʒ/, as in [su] for *shoe*; assimilations, especially regressive and particularly nasal, labial, and velar; and metathesis, as in [mæks] for *mask*. The only process shared by all of the intelligible children was devoicing of final consonants, which does not interfere with intelligibility. (This process was seldom exhibited by the unintelligible children because they tended to delete final consonants.)

Most of the processes that were common for the unintelligible children did not occur at all in the phonologies of the normal 4-year-olds. Moreover, Hodson and Paden note (p. 372) that the two groups exhibited different "strategies" for dealing with certain classes of phonemes and that they applied their processes differently. To illustrate, children in both groups had difficulty with the interdental fricatives /θ, ð/, but the intelligible children tended to maintain continuancy (and add stridency) while the unintelligible children often used stop substitutes. Prevocalic liquids were more problematic for the unintelligible children (who frequently used glide substitutes) than for the normal 4-year-olds, and the unintelligible group exhibited more assimilations, including progressive as well as regressive assimilations. Whereas stridency and continuancy were found to be well established for the normal 4-year-olds, stridency was used only by the older unintelligible children (in word-initial sounds). Cluster reduction, especially involving /s/ clusters, was exhibited by all the unintelligible children, but it was uncommon for the normal 4-year-olds.

Among their conclusions, Hodson and Paden (p. 373) list the following processes as particularly differentiating the unintelligible children from the normal 4-year-old children in their study: cluster reduction, stridency deletion, and stopping, all of which were exhibited by all 60 unintelligible children but by fewer than five of the intelligible children, and final consonant deletion, fronting of velars, backing, syllable reduction, prevocalic voicing, and glottal replacement, which were extremely rare in the speech samples from the normal children but were commonly exhibited by the unintelligible children (i.e., one or more of these processes were used by about two-thirds of the unintelligible group). Thus the authors conclude (p. 373) that the processes exhibited by unintelligible children differ in "number and kind" from those characterizing the speech of intelligible 4-year-olds.

CONCLUSION

Procedures for assessing the speech of people with communicative disorders have closely followed developments in phonological theory. For nearly 40 years, articulation assessment procedures placed exclusive emphasis on the segment. The assumption was that children's speech sound errors reflected imperfect learning of the adult system; the assessment task was to describe as precisely as possible how a child was "misarticulating" adult forms. Beginning in the 1970s, alternative procedures were introduced in the literature at a fairly rapid rate. These procedures reflected, in turn, the constructs of the distinctive feature, the generative rule, and most recently the phonological process as organizing units to describe speech sound errors. In this chapter we have sketched the main outlines of this history, with more detailed coverage in Appendix D of several clinical procedures for phonological analysis of children's speech sound errors.

One important topic that could not be included within the scope of this text concerns associations among structural and grammatical complexity and speech production errors. Suggested readings include Haynes, Haynes, and Jackson (1982), Paul and Shriberg (1982), Panagos and Prelock (1982), and Shriberg (1982a).

FOOTNOTES

[1]In the notation used by Haas, $\{^d_t \, {}^{(b)}\}$ apparently indicates that [t] varies with (or even combines with) [ḍ], and [b] occurs less frequently, varying with [ḍ].

[2]Although Singh and Frank claim to be talking about "distinctive" features, they are not using a traditional distinctive feature system, such as that of Jakobson, Fant, and Halle (1952), or Chomsky and Halle (1968), and their features are not "binary" ($\pm$). They reject traditional distinctive features as being "impractical" for describing children's substitutions or the development of the phonological system. Instead, they use nonbinary articulatory features of place, manner, and voicing, as did Fisher and Logemann (1971) (see Appendix D).

[3]Leonard cautions that these results are based on an articulation test, and thus exceptions may not be as evident as if larger samples were used. Moreover, these may be the most severe cases, which could not be handled in the schools.

[4]In Compton's feature system [place₅] indicates palatal and [place₄] indicates alveolar. The alpha (α) variable is a notational convention indicating that the feature has the same value ($+$ or $-$) as the value specified on the left of the arrow (see Appendix A). It should be noted that Compton's use of the alpha variable is somewhat different from its use in generative phonology.

[5]See Ingram's (1976) book for a critique of Compton's (1970) paper and a partial reanalysis of the data.

[6]The rules listed here apply in counterfeeding order for this child because if the ordering were reversed, the first rule would feed or produce input for the second: tʃ→ʃ and ʃ→t (or tʃ→ʃ→t). Rule ordering is discussed in Appendix B.

[7]The features used by Lorentz in his rule formulations are not really distinctive features (as in Chomsky & Halle 1968), even though they are written with plus signs and minus signs.

[8]Note that even the fricative components of the affricates /tʃ, dʒ/ undergo this change.

[9]The optional C in the environment of this rule allows /ʃ/ and /ʒ/ to undergo this change even when they occur in word-initial affricates.

[10]In a 1982 book, Grunwell discusses in much more detail her views of phonological analysis.

[11]The "processes" that Grunwell discusses would not qualify as "natural processes," and, in fact, it is not clear how she is using the term process, as she does not define it.

[12]Note here that tʃ→j is predicted from the process, but apparently it is not part of this child's rule system.

[13]It is not entirely clear why Ingram chooses to classify such cases as involving partial reduplication. In each example that he gives, the adult form also ends in [i].

[14]These are also called *progressive idioms*. In contrast, early forms that persist are called *frozen forms* or *regressive idioms*.

[15]As discussed earlier, a *phone class* is said to be made up of a sound produced by a child in a certain position, along with all the other sounds that vary with that sound in that position. To illustrate, one word-initial phone class might be |t ~ d ~ s ~ φ|.

[16]For a process to be considered productive for a child, two occurrences of that process had to be observed (Schwartz et al., 1980, p. 362).

[17]Not all researchers (e.g., Edwards, 1980b) would want to consider systematic sound preference as a process, but this is Weiner's approach.

[18]In her 1980b discussion of sound preferences or "favorite sounds," Edwards, unlike Weiner, includes cases that can be accounted for by regular processes, as well as those that cannot be.

[19]Again, the suggestions made by Edwards (1980b) are different. She recommends first contrasting the preferred sound with the one collapsed sound to which it is most similar and then contrasting it with a less similar sound, and so on, until it is contrasted with all of the collapsed sounds. For sound preferences that result from the interaction of regular processes, she recommends remediating the processes one at a time, starting with one that occurs by itself and/or one that affects several target sounds.

[20]The process that is called vowelization by Hodson and Paden (1981) is similar to vocalization.
[21]Only 10 of the 60 unintelligible children had all of these processes. Hodson and Paden note (p. 371) that most of the children showed preferences for certain ones.

8

Other
Communicative
Disorders

This concluding chapter reviews some studies in areas other than developmental phonological disorders. We have selected as representative, papers describing the phonology of adult aphasia, hearing impairment, and mental retardation.

ADULT APHASIA

Segment-Based
Phonological Studies

The speech of adult aphasics often contains many articulation errors. Since Broca's (1863) early description of aphasia, which focused on the loss of articulatory ability, numerous investigators (e.g., Head, 1926; Goldstein,

1948; Critchley, 1952; Jackson, 1958; Johns & Darley, 1970) have commented on articulatory problems in aphasia, and most often their descriptions have involved sound segments.

As Blumstein (1973a, p. 21) pointed out, early discussions of articulatory problems related to aphasia were associated with diagnostic descriptions. There was "no concept of the phonological system as a linguistic organization, and thus, no systematic study of phonological errors." However, a number of the studies published after 1925 (e.g., Alajouanine, Ombredane, & Durand, 1939; Fry, 1959; Shankweiler & Harris, 1966) were conducted for the purpose of investigating sound production errors. Although the researchers used different methods, their observations were quite consistent. The aphasic patients seemed to make similar types of phonological errors, including sound substitutions, the addition or loss of phonemes, and phonemic sequencing errors. Moreover, these investigators noted that substitution errors seemed to involve similar phonemes, e.g., homorganic voiceless and voiced stops (Blumstein, 1973a, p. 22).[1]

Segmental errors are also mentioned in later studies that are phonologically based, e.g., Blumstein's (1973a) study that is discussed next. See MacMahon (1972) for an overview of studies dealing with the sound errors of adult aphasics.

Feature-Based
Phonological Studies

Blumstein (1973a)

Blumstein's study (1973a) is probably the most detailed investigation of aphasic phonology. Her work had three objectives (1973a, p. 31): (1) to discover and systematically characterize the error categories that make up the phonological patterns of aphasic speech; (2) to find out what relationships, if any, exist between patterns of disintegration and areas of brain pathology; and (3) to use evidence from aphasia to test certain linguistic assumptions. In pursuing these goals, Blumstein worked within the distinctive feature framework of generative phonological theory.[2]

Blumstein's subjects were 17 aphasics in three diagnostic groups: six Broca's, six Wernicke's, and five Conduction aphasics, classified according to the system devised by the Aphasia Research Center in Boston. Blumstein described the characteristics of the three groups as follows. The Broca's aphasics, in whom damage is in the third frontal convolution of the speech area, display a "contiguity" or "expressive" disorder

(1973a, p. 28). Words such as articles, pronouns, and connectives are often omitted. Speech may be dysarthric, e.g., intonation patterns may be distorted, and there may be many phonetic errors.[3] Comprehension and naming may be "mildly impaired," and errors are about the same in repetition as in spontaneous speech. Because of their dysarthric impairment, Broca's aphasics may make both phonetic and phonemic errors. In her analysis, Blumstein considered only the latter (i.e., errors that affect the distinctive values of phonemes).

Conduction aphasics, whose damage is located in the *acuate fasciculus* (a band of fibers that is considered to be the "bridge" between Wernicke's area and Broca's area) have good comprehension and fluent speech, although they have some naming problems. They display many phonemic substitutions (literal paraphasias) but fewer instances of verbal paraphasia (the substitution of one lexical item for another) (1973a, p. 29).

Wernicke's aphasics, whose damage is in the first temporal gyrus, have fluent speech but display problems in naming, repetition, and comprehension. Their spontaneous speech contains circumlocutions (due to word-finding problems) and is often "void of specific semantic content" (Blumstein, 1973a, p. 30). They frequently cannot inhibit their speech and often substitute one lexical item for another. Some Wernicke's aphasics produce phoneme sequences that are not identifiable as English words. The amount of such "neologistic jargon" is said to vary from patient to patient.

Blumstein's data consisted of transcriptions of open-ended conversations with each patient. Each sample contained at least 2,000 words. Phonological errors (not including very distorted words, neologisms, and verbal paraphasias) were categorized as follows (1973a, pp. 37–38):

A. phoneme substitutions

B. simplifications (loss of a phoneme or syllable)

C. additions (of a phoneme or syllable)

D. environmental errors

   1. intramorphemic blends (assimilation errors triggered by a phoneme in the same word)

   2. intermorphemic blends (assimilation errors triggered by sounds or syllables in neighboring words)

   3. metatheses

Blumstein found that the Broca's aphasics made the largest number of phonological errors—more than three times as many as the Conduction aphasics, who made twice as many (analyzable) errors as the Wernicke's aphasics. However, the same ordering of types of phonological errors was found for each group: substitutions>simplifications>environmental errors>additions. This result indicates that "the phonological errors characteristic of aphasic speech reflect a systematic disorganization of phonology which is independent of . . . lesion site" (Blumstein, 1973a, p. 47).

Concerning substitutions, Blumstein found that errors of a single distinctive feature were the most frequent for all groups, and moreover, there was a general pattern in the "hierarchical organization" of errors. The features most commonly incorrect in each group were [continuant] and [compact]. Fewest errors were made on the [strident] and [nasal] features. Marked consonants were found to be incorrect more than unmarked consonants, and unmarked consonants tended to be substituted for marked. For the Broca's and Conduction aphasics, most phoneme substitution errors occurred in initial position, whereas for the Wernicke's aphasics, slightly more substitution errors in final position. For all groups most substitution errors involved singleton consonants rather than clusters.

Blumstein (1973a, p. 60) reports that most simplification errors were found in clusters, and they were distributed quite evenly across word positions. Simplification errors involving singleton consonants usually occurred in word-final position. These facts indicate that for Blumstein's subjects, the tendency was for marked syllable structures to become unmarked (CV).

There were few addition errors, and most of these errors occurred in consonant clusters (a finding that apparently contradicts the statement above concerning markedness). For example, a liquid or semiconsonant was often added to a stop or continuant, as in [trami] for *Tommy*. Sometimes an initial consonant was added to a word beginning with a vowel, as in [dʒarmi] for *army*, giving the basic CV structure. (Only consonant additions are discussed by Blumstein).

Most intramorphemic and intermorphemic blend errors involved single consonants. Generally more regressive assimilation errors occurred than progressive assimilations. This suggests, according to Blumstein (1973a, p. 65) that the difficulty is related to the programming of utterances. This, in turn, supports the claim that the phonological patterns of aphasic speech reflect a phonological rather than just a phonetic disturbance. Most intramorphemic assimilation errors occurred when no consonant phonemes intervened (e.g., [bɪb] for *big*) as did most metatheses (e.g., [klots] for *colts*). For intermorphemic blend errors, the assimilated sound was usually in the same relative place in the word as the "contaminating" phoneme, as in [bɪstrɪ bʊks] for *history books.*

Blumstein found that her subjects produced very few non-English sequences, supporting Whitaker's (1969) claim that morpheme structure rules remain intact in aphasia. Blumstein's most striking finding, however, was the uniformity of error types and directions among the three groups of aphasics (p. 73). This, in her view, suggests that the phonological system is hierarchically organized.

Blumstein states (1973a, p. 79) that her analysis of aphasic speech supports many of the theoretical assumptions on which the concept of "distinctive feature" is based, partly because most sound errors made by her subjects involved one feature change. Moreover, her data demonstrate a need for the feature [sonorant]. Blumstein argues that substitutions such as l→w, r→w, and w→m, which were fairly common in her data, cannot be adequately accounted for without the feature [sonorant]. (These substitutions involve several feature changes.) In addition, Blumstein shows that the existing feature system is inadequate because it does not capture the fact that a substitution such as r→w is more typical than one such as p→u. (Both involve changes in the features [consonantal] and [vocalic].) Thus she proposes that each sound should be marked as belonging to at least one of the three main sound classes—consonant, vowel, or sonorant. In addition, the theory should be modified so that a substitution involving a major class feature would be "highly marked," implying that such changes rarely occur (Blumstein, 1973a, p. 87).

Blumstein found that patients who could monitor their output often made successive attempts at reaching the target, and the final attempt was usually closer, in terms of distinctive features, than the first attempt. In addition, only a single feature specification was generally changed with each successive attempt. This, in Blumstein's view, demonstrates that the binary feature is an integral part of the phonological system of a speaker. The fact that the subjects in this study tended to replace /t/ by [p] suggests that labial plosives are unmarked and dental plosives are marked (p. 111). See Blumstein's (1973a) Chapters 7, 8, and 9 for a detailed discussion of how her results relate to various aspects of distinctive feature theory. For example, she found that her subjects' substitution errors were based both on redundant features and distinctive features (p. 110).

Although Blumstein's study makes some important contributions, there are limitations. For instance, the type of analysis that is presented does not indicate how various errors are related. Statements like "75% of the substitution errors in all groups occurred within single consonants" present only part of the picture. Blumstein does not indicate whether the phonological problems of one particular patient fit together into a system, and if so, to what extent and how. Although there are some examples, there are not enough to make reanalysis possible. One example of simplification is [si] for *ski*. This error is different from the errors usually made by children and goes against the notion of markedness. However, Blumstein did not note if this was a typical sort of error, i.e., if some patients consistently retained the sibilant in such clusters. Similarly, one example given under successive attempts was *flood⟩* [tlɑd]⟩ [plɑd], but Blumstein did not state whether all errors such as [tlɑd] (involving non-English sequences) were produced as first approximations and were later changed to obey the phonotactic constraints of English. Again, it would have been helpful to have more data.

See Lecours and Caplan (1975) for a review of Blumstein's book that takes an aphasiological (rather than a linguistic) point of view.

Suprasegmental-Based Studies

Although there are apparently no studies of aphasia that focus specifically on prosodies or suprasegmentals, they are sometimes mentioned in studies of aphasic phonology. For example, in describing the characteristics of Broca's aphasics, Blumstein (1973a, p. 28) noted that their speech is sometimes dysarthric, being characterized by distorted intonation patterns, and a slow rate, as well as frequent phonetic errors. Sparks and Holland (1976) and others have proposed a form of suprasegmental training that reportedly facilitates "linguistic learning" in the adult aphasic.

Phonological Rule- and Phonological Process- Based Studies

Quite recently a few linguists have attempted to describe the phonological errors of adult aphasic patients from the viewpoint of generative phonology. These include Whitaker (1969), Schnitzer (1972), and Blumstein (1973a), whose study was discussed under features.

Whitaker (1969)

Whitaker (1969) attempted to establish the study of adult aphasia as providing useful data for constructing psycholinguistic models and for investigating the neurological bases of language (Schnitzer, 1972, p. 4). (See also Whitaker, 1970.) He stated that aphasic errors may reveal aspects of the linguistic structure of the mental grammar and may even give insight into which parts of the brain underlie specific components of the grammar.

Whitaker discussed four aspects of grammar that he called "functionally independent levels": (1) the physical phonetic level; (2) the surface structure or phonological representation;[4] (3) the deep structure; and (4) semantic features. He argued that each of these levels can be impaired independently of the others. For example, only the phonological representation of utterances or words may be impaired, or on the other hand, the phonological representation may remain intact while the syntactic and/or semantic features are disrupted. Because dysarthria affects only the actualization of utterances, it involves only level 1 (i.e., the physical phonetic level). Whitaker claims that phonological representations are "neurologically distinct" and more peripheral than semantic and syntactic representations. In fact, he claims that they are "properties of Broca's area and Heschl's Gyrus" (p. 107). In his thesis, Whitaker discusses each type of representation and gives evidence for the autonomy of each level.

Whitaker views morpheme structure rules as part of performance ("neuromuscular habits") and phonological rules (which convert lexical representations to phonetic representations) as part of competence. Phonological rules are divided into two groups: (a) more abstract ones, such as the stress rule and the rule deleting /g/ in words such as *resign*, and (b) low level phonetic rules, such as the aspiration of voiceless stops before stressed vowels. Whitaker claims that low level phonetic rules are not disrupted in nondysarthric patients and that morpheme structure rules also remain intact, whereas actual phonological rules, like the stress rules, are more likely to be disrupted. He sees this as evidence for a complex competence/performance interrelationship in aphasia. In his view (p. 86), aphasia is more than just a performance problem.

Broca's aphasia, according to Whitaker, is strictly a phonetic (level 1) problem, equated with apraxia of speech. One indication of this is that patients with this disorder are often upset by their errors. If the disruption was phonological, Whitaker argues, patients would not know that they were making errors because their problem would encompass perception as well as production.

Patients who display a combination of apraxia and auditory verbal agnosia produce some normal speech but then produce one or two garbled words. As some of their speech is normal, Whitaker says (1969, p. 89) that the whole level (level 2) of phonological representation cannot be impaired. And because it is hard to imagine (in his view) how the phonological rules could be impaired for one word and not another, he hypothesizes (p. 89) that the problem may be in the "tracking mechanism," which relates lexical representations to neuromuscular commands, or it may be a disruption of the "neuromuscular specification" of a lexical representation.[5] So, the lexical representation itself may be disrupted, or "blocking" may make it impossible for the patient to "retrieve" a lexical representation. Moreover, this problem may be limited to a particular class of lexical items. For example, *anomia* is viewed as a loss of the lexical representations of nouns (p. 90). In addition, access to phonological representations may be disrupted in the visual as well as the auditory modality. If access is disrupted only in the auditory modality, visual stimuli may serve a deblocking function. In this case, the disorder is a performance problem because the underlying phonological representations are intact.

Schnitzer (1972)

Using performance data from one aphasic patient, Schnitzer (1972) attempted to give evidence for the "psychological reality" of the phonological component of grammar, particularly at the word level (p. 3). More precisely, he tried to show that the systematic phonemic representations and phonological rules of English (as presented by Chomsky & Halle, 1968) "must undoubtedly be credited as having psychological reality" (p. 5).

Schnitzer's subject was RGMS, a 22-year-old woman whose aphasia was caused by a large hematoma in the left parietal region of the brain. After removal of the hematoma, her aphasia improved greatly. At the time of data collection (6 to 10 months after she was first admitted to the hospital) her aphasia was reportedly so minimal that she was able to hide it under normal circumstances. Schnitzer had his subject read a list of 500 words at her own rate, and at another session 1 to 3 months later, she read aloud a list of approximately 200 additional words. When she was asked to read these complex words (e.g., *repetitious*, *admirable*) that she could avoid in ordinary conversation, the extent of her aphasia was apparent. Other tests showed that her behavior was also affected in more normal situations whenever such words could not be avoided. Her problem was determined to be one of using (i.e., speaking, reading, writing, or spelling) "literary" words of more than two syllables (p. 6).

In Schnitzer's book, examples of RGMS's words are presented that "deviate radically" from accepted pronunciation. In each case Schnitzer shows that by assuming a "minor error" in the underlying representation and by assuming correct application of the appropriate rules of *The Sound Pattern of English* (Chomsky & Halle, 1968), the subject's surface form can be derived. He gives examples of errors related to, for example, vowel tenseness, part of speech, deletions, spoonerisms, and boundary phenomena. In his view, this evidence demonstrates the "psychological reality" of the underlying level because slight errors made at this level can account for widespread and apparently random phonetic errors. Such evidence is said to indirectly support the phonological rules that are needed to derive the phonetic forms from the underlying representations.

To illustrate, RGMS read *telekinesis* as [tĕlkinəsəs]. Schnitzer accounts for this form by positing an underlying lax /e/ in the stem rather than a tense /ē/. (The underlying form is /tele + kinēt + is/$_N$.) The SPE rules then apply normally. He says (1972, p. 11) that this example provides evidence for the psychological reality of the underlying feature [±tense], the stress cycle, and the vowel reduction rule.

Democratize was read as a noun [dĕməkrēĭʃən] "democration," which does not exist in English. To explain this form, schnitzer hypothesizes that his subject replaced a verbal suffix (-ize) with a nominal one (-ion). Then by assuming regular application of the SPE rules (including the main stress rule, stress adjustment, spirantization, palatalization) he is able to derive the phonetic form (p. 19).

To derive the form [kæθəlaɪz] for *catholicize*, Schnitzer (1972, pp. 24–25) assumes that his subject deleted /ik/ from the underlying representation. Thus her underlying form was /kæθɔl + iz/$_V$. Then the normal application of several SPE rules gives her surface form.

The word *endomorph* was said by RGMS as [əndōrməf]. To derive this form, Schnitzer assumes that his subject "anticipated the underlying /ɔr/ syllable" (p. 39). Her supposed underlying form is therefore /endɔrmɔf/$_N$.

Schnitzer also presents a smaller number of examples which contain phonetic errors that are traceable to omissions or misapplications of phonological rules. Again, he attributes widespread phonetic errors to minor errors at a more abstract level. These examples are said to provide direct evidence for the psychological reality of certain phonological rules. For example, Schnitzer shows how RGMS's [kəmpʌlsŏrīy] for *com-pulsory*, [səksīyʃən] for *succession*, and several other forms can be accounted for by her failure to apply the SPE laxing rule. A few forms such as [lāgizəm] for *logicism* and [ælədʒŏriy] for *allegory*, are accounted for by misapplication of velar softening. To illustrate, Schnitzer (p. 79) assumes that RGMS has the correct underlying form for *allegory*: /æleg + ɔr + y/ₙ. Her surface form is derived almost exactly as it should be, except that velar softening applies to the /g/, giving [dʒ]. This is a misapplication of velar softening because it should not apply before a low back vowel. This part of Schnitzer's study supports Whitaker's claim that phonological rules may be impaired in aphasia.

Although Schnitzer's investigation is said to demonstrate the psychological reality of generative phonology, he states (1972, p. 87) that the evidence does not necessarily show that the brain "performs" word-level phonological rules as a regular part of speech production. Schnitzer also concedes that surface representations may not have to be derived from underlying representations every time a person speaks; perhaps underlying forms and derivations are used only when the speaker is making up new words or is having a problem producing a phonetic form. This would account for the "large number of mistakes" (in Schnitzer's corpus) that could not be analyzed as errors in either underlying representations or rules (p. 88).

Schnitzer showed that it is possible to account for one aphasic patient's renditions of a list of literary words within the framework of a strict *SPE* approach to phonology. However, as he pointed out, many of his subject's errors could be accounted for simply as surface errors due to orthographical factors. Many errors also could be accounted for by assuming incorrect stress placement and omission of an unstressed vowel or syllable on the surface level (e.g., [plūwrəltīy]), and in some cases the incorrect stress could be due to the stress pattern of a more common related form (e.g., plural). Thus Schnitzer's data do not necessarily support his strong claims concerning the psychological reality of abstract underlying representations and generative phonological rules.

Schnitzer's approach left a large number of his subject's errors unaccounted for, and in some instances he still had to make arbitrary assumptions or appeal to phonetic-level rules in order to perform the desired derivations. For instance, in deriving *Canadian* (p. 83) he was able to come up with [kənēīʒən], but the form actually pronounced by RGMS was [kənēīʃən], which Schnitzer said could be due to "phonetic-level devoicing."

Some of Schnitzer's data actually seem to indicate that certain *SPE* rules are not psychologically real. For example, although there are many forms that give evidence for spirantization and palatalization (e.g., *democration*), there are no forms that give evidence for the psychological reality of velar softening. In fact, there are several forms in which this rule should apply but does not (e.g., *logician*) and it applies incorrectly in *allegory*. What these data appear to indicate is that palatalization is a natural and productive phonological process, whereas velar softening is not. In fact, these are two changes that Stampe discusses in illustrating the difference between natural processes (which the speaker brings to the language) and rules (which the language imposes on the speaker and which therefore have to be learned).

The studies discussed above have shown that the constructs of generative phonology can be used in the description and explanation of the phonological errors of adult aphasic patients and that evidence from aphasia can shed light on theoretical issues in phonology. They have also described and defined the types of phonological errors likely to occur in aphasic speech more explicitly than have previous studies.

Edwards (1978)

In an unpublished paper, Edwards (1978) attempted to apply the principles of natural phonology in analyzing the sound errors of three adult aphasic patients. She reasoned that if natural phonological processes are innate and govern phonetic behavior, as Stampe claimed, then there should be evidence for them in the speech of adult aphasics, and natural processes should show up more frequently than unnatural processes. She went on to argue that if this is not the case, we either have to revise our notion of natural processes or abandon the idea that aphasic disturbances are governed by the same principles that govern language acquisition and language change, i.e., that aphasia is a "natural phenomenon" (Blumstein 1973a, p. 8).

The subjects in this study were three adult aphasic patients, one Broca's, one Wernicke's, and one Conduction (as defined by Blumstein, 1973a). Each subject was asked to repeat a list of 84 phrases and sentences of varying lengths (totaling about 450 words) that were formulated to elicit all phonemes of American English. The data for each subject consisted of broad phonetic transcriptions of these 84 sentences and phrases.[6]

An attempt was made to discover the phonological processes underlying the consonantal substitutions and omissions made by each subject. For instance, if a subject substituted [s] for /ʃ/ and [z] for /ʒ/, he was said to have a depalatalization process, and if he eliminated one element of a cluster, he was said to have a process of cluster reduction.

Processes for each subject were divided into three categories: natural, unnatural, and indeterminate. As no one had previously attempted to make an extensive list of natural (or unnatural) processes, some rather arbitrary decisions were involved in this classification, although all were based on the work of Stampe (1969, 1972a, and class lectures at the Ohio State University, 1969–1970). However, Stampe did not claim to have discussed all the possible natural phonological processes, and he did not discuss indeterminate processes at all. In Edwards' study, a change was generally called natural if it involved similar sounds (differing by just one or two features), but context was sometimes considered. For instance, voicing was classified as unnatural if it affected final segments, but natural if it affected intervocalic segments.

Subjects were given credit for having certain natural processes even if the surface substitutions were not the ones that would normally result from the operation of those processes. To illustrate, the process of depalatalization would be expected to result in an [s] substitute for /ʃ/. If voicing also applied, the substitute would be [z], and if despirantization (i.e., stopping) applied as well, [d] would result. Depalatalization and despirantization without voicing would give a [t] substitute for /ʃ/. However, in some cases palatals were replaced by labiodental or interdental fricatives or even bilabial stops. Because the function of depalatalization is "to eliminate the fronted and raised tongue posture of [ʃ, ʒ] etc." (Stampe 1972a, p. 13), these subjects were given credit for having the natural process of depalatalization even if the resulting substitute was not always an alveolar. Similar cases were handled in a comparable way.

Edwards found that there were many similarities and also many differences among her three aphasic subjects. Concerning total number of words mispronounced (not including obvious cases of verbal paraphasia), the Broca's aphasic incorrectly produced nearly as many (about 190) as the Wernicke's (about 200). The Conduction aphasic mispronounced fewer words, approximately 70.

An analysis of repeated attempts and error corrections revealed considerable differences in awareness of sound errors and ability to correct them. The Conduction aphasic appeared to have the greatest ability in this regard, as he attempted to correct 71% of his mispronounced words and actually corrected 80% of the words he attempted more than once. The Broca's aphasic was apparently aware of his sound errors, as he attempted to correct about half of them, producing many words in several forms. However, his ability to correct his sound errors was quite poor, and his repeated attempts were sometimes further from the target word than his first attempt. The Wernicke's aphasic appeared to be least aware of his errors. Although he made the largest number of word errors, he attempted to correct very few, and only one word was rendered correctly on the second or third try. Although nine other words improved, just as many got worse or were equally far from the target. This supports Blumstein's (1973a, p. 8) statement that for Wernicke's aphasics "the disordered selection and sequencing of sounds and syllables appears to be part of a broader disorder in which the inner acoustic image of the word is weakened."

All three subjects exhibited many natural phonological processes: 33 for the Broca's aphasic, 30 for the Wernicke's aphasic, and 22 for the Conduction. Moreover, all subjects shared 21 of the natural processes, including: depalatalization, fronting of velars, cluster reduction, obstruent devoicing, assimilatory voicing, final consonant deletion, weak syllable deletion, despirantization, the substitution of fricatives for affricates (i.e., weakening of affricates), and the substitution of fricatives for glides. All three patients exhibited all fronting processes and virtually all processes giving rise to CV syllables, as well as obstruent voicing changes.

All three subjects also shared some of the same unnatural and indeterminate processes. For instance, they all produced some clusters in place of single consonants, and all three patients also omitted initial consonants occasionally. They shared one unnatural weakening process (stop ⟩ liquid), and all had some unnatural strengthening processes. All three exhibited some metatheses, substituted affricates for fricatives, and substituted labial nasals for alveolar nasals. Although the Broca's aphasic had the largest number of phonological processes (55), followed by the Wernicke's (48), and the the Conduction aphasic (36), the fact that many of the individual processes were shared by all three patients seems to indicate that "the patterns of phonological disintegration," at least in terms of phonological processes, may be similar across subjects, regardless of area of brain lesion.

Although the three patients shared many natural processes and also some unnatural and indeterminate processes, they also frequently exhibited different changes or different types of examples of a more general common process. Edwards presents a table of "distinguishing characteristics" for the three aphasic patients that she studied.

One objective of this study was to determine if certain theoretical assumptions about natural phonological processes would be supported by evidence from adult aphasia. One hypothesis was that more natural processes than unnatural processes would be found to underlie the surface substitutions and omissions in the speech of these three adult aphasics. Considering data from all three patients, there was evidence for a total of 61 phonological processes, 34 of which (55.7%) could be classified as natural. In other words, over half of the phonological processes for which there was evidence (for each subject and also across subjects) were natural phonological processes like those that are found in language acquisition and language change. Unnatural processes made up less than 30%. In addition, if each process is counted each time it applies (i.e., if the total number of applications is computed for each process), the percentage of natural changes found for each subject is even higher, amounting to 74.5% for the Broca's patient, 70.9% for the Wernicke's, and 77.2% for the Conduction aphasic.

Although each patient exhibited more natural processes than unnatural processes, some of the natural processes had unexpected results or were limited in unpredicted ways. For instance, although cluster reduction was quite prevalent, the deleted segment was not always the expected (or marked) one (e.g., sometimes a stop was deleted rather than a fricative).

Stampe (1969) stated that natural processes are limited according to certain hierarchies. For example, obstruent devoicing may be limited to voiceless contexts but not to voiced contexts, and obstruent voicing may be limited to intervocalic position. However, none of the three subjects studied by Edwards limited their processes according to Stampe's proposed hierarchies. Thus even their natural processes were sometimes unnatural in certain respects.

In Edwards' view, the most surprising finding was the similarity in the percentages of the various types of phonological processes across subjects. Although the Broca's and the Wernicke's aphasics mispronounced many more words than did the Conduction aphasic, and although the number of sound errors varied considerably for all three subjects, the percentages of processes that were natural, unnatural, and indeterminate were very similar across subjects. This appears to indicate that it is not possible to differentiate among clinical types of aphasic patients on the basis of percentage of natural, unnatural, and indeterminate processes that they exhibit, i.e., there may be no relationship between area of brain pathology and type of phonological process most frequently exemplified. The differences are somewhat greater if total number of process applications is considered. However, the differences are still very slight and thus could not be used to differentiate among these three clinical types of aphasics.

The results of this study also indicate that the sound errors found in adult aphasia result from a phonological disturbance related to the programming of speech, as evidenced by the numerous cases of distant regressive assimilation. Moreover, the comparable processes and percentages of various types of processes for the three patients indicate that, on that level at least, the phonological disintegration is determined by common principles.

In spite of the similarities in phonological processes, there were also differences among the three aphasic patients in Edwards' study (e.g., concerning number of sound errors and correction of errors). However, Edwards notes that these differences should not be used to form generalizations about characteristics of Broca's, Wernicke's, and Conduction aphasics. First, because a repetition task was used to elicit these data, results may differ from results based on spontaneous utterances. Second, the subjects in this study were asked to repeat entire phrases and sentences, and therefore the effects of short term memory and/or of processing whole utterances may have influenced the results. Finally, the three subjects may not be representative of other similarly classified aphasic patients. Additional research with many more subjects should indicate whether the distinguishing characteristics discussed by Edwards are in fact more general characteristics or are simply idiosyncratic to her subjects.

Other studies of adult aphasia that deal at least partly with phonology include those of Poncet, Degos, and Deloche (1972); Lecours and Lhermitte (1973); Martin and Rigrodsky (1974); Halpern, Keith, and Darley (1976); Dunlop and Marquardt (1977); Ireland, Klich, and Panagos (1977); Blumstein (1978); Klich, Ireland, and Weidner (1979); and Buckingham (1980).

HEARING-IMPAIRED

Segment-Based Phonological Studies

Traditionally, studies of the hearing-impaired have commented on their problems with articulation, and most of these studies have focused on sound segments. Silverman (1963), in his review of some of the relevant literature, noted that the speech of the deaf is characterized by misarticulations, difficulty with the voicing contrast, omissions (especially of consonants in clusters), and problems with vowels and diphthongs. It also has been noted that the hearing-impaired may omit initial consonants, add vowels and syllables, and nasalize or neutralize vowels.

Among the many segment-based phonological studies of the speech of
the deaf are those of Hudgins, 1934; Hudgins and Numbers, 1942; Carr,
1953; Markides, 1970; and Levitt and Smith, 1972. Space limitations allow
discussion of only one interesting paper by West and Weber, 1973.

West and Weber (1973)

In an article published in 1973, West and Weber presented a linguistic
analysis of the speech of a 4-year-old (4;3) girl with a moderately severe
bilateral hearing loss. Their subject had attended a class for the deaf for
10 months and before that had received speech therapy briefly. West and
Weber used an approach that is utilized in field linguistics, with the child
as informant. (This approach is like that used by American descriptive
linguists.) Their purpose was to find the phonological structures used by
their subject and to investigate her phonemic development. They also
hoped to demonstrate the usefulness of a linguistic analysis.

The data used in this study consisted of narrow transcriptions of spontaneous speech samples elicited in six play sessions (looking at pictures
and playing with objects) over a period of several weeks. The data were
divided into three groups: comparative utterances, or those that could be
compared to corresponding adult forms, noncomparative utterances, or
those whose meaning could not be determined and which thus could not
be compared to the adult English forms, and interjections or emotive
utterances. It was noted that this child used about half comparative
utterances.

The subject's comparative utterances were analyzed to derive her phoneme inventory. The researchers determined the allophones that were
used to represent each English phoneme in initial, medial, and final positions. Phonemes were classified as "firmly established" if there was consistent use of appropriate allophones, "fairly well established" if
there was frequent use of expected allophones, "partially established" if
the child used a number of appropriate allophones, and "not established" if appropriate allophones were not used (p. 28). (Each category was
actually defined somewhat more precisely.)

Phoneme classes that were found to be fairly well established were /p,
b, k, m, n, w, h/. Partially established phonemes included /t, d, tʃ, f, r,
l, j/. The phonemes that were not established included /s, θ, g, dʒ, v, ð,
z, ʃ, ʒ, ŋ/. (/dʒ, ʒ, ŋ/ were not tested at all.) No adult phonemes were
firmly established. West and Weber (1973, p. 30) noted that more
resonants were established than stops and more stops than fricatives or
affricates. Regarding place of articulation, more bilabial sounds were
established than sounds produced at any other place (/p, b, m, w/).

The subject's vowel production was noted to be quite good, with all phoneme classes being firmly established.

The authors report (1973, p. 30) four "obvious systematic deviations" from adult English: (1) More deviations occurred in final position than in other positions. (2) Final consonant omission was often accompanied by a modification of the preceding vowel (e.g., elongation or nasalization). (3) Voiced fricatives were seldom used. (4) Back voiced consonants were rarely used.

West and Weber also analyzed the phonetic structure of their subject's noncomparative utterances, and they list the sounds that she used in initial and medial positions; for example, both voiced and voiceless labial and alveolar stops appeared in these positions. Fewer sounds were used in final position, and all were voiceless. Glottal stops were used extensively in both initial and final position. Fricatives appeared rarely, with the labiodentals being used the most. Although resonants occurred in all positions, the velar [ŋ] never appeared. Bilabial semivowels were used frequently, and [ə] was the most frequent vowel sound, although many other vowel sounds also appeared.

More phones were reportedly used in the noncomparative utterances than in the comparative utterances (an average of 4.7 vs. 3.7). In addition, certain phones, such as bilabial semivowels and glottal stops, occurred more frequently in the noncomparative utterances. However, there were also "notable similarities" between the two groups of data (p. 32). Specifically (a) more stops and resonants than fricatives were used; (b) fewer stops occurred in final position than in medial and initial positions; (c) few (or no) final voiced stops occurred; (d) all types of vowels and diphthongs were used in both groups of data; and (e) most consonants occurred in both groups, with some exceptions (e.g., [θ] appeared only in the comparative utterances).

Regarding the category of interjections, it was found that most consisted of glottal stops and back vowels. The most frequently used interjection was [ʔoʔ], which accounted for 26 out of the 70 interjections in this sample.

West and Weber (1973, p. 32) discuss their subject's phonemic development in terms of the "principle of contrast" discussed by Leopold (1966) [based on Jakobson's theory of acquisition]. This involves learning "coarser contrasts" first, then "more refined differentiations." The authors report that most of their subject's consonant phoneme contrasts were "coarse" contrasts between stops and resonants and between labial and nonlabial consonants.

Based on the similarities between their subject's comparative and noncomparative utterances, West and Weber hypothesize that her noncomparative utterances, like her comparative utterances, were "linguistically structured," although they were not comprehended by the researchers because they did not closely resemble specific adult forms.

The conclusions drawn by West and Weber (1973, p. 34) include the following. First, various stages of acquisition can be discovered for phonemes. For example, some phonemes were fairly well established, some were partially established and others were not established for the subject in this study. Second, the order of acquisition of phonemes is governed by the principle of contrast, with coarser contrasts being learned first. Third, it is sometimes possible to discern "rudimentary patterns" such as vowel elongation, which may "signal future linguistic development."

Concerning therapy applications, West and Weber suggest teaching contrasts, for instance, making the child aware of stop vs. resonant contrasts, and later introducing fricatives, which are between stops and resonants. In their view (p. 34), linguistic patterns should be taught, rather than individual sounds. For example, to teach frication, /s/ and /z/ might be contrasted to stops. Other therapy suggestions include helping the child to stabilize her "fairly well established" phoneme classes and teaching her to use final consonants more consistently. They also suggest rewarding the child for any linguistic structures that are utilized, even if they do not correspond to standard adult English.

Feature-Based Studies

As far as we know, there are few, if any, studies of the speech of the hearing-impaired that have as their focus distinctive features.

Suprasegmental-Based Studies

In many studies of the speech of the hearing-impaired, characteristics involving suprasegmentals have been mentioned. Ingram (1976, p. 128) in his review of the literature noted that children with impaired hearing typically have slow arhythmic speech and an abnormal voice quality. Silverman (1963) reported arhythmia, vowel elongation, lack of pitch variation, and nasality as being characteristic of the speech of the deaf. Unusual sound prolongations also have been noted, e.g., by Calvert

(1962) and Quigley (1966). "Time distortions" are discussed by John and Howarth, (1965). Bush (1979, p. 1) observed that the intrinsic differences in fundamental frequency for high and low vowels may be exaggerated by some profoundly deaf speakers. Although the babbling of deaf infants is said to be like that of hearing infants, the intonation patterns of the two groups have been noted (e.g., by Downs, 1968) to diverge sometime before the age of 1 year.

Phonological Rule- and Phonological Process- Based Studies

Oller and Kelly (1974)

In a 1974 article, Oller and Kelly used "substitution processes" in analyzing the phonology of a hard-of-hearing child. Although they were influenced by Stampe's (1969, 1972a) theory of natural phonology, they followed primarily a generative phonological approach. In fact, one of their purposes was to investigate the usefulness of describing the speech of hard-of-hearing children in terms of generative phonology (p. 65).

The subject in this study was a 6-year-old (6;2) girl named Ann who had a moderately severe sensorineural hearing loss. She had never had speech therapy. The child was asked to repeat the names of pictures taken from the *Photo Articulation Test* (Pendergast, Dickey, Selmar, & Soder, 1965) and McDonald's (1968) *A Screening Deep Test of Articulation.*

Substitution processes (formalized as generative phonological rules) were then formulated to capture the relationship between the adult forms and the child's phonetic forms. Several of the rules postulated for the subject in this study were reportedly similar to those found for younger normally developing children, for example, final devoicing. Oller and Kelly (1974, p. 65) found it necessary in some cases to "invoke . . . ordering restrictions" on the application of rules.

The authors describe their subject's phonology in terms of common types of processes, such as liquid and glide processes, voicing avoidance, and fronting of consonants, and they report only her more pervasive processes.[7] For instance, Ann exhibited an obligatory process of preconsonantal and final liquidation:

$$[+\text{liquid}] \longrightarrow \begin{bmatrix} -\text{consonantal} \\ +\text{round} \\ +\text{mid} \\ -\text{back} \end{bmatrix} \Big/ \underline{\quad\quad} \begin{Bmatrix} C \\ \# \end{Bmatrix}$$

by which all preconsonantal and final liquids were replaced by mid rounded vowels (p. 69). She also devoiced word-final obstruents:

$$[+ \text{obstruent}] \longrightarrow [-\text{voice}]/\underline{\quad} \#$$

For Ann, postvocalic palatals and velars were fronted to alveolars (as in [wɪts] for *witch* and [kʰeɪtʰ] for *cake*), and alveolars were dentalized. There was also some evidence of cluster reduction, assimilation, stopping, vowel substitution, and fricativization (of certain stops). Oller and Kelly found no evidence for processes that do not also occur in the development of children with normal hearing.

Regarding the formulation of processes, Oller and Kelly (1974, p. 68) note that if the same surface sound is found for two underlying (adult sounds, then there has to be a common "nonsurface" form at some point in the derivation. For example, in place of both adult /r/ and /w/, Ann used a [w]-like glide without full lip rounding, but with the appropriate velar tongue position. (This sound is represented as [w̵].) Therefore, both *ring* and *wing* were produced as [w̵ɪn]. Oller and Kelly argue that formulating two separate rules such as r → w/#__ V and w → w̵#/__ V would imply that these two underlying sounds (/r/ and /w/) are produced the same "by accident." Instead, they postulate two rules, both of which apply whenever they can. (These rules are said to be "intrinsically ordered.")

(1) r → w/__ V   Prevocalic liquidation

(2) w → w̵/__ V   Depursing

Prevocalic liquidation changes /r/ to /w/; then depursing applies, and all /w/s (whether from adult /w/ or /r/) are rendered as [w̵]. Thus, adult /r/ and /w/ have a common nonsurface form (/w/) before depursing applies. Oller and Kelly (1974, p. 68) point out that this formulation "expresses the relatedness of [w̵]s derived from both /r/ and /w/." In their view, "a description of phonological changes is most powerful when it accounts for the underlying relatedness of surface shapes," as in this example. (Note that they assume that the child has underlyingly, /r/ and /w/.)

Although Oller and Kelly do not discuss therapy, they note (p. 65) that this type of description may have "possible clinical usefulness" because it provides a "detailed diagnosis" within the framework of generative phonology.

Dodd (1976b)

Dodd (1976b) reported a study in which she investigated the possibility that profoundly congenitally deaf children may acquire some "consistent phonological behavior" (p. 185). The subjects in her study were 10 profoundly congenitally deaf children between the ages of 9;5 and 12;4. Various etiologies were represented. The subjects attended a London school in which lipreading and spoken language were encouraged.

The subjects in Dodd's study were asked to name 45 pictures. Then they were asked to say each name again. Dodd used only those words that were said the same on both tries and that were transcribed the same by two trained transcribers because she wanted to discover "consistent phonological behavior" (p. 186).[8]

Phonological rules were formulated to account for each subject's sound errors. However, Dodd (1976b, p. 188) presents only those rules that were shared by two or more subjects. To illustrate, all 10 subjects had a rule for nasal cluster reduction, as in [hæd] for *hand*, and /s/-cluster reduction, deleting /s/ preconsonantly, as in [pun] for *spoon*. Nine subjects reduced clusters made up of /k/, /t/, or /g/ plus /l/, /r/, or /w/, as in [gæs] for *glass*. Eight children simplified /l/ plus consonant clusters, and three of those children deleted /l/ preceding /d/ or /k/.

Dodd's rules are not stated formally and do not utilize distinctive features. Rather they are statements such as the following (1976b, p. 188):

/r, l/ are deleted after /b, p, t, d/ (8 subjects)

/n/ is replaced by [d] initially (7 subjects) (The "rule function" here is said to be nasal simplification.)

/dʒ, tʃ, θ, ð, ʃ/ are replaced by [d], as in [dæm] for *jam* (7 subjects) (The "rule function" is the simplification of nonsonorant consonants.)

Dodd reports the number of subjects erring on each phonological configuration (e.g., /s/ plus consonant) and exhibiting each rule (e.g., /s/ is deleted preconsonantly).

The results of Dodd's study show that hearing is not necessary for the acquisition of sounds or for the development of a phonological system that is "at least partially rule governed" (p. 189). Eight of her subjects produced nearly all the consonant sounds of English. In addition, all of the phonological rules found for these deaf children are also found for hearing children.

Dodd (1976b, p. 190) proposed two hypotheses to account for the rule-governed nature of the phonological systems of her deaf subjects. First, these children could be "internalizing an incomplete acoustic trace . . . using [their] residual hearing," as argued by Fry (1966). They could then map their output from this information. However, this would predict less homogeneity than was found in Dodd's study. Moreover, there were no patterns in the children's "phone repertoires" that would indicate difficulty with sounds of particular frequencies. Dodd's second hypothesis, which she says is more likely, is that deaf children internalize a "lip-read trace" for words and "use this visual input as the primary source of information from which to map their vocal output." Support for this hypothesis comes from their treatment of velar stops, which are hard to lip-read. These sounds tended to be deleted in clusters and in word-final position where they are very difficult to see. (In addition, seven subjects did not use [ŋ].)

A second study was undertaken by Dodd to lend support to the findings of her first study and to determine the role of lipreading as input. Two specific hypotheses were tested (p. 190): (1) the rules that were used often by the deaf subjects in the first study will predict the errors of other deaf children, and (2) different types of input (reading vs. lipreading] will affect output.

The subjects in the second study were eight "profoundly and prelinguistically" deaf children and two severely deaf children. Again, etiologies varied. The age range of 12;9 to 16;11 was higher in this study because the subjects had to be able to read. As in the first study, all subjects attended a London school for the deaf in which spoken language and lipreading were encouraged.

Thirty-six nonsense words of various syllable shapes were made up to test nine rules that were used by at least seven children in the first study. To illustrate, two nonsense words made up to test the deletion of nasals before consonants were *vump* and *gunka*. (The subjects were told that the words were made up.) Half of the subjects had to read the words aloud and then repeat them after lip-reading the adult's production. The others had to lip-read first.

Six of the nine rules were found to have "predictive value" in the lipreading condition. That is, they appeared more than any other type of error (p. 192):

1. Nasals delete before consonants.

2. /s/ deletes before consonants.

3. /l, r/ delete after labial stops.

4. /m/ is replaced by [b].

5. /k, g/ are replaced by [t, d].

6. /k, g/ delete word-finally.

Five of the nine rules had predictive value in the reading condition. These included all the rules listed above except rule 5. Also, one rule (predicting the deletion of velar stops before /l, r, w/) was replaced by its opposite. In other words, /l, r, w/ were deleted after /k, g/.

Statistical analyses indicated that subjects performed significantly differently in the two conditions only on certain features (p. 194): (1) Velar stops preceding /l, r, w/ were deleted more frequently in the lipreading condition. (2) There were more initial /k, g/ errors in the lipreading conditions. (3) Final /k, g/ were more often deleted in the lipreading condition. (4) Final /n/ was more often deleted in the lipreading condition and was more often correct in the reading condition.

Dodd proposed three explanations to account for the fact that some rules were not "validated" in the lipreading condition (p. 195): (1) The rules may not have been stated precisely enough. (b) After learning to read, children may no longer use some of the rules consistently. (c) The nonsense words may have been too simple. (Most were one-syllable CVC's).

The fact that most of Dodd's rules did have predictive value is said to indicate that deaf children acquire a phonological system that is (at least partially) rule-governed. In addition, as most features were not affected by the type of input, the phonological systems of these children appear to be "relatively stable." However, some sounds that are difficult to lip-read (e.g., velar stops) are affected by the type of input.

According to Dodd (1976b, p. 195), it is significant that older children who lip-read treat velar stops (/k, g/) in much the same way as do younger children in their spontaneous speech. This may indicate that lipreading is "a primary source of information which deaf children use for partially governing their phonological output." Dodd states (p. 196) that these results, if they are supported further, will have two implications for a general theory of phonological acquisition. First, vision may be more important in phonological acquisition than has been thought (cf. von Raffler Engel, 1965). Second, the processes that govern output may be somewhat "independent of input modality."

To summarize, the results of Dodd's work indicate that the deaf have at least partially rule-governed phonological systems. Although they appear to depend somewhat on lipreading for input, information from orthographic representations may also be important.

Oller, Jensen, and Lafayette (1978)

Following a generative phonological approach, Oller, Jensen, and Lafayette (1978) presented evidence to show that a hearing-impaired child may have phonological processes that are like those of younger normally developing children. An additional purpose was to demonstrate that the child's phonological system consists of groups of related processes, each of which "operationalizes" a particular phonetic preference, such as a preference for a CV syllable structure (p. 98).

The subject in this study was a 6-year-old boy (6;1) named Freddie who had a profound bilateral sensorineural hearing loss. He had normal intelligence and was enrolled in a public school with an oral approach. He had been in a public school program since the age of 3½.

Freddie was presented with items from the *Photo Articulation Test* (Pendergast, Dickey, Selmar, & Soder, 1965) and was asked to repeat the name of each item after his teacher. Sometimes a second and even a third attempt was requested. Composite transcriptions from three transcribers were used as a basis for the phonological analysis.

The results of the analysis indicated that Freddie's phonological processes were very similar to those found for younger normal children and also for language delayed children. Moreover, it was found that his phonological processes fit together into groups, with each group "operationalizing some phonetic preference" (p. 97).

Specific processes found to be operating for Freddie included the following. Freddie preferred singleton consonants, exhibiting at least 30 examples of cluster reduction, as in [ʈɑ] for *star*. Fricative plus stop clusters were generally reduced to the stop, as were nasal plus stop clusters and liquid plus stop clusters. In the view of Oller, Jensen, and Lafayette (1978, p. 100) all of Freddie's cluster reduction processes operationalize a constraint against consonant clusters in his phonological system.

Two additional processes are said to operationalize Freddie's restriction against word-final voiced consonants. That is, they work together to avoid voiced consonants in word-final position (cf. Oller & Kelly, 1974). His final consonant deletion process, as in [ti] for *keys*, affected 80% of all final voiced consonants, as compared to 30% for final voiceless consonants. There were eight instances of final devoicing, which was his other way of avoiding final voiced consonants.

Freddie also avoided velar plosives in word-final position. Three processes fell into this group. Final velars were often deleted by final consonant deletion (while final coronal consonants tended to be retained). Sometimes velar plosives were fronted to alveolars (velar fronting), as happens for younger normal children. In addition, final velar stops were sometimes changed to fricatives. (This type of *fricativization* change is rare in normal development.)

Freddie exhibited a "general preference" for more fronted consonants (p. 101). This was exemplified by three processes that are found in both normal and disordered development. Labiodentals were fronted to bilabials (as in f→ɸ); palatals and alveolars were fronted to dentals; and velars were often fronted to dentals, as in [d̪ʌ̃n] for *gun* and [t̪wa̪t̪ʊ] for *cracker*.

Stopping affected all initial and medial fricatives and often also final fricatives (although other processes also applied in final position). There were 37 cases of stopping, as in [tu] for *shoe* and [haʊt] for *house*. In word-final position, Freddie seemed to have a preference for a "bladed alveolar affricate" (in place of stops and fricatives). The authors claim (p. 103) that stopping and cluster reduction work together to operationalize a preference for stops, as opposed to fricatives.

Liquids were often replaced by glides in prevocalic position and by mid to back vowels in postvocalic position, as in [bwɔts] for *blocks*, [weɪo] for *radio*, and [d̪ɪtə] for *scissor*. The authors call this process liquidation (others use the term liquid simplification for such liquid errors). In addition, liquids were sometimes deleted in word-final position and in clusters. Thus, several processes are said to avoid the production of liquid consonants.

Other less general processes that affect just a few words include assimilation, as in [næm] for *lamb*, and deaspiration of initial stops. Oller, Jensen, and Lafayette (1978, p. 103) also note that their subject exhibited a few "strange" processes for which there is no apparent phonetic reason. However, they say that such processes sometimes show up in studies of normal development as well. (Examples are not given.) The authors do not try to relate Freddie's phonological processes to the configuration of his hearing loss. In their view, his loss has simply delayed his phonological development.

In discussing the implications of this study for a theory of phonological acquisition, particularly Stampe's (1969, 1972a) theory of natural phonology, the authors state that several phonological processes often work together to achieve a common goal. Thus, they argue that children's phonological processes are organized into "strategy groups," and they hypothesize that the processes themselves are not innate (as Stampe claims). Instead, the child is born with a set of phonetic preferences and has the capacity to "construct" processes that operationalize these preferences (p. 104).[9]

MENTAL RETARDATION

Segment-Based Studies

Studies of mentally retarded children have typically reported a high incidence of articulation problems, although these studies usually do not provide much detail. (It should be noted here that the cover term mental retardation includes an extremely heterogeneous population.) Studies that discuss the speech development of mentally retarded children from a sound segment viewpoint include those of Sirkin and Lyons (1941), Bangs (1942), Irwin (1942), Karlin and Strazzula (1952), Schlanger (1953a, 1953b), Schlanger and Gottsleben (1957), Blanchard (1964), Sheehan, Martyn, and Kilburn (1968), and Fitzgerald, Brajović, Djurdjić, and Djurdjević (1979). (See Zisk & Bialer, 1967, for a review of the literature to that time.) According to Ingram (1976, p. 122), such studies generally have shown a similarity between the sound errors of mentally retarded children and those or normally developing children. That is, mentally retarded children seem to exhibit a delay in articulatory development (cf. Zisk & Bialer, 1967). However, Lenneberg (1967) found that Down's syndrome children had particularly poor articulation. In general, Down's syndrome children are reported to have very severe speech problems. Their speech, which is often hard to understand, may be characterized by "grunt-type sounds" and unusual intonation patterns. These children also may have harsh or husky voices (Ingram, 1976, p. 126).

In a 1953 study of 40 children with Down's syndrome, Strazzula reported that most of their errors involved velar stops, fricatives, and affricates. (See also Zisk & Bialer, 1967, and Lenneberg, Nichols, & Rosenberger, 1964.)

Bangs (1942)

Bangs (1942) studied the articulation errors of 53 mentally retarded individuals living at a residential school. Each subject was asked to name familiar objects pictured on 65 stimulus cards. Bangs reported their major sound errors in initial, medial, and final positions. In initial position, the "preferred substitution" (exhibited by 60% of the subjects) involved the use of [w] for /r/. Second in frequency was the use of [f] for /θ/, exhibited by 49% of the subjects. (The f/θ error was found to be the most frequent substitute, across positions, occurring a total of 65 times.)

In medial position, the preferred substitute involved the use of [d] for /ð/, exhibited by 41% of the subjects. The use of [f] for /θ/ was the second most frequent error in medial position, and [w] for /r/ and [t] for /θ/ were also common substitutions, being used by over 30% of the subjects.

In word-final position, f/θ was the preferred substitute, occurring much more frequently than any other substitution error. Thirty-five percent of all errors in final position involved omissions, with /d/ being omitted by the largest number of subjects, followed by /t/ and /k/ and then /p/.

Based on the results of his study, Bangs (1942, p. 355) stated that the most frequent substitution errors of mentally retarded individuals appear to be very similar to those reported for normally developing children, although many of the "minor substitutions" are not. Commenting on the large number of omissions exhibited by the subjects in his study (21% of all errors, across positions), Bangs concluded (p. 356) that omissions are a significant characteristic of the speech of the mentally retarded (cf. Karlin & Strazzula, 1952).

Bodine (1974)

Bodine (1974) described the phonological systems of two English-speaking children with Down's syndrome, Tommy, aged 5;9, and David, aged 6;1. Both children were being raised at home. Bodine's analysis was based primarily on 2 to 4 hours of conversational speech, recorded in the child's own home.

Bodine used two approaches in her analysis. She first analyzed each child's phonology as a "self-contained system, without reference to the model language" (p. 5). That is, she sought to determine the child's significant sound differences. In the second type of analysis (a "correspondence analysis") Bodine identified the correspondences between the child's sounds and the "model" (adult) sounds.

In her study, Bodine also attempted to deal with each child's "sound fluctuations." She first identified all the sound differences that functioned to keep forms apart, and then she identified the "wide and narrow phonetic ranges" of those sounds. For both children, she reports the distinctive sounds and the phonetic ranges of each. For example, Tommy's /g/ "phoneme" was realized as [g] or [ŋg] in initial position and was realized as [k] in final position.

Neither child in this study had the hoarse voice quality that is said to be characteristic of children with Down's syndrome. However, Tommy was found to use [ʔ] as a "generalized" consonant that occurred "whenever another initial consonant was omitted" (p. 9). In addition, 25% of Tommy's first 270 utterances contained a "strong glottal stop" followed by an oral or nasal mid-front or mid-central vowel. Bodine divides these "communicative grunts" into 10 semantic categories, some of which also exist in the adult language (e.g., "pause-filler"). For example, there were 17 occurrences in Tommy's sample of [ʔəʔə], [ʔʰɪ] or [ʔʊʔ] being used as "concentration sounds" (p. 13).

Bodine presents model and replica charts (Ferguson, 1968) to show the "usual correspondence" between each adult vowel, consonant, and consonant cluster and the vowels and consonants of the child's speech. To illustrate, in initial position, Tommy's [m] and [n] corresponded to adult /m/ and /n/, but his initial [b] corresponded to adult /p/ and /b/. In general, Tommy's consonants were voiced in initial and medial positions but voiceless in final position. So, for instance, he used [dʒ] for medial /tʃ/ and [p, t, k] for final /b, d, g/ (p. 11). Tommy sometimes used [w] in place of initial /r/ and [d] was sometimes used in place of initial velar stops, as well as palatal affricates and coronal fricatives /θ, ð, s, z, ʃ/.

Bodine reports (p. 12) seven "multiple correspondences" for Tommy. That is, "seven model-language sounds are each regularly represented by two different sounds in Tommy's speech, depending on the form." For example, adult initial /k/ was produced by Tommy as [d] in three words and as [g] in two words.

David was more intelligible than Tommy and used fewer glottal stops. Bodine shows the wide and narrow phonetic ranges for David's consonants, clusters, and vowels. To give an example, David's "phoneme" /b/ was realized phonetically as [b] or [β] in initial and medial positions.

Model and replica charts show that many adult sounds were produced correctly by David. For instance, initial [p, b, t, k, g, θ, m, n] corresponded to the appropriate adult sounds; [f] was correct in all positions and also replaced adult /v/ in final position. Similarly, [s] was correct in all positions and replaced /z/ in final position. It also replaced /ʃ/ in initial and final positions. Additionally, [l] was correct in medial position and sometimes in initial position, but it was deleted word-finally. Also /r/ was replaced by [w] medially and sometimes initially, but it was replaced by a vowel in final position.

David was found to produce many more clusters than Tommy. For example, his initial /s/ plus stop clusters were generally produced correctly. However, liquids were usually omitted in initial clusters, and initial /tr/ clusters were produced as [f].

Bodine (1974, p. 20) concludes that children with Down's syndrome have "rudimentary patterned and meaningful language." Their utterances are said to show "regular correspondences" with the adult language.

Feature-Based
Studies

We do not know of any studies of the speech of mentally retarded children that have distinctive features as their basic unit of analysis.

Suprasegmental-Based
Studies

We are not aware of studies of the phonological production of mentally retarded children that focus on suprasegmentals. However, as mentioned earlier, it has been noted that children with Down's syndrome may have unusual intonation patterns and may have harsh or husky voices. In their review of the literature dealing with speech and language problems related to mongolism (Down's syndrome), Zisk and Bialer (1967, p. 240) note that both the rhythmic deviations and the phonation problems reportedly associated with mongolism need to be researched further, especially the hypothesis that specific voice problems may be linked to certain anatomical-physiological characteristics of Down's syndrome. (See Cantor and Girardeau, 1959, for a study of rhythmic discrimination in Down's syndrome children.)

Phonological Rule-
and Process-Based
Studies

Dodd (1976a)
Dodd (1976a) compared the phonological errors (in spontaneous and imitated speech) of 10 normally developing children, 10 Down's syndrome children, and 10 "severely subnormal" (SSN) non-Down's syndrome children. All groups were matched for mental age. Each child was asked to name 45 pictures of familiar objects and then to imitate the picture names after the examiner. Finally, each child had to again name the picture spontaneously. So, for each subject there were two spontaneous trials and one imitation trial.

Phonetic transcriptions of the subjects' productions were analyzed for evidence of several kinds of errors: cluster reduction (four specific types); consonant harmony (two types); seven types of "systematic simplification," including deletion of initial unstressed syllables, deletion of initial /h/, deletion or replacement of /l/, and deletion of final /s, z/.

Dodd (1976a, p. 34) found that the normal subjects used the "same number of error types" on all three trials. However, they made fewer errors on the second spontaneous trial than on the first. Only 49 errors were not accounted for by the above categories.

For the Down's syndrome children, like the normal group, the number of error types was not significantly different across trials, but the Down's syndrome children made fewer errors on the imitated trial than on the first spontaneous trial. In addition the Down's syndrome children made many errors (148) that could not be accounted for by the error categories listed above. These additional errors included 104 "inconsistent substitutions and omissions," which Dodd (p. 35) calls "random errors."

The severely subnormal children did not perform significantly differently (in terms of number of errors) on the various trials, and the number of error types was not significantly different across trials. The 47 errors that were not accounted for by the original error categories included 23 inconsistent substitutions and omissions or random errors.

Statistical analyses showed that the Down's syndrome children made significantly more errors than either the normal group or the SSN group. (There was no signficant difference in number of errors for the other two groups.) In addition, the Down's syndrome children exhibited more types of errors than the other two groups. The normal and SSN groups did not differ significantly from one another regarding the number of error types. Children in the Down's syndrome group also were found to exhibit significantly more random errors than either of the other two groups.

In summary, Dodd found that the Down's syndrome children made more errors and exhibited less consistency than the other two groups, whose performance was comparable. However, the productions of the Down's syndrome children improved in imitation. These results suggest, according to Dodd (1976a, p. 40), that the articulation problems of Down's syndrome children may be at least partly "due to difficulties in programming the motor movements of speech" rather than resulting from their mental deficits (cf. Firth & Firth, 1974). That is, if their articulation problems were a direct result of their mental deficits, we would not expect to find improvements in imitation. This general conclusion was also reported earlier by Dodd (1975).

Based on the similarities in performance for normally developing and mental-age matched severely subnormal children (without Down's syndrome), Dodd (1976a, p. 41) concludes that non-Down's syndrome severely subnormal children have mental-age appropriate phonological abilities. That is, level of phonological development is closely tied to general mental development for these children.

Stoel-Gammon (1980)

Stoel-Gammon (1980) studied four monolingual English-speaking Down's syndrome children between the ages of 3;10 and 6;3. All four children were being raised at home and all were said to have a "mild deficit in adaptive behavior" (pp. 32–33). Stoel-Gammon analyzed the spontaneous utterances of these children (250 to 290 utterances per child) produced at home and in their preschools. She determined each child's phonetic inventory and compared each child's productions to the corresponding adult sounds. In addition, phonological processes were determined for each subject.

Stoel-Gammon found that these children, who were in Brown's (1973) Stage I (with MLU's between 1.22 and 2.06), made errors primarily on consonants; 90% of their errors involved consonant production (p. 35). Therefore her analyses focused on consonants.

Concerning the phonetic inventories of these four Down's syndrome children, Stoel-Gammon found that, as a group, they could produce stops and front nasals (not /ŋ/) in all positions. Their production of fricatives, affricates, liquids, and glides was more variable.

A comparison of the children's productions to the corresponding adult sounds revealed that many adult sounds (e.g., stops and nasals) generally were produced correctly. Stoel-Gammon also found specific substitution and deletion patterns. There was some variation among subjects, for instance in the production of initial clusters.

The phonological processes postulated for these children are said to be similar to those found in normal development. Few phonological processes were obligatory, but several were exhibited by at least three of the children in this study. These included: deaspiration of initial stops, stopping of initial fricatives and affricates, voicing of intervocalic stops (as in [sʌbɚ] for *supper*), gliding of initial liquids, vocalization of final syllabic liquids, devoicing of final stops and fricatives, glottal replacement of final voiceless stops, as in [bʌʔ] for *book*, and omission of final nasals, with nasalization of the preceding vowel, as in [dʌ̃] for *done*. Stoel-Gammon's subjects often simplified clusters, exhibiting a preference for CV syllables or syllables made up of C + glide + V (p. 42). /s/-cluster reduction, as in [teɪk] for *steak*, was common and liquid cluster reduction, as in [pis] for *please* also occurred, but liquids in clusters were sometimes replaced by glides, as in [fwæg] for *flag*, and in some cases, an epenthetic vowel was inserted, as in [dᵊwəs] for *dress*, and [bᵊlu] for *blue*.

Additional processes that applied for individual children and that also appear in normal development include: depalatalization, as in [was] for *wash*, metathesis (or migration of initial /s/ in clusters) as in [dʌks] for *stuck*, denasalization of initial nasals, as in [dos] for *nose*, and initial voicing, as in [gʌlɚ] for *color*.

The fact that Stoel-Gammon's subjects were able to produce nearly all the sounds of adult English suggests that their articulation problems cannot be due primarily to oral-motor deficits (cf. Strazzula, 1953, and Dodd, 1976a).

Stoel-Gammon found the productions of her subjects to be regular and systematic, i.e., they were related systematically to the adult forms. Most of their sound patterns also have been reported in studies of normally developing children. Findings not reported in previous studies of mentally retarded children include: voicing of intervocalic consonants, deletion of alveolar flaps, and weakening of word-final consonants (p. 46).

In Stoel-Gammon's view, the articulatory abilities of her four retarded subjects were as good as the abilities of normally developing children at a comparable stage of language development (Brown's Stage I). In other words, her results support the view that Down's syndrome children have delayed language development.

Other phonological studies of the speech of mentally retarded children include those of Bleile (1982) and Prater (1982).

CONCLUSION

In this concluding chapter we have discussed the application of phonological theory to only three conditions associated with disordered communication—aphasia, hearing impairment, and mental retardation. Phonological analyses of the types described here also have been reported for virtually every other type of speech disorder, including those associated with speech flow (stuttering, cluttering), speechmotor control (e.g., dysarthria, dyspraxia) and emotional disturbance (e.g., autism). Future directions in the study of both normal and disordered speech development and performance include increased use of physiological and acoustic phonetics (e.g., Elbert, Dinnsen, & Weismer, to appear) and computer-assisted analysis procedures (e.g., Shriberg, 1982b). As suggested at the outset of this book, it is hoped that the application of phonological theory to applied concerns will continue to provide significant insights into the nature and treatment of communicative disorders.

FOOTNOTES

[1]It should be noted that some researchers, such as Critchley (1952) have not subscribed to the view that the phonological errors of aphasic speech are systematic.

[2]This review and the later discussions of work by Whitaker (1969) and Schnitzer (1972) are taken from an unpublished paper by the first author titled "Generative Phonology and Adult Aphasia," Stanford University, 1977.

[3]In dysarthria, articulation errors are said to be due to neuromuscular deficits including slowness, weakness, incoordination, or loss of the tone of the speech musculature.

[4]Actually Whitaker uses the term *phonological representation* to refer to both the lexical and the surface structure representation.

[5]It is not clear why Whitaker says that the phonological rules could not be impaired for one word and not another. Schnitzer (1972) presents evidence from aphasia that goes against this claim, and data from language acquisition indicate that children may apply a rule to one lexical item and not to another similar lexical item.

[6]These data were collected by Sheila Blumstein, who did not use them in her 1970 dissertation (published as 1973b). They were later sent to M. L. Edwards to be utilized in her study.

[7]In this paper only a few of the child's processes are given. Thus the authors do not provide a complete picture of their subject's phonological system.

[8]It should be noted that Dodd may have missed some important variability by using this procedure. See Ingram (1982) for a discussion of methodological issues of this type.

[9]How the results of this study led the authors to this conclusion is not made explicit. No evidence is presented to argue for this view in contrast to Stampe's view of innate natural processes. It would seem that other types of evidence are necessary before a view of the child as an active "constructor" is taken.

APPENDIXES

Appendix A

Notational Devices in Generative Phonology

Generative phonologists use many notational devices and conventions in writing phonological rules. These abbreviatory devices allow phonologists to collapse or combine similar rules or rules involving the same phonological process. Thus they help in capturing and expressing linguistic generalizations. Of course, distinctive features also do this to a certain extent because they help phonologists capture natural classes. Some important notational devices and conventions are described in this appendix.

Subscripts and Superscripts

Subscripts and *superscripts* are sometimes used in writing rules. For example, C_1 means "one or more consonants up to an infinite number." So, a subscript represents the minimum number of segments. Schane

(1973, p. 63) gives an example of an umlaut rule (an assimilation rule that fronts vowels before /i/) which is written using a subscript:

$$V \longrightarrow [-back] \, / \underline{} \, C_0 \begin{bmatrix} V \\ +high \\ -back \end{bmatrix}$$

This rule says that a vowel is fronted preceding a high front vowel, and there may be zero or any number of consonants intervening between the high front vowel and the vowel that is umlauted. (No maximum number is specified.) Another example of a rule using subscripts is the trisyllabic laxing rule in English. This rule accounts for the antepenultimate lax vowel in forms like div*i*nity and ser*e*nity (Schane, 1973, p. 81):

$$V \longrightarrow [-tense] \, / \underline{} \, C_0 V C_0 V C_0 \, \#$$

This type of notation allows us to abbreviate several different environments, such as CC, CCC, CCCC, etc.

Whereas a subscript indicates the smallest number of segments necessary, a superscript is used to indicate the maximum number of segments possible. So, C_0^1 (or more formally $[+consonantal]_0^1$) is read as "zero or one consonant"; C_2^3 means "no fewer than two and no more than three consonants"; C_0^2 means "between zero and two consonants," etc. A superscript with no subscript indicates exactly that number of segments, so C^2 means "exactly two consonants" or CC (Schane, 1973, p. 72).

Parenthesis Notation

Instead of using a subscript and a superscript, phonologists may use *parentheses*. For instance, C_2^3 can be written as CC(C). The element in parentheses is understood as being optional. By using parentheses, we can combine two related rules and thus capture a generalization by expressing their relatedness in a formal way. One of the rules includes an element or restriction that is not included in the other. To illustrate:

$$V \longrightarrow [-back] \, / \underline{} \, (C) \begin{bmatrix} V \\ +high \\ -back \end{bmatrix}$$

is an umlaut rule very similar to the one just discussed. This rule says that a vowel is fronted when it precedes a high front vowel, even if there is a consonant intervening between the two vowels. This rule has two expansions, one including the part in parentheses, and one without it. At least some generative phonologists claim that the two expansions are related in a certain way. When parentheses are used, it is understood that the longest expansion applies first if it can, and if it does apply, the shorter expansion cannot apply to the same elements (Sloat, Taylor, & Hoard, 1978, p. 154). The expansions are said to be *disjunctively ordered* (for discussion of this term, see Appendix B).

Braces Notation

Another way of collapsing structurally related rules is by using *braces*. Like the use of parentheses, the braces notation makes claims about the application of processes, i.e., that processes may apply to strings that are partly the same (Schane, 1973, p. 73). It is understood that no other rules can be ordered between two rules that are collapsed by braces (Hyman, 1975, p. 118). The use of braces allows us to collapse rules that involve the same change but different environments. To give an example, the following rule is often postulated for children:

$$r \longrightarrow \phi \ / \ \underline{\hspace{1cm}} \ \begin{Bmatrix} \# \\ C \end{Bmatrix}$$

This rule says that /r/ is deleted when it precedes either a word boundary (___ #) or a consonant (___ C). The environments in this rule do not comprise a natural class. Rather, each contains a restriction that is not found in the other. (Yet the two strings that are involved are partly the same.) Braces are said to involve a *disjunction* (Hyman, 1975, p. 118). Either one expansion or the other applies. (Schane, 1973, p. 90, disagrees. He says that both parts of the rule may apply in the same derivation). A rule with braces on each side of the arrow would be interpreted as follows:

$$\begin{Bmatrix} r \\ l \end{Bmatrix} \longrightarrow \phi \ / \ \underline{\hspace{1cm}} \ \begin{Bmatrix} \# \\ C \end{Bmatrix}$$

says that /r/ is deleted preceding either a word boundary or a consonant and that /l/ is deleted in the same environments.

In the phonological description of a language or variety of a language, usually only a few rules are written using braces because most rules should involve natural classes. In fact, some phonologists do not allow any rules using this notation because they believe that such rules do not capture linguistically significant generalizations.

Bracket Notation

Some generative phonologists also use the *bracket notation*. This convention, which requires that segments be matched horizontally, is said to be more restricted than the braces notation (Hyman, 1975, p. 119). For example, the following rule (written informally)

$$\begin{bmatrix} l \\ r \end{bmatrix} \rightarrow \phi \Big/ \underline{\hspace{1cm}} \begin{bmatrix} \# \\ C \end{bmatrix}$$

says that /l/ is deleted preceding a word boundary (i.e., in word-final position) and /r/ is deleted preceding a consonant. That is, the following two rules are collapsed:

(a) $l \rightarrow \phi / \underline{\hspace{1cm}} \#$ (b) $r \rightarrow \phi / \underline{\hspace{1cm}} C$

Angled Brackets

Angled brackets are also used by generative phonologists to capture generalizations. By using angled brackets, we can show "an interdependency between two feature specifications" (Hyman, 1975, p. 120). According to this convention, a rule is read twice, once with all the features in angled brackets included, and once with all the features in angled brackets excluded. This device, like the others already discussed, is said to collapse related rules. To illustrate, Oller (1973) in a study of the speech of five children with delayed phonology used the angled bracket convention (as well as others from generative phonology). One of his rules (discussed in Chapter 7 of this book) was similar to the following (Oller, 1973, p. 41):

$$\begin{bmatrix} -\text{vocalic} \\ +\text{coronal} \\ \langle +\text{anterior} \rangle \end{bmatrix} \rightarrow \begin{bmatrix} -\text{continuant} \\ \langle -\text{strident} \rangle \end{bmatrix} \Big/ \# \underline{\hspace{1cm}} \langle \text{optional} \rangle$$

This rule captures the fact that coronal consonants become noncontinuant in initial position. Coronal consonants that are also [+ anterior] optionally lose their stridency (i.e., become true stops). Oller points out (p. 41) that there is some controversy as to whether the generalizations captured by such devices are real generalizations or only "spurious" ones. As this rule is actually formulated by Oller (1973, p. 41) the ⟨ + anterior⟩ feature does not appear on the left of the arrow; instead, it appears as part of the environment, i.e.,

$$/ \# \; [\overline{\langle + \text{anterior} \rangle}]$$

This simply indicates that the sound that is changed is [+ anterior]. In other words, this feature is part of the specification of the input. So, these two ways of formalizing this rule are equivalent. (See Hyman, 1975, p. 124.)

Negative Constraints

Generative phonologists sometimes use a notational device that specifies the environment in which a rule does not apply. The negative symbol (~) is used before the environment that is excluded. This device (or *negative constraint*) is used when the elements that make up the environment in which a rule does *not* apply comprise a natural class (Sloat et al., 1978, p. 157). For example, if a child deletes /l/ everywhere except preceding high front vowels (as in *leaf*), the rule could be stated as follows:

$$/l/ \longrightarrow \phi \; / \; \underline{\hspace{2cm}} \quad \sim \begin{bmatrix} + \text{vocalic} \\ - \text{consonantal} \\ + \text{high} \\ - \text{back} \end{bmatrix}$$

The environment in which /l/ is actually deleted (e.g., in word-final position and preceding front low vowels and all back vowels) cannot be captured nearly as neatly as the environment in which it is not deleted.

Alpha Variables

Alpha variables, which are Greek letters such as α, β, γ, etc. are also widely used by generative phonologists in rule writing. They allow us to combine two rules that are identical except for the + or − values assigned to a certain feature. Each instance of a particular variable on either side of the arrow in a particular rule is read the same way (+ or −).

Alpha variables are very useful for formalizing certain kinds of processes, such as assimilation processes, by which a segment takes on feature values of (or assimilates to) a neighboring segment. To illustrate, it is natural for two obstruents that occur together in a cluster to agree in voicing, and often the first obstruent takes on the voicing feature of the following obstruent. This is an example of regressive voicing assimilation. So, in a language having this process, an underlying /gt/ cluster would be realized as [kt], and an underlying /pz/ cluster as [bz], etc. Without α variables, it would be necessary to write two separate rules, one by which a voiced consonant assimilates to a following voiceless consonant, and one by which a voiceless consonant assimilates to a following voiced consonant, as in the examples just given. However, by using α variable notation, we can capture the generalization that the first obstruent agrees in voicing with the second. This rule could be formalized as follows (Schane, 1973, p. 69):

$$[-\text{sonorant}] \longrightarrow [\alpha \text{ voice}] \ / \ \underline{\hspace{2cm}} \begin{bmatrix} -\text{sonorant} \\ \alpha \text{ voice} \end{bmatrix}$$

When a variable is used, it is understood that the variable has the same value (+ or −) wherever it occurs in a particular rule, as mentioned above. For instance, in the rule just given, if [α voice] has the value [+ voice] in the environment, it also has the value [+ voice] in the output (immediately to the right of the arrow), and likewise for [− voice].

If two features in a rule must have opposite values, α and − α are used. If α is +, − α is −, and vice versa. Alpha variables of this type can be used in the formalization of dissimilation processes, processes by which one sound becomes less like a neighboring sound. Schane (1973, p. 70) gives the following example of a continuancy dissimilation rule:

$$[-\text{sonorant}] \longrightarrow [-\alpha \text{ continuant}] \ / \ [\alpha \text{ continuant}] \ \underline{\hspace{1cm}}$$

This rule says that an obstruent ([− sonorant]) becomes [− continuant] when it follows a [+ continuant] segment, and conversely, an obstruent becomes [+ continuant] when it follows a [− continuant] segment. For example, in a language with this rule, an underlying /fs/ sequence would be realized as [ft], /kt/ as [ks], etc.

Alpha variables also can be used in other types of rules, in addition to assimilation and dissimilation, e.g., deletion, insertion, and coalescence rules. An example of a deletion rule using α variables is the following:

$$
\begin{bmatrix} -\text{sonorant} \\ \alpha \text{ anterior} \\ \alpha \text{ coronal} \end{bmatrix} \rightarrow \phi \Big/ \begin{bmatrix} +\text{consonantal} \\ \alpha \text{ anterior} \\ \alpha \text{ coronal} \end{bmatrix} \underline{\hspace{2cm}}
$$

This rule says that an obstruent ([– sonorant]) is deleted when it follows a consonant that agrees with it in the values (+ or –) for the [anterior] and [coronal] features. In addition, because α is used for both features, both must have the same value. So, an alveolar obstruent ([+ anterior] and [+ coronal]) is deleted following another alveolar consonant, as in a child's production of [bɛs] for *best* or [sæn] for *sand*. Similarly, a velar obstruent ([– anterior], [– coronal]) is deleted after another velar, as in [sɪŋ] for *sink*.

A rule may have more than one variable. In such cases, other Greek letters are used besides α. (α is used if a rule has one variable, α and β if it has two, etc.) The value of each variable is consistent throughout each reading of a rule, but two variables can have opposite values. For example, α may have a + value, while β has a – value throughout the rule. English has a nasal assimilation rule by which a nasal consonant becomes homorganic to (takes on the place feature of) a following obstruent. This rule is usually written with two variables, as follows (from Sloat et al. 1978, p. 151):

$$
\begin{bmatrix} +\text{nasal} \\ +\text{consonantal} \end{bmatrix} \rightarrow \begin{bmatrix} \alpha \text{ anterior} \\ \beta \text{ coronal} \end{bmatrix} \Big/ \underline{\hspace{1cm}} \begin{bmatrix} -\text{sonorant} \\ \alpha \text{ anterior} \\ \beta \text{ coronal} \end{bmatrix}
$$

This is actually a collapsed form of four nasal assimilation rules. α can have any value, as can β, and the two do not need to agree. So, the values can be [+ anterior], [+ coronal] (for alveolars), [– anterior], [+ coronal] (for palatals), [+ anterior], [– coronal] (for labials), or [– anterior], [– coronal] (for velars).

Alpha variables are also used for switching rules, also called exchange rules, or flip-flop rules (Schane, 1973, p. 71). In these rules, two things happen at the same time; an element that was + some feature becomes – , while an element that was – a feature becomes + . For example, [α high] → [– α high] is a shorthand way of collapsing two rules:

(a) [+ high] → [– high]   and   **(b)** [– high] → [+ high]

These rules capture the fact that [+ high] sounds become [– high] and [– high] sounds become [+ high].

Certain constraints can also be formalized using alpha variables. For instance, nonlow vowels frequently agree in backness and rounding, as they do in English. That is, [– back] (front or central) vowels are [– round], and [+ back] vowels are [+ round]. Hyman (1976, p. 122) states this constraint somewhat as follows:

$$
\text{If:} \quad
\begin{bmatrix}
+\,\text{syllabic} \\
-\,\text{consonantal} \\
-\,\text{low} \\
\alpha\ \text{back}
\end{bmatrix}
$$

$$\Downarrow$$

$$\text{Then:} \qquad [\alpha\ \text{round}]$$

In other words, if a nonlow vowel is [+ back] it is also [+ round], and if it is [– back] it is [– round].

Mirror Image Rules

Another notational device used in rule writing is the notation for *mirror image rules*. Mirror image rules are rules in which the environment may be read either from left to right or from right to left (Sloat et al. 1978, p. 152). For example, in English velar stops tend to be fronted when they come immediately before or after a front vowel. This can be captured in one rule using the mirror image convention. An asterisk may be placed before the environment to indicate that is can be read either forwards or backwards, or the environment slash (/) may be replaced by double diagonal lines (//) or by a percentage sign (%) (Sommerstein,

1977, p. 142). Thus the rule just mentioned can be formalized as follows (Sloat et al., 1978, p. 152):

$$
\begin{bmatrix}
+\text{consonantal} \\
-\text{anterior} \\
-\text{coronal} \\
+\text{back}
\end{bmatrix}
\rightarrow [-\text{back}]^*\Big/ \underline{\quad}
\begin{bmatrix}
-\text{consonantal} \\
-\text{back}
\end{bmatrix}
$$

In this rule,

$$
^*\Big/ \underline{\quad}
\begin{bmatrix}
-\text{consonantal} \\
-\text{back}
\end{bmatrix}
\text{ is read as } \Big/ \underline{\quad}
\begin{bmatrix}
-\text{consonantal} \\
-\text{back}
\end{bmatrix}
$$

and also as

$$
\Big/
\begin{bmatrix}
-\text{consonantal} \\
-\text{back}
\end{bmatrix}
\underline{\quad} .
$$

Sloat et al. (1978, p. 153) point out that in rules of this type (*neighborhood rules*), in which the environment on just one side of the sound is relevant, the asterisk and the horizontal line (*underscore*) can be omitted. The environment of the rule just discussed could therefore be represented as:

$$
\Big/
\begin{bmatrix}
-\text{consonantal} \\
-\text{back}
\end{bmatrix}
$$

This environment is read as "next to a front vowel." However, mirror image rules cannot be represented this way if the environment on each side of the sound is relevant. It should be noted that the mirror image device is not accepted by all phonologists (e.g., Dinnsen, 1979).

In her phonological analysis of the speech of a misarticulating child, Maxwell (1979) used many of the notational devices and conventions just discussed. For example, one of the rules postulated by Maxwell (1979, p. 193) is called *least anterior deletion*. It is stated as follows:

$$
\begin{bmatrix} -\text{sonorant} \\ \langle +\text{anterior} \rangle \end{bmatrix} \rightarrow \phi \ \% \ + \text{X} \underline{\quad} \$ \begin{bmatrix} -\text{sonorant} \\ +\text{anterior} \\ \langle -\text{coronal} \rangle \end{bmatrix} \text{Y} +
$$

This rule captures the fact that [+ anterior] obstruents are deleted in the neighborhood of (%) labial obstruents that are not in the same syllable; and velar obstruents are deleted in the neighborhood of labial and dental obstruents ([+ anterior], [- sonorant]) across syllable boundaries. In other words, when two obstruents occur side by side, with a syllable boundary intervening, it is always the least anterior obstruent that is deleted, as in [kæpɪn] for *captain* and [æfə] for *after* (Maxwell, 1979, p. 191). By using the mirror image device (% is used here) and angled brackets (⟨ ⟩), Maxwell was able to collapse four rules into one.

Conventions for Phonological Domains and Boundaries

Each phonological rule has a domain or scope within which it applies. This may be a word, syllable, morpheme, etc. If no boundaries are specified in a rule, the domain of the rule is understood to be a single syllable. Other domains have to be specified (Sloat et al., 1978, p. 143). So, if we want to state that a rule operates across a syllable or word boundary, that boundary must be specifically mentioned in the rule, as in the example from Maxwell (1979) given above.

Chomsky and Halle's (1968, pp. 12, 13) boundary convention has the function of assigning boundaries. Each word, phrase, sentence, etc. is said to be bounded by external junctures. Only one juncture (#) comes between a stem and and an affix, but each full word is bounded by at least two external junctures (# #) (Sloat et al., 1978, p. 144). (In practice, however, a single # is often used to represent a word boundary.)

Some linguists use + for internal junctures, which separate morphemes that are more closely connected than those separated by #. According to Chomsky and Halle (1968), any sequence of XY in a rule is assumed to have an optional internal juncture (+). Thus any rule that applies to XY, will also apply to X + Y. However, a rule that has an internal juncture specified (X + Y) does not apply to the sequence (XY) without the juncture (Sloat et al., 1978, p. 155). In other words, if a boundary is specified in the environment of a rule, the rule will not apply to sequences that do not contain that boundary (Schane, 1973, p. 94).

Many types of boundaries have been proposed. For instance ‖ has been proposed as a phrase boundary or pause (Schane, 1973, p. 64). As just mentioned, a full word boundary is usually represented by *##*, as in *##bring##her##*. An internal word or stem boundary is then represented by *#*, as in *##sing#er##* (Hyman, 1975, p. 77). However, *#* is used by some generative phonologists (e.g., Schane, 1973) to represent any word boundary, as noted above, and Sloat et al. (1978, p. 155) use *#* to represent what they call external juncture. A morpheme boundary (or internal juncture) is represented by +, as in *##long + er##*. Syllable boundaries are most often represented as $, although other conventions (e.g. .) are sometimes used.

Boundaries are grammatical (morphological/syntactic) elements, but they are sometimes important in phonological rules. For example, grammatical information is important in the rules of stress assignment in English, and in some languages a full word boundary blocks assimilation rules. Many rules need to be stated with grammatical boundaries because many processes seem to be sensitive to boundaries. Boundaries may condition rules (e.g., word-final obstruent devoicing) or block rules (e.g., assimilation rules) (Hyman, 1975).[1]

According to Hyman (1975, p. 196), + is a weaker boundary than *#* or *##*, and *##* is the strongest. That is, + cannot block rules, and *##* is most likely to block or condition rules. For example, obstruents may undergo voicing assimilation across morpheme boundaries, but not across full word boundaries. Hyman (1975, p. 197) states that the rule deleting /g/ from /ng/ sequences must be sensitive to boundaries because it does not apply in *finger*, where there is no boundary, or *longer*, in which there is a morpheme boundary. However, it does apply in the cases where there is an internal word boundary, as in *singer*, or a full word boundary, as in *bring her*. Because boundaries are erased as the last step in a derivation, they do not appear in surface representations.

FOOTNOTE

[1]American descriptive linguists talked about phonological juncture instead of grammatical boundaries because they did not want to mix levels. That is, they did not want to include grammatical (boundary) information in their phonological descriptions (Hyman, 1975, p. 78).

Appendix B

Rule Ordering in Generative Phonology and Evaluation Metrics

Rule ordering issues and ways to evaluate grammars are central concerns in generative phonology. This appendix discusses major issues associated with rule ordering and simplicity. (See Appendix A for a review of notational conventions.)

Overview

In any phonological analysis, there are some rules that can apparently apply in any order. Thus only certain sets of rules may need to be ordered. Two rules are said to be critically or crucially ordered if applying them in a different order gives the incorrect output. Several examples of ordering are given here.

In English, vowels are nasalized before nasal consonants. In addition, nasal consonants may be deleted before voiceless obstruents, so *can't* may be pronounced as [kʰǣt]. The nasalization rule must precede the nasal deletion rule or the incorrect output will be derived (e.g., [kʰæt]). (See Sloat et al., 1978, p. 146).

Phonological rules for children's speech sometimes have to be ordered. To illustrate, some young children say [gɑ] for *dog*. In order to derive this form, two rules have to be ordered: regressive velar assimilation, then final consonant deletion. If final consonant deletion preceded velar assimilation, the surface form would be [dɑ]. The derivation of [gɑ] is given below. (The child's underlying representation is taken to be the adult surface form.)

Child's underlying form	/dɔg/
Regressive velar assimilation	/gɔg/
Final consonant deletion	/gɔ/
Vowel modification	/gɑ/
Child's surface form	[gɑ]

Two dialects of a language may differ only in the order in which certain rules apply. (The same rules may apply, but in a different order.) For instance, in some dialects of English, *writer* and *rider* are both pronounced as [rɑːɾɚ], while in other dialects, *writer* is pronounced as [rāɪɾɚ], but *rider* is [rɑːɾɚ], with lengthening of the vowel. The two rules of interest here are vowel lengthening and flapping, which may be formulated as follows (Schane, 1973, p. 85):

$$\text{(a)} \quad V \longrightarrow [+\text{long}] \; / \; \underline{\hspace{1.5cm}} \begin{bmatrix} C \\ +\text{voice} \end{bmatrix}$$

$$\text{(b)} \quad \begin{Bmatrix} t \\ d \end{Bmatrix} \longrightarrow \mathfrak{r} \; / \; V \underline{\hspace{1.5cm}} \begin{bmatrix} V \\ -\text{stress} \end{bmatrix}$$

In the first group of dialects, flapping (b) precedes vowel lengthening (a), and the voiced flap causes the stressed vowels in both *writer* and *rider* to be lengthened. In the other dialects, however, vowel lengthing applies first, and therefore does not affect the vowel in *writer*. In these dialects, the underlying contrast between /t/ and /d/ (one of voicing) is realized on the surface as a difference in vowel length. (This can be considered a displaced contrast.)

Similarly, two children may have the same rules but in a different order. To give an example, child A may have [pɪŋ] for *swing* and [pɪ̩ŋə] for *finger*, while child B has [fɪŋ] for *swing* but [pɪŋə] for *finger*. Both children have the following rules, stated informally:

(a) sw → f/#____   (b) f → p / #____

For child A, the rules apply in the order (a, b), and the output of rule (a) undergoes rule (b), but for child B, the rules apply in the opposite order (b, a), and therefore the output of (a) does not undergo (b). (Stampe, 1969, 1972a, would say that for child A the rules are unordered, and each applies whenever it can.)

With these examples in mind let us now look at the issues.

The Linear Ordering Hypothesis

Many generative phonologists operate under the assumption that the phonological rules that are postulated for a language must be linearly ordered. After the first rule in a derivation applies, changing the underlying representation somehow, the second rule applies (if it is applicable) and so on, with rules applying in sequence until the surface representation is derived. Thus the output of one rule serves as the input to the next applicable rule (Sloat et al., 1978, p. 146). This view of rule ordering, put forth by Chomsky and Halle (1968), is called the *linear ordering hypothesis*. According to this hypothesis, "every pair of rules in a language has an invariable ordering relationship," and the relationship between two rules holds throughout the language; if two rules apply in one order to one set of forms, they cannot apply in the opposite order elsewhere. In addition, ordering relationships are *transitive*; this means that if rule A precedes rule B, and rule B precedes rule C, then rule A must also precede rule C (Sommerstein, 1977, p. 174).

In the linear ordering view of rule application, if a form meets the structural description of two rules, A and B, only the first (A) applies. This is called the *precedence constraint*. Also, if a form has undergone rule B, it cannot undergo A. This is called the *blockage constraint* (Sommerstein, 1977, p. 177).

Since *The Sound Pattern of English* was published in 1968, the "across-the-board" property of rule ordering has been disconfirmed for some forms, and many "ordering paradoxes" have been discussed which show that Chomsky and Halle's hypotheses regarding rule application cannot be completely correct (e.g., Anderson, 1969). Therefore, many alternative hypotheses have been proposed, and most of these proposals include some type of *iterative rule application*. Some of these alternative proposals are discussed here. (Also see Sommerstein, 1977.)

Alternatives to the Linear Ordering Hypothesis

Iterative Application

Iterative application allows rules to apply more than once in the same derivation, i.e., a rule can apply to its own output. A rule applies first to an appropriate segment at one end of a form, and then it progresses toward the other end, applying to each appropriate segment until it can no longer apply. Both right-to-left iterative application and left-to-right iterative application are possible. Assimilatory nasalization in English is an example of right-to-left iterative application. A sonorant is nasalized when it precedes a nasal sound. This rule applies to as many segments as it can, starting with the sonorant immediately to the left of the nasal (Sloat et al., 1978, p. 149). Rules for stress assignment are often left-to-right iterative rules, starting at the beginning of a word.

Anderson (1974) claimed that rule application is either *simultaneous-once-only* or *simultaneous iterative*, with each rule marked for one of these types of application. In simultaneous-once-only application, all rules apply at one time and only once to underlying representations. However, in simultaneous iterative application, a rule can apply to its own output, and at each iteration, all applicable rules apply at once (Sommerstein, 1977, p. 174).

Partial Ordering

Sommerstein (1977, pp. 176–180) discusses another alternative to the *SPE* view of rule ordering. It is called *partial ordering*. Like the linear ordering hypothesis, it includes precedence and blockage constraints. That is, rule A may "take precedence over" rule B, and if rule B has already applied, it blocks the application of rule A. According to the partial ordering hypothesis, there are some cases in which explicit statements have to made regarding the application of pairs of rules. In addition, all statements about ordering are considered to hold across-the-board. In other words, the relationship between two rules is seen as being constant throughout the language. According to Sommerstein (1977, p. 180), the partial ordering hypothesis differs from the linear ordering hypothesis only in separating the precedence and blockage functions of ordering and in allowing rules to be unordered.

Local Ordering

Another hypothesis regarding rule application is called *local ordering* (e.g., Anderson 1969, 1970, 1972a, 1974). The local ordering hypothesis includes three types of ordering constraints, one of which must hold for every pair of rules (unless they never have to apply in a specific order). The first constraint is: Rule A precedes rule B, across-the-board. The second constraint is: Rules A and B apply in the unmarked order, whatever that is. (This allows the order of application of two rules to differ for different forms.) If an unmarked order cannot be found for a pair of rules, the contingent ordering constraint imposes an order (Sommerstein, 1977, pp. 181–183).

Extrinsic and Intrinsic
Rule Ordering

Extrinsic rule ordering is ordering that is governed by explicit statements about particular rules in a particular language (Sommerstein, 1977, p. 184). In contrast, *intrinsic ordering* is imposed by the forms of the rules themselves so that no explicit statement of their ordering is necessary. Two rules are intrinsically ordered if they can apply in only one way because of their form (Hyman, 1975, p. 129). If rules are extrinsically ordered, each applies just once at a specific point in a derivation. Two rules are said to be extrinsically ordered if they must apply in a particular order to give the correct output and if the order does not follow from the form of the rules themselves or from universal principles (Sommerstein, 1977).

Some phonologists have argued against extrinsic ordering, claiming that rule application should be restricted only by universal principles. One proposal that does not allow extrinsic ordering is called *unordered semisimultaneous rule application* (Pullum, 1975, discussed by Sommerstein, 1977). This proposal says that all rules whose structural descriptions are met apply simultaneously, and then any that can apply again do so. This goes on until no rules can apply. Only universal principles can modify this system of rule application, it is claimed. One such universal principle is called Proper Inclusion Precedence (Koutsoudas, Sanders, & Noll, 1974). According to this principle, if every form that meets the structural description of Rule A also meets the structural description of Rule B, but the opposite is not true, Rule A has precedence over Rule B (Sommerstein, 1977, p. 186). In other words, the less general rule precedes the more general rule. It is argued that many cases of rule ordering can probably be accounted for by this constraint.

The need for extrinsic ordering has been questioned a great deal. In Hyman's (1975, p. 129) view, there are no clear cases that show that extrinsic ordering is absolutely necessary, although there are some fairly convincing cases.

Extrinsic rule ordering is related to simplicity. By imposing an extrinsic order, we can often simplify rules considerably. In many cases, rules have to be made more complicated if extrinsic rule order is to be avoided. For example, a whole set of rules may be allowed to apply simultaneously to underlying representations. This avoids imposing an extrinsic order, but such rules are often very complex and have unusual environments. Ordering rules allows us to simplify environments and capture generalizations (Schane, 1973, p. 88).

Random Sequential
Rule Ordering

Another way of avoiding extrinsic rule order is to allow *random sequential ordering*. In random sequential ordering, rules apply whenever they can—whenever the appropriate conditions are met, but only one rule can apply at each stage of a derivation (Sommerstein, 1977, p. 184). This type of rule application often requires making environments more complicated, however. In addition, underlying representations have to be less abstract than they can be if extrinsic rule ordering is allowed.

In some instances, we cannot avoid imposing an order by making rules more complicated. In these cases, phonologists may resort to using rule features, marking certain forms in the lexicon as undergoing or not undergoing particular rules. Thus there are cases in which extrinsic rule order is necessary or can only be avoided by complicating the grammar. As Hyman (1975, p. 129) points out, only by means of extrinsic rule order can we (reasonably) prevent a rule from applying when its structural description is met.

Interacting Rules

Two rules are said to *interact* if their order of application affects the number of forms to which one of them applies (Chafe, 1968; Sloat et al., 1978, p. 160). Several types of order have been distinguished for interacting rules.

Feeding and
Bleeding Orders

Kiparsky (1968b) distinguished *feeding order* from *bleeding order*. Rule A feeds rule B if it creates new input or new environments for B. That is, A increases the number of items to which B can apply. An example of feeding order was given above. If a child has two rules: (a) sw→f/#____ and (b) f→p/#____, and if the rules apply in the order (a, b), then (a) produces new instances of /f/ to undergo rule (b), along with underlying (adult) /f/. In other words, rule (b) applies to all instances of underlying /f/, and in addition, it applies to those new instances of /f/ generated by the application of rule (a).

Another example from child phonology is the following. If a child has [su] for *shoe* and [seɪə] for *chair*, the two rules given below apply in the order (a, b). Rule (a) feeds or creates new input for (b).

$$\textbf{(a)} \quad t\!\int \rightarrow \int / \# \underline{\qquad} \qquad \textbf{(b)} \quad \int \rightarrow s / \# \underline{\qquad}$$

If all of the inputs for a rule B are created by a rule A, rule A is said to *absolutely feed* rule B. If it were not for rule A, rule B would have nothing to apply to (Hyman, 1975, p. 130).

A rule that creates environments for its own later application is called *self-feeding* (Sloat et al., 1978, p. 160). The vowel nasalization rule discussed earlier is such a rule because once a vowel (or sonorant) is nasalized preceding a nasal consonant, it can then cause the sound preceding it to be nasalized.

Rule A *bleeds* rule B if it either removes environments or changes segments that could have undergone rule B. It decreases the number of items to which B can apply or the number of environments in which it is applicable. For example, a child may have [fwɪm] for *swim*, but [noʊ] for *snow* and [laɪd] for *slide*. In this case, we say that rule (a) below bleeds rule (b) because it decreases the number of forms to which (b) may apply:

$$\textbf{(a)} \quad s \rightarrow f / \# \underline{\qquad} w \qquad \textbf{(b)} \quad s \rightarrow \phi / \# \underline{\qquad} C$$

When two rules are in a bleeding relationship like this, the more specific rule generally applies first. So, in this example, the more specific rule is the one affecting just /sw/ sequences.

Absolute bleeding is not allowed because in such a case rule A would take away all inputs from rule B, and thus there would be no reason to posit rule B (Hyman, 1975, p. 130).

Other types of ordering have also been discussed. These include *counterfeeding* and *counterbleeding* (Newton, 1971). If two rules are ordered such that rule A would feed rule B if the order were reversed, they are in counterfeeding order (Sloat et al. 1978, p. 160). To illustrate, using an example given at the beginning of this discussion on rule ordering, if a child has [pɪŋə] for *finger* but [fɪŋ] for *swing*, the two rules listed here are said to be in a counterfeeding relationship with (a) preceding (b):

(a) f → p / # _____   **(b)** sw → f / # _____

This order prevents (b) from feeding (a). If the order were reversed, (b) would feed (create new input for) (a), and *swing* would be [pɪŋ].

Two rules are in counterbleeding relationship if, in the opposite order, one would take input away from (bleed) the other. Earlier, an example was given in which a child's form for *dog* was [gɑ]. In this example, velar assimilation had to apply before final consonant deletion. This is an example of counterbleeding order. If the rules applied in the opposite order, final consonant deletion would bleed velar assimilation, and velar assimilation could not apply to this form. The output would then be [dɑ], as shown in the following derivation:

Child's underlying form	/dɔg/
Final consonant deletion	/dɔ/
Velar assimilation	—
Vowel modification	/dɑ/
Child's surface form	[dɑ]

Note that counterbleeding is not equivalent to feeding. So, in the [gɑ] example, the application of velar assimilation did not feed final consonant deletion.

Feeding and counterbleeding orders increase the application of a rule, while bleeding and counterfeeding orders decrease the application of a rule. Because the natural state of affairs is for rules to apply to as many forms as possible, phonologists often consider feeding and counterbleeding orders to be natural or favored, while the other orders are considered to be marked. Supporting evidence comes from historical language change. According to Kiparsky (1968b), when rules are reordered in historical change, they tend to shift into orders that allow for their maximum application (Schane, 1973, p. 87).

Concerning phonological acquisition, phonological rules (or processes) at first apply in a feeding order, according to Stampe (1969, 1972a), because it is natural for rules to apply whenever the appropriate conditions are met. (He calls this unordered application.) At later stages, *antisequential constraints* are imposed, and rules are put into a counterfeeding relationship. This is necessary if children are to represent as many contrasts as possible. For example, the following two rules might apply in a feeding order early on for a child:

$$\text{(a) } t\int \rightarrow \int / \#\,\underline{\hspace{1cm}} \qquad \text{(b) } \int \rightarrow s / \#\,\underline{\hspace{1cm}}$$

Thus the child would produce [su] for *shoe* and [seɪə] for *chair* as noted above, because the output of (a) would undergo rule (b) along with underlying (adult) /ʃ/. If the child imposed an antisequential constraint at a later stage, the rules would be put in a counterfeeding order; (b) would apply before (a). At this stage, *shoe* would still be [su], but *chair* would be [ʃeɪə]. At this later stage, the child would be said to exhibit a *displaced contrast* (Kiparsky & Menn, 1977). The adult contrast between /tʃ/ and /ʃ/ would be realized by the child as a contrast between [ʃ] and [s].

Disjunctive and
Conjunctive Ordering

Disjunctive ordering is a constraint on the ordering of some rules such that only the first applicable rule in an ordered set applies. The application of the first rule blocks the application of the second; the two rules are mutually exclusive (Schane, 1973, p. 89). In *The Sound Pattern of English*, disjunctive rule application was related to specific formal devices. Two rules were disjunctively ordered if they could be abbreviated by means of either the *parenthesis* or the *angled-bracket* convention (Sommerstein, 1977, p. 188). When the parenthesis notion is used, it is understood that the rule applies first with the longer environment (including the part in parenthesis), if it is applicable. Schane (1973, p. 89) gives an example from French:

$$V \rightarrow [+\text{stress}] / \underline{\hspace{1cm}} C_0 \left(\begin{bmatrix} V \\ -\text{tense} \end{bmatrix} \right) \#$$

This rule assigns stress to the next to the last vowel if a word ends in a lax vowel (i.e., the rule is read with the part in parentheses). If this expansion of the rule is not applicable, the rule is read without the part in parentheses, and stress is assigned to the last vowel.

Schane (1973, p. 90) argued that the parenthesis convention is the "appropriate formalism for showing disjunctive ordering." However, Sommerstein (1977, pp. 188–189) stated that it has been discovered that some pairs of rules have to apply disjunctively even though they cannot be abbreviated by using parentheses or angled brackets, and that use of the parenthesis notation does not always give the correct results.

In *conjunctive ordering*, two rules or two expansions of a rule apply to the same form (in the same derivation) and are ordered (Hyman, 1975, p. 124). Conjunctively ordered rules can be collapsed using the braces notation, according to Schane (1973, p. 90). In interpreting the braces notation, we allow both parts of the rule to apply. After one part applies, starting at the top, the others also apply if the conditions are met. The following example from French is given by Schane (1973, p. 90):

$$C \longrightarrow \phi \: / \: \underline{\hspace{1cm}} \: \begin{Bmatrix} + \\ \# \end{Bmatrix} \: C$$

This rule says that a consonant is deleted when it precedes a morpheme boundary (+) followed by another consonant, and then before a word boundary (#) followed by another consonant. So, in the derivation of French [pətigɑrsɔ̃] "little boys" from #pətit + z # gɑrsɔ̃ #, the final /t/ of /pətit/ is deleted before the morpheme boundary (+) and then the plural ending /z/ is deleted preceding the word boundary (#). If the subparts of this rule applied in the opposite order, the /z/ would be deleted first, and then there would be no consonant after the (+) to allow the final /t/ of /pətit/ to be deleted. Thus both parts of the rule apply, and they have to apply in a specific order.

Cyclic Rule
Application (The
Transformational Cycle)

The principle of *cyclic rule application* or the *transformational cycle*, another ordering principle, was proposed by Chomsky and Halle (1968). According to this principle, an entire set of rules applies to the smallest possible unit and then reapplies within increasingly larger units (Schane, 1973, p. 103). The domains for the phonological cycle are syntactic constituents (nouns, verbs, etc.). The rules in an ordered set apply first to the most deeply embedded constituent (which does not include any other). After all applicable rules have applied, the inside brackets are erased. Then the rules apply over again, in the same order, within the next larger unit (i.e., they apply to derived elements). Chomsky and Halle (1968) proposed cyclic rule application for the rules assigning stress in English. The rules assigning stress first apply to the innermost element of words. To give a simple example, the stress pattern of the compound noun *blackbird* is derived as follows. This compound noun consists of an adjective (*black*) plus a noun (*bird*). This is indicated by bracketing:

$$\left[\quad [\text{black}]_A \quad [\text{bird}]_N \quad \right]_N$$

(A stands for adjective and N stands for noun.) The *lexical stress rule* assigns primary stress to both elements of the compound noun and erases the innermost brackets. The *compound stress rule* then assigns primary stress [1 stress] to *black*, and reduces the stress of *bird* (to [2 stress]). This gives the correct stress pattern: *bláck bìrd* (Hyman, 1975, p. 201). More complicated examples of stress assignment are given, for example, in Hyman (1975, 198–203) and Sommerstein (1977, pp. 163–165). Although some linguists have argued against cyclic stress assignment, the principle of cyclic rule application is subscribed to by many generative phonologists.

Additional Properties of Rules

Derivational Constraints
Kisseberth (1970) introduced *derivational constraints* in order to capture, formally, the *functional relatedness* of rules (as many of the conventions and notations that have already been discussed capture *structural relatedness*). A derivational constraint, which is assumed to be in effect throughout the operation of a sequence of rules, has the function of triggering rules (i.e, making them apply) or preventing rules from applying if their output is not permissible in the language (Hyman, 1975, p. 137). To illustrate, if sequences of three consonants are not permitted in a language, any rule that would produce such sequences may be prevented from applying by a derivational constraint. Derivational constraints allow us to state rules more simply than we otherwise could, but as Hyman (1975, p. 137) points out, there is some controversy as to whether the functional relatedness of rules should be captured formally.

Global Rules
Some phonologists (e.g., Kisseberth, 1973a, 1973b) have proposed that languages have *global rules* or rules that can refer to earlier stages of a derivation, even if those earlier stages are no longer evident. In this view, information from the *systematic phonemic level* is available throughout

a derivation (Hyman, 1975). So, a rule can refer to an element in the underlying form, even if it has been deleted. With global rules, extrinsic rule order may not be necessary. For instance, in the *writer/rider* example discussed earlier, vowel lengthening could be allowed only before underlying voiced consonants. By postulating global rules, we imply that speakers "have access to underlying forms at all stages of the derivation" (Hyman, 1975, p. 132). This is consistent with the claim that underlying forms are "psychologically real."

**Opacity and
Transparency**

Opacity and *transparency* are two additional properties of rules that have been discussed by generative phonologists (e.g., Kiparsky, 1971). A rule is opaque if it does not capture a "true surface generalization" (Sommerstein, 1977, p. 245). That is, certain forms that look as though they were derived by it actually were not (as is the case with neutralization rules), or forms underwent it even though they look as though they should not have. Stated differently, a rule of the form $X \rightarrow Y \; / \; A \underline{\hspace{1em}} B$ is opaque if there are surface representations AXB that did not undergo this rule (i.e., exceptions) or AYB that were not derived by this rule. Marked orders are said to lead to a rule becoming opaque, while unmarked orders "maximize transparency" (Kiparsky & Menn, 1977, p. 73). In general, a rule is transparent if we can infer its existence from the surface representations. Transparent rules are said to be more natural than opaque rules. Thus opaque rules tend to be lost historically, and rules tend to shift into an order that maximizes their transparency (Sommerstein, 1977, p. 245). There are still many unresolved problems or paradoxes in rule application, and, according to Sommerstein (1977), it is unlikely that any single method of rule application will prove to be universally valid.

Simplicity and the Evaluation Metric

In this last section we consider the more general problem of evaluating phonological grammars.

Generative linguists distinguish three levels of adequacy: *observational*, *descriptive*, and *explanatory*. A grammar (or an analysis) of a language that is observationally adequate "correctly describes the data

. . . and nothing more." A grammar that is descriptively adequate is said to be psychologically real. It describes the data correctly and also captures the "tacit knowledge of native speakers" (Chomsky & Halle, 1968, p. 458). A grammar is said to have explanatory adequacy if it provides a way for linguists to choose the best solution from two or more descriptively adequate solutions (Hyman, 1975, p. 102).

Hyman (1975) points out that generative linguists want to write grammars that are psychologically real, and they also want to devise the best grammar possible. Thus they need ways of deciding among alternative solutions. Chomsky (1962) argued for choosing the simplest solution. Subsequently, *simplicity* became a very important concept in generative phonology. The *simplicity metric* allows linguists to evaluate different solutions (i.e., grammars) and to choose the simplest or most general solution of all those that are descriptively adequate.[1] This makes the claim that the simplest phonological solutions are preferred by speakers and are also perhaps learned most easily by children (Hyman, 1975).[2]

As Hyman (1975) observed, simplicity in one part of the grammar may lead to complexity elsewhere in the grammar. Therefore, simplicity must be considered with reference to both underlying (lexical) representations and phonological rules. The simplicity metric used by generative phonologists is based on *feature counting*. That is, simplicity is considered to be closely related to the number of features needed to capture a generalization (Hyman, 1975, p. 103).[3]

As mentioned in an earlier section, redundant feature specifications are omitted from lexical representations. Only features that are distinctive and cannot be predicted are specified; others are left unspecified and are filled in later by morpheme structure rules (or are specified by morpheme structure conditions). This is done because of the feature counting simplicity metric. To illustrate, because English has only two affricates, the only distinctive features needed in their lexical representations are [− continuant], [+ delayed release], and either [+ voice] or [− voice]. All other features are predictable and can therefore be omitted. Similarly, features that can be predicted from the *sequential constraints* of a language can also be omitted from underlying representations (Hyman, 1975, p. 104). For instance, only vowels can follow affricates in English. Therefore, only the distinctive features of a vowel following an affricate need to be specified in the underlying representation.

Generative phonologists have focused more on counting features in phonological rules than in lexical representations. The crucial assumption (questioned by some linguists) is that a rule with fewer features is simpler, i.e., "costs less," than a rule with more features (Hyman, 1975,

p. 113). This feature counting metric is supposed to help linguists distinguish "linguistically significant generalizations" from false or "spurious" generalizations. However, according to Contreras (1969, p. 1), rules that are more general do not always appear simpler in terms of the number of features needed to formalize them. In addition, although feature counting has been used quite effectively to distinguish natural from "crazy" rules, it cannot help us choose the best rule from two or more natural rules. So, feature counting does not work in all cases (Hyman, 1975, 113–114).

Hyman (1975) points out that this concern with simplicity, as measured by feature counting, has greatly influenced the development of generative phonology. For one thing, it is assumed that the notational devices and formalisms that are used in rule writing should capture significant generalizations, and many abbreviatory conventions have been proposed with the express purpose of "saving features."

As discussed, earlier, phonological rules are written in such a way that segments and feature values are not repeated unless absolutely necessary. For example, the environment of a sound change is stated just once in a rule instead of appearing on both sides of the arrow (e.g., p→b/#___V instead of #pV→#bV). Also, only features whose values change are written on the right of the arrow, and the opposite feature values are not explicitly stated in the input (Hyman, 1975, p. 116). To illustrate, for final devoicing, we write [– sonorant]→[– voice] / ___ #. None of the other obstruent features are listed in the output, and [+ voice] is not included in the input. Using the conventions of generative phonology allows us to save many features and also to capture the fact that this rule formalizes a real linguistic generalization (in fact, a natural process). Rules that do not express linguistically significant generalizations cannot be simplified in this way. For example, a rule such as /bi/→[sɑ] could not be simplified by using the conventions of generative phonology because it does not capture a real generalization. The notational devices discussed in Appendix A (e.g., parentheses, braces, and angled brackets) also allow us to combine structurally related rules and therefore come up with simpler solutions.

Generative phonologists assume that the notational devices used to formalize a process should reflect the complexity of that process. For example, it should be possible to formalize a natural rule using fewer features than would be needed for a less natural rule (Hyman, 1975, p. 133). As demonstrated earlier, this works in some, but not all, cases. Feature counting does favor more general processes, but these are not always more natural.

There are also other problems with an evaluation metric based on feature counting. For instance, feature counting does not adequately account for natural classes because the simplest classes, in terms of features, may not be the most natural. To illustrate, the class defined by the feature [+voice] is very general, including vowels, glides, liquids, nasals, and voiced obstruents, and almost no phonological rules refer to this class. However, more rules refer to voiced obstruents, voiced stops, and other subclasses which must be specified with more features than just [+voice] (Hyman, 1975, p. 140).

As already noted, we cannot always adequately capture the simplicity or naturalness of a particular phonemic inventory by counting features. For instance /p, t, k/ is a more natural series of voiceless stops than /p, t, c/ (/c/ being a palatal stop), but this is not evident from counting features. The criterion of feature counting also does not help us decide whether to postulate one phoneme or two for certain phonetic units (see Hyman, 1975). For example, should affricates be analyzed as single phonemes (such as /tʃ, dʒ/) or as sequences of two phonemes (/t/ plus /ʃ/, /d/ plus /ʒ/, etc.)? Another problem is that feature counting does not show the functional unity of rules (Schane, 1973, p. 119).

Linguists to not agree regarding the simplicity metric, particularly as defined by feature counting. Some linguists want to reject it completely, while others just want to modify it. As Hyman (1975) points out, in recent years, there has been a shift away from feature counting. Phonologists are now more concerned with naturalness and finding ways to capture naturalness and to relate it to simplicity. When the evaluation metric (i.e., feature counting) fails to show that a natural rule or property is "simpler" than an unnatural rule or property, the evaluation metric is assumed to be incorrect (Hyman, 1975, p. 139). Naturalness issues are the subject of Chapter 5. To conclude this appendix, however, a brief discussion of markedness is warranted.

Markedness

There has been a great deal of interest in characterizing phonological naturalness (see Chapter 5). It has been argued that the concept of markedness allows phonologists to capture naturalness, that is, to explain why some segments are acquired earlier, occur in more languages, and more frequently result from historical change. The concept of markedness, as introduced by the Prague school (see Chapter 3) was a language-specific property related to neutralization (Hyman, 1975,

p. 144). When two segments are neutralized or merge, they merge to the unmarked member. For example, voiced and voiceless obstruents in German merge to voiceless obstruents in final position. So, the unmarked member of an opposition is the one found in the position of neutralization (Hyman, 1975, p. 143). However, there are problems with this view because it is often necessary to take environments or contexts into consideration. For example, in final position voiceless obstruents are unmarked, but in intervocalic position, voiced obstruents may be unmarked because they may take on voicing from the surrounding vowels. Thus assigning markedness values is not always as simple as it might seem (Hyman, 1975).

The concept of markedness was revised by Chomsky and Halle (1968) in an attempt to make naturalness more explicit and to alleviate some of the problems created by the fact that the plus (+) and minus (−) values of a feature are not necessarily equally natural. A big difference between the Prague view of markedness and the generative phonologists' view is that generative phonologists see markedness values as being *universal* and *innate*—not language-specific. For instance, voiceless obstruents are said to be universally less marked than voiced obstruents (Hyman, 1975, p. 147).

Markedness has played an important part in generative phonology since 1968, but the term *marked* has not been used in a consistent way. In one interpretation, it means that an extra feature (e.g., palatalization) has been added. In another view, it has to do with frequency of occurrence; the unmarked member of a pair of sounds occurs more frequently than the marked member. Still other interpretations are possible (Hyman, 1975, p. 145). In the most common view of markedness, the unmarked member of a pair of sounds is said to be less complex and also more normal or expected (Schane, 1973, p. 112). A certain segment is considered to be marked or unmarked for a particular feature (e.g., nasalization or voicing). For example, oral vowels are unmarked or natural in comparison to nasal vowels. The feature *nasal* differentiates them. So, for nasalized sounds (and other sounds with secondary articulations), unmarked is minus (−). Nasalized vowels are marked for nasality.

In the epilogue of *SPE*, Chomsky and Halle (1968) proposed replacing the pluses and minuses in underlying representations by *U*'s and *M*'s (for unmarked and marked) in order to "evaluate the content of features" and to show the relative naturalness of certain classes (Hyman, 1975, p. 147). This also "saves features," since *U* "costs" nothing. (+ , − , and *M* cost one point each.) To illustrate, consonants articulated in the front of the mouth (labials and dentals) are unmarked for anterior or [U anterior] because the optimal consonants are articulated in the front of the mouth (Schane, 1973, p. 113). Alveolars (/t, d, s/, etc.) are unmarked for both anterior and coronal: [U anterior], [U coronal]. Palatals and velars, articulated further back in the mouth, are marked for anterior [M anterior]. Labials are [M coronal] because for anterior consonants, an articulation is more natural if it involves the tongue blade (Schane,1973). Similarly, nasal vowels are [M nasal] because they are less natural than oral vowels, and voiced obstruents, being less natural than voiceless obstruents, are [M voice].

Marking conventions that are universal—given once for all languages—convert the *U's* and *M's* of underlying representations to +'s and −'s (Schane 1973, p. 133).[4] Marking conventions are statements such as (Hyman, 1975, pp. 148, 149):

(1) [U back] → [+back] / [$\overline{+\text{low}}$]

This convention indicates that the unmarked value for *back* is [+back] for segments that are also [+low]. It captures the fact that the natural vowel /ɑ/, which [+low], is also [+back].

(2) [U round] →
$$\begin{cases} [\alpha \text{ round}] \ / \ \begin{bmatrix} \overline{\alpha \text{ back}} \\ -\text{low} \end{bmatrix} & \textbf{(a)} \\ [-\text{round}] \ / \ [\ \overline{+\text{l o w}}\ ] & \textbf{(b)} \end{cases}$$

(2a) says that the unmarked value for *round* is [+round] for segments that are also [+back], [−low] and is [−round] for segments that are [−back], [−low]. (2b) says that the unmarked value for *round* is [−round] for segments that are [+low]. So for instance the unmarked value for *round* would be [−round] for the [+low] segment /ɑ/, and [U round] for /u/ would be [+round] because /u/ is a [+back], [−low] segment.

Marking conventions appear in *ordered pairs*. For example, the marking conventions for the feature *anterior* apply before those for the feature *coronal* because the unmarked value for coronal depends on the value for anterior. These marking conventions are formalized as follows (Schane, 1973, p. 113):

(1a) [U anterior] → [+anterior]

(1b) [M anterior] → [−anterior]

(2) [U coronal] → [α coronal] / [$\overline{\alpha \text{ anterior}}$]

Convention (2) just above states that the unmarked value for coronal is [+ coronal] for segments that are [+ anterior] and is [- coronal] for segments that are [- anterior].

Similarly, the universal marking conventions assigning values to the feature *sonorant* must apply before those assigning values to the feature *voice* because [U voice] is [+ voice] for sounds that are [+ sonorant] but is [- voice] for [- sonorant] sounds (Schane, 1973, p. 114):

$$[\text{U voice}] \longrightarrow [\alpha \text{ voice}] \; / \; [\overline{\alpha \text{ sonorant}}]$$

As noted above, it is sometimes necessary to take environments into consideration in assigning markedness values. For instance, [U voice] may be [+ voice] for intervocalic obstruents, while it is [- voice] for final obstruents. Thus, as noted by Schane (1973, p. 114) marking conventions have to "be sensitive to" other factors, such as the features of neighboring sounds.

Data from linguistic universals, language change, and language acquisition are relevant to markedness. In historical sound change, we expect that marked segments may become less marked, and in phonological acquisition, unmarked sounds should be acquired before the corresponding marked sounds, e.g., voiceless obstruents before the corresponding voiced obstruents and anterior consonants before similar nonanterior consonants. The unmarked sounds should also be more widespread in languages of the world.

FOOTNOTES

[1]Hyman (1975, p. 103) points out that although contemporary linguists do not agree regarding the usefulness of a simplicity metric, most operate as though one were necessary.

[2]In Chomsky's view, such an evaluation procedure is available to language-learning children, allowing them to construct the grammar that is best (simplest), based on their exposure to their native language (Hyman, 1975, p. 103).

[3]Simplicity can be interpreted in various ways, as noted by Hyman, (1975, p. 100). For example, it can be interpreted as equivalent to economy. For the American descriptive linguists, a solution with fewer phonemes was considered to be more economical. Similarly, an analysis that requires fewer rules could be considered to be more economical than another. However, simplicity can also be interpreted as being equivalent to generality. So, a simpler solution may be one that makes more general use of certain features. According to Hyman (1975), considerations of economy and generality do not always lead to the same conclusions. For instance, an economical phonemic solution may be less general than another solution and may require additional constraints or rules.

[4]Schane (1973, p. 120) argues that what he calls *naturalness conditions*, or constraints that govern both underlying and derived structures, are "embodied" in universal marking conventions and natural phonological rules.

Appendix C

Aspects of Speech Development

STAGES OF
PHONOLOGICAL
ACQUISITION

What follows is a composite chart summarizing the "stages" of pre-linguistic and linguistic development. This chart is based on data and discussions in McCarthy (1954), Templin (1957), Oyer (1966), Lenneberg (1967), Wolff (1969), Eisenson and Ogilvie (1971), Kaplan and Kaplan (1971), Stark et al. (1975), Dale (1976), Ingram (1976), Shriberg and Kwiatkowski (1980), and others. It should be kept in mind that the ages at which certain types of vocalizations or certain sounds are said to appear varies somewhat depending on the particular source that is consulted. As a result, there is some overlap among the "stages" presented here.

Stages of Prelinguistic
and Phonological Development

I. Birth-1;0—Prelinguistic vocalization and perception (Ingram, 1976, p. 15)

A. *Crying* (Dale, 1976, p. 204)
0–4 weeks—birth cry; undifferentiated crying with rising and falling pitch contours, repeated once per second; egressive air flow; crying may begin to be differentiated (e.g., for pain vs. anger).

B. *Other vocalizations and cooing* (Dale 1976, p. 205)
Other vocalizations besides crying, e.g., discomfort sounds and vegetative sounds appear at end of first month; there is more variety due to use of articulators. At 4–6 weeks, crying is more clearly differentiated (for pleasure, distress, etc.). Cooing, which involves [u]-like vowel sounds and seems to express pleasure, appears at 2–3 months. At 3–4 months, the child coos and chuckles; some back consonants (e.g., velars) are produced. Crying decreases. By 5 months, nasals, labials, and front vowels appear. Infants can discriminate between sounds.

C. *Babbling* (Dale 1976, p. 205)
By 5–6 months, babbling ("vocalizations with at least one C and one V") appears; it predominates until about 12 months. Babbled utterances are speech-like and resemble one syllable CV utterances, though VC sequences may also occur. Toward the end of the period, intonation may sound adult-like. Most consonants are front consonants, (e.g., [m, n, p, b]) and most vowels are front vowels. Between 9–12 months, *echolalia* occurs; the child repeats sounds made by self or others, approximates adult sounds, and responds to adult stimuli. Consonants begin to outnumber vowels. The child may begin to use *phonetically consistent forms* or *vocables* (*proto-words*).

D. *Patterned speech* (Dale 1976, p. 205)
"Patterned," or true speech, begins with the appearance of the first real word for identification at any time from age 10 months on. Babbled utterances as well as phonetically consistent forms may continue to occur.

II. 1;0-1;6—Phonology of the first 50 words (Ingram 1976, p. 17)
Intentional use of speech; *holophrastic* speech; utterances are one word long; most words have 1-2 syllables and consist of CV or reduplicated CVCV. Front stops and /m/ are used; /h/ and /w/ may also appear as well as a few front fricatives. The first vowel is /ɑ/, followed by /i/ and /u/. Children may actively "select" words for production. The child has a vocabulary of up to 50 words. There may be much inter- and intra-word variability. Words are important units of acquisition and phonological development is closely tied to lexical development. *Progressive idioms* may occur.

III. 1;6-4;0—Phonology of simple morphemes (Ingram, 1976, p. 22)
Perception continues to develop. The sound inventory expands. Nasals are acquired early followed by glides and most stops. Some fricatives and affricates are acquired. Clusters begin to appear. Consonants are generally acquired earliest in initial position (especially stops), but fricatives may be learned first in postvocalic positions. Acquisition is gradual and there is much individual variation. The child develops a system of phonemic contrasts. Substitutions (simplification processes) predominate (see Ingram, 1976).

Until 2;0 speech is "egocentric"; some two-word utterances appear. At 2;0, the child has a vocabulary of over 50 words for naming and effecting results; the child produces "novel" two-word utterances. Between 2;0-3;0, speech becomes more intelligible and differentiated; 3-4 word utterances appear; the child has a vocabulary of up to 900 words; two-thirds of the adult sounds are mastered. At 3;0 most utterances are intelligible to adults; all vowels are acquired. Between 3;0-4;0, language becomes more developed and complex. It is used to narrate, describe, explain, request, etc.; the child has a vocabulary of up to 1,500 words; 4-8 word utterances appear; by 4;0 most simple words are produced correctly, but many clusters and some singleton consonants are not yet acquired.

IV. 4;0-7;0—Completion of phonetic inventory (Ingram, 1976, p. 44)
Between 4;0-5;0 language becomes more complex more abstract, and less egocentric; the child has a vocabulary of up to 2,500 words; utterances may be 7 words long; most basic syntactic rules are acquired; more two- and three-consonant clusters appear;

a few fricatives are still problematic. Between 6;0-7;0, language becomes more symbolic; most sentences are approximately 6.5 words long. Most children have acquired the entire phonetic inventory. Some morphophonemic development occurs (e.g., involving regular past tenses).

V. 7;0-12;0—Morphophonemic development (Ingram 1976, p. 45) The child learns more complex derivational structures and morphophonemic rules. A few remaining clusters may be mastered. The child is fluent.

VI. 12;0-16;0—Spelling is mastered (Ingram, 1976, p. 11)

SOME COMMON PHONOLOGICAL PROCESSES[1]

A. *SYLLABLE STRUCTURE PROCESSES*

1. **Weak syllable deletion** *(WSD)*—An unstressed syllable is deleted.

   banana [nǽnə]   *umbrella* [bʌ́lə]

2. **Reduplication** *(R)*— An entire syllable or part of a syllable is repeated.

   pudding [pʰúpu]   *water* [wáwɑ]

3. **Cluster reduction** *(CR)*—A sequence of two (or more) consonants is simplified, usually by deletion of the more marked or difficult element.

   a. **/s/-cluster reduction**— Usually the /s/ is deleted, especially in initial clusters.

   spoon [pun]   *box* [bɔk] or [bɔs]

   b. **Liquid cluster reduction**—The liquid is generally deleted.
   frog [fɑg]   *block* [bɑk]
   corn [kɔn]   *milk* [mɪk]

   c. **Nasal cluster reduction**—The element that is deleted may depend on the voicing of the obstruent.

   pink [pɪk]   *hand* [hæn]

d. **Coalescence**—Features from two adjacent segments or syllables combine.[2]

swing [fɪŋ]   *snow* [n̥o͞o]   *banana* [bǽnə]

4. **Final consonant deletion (FCD)**—A word or syllable-final consonant is deleted. Weiner (1979) includes examples with [ʔ] in final position, as in [bɛʔ] for *bed*.

dog [gɑ]   *fish* [bɪ]   *doggie* [dɑːi]

5. *Epenthesis*— A segment is inserted in the middle of a word; usually [ə] is inserted between two elements of a cluster.

blue [bᵊlu]   *green* [gᵊwin]

6. *Reordering of segments*

a. **Metathesis**—Two sounds (which may be adjacent or nonadjacent) are reversed.

ask [æks]   *pencil* [pɛ́snə]
blue [bul]   *animal* [ǽmənʊ]

b. **Migration**—One sound migrates to another position in the word.

snake [ne͞iks]   *snow* [no͞os]

B. *ASSIMILATION OR HARMONY PROCESSES*—One sound is influenced by another sound that is nearby and becomes more similar (or identical) to it.[3]

1. *Velar assimilation (VA)*—A sound becomes a velar due to the influence of another velar sound.

dog [gɔg]   (regressive, noncontiguous, complete)
snake [ŋe͞ik]   (regressive, noncontiguous, partial)

2. *Labial assimilation (LA)*—A sound becomes a labial due to the influence of another labial sound.

swing [fwɪŋ]   (regressive, contiguous, partial)
table [be͞ibʊ]   (regressive, noncontiguous, complete)

3. *Nasal assimilation (NA)*—A sound becomes a nasal due to the influence of another nasal sound.

lamb [næm]   (regressive, noncontiguous, partial)
candle [nʌ́no]   (regressive, noncontiguous, complete)

4. *Liquid assimilation*—A sound becomes a liquid due to the influence of another liquid sound. (Weiner, 1979, includes this under alveolar assimilation.)

yellow [lɛ́lo]   (regressive, noncontiguous, complete)

5. *Assimilation between a consonant and a vowel*

   a. **Place assimilation**—The place of articulation of a consonant changes due to the influence of a neighboring vowel.
   puddle [pʌgu], *middle* [mígu] (regressive, contiguous, partial)

   b. **Voicing assimilation**—A consonant takes on the voicing feature of a neighboring element. (These changes are not always classified as assimilation).

      1. **Prevocalic voicing (PV)**—Voiceless obstruents are voiced preceding a vowel.

         tail [déɪu]   (regressive, contiguous, partial)
         zipper [díbʊ]   ("double," contiguous, partial)

      2. **Final devoicing (FD)**—Obstruents are devoiced in word-final position (i.e., they assimilate to silence.)

         nose [nos]   *pig* [pɪk]   (regressive, contiguous, partial)

C. CHANGES IN PLACE OF ARTICULATION

1. *Fronting processes*—Sounds are replaced by others produced farther forward in the mouth.

   a. **Depalatalization (DP)**—Palatals are fronted, usually to alveolars ("palatal fronting").
   shoe [su]   *watch* [wɑts]

   b. **Fronting of velars (VF)**—Velar sounds are replaced by alveolars ("velar fronting").
   cookie [tʊ́ti]   *book* [bʊt]

2. *Alveolarization (A)*—Interdental or labial sounds are replaced by alveolars. This also involves a change in stridency for interdentals.)
   thumb [sʌm]   *bath* [bɑs]   *leaf* [lis]

3. *Labialization (L)*—A nonlabial sound is replaced by a labial.
   chair [féɪə]   *glasses* [gwǽfɪ]   *thumb* [fʌm]

D. *CHANGES IN MANNER OF ARTICULATION*

1. *Stopping (ST)*—Fricatives or affricates are replaced by stops.
   see [ti]   *juice* [dus]

2. *Affrication (AF)*—Fricatives are replaced by affricates. (This could be considered partial stopping.)
   shoe [tʃu]   *fish* [pfɪs]

3. *Gliding of liquids (GL)*—Liquids are replaced by glides.⁴
   red [wɛd]   *car* [kɑʊ]
   light [jaɪt]   *milk* [mɪʊk]

4. *Gliding of fricatives (GF)*—Fricatives are replaced by glides.
   jet [djɛt]   *fork* [wʊk]   *shoe* [ju]

5. *Deaffrication (DA)*—Affricates are replaced by fricatives.
   page [peʒ]   *watch* [wɔʃ]

6. *Denasalization (DN)*—Nasal consonants are replaced by homorganic oral stops.
   moon [bud]   *knife* [daɪp]

7. *Vocalization (V)*—Syllabic liquids or nasals are replaced by vowels, usually [ə] or [ʊ] (or [ʊə], [oə] if the target sound is stressed).
   bottle [bádʊ]   *bird* [buəd]
   mitten [mɪʔə]   *other* [ʌdə]

SOME UNUSUAL SOUND CHANGES⁵

1. *Deletion of the unmarked element of clusters* (e.g., Ingram, 1976).
   story [sóri]   *snake* [sẽk]

2. *Nasal intrusion*—A homorganic nasal is inserted before an obstruent (e.g., Edwards & Bernhardt, 1973a).
   red [wæɪnt]   *bridge* [pfwɪnt]

3. *Initial consonant deletion*—A word-initial consonant is deleted (e.g., Hodson, 1980).

   gun [ʌn]   *shoe* [u]

4. *Final vowel addition*—A vowel, usually [ə], is added to the end of a word (Edwards & Bernhardt, 1973a).

   comb [kɔ́mə]   *shoe* [ʃúwə]

5. *Glottal replacement*—A consonant in intervocalic or final position is replaced by a glottal stop [ʔ] (e.g., Edwards & Bernhardt, 1973a; Weiner, 1979).

   happy [hǽʔi]   *honey* [hɑ́ʔi]   *bed* [bɛʔ]

6. *Tetism*—[t] is used in place of other sounds, especially [f] (Panagos, 1974; Ingram, 1976).

   fish [tɪʃ]   *fall* [tɑo]

7. *Lateralization*—A lateral fricative [ɬ] is used in place of some or all sibilants, or sibilants are produced with lateral frication (e.g., Pollack & Rees, 1972; Edwards & Bernhardt, 1973a).

   saw [ɬɔ]   *shoe* [su̲]

8. *Nasal substitution*—Obstruents are replaced by nasal consonants (e.g., Edwards & Bernhardt, 1973a).

   juice [nĩjús]   *star* [ŋɑə]   *crib* [ŋɪp]

9. *Gliding of intervocalic consonants*—Consonants in intervocalic position are replaced by glides (e.g., Edwards & Bernhardt, 1973b).

   T.V. [tʰíji]   *bottle* [bɔ́wo͞u]

10. *Velarization*—Front consonants are replaced by velar stops (Edwards, 1980a).

    feather [fɛ́gə]   *nose* [nog]   *button* [bʌ́kɛn]

11. *Neutralization*—Several adult sounds in one or more positions are replaced by one sound or by two similar sounds, i.e., adult contrasts are neutralized (e.g., Weiner, 1981; Edwards 1980b). For example:

    a. Noninitial voiceless fricatives are replaced by [ʰ] (Lorentz, 1974).

       if [ɪʰ]   *wish* [wɪʰ]   *nothing* [nʌʰɪŋ]

b. Initial labials are replaced by [w] (Edwards & Bernhardt, 1973a).

   fish [wæ²]   *bottle* [wɑ́do]

c. Final sibilants are replaced by a voiceless nasal fricative [f̥̃] (Edwards & Bernhardt, 1973a).

   brush [bʌf̥̃]   *watch* [jʌtf̥̃]

d. Initial and postconsonantal continuants (except vowels) are replaced by [l] (Lorentz, 1974).

   sing [lɪŋ]   *chin* [tlɪn]   *twelve* [tlɛl]

FOOTNOTES

[1]This list is a collection of entries that have occurred in the literature. It represents just one possible system of classification. Several of the processes listed here are handled differently by different researchers, e.g., alveolarization and labialization. Vowel changes are not included. The initials following the name of a process are primarily those used by Weiner (1979).

[2]Examples of coalescence may be seen as involving assimilation followed by deletion (e.g., see Schane, 1973). For instance, the [fɪŋ] for *swing* example could be accounted for by (a) regressive labial assimilation (s→f /#____w) and (b) cluster simplification (w→∅/#f____). This analysis has the advantage of capturing the relatedness of [fwɪm] for *swim* and of [fɪŋ] for *swing*, which may co-occur in a child's speech.

[3]*Reduplication*, which is also called syllable harmony, could be discussed in this section instead of under syllable structure processes.

[4]Child phonologists do not agree concerning how to classify the substitution of vowels for nonsyllabic liquids, as in [bɔʊ] for *ball*. Here, such cases are included under gliding of liquids. However, vocalization (#7 below) is sometimes defined to include them. Liquid simplification might be a better cover term for all of these changes.

[5]This is a list of some of the unusual sound changes that have shown up in studies of developmental phonological disorders. Some of these were discussed in Chapter 7. At the present time, we can not say positively what is normal and what is not, but these unusual patterns (or "deviant rules") have been reported rarely, if ever, in studies of normal development.

Appendix D

Some Procedures for Phonological Analysis

FISHER-LOGEMANN (1971)

The *Fisher-Logemann Test of Articulation Competence* (1971) claims to provide a distinctive feature analysis of articulation errors. According to the manual (p.1), this test allows the therapist to "examine the client's phonological system in an orderly framework" and to formulate an "accurate and complete" analysis of errors. The clinician discovers not only if sounds are correct, but also what the substitutions are.

In the view of the designers of this test (p. 24), "real" distinctive features (for example, those put forward by Jakobson et al., 1963) are too complex for routine articulation testing. So the features on which their test is based are traditional articulatory features (involving place, manner, and voicing) rather than binary distinctive features.

In both the picture form of the test and the sentence form, in which sentences are read by the client, all English consonant phonemes are tested in various "syllabic functions." The syllable positions tested are prevocalic, postvocalic, and intervocalic. In addition, each phoneme is positioned on the record sheet such that the features characterizing that phoneme are evident. Consonants are organized according to a three-parameter system of features: (1) manner of articulation (on the vertical dimension), (2) place of articulation (on the horizontal dimension), and (3) voicing. (Each row is split into two lines for voiced and voiceless.) The client's misarticulations can therefore be summarized by the "distinctive features" that are in error. (However, allophonic errors are also recorded and diacritics are provided in the manual for this purpose.)

Four features are used in the analysis of vowel errors: (1) tongue height (high, mid, low), (2) place of articulation (front, central, back), and (3) degree of tension in the lingual muscles (tense vs. lax).

The type of feature analysis proposed by Fisher and Logemann is said to allow the examiner to view a person's sound errors as part of a "systematized phonology." It should help in planning therapy, they claim, because it enables the clinician to understand the nature of the incorrect productions. That is, the analysis specifies the particular aspect (feature) of the client's production that is wrong, and therapy can then be directed toward that incorrect feature. Moreover, if the clinician can identify feature problems that are common to several phonemes, therapy can be facilitated because, theoretically, when the client learns to modify a feature in one phoneme, this can be transferred to similar phonemes.

McREYNOLDS AND ENGMANN (1975)

In their 1975 book titled *Distinctive Feature Analysis of Misarticulations*, McReynolds and Engmann first discuss distinctive feature theory, focusing on the feature system of Chomsky and Halle (1968), which is the system they use. They then present their own procedures for a distinctive feature analysis of articulation errors. They use articulation test results from two children to teach their procedures in a programmed instruction format. The last section of the book is devoted to the development of training programs using information derived from distinctive feature analysis.

In the second section of the book, which contains the actual procedures for distinctive feature analysis, one brief chapter shows how to use a distinctive feature table (based on Chomsky and Halle) to determine the features that make up each English consonant and vowel and also to specify the features that differentiate two sounds. To illustrate, /tʃ/ and /ʃ/ are differentiated only by the continuant feature; while /ʃ/ is [+continuant], /tʃ/ is [−continuant].

Regarding the type of articulation sample that should be used for a distinctive feature analysis, the authors recommend using a "comprehensive" sample, either from spontaneous speech or from articulation test responses. The important point is that each phoneme should be sampled several times, not just once in each word-position in which it occurs. Because distinctive feature analysis involves looking for "systematic patterns of feature errors" across all the phonemes containing each feature, both appropriate and inappropriate feature use have to be noted. In their analysis, the authors use the *McDonald Deep Test of Articulation* (1964) because it samples each phoneme many times in both the releasing position and the arresting position. However, if a child produces consistent error patterns on 10 items, they state that it is probably not necessary to elicit a more extensive sample.

For a distinctive feature analysis, the clinician must transcribe a child's responses, using the International Phonetic Alphabet or a similar transcription system. In this way, a comparison can be made between the features of the test phoneme and the child's response. However, only correct productions, omissions, and substitutions can be utilized. If distortions are produced whose features cannot be specified, the production has to be deleted from the analysis or scored as an omission, or another feature system must be used that allows for the specification of the distorted sound.

Each response produced by the child for each target phoneme is listed under "arresting position" or "releasing position." The next step involves transferring correct responses and substitutions to a Distinctive Feature Analysis Worksheet. The features of each test phoneme and each substitution are then recorded, and correct feature usage is analyzed. Each phoneme has a separate worksheet, divided into four columns. Down the left side, the 13 Chomsky and Halle features are listed. In the first column is written the test phoneme and the number of times that phoneme was used correctly.

The second column contains a list of all the substitutions that occurred for that phoneme, along with the number of times each occurred. For example, if a child produced [b] in place of the test phoneme /p/ 36 times, [b] would be written in column two, along with "36." In the third column is written the number of times that the test phoneme was omitted.

Before completing the fourth column, the examiner has to indicate the + or − aspect of each feature of the test phoneme and each substitution. To illustrate, for the test phoneme /p/ the features [vocalic], [consonantal], and [high] would be specified as −, +, and −, respectively. The [b] substitution for /p/ would have the same values for these three features.

In column four, the examiner lists the number of times each feature aspect (+ or −) was produced correctly in response to the test phoneme. (This number is derived by adding the correct + or − feature values across the columns.) For example, the child discussed by the authors produced /p/ correctly 10 times, and produced [b] as a substitute for /p/ 36 times. Since both /p/ and /b/ are [−vocalic], the [−vocalic] feature was correct a total of 46 times when /p/ was tested. However, the [−voice] feature was correct only 10 times because the [b] substitute is [+voice].

The last step in distinctive feature analysis is the completion of a Distinctive Feature Analysis Sheet. This step involves computing, across all phonemes, the percentage at which each feature is incorrect. First, the total scores from each worksheet are transferred to the analysis sheet. (A separate analysis sheet has to be completed for each feature.) Each sheet is divided into two sections, one for the + aspect and one for the − aspect of the feature. In the first column is listed each test phoneme containing the feature value in question (e.g., [+continuant]). In the second column is written the number of possible occurrences (i.e., the total number of times the feature could have been correct for each test phoneme). For instance, if /f/ is tested a total of 46 times, the [+continuant] feature could be correct 46 times for /f/. In the last column, the examiner lists the number of correct occurrences for the feature aspect in question (transferred from the completed worksheets for each phoneme).

Next, the examiner totals the numbers in the columns with the headings "Number of Possible Occurrences" and "Number of Correct Occurrences" for both feature values (+ and −). The total for the number of correct occurrences is then divided by the total for the number of possible occurrences. This gives a percentage of correct feature production. To find the percent incorrect, the dividend is subtracted from 100. The percent incorrect figures for each aspect of each feature are said to "provide a profile of a child's distinctive feature development and usage" (p. 63).

After the examiner completes an analysis sheet for each feature, the results can be shown on a Summary Sheet. The features used in the analysis are listed down the left, with the + and − aspects listed separately. Across from each feature aspect is listed the percent incorrect (obtained from the analysis sheets for each feature). This Summary Sheet provides a starting point for deciding which feature should be trained. (However, detailed information regarding the phonemes and contexts within which each feature was tested has to be obtained from the original articulation test data).

In the last section of their book, McReynolds and Engmann present guidelines for planning a distinctive feature training program. Criteria to be used in selecting a feature to train include the following: An error percentage of 80% or higher indicates that the feature in question has not been acquired and "should receive high priority for training" (p. 103). In contrast, an error percentage of 25% or lower indicates that the feature is acquired, and training is not required. An error percentage of about 65% shows inconsistent production, and thus the feature in question should be considered for training. An error percentage of 40% to 50% may be indicative of various patterns. For example, the feature may be produced consistently in some but not all phonemes containing it, or the feature may be established only in certain positions. McReynolds and Engmann recommend training first on features that are in error at the 80% level. If no features reach that level, a feature may be selected that is in error at the 50% or 60% level. Training would aim toward stabilizing that feature across phonemes or positions.

After a feature has been selected, a pair of phonemes is chosen for training the feature contrast. That is, a target phoneme that contains the + aspect of a feature is paired with a phoneme containing the − aspect of the feature. An appropriate phoneme pair should differ only in the feature contrast to be learned. To select an appropriate phoneme pair, the clinician examines each substitution for each test phoneme containing the feature to be trained. If one of the consistent substitutions differs from its target phoneme only in the crucial feature, the two phonemes (target and substitute) may be an appropriate pair for training. Exercises are given that illustrate the procedures for selecting appropriate features and phoneme pairs.

McReynolds and Engmann point out that in some cases it may be necessary to train on phoneme pairs that differ from each other on two feature contrasts. Moreover, if a child has more than one feature in error a high percentage of the time, it may be more effective to train the two feature contrasts simultaneously. To illustrate, if a child had a high error rate for both continuancy and stridency, two phonemes differing in both feature contrasts (but only those features) would be selected. The selection would be made after a close examination of all the test phonemes and the substitutions. Exercises are presented that demonstrate the development of a training program when more than one feature contrast is to be trained simultaneously.

McReynolds and Engmann also present a program for training distinctive features that was designed for a study by McReynolds and Bennett (1972). However, they do not advocate adopting all details of this program for clinical use because it was designed for research purposes.

The authors of this procedure caution that a distinctive feature analysis is time-consuming, and they state that it should be completed primarily when children have several (more than four) sounds in error. For such children, it is claimed that an in-depth feature analysis may lead to more effective and efficient therapy.

LUND AND DUCHAN (1978)

After discussing some of the shortcomings of the "traditional" approach to articulation testing, Lund and Duchan (1978, p. 119) argue for what they call a "multifaceted approach" to phonological analysis. This approach is said to incorporate some of the strengths of traditional approaches and feature approaches while avoiding their weaknesses (See also Lund and Duchan, 1983.) First, several examples of each target sound are obtained in spontaneous speech and in a test situation, and narrow transcriptions of whole words are then derived so that allophonic variants can be described and the "distortion" category can be avoided. Lund and Duchan discuss three types of analysis, but they note that this is not intended to be an exhaustive list.

The first type of analysis is called a *substitution analysis*. This is a modified version of traditional substitution analysis procedures. In this analysis, sound errors, including distortions or allophonic substitutions, are analyzed in terms of "feature substitutions" or "feature-plus-position regularities" (i.e., feature substitutions that occur only in certain syllable positions).[1] That is, the child's errors are compared with the adult target sounds and the feature differences are described. This is done for within-phoneme as well as across-phoneme substitutions (p. 121). Lund and Duchan claim that their substitution analysis allows the clinician to capture regularities that may not be noticed if only phonemic substitutions are listed.

The second type of analysis is called *context sensitive analysis*. This takes into account the fact that sounds and syllables in connected speech may influence each other. Possible effects of context are considered, and processes such as weak syllable deletion, assimilation, coalescence, and reduplication are isolated.

The last type of analysis procedure is called *idiosyncratic structure analysis*. In this analysis, any errors that are due to the child's idiosyncratic production of certain words are discovered, and structures that are unique to particular children are described. The authors state (p. 125) that this helps to account for cases in which there is not a one-to-one match between the adult form and the child's production. Examples of "unique phonological structures" include two syllable structures such as CVʔV (as in [wʌʔĩ]) and [dʌʔĩ]) and nasal structures, such as Waterson's (1971a) son's [ɲV(:)ɲV], which was used for several adult words containing nasals, e.g., [ɲeːɲe] for *window* and [ɲaɲo] for *Randall*.

To summarize, Lund and Duchan suggest a set of steps to be followed in analyzing a child's sound errors. If such a "multifaceted approach" to analysis is followed, they claim that the clinician will probably discover more regularities than at first appeared and may also discover additional types of patterns that need to be described.

FOOTNOTE

[1]*Feature* here refers to place, manner, and voicing characteristics rather than "distinctive features."

COMPTON-HUTTON (1978)

The *Compton-Hutton Phonological Assessment* procedure was published in 1978. Its purpose is "to provide a structured, step-by-step approach for linguistic analysis of misarticulations" (Compton & Hutton, 1978, p. 1). Fifty simple black and white line drawings of familiar objects are used to elicit a "representative" sample of English consonants in word-initial and word-final position and in blends. All English vowels are also represented. Medial position is not assessed, and, in fact, only five two-syllable words are included.[1] In each word, both the initial and final consonants or blends are tested. For instance, in the test item *spring* (#5), both the initial /spr/ cluster and the final /ŋ/ are assessed, and in test item #8, *zipper*, both the initial /z/ and the final /ɚ/ are assessed (but not medial /p/). The stimuli are presented in an order that is supposed to minimize the chances of assimilation or interference between words.

The response/analysis form has three sections. Section I, labeled "Responses," contains a list of a 50 stimulus words. Beside each word is space to transcribe two renditions of each target sound or blend and to note comments. (The child is instructed to say each word twice.) There is also a column labeled "Model" which is used to indicate if a spoken (adult) model was required. Any additional misarticulations that are observed in conversational speech are noted at the end of the word list.

Section II of the response/analysis form, labeled "Pattern Analysis," is divided into three main columns, one for initial consonants, one for final consonants, and one for blends. All target sounds are listed by class, and all target blends are listed by type. To illustrate, the first class of sounds in column one is the stop class, and all six English stop consonants are listed. The stops are followed by nasals, "frictions," affricates, liquids, etc. Similarly, in the third column under "Blends" are listed eight /r/-blends, five /l/-blends, seven two-element /s/-blends, etc.

According to Compton and Hutton (1978, p. 1) the purpose of the pattern analysis is to summarize and organize the data from the transcription section "in such a way that the phonological patterns of the child's misarticulations become evident." The examiner is instructed to record correct responses on this form in blue or black ink and to record error responses in red. Tally marks are put after each phonetic symbol to indicate the number of times that sound occurred (whether as a correct production or as a substitute). For instance, if initial /g/ is produced correctly twice, the symbol [g] followed by two tally marks, is written in black or blue across from /g/ in the column labeled "Initial Consonants." Similarly, if a child produced [p] in place of initial /fl/ twice, [p] *//* is written in red beside /fl/ under "Blends." Compton and Hutton discuss a sample pattern analysis.

If there are noticeable differences between a child's unmodeled sin-gle-word responses and either the modeled responses or conversational speech, these discrepancies are noted for later use in planning therapy (Compton & Hutton, 1978, p. 6). Any "atypical" patterns should also be identified during the pattern anaysis. Finally, the examiner summarizes his or her observations of the child's patterns. This is supposed to help establish an objective base for planning therapy (Compton & Hutton, 1978, p. 10). An example of a summary statement might be: "/f/ is replaced by [p] in [initial] blends" or "final frictions and affricates are omitted."

Section III of the response/analysis form is called "Phonological Rule Analysis." This section contains a list of 40 "Common Deviant Phono-logical Rules."[2] Rules are listed separately for initial consonants and blends and for final consonants. Within each position category, rules are organized according to the types of sounds they affect. For example, under "Initial Consonants and Blends" is the subheading "Liquids (Non-blends)," followed by three rules:

1. $\begin{bmatrix} l \\ r \end{bmatrix} \longrightarrow$ w

2. [l] $\longrightarrow \phi$

3. [l] $\longrightarrow$ [j]

The examiner is instructed to circle all rules or parts of rules that apply. Thus, if a child substituted [w] for initial /r/, but substituted [j] for in-itial /l/, the second part of rule 1 (above) would be circled, along with rule 3.

This "Phonological Rule Analysis" is said to be optional. The authors state (p. 1) that it is included for the benefit of clinicians who want "a more precise characterization of the phonological principles underlying the child's misarticulations." In fact, the phonological rules listed by Compton and Hutton are basically just substitution rules, with the adult sound on the left of the arrow and the child's rendition of that sound on the right of the arrow, as in /tʃ/$\longrightarrow$ [ʃ].[3] Some of the rules that are listed do capture generalizations to a small extent, however. To give an example, their rule #8 (under initial stops) is:

$$\begin{bmatrix} k \\ g \end{bmatrix} \rightarrow \begin{bmatrix} t \\ d \end{bmatrix} \quad \begin{matrix} \text{B (Blend)} \\ \text{NB (Nonblend)} \end{matrix}$$

In other words, velar stops are replaced by alveolars. Similarly, their rule #36a (under final affricates) is:

$$\begin{bmatrix} t\int \\ d_3 \end{bmatrix} \rightarrow \begin{bmatrix} \int \\ 3 \end{bmatrix}$$

That is, word final affricates are replaced by the corresponding fricatives. While these rules capture parallel changes that affect both members of a cognate pair, the authors do not indicate how they "characterize the phonological principles that underlie the child's misarticulations." This is especially evident in the case of rules such as #36b (under final affricates):

$$\begin{bmatrix} t\int \\ d_3 \end{bmatrix} \rightarrow \begin{bmatrix} s \\ z \end{bmatrix}$$

In this example, there is a change in both place and manner of articulation. It is not clear what the "underlying phonological principle" is supposed to be in a case like this. Moreover, because rules are listed separately for initial and final positions, the examiner may not be encouraged to look for larger generalizations that encompass both word-positions. To illustrate, if a child replaced /tʃ/ and d3/ with [t] and [d], respectively, in both initial and final positions, two rules would be circled, rule #19 for initial position, and rule #37 for final position.

The authors point out that summary statements based on the pattern analysis can be used in completing the phonological rule analysis. They suggest comparing the rules listed in Part III of the response/analysis form with the completed pattern analysis. In this way, the clinician can determine whether or not each rule is evident in the child's speech. If it is, the rule (or the part that is applicable) is circled. If any misarticulations remain that are not accounted for by the rules that are listed, the clinician has to devise his or her own rules. These rules are inserted in the appropriate places on Section III of the response/analysis form.

Any rule that applies in all possible cases is designated as "obligatory" and rules that apply only part of the time are labeled "optional." If a rule applies only in specific phonetic contexts, these contexts are written beside the rule. Examples are provided that illustrate a completed phonological rule analysis.

According to Compton and Hutton (p. 11), the clinical advantages of phonological rule analysis include the following:

(a) The child's phonological patterns can be stated more precisely.

(b) Using phonological rules can "facilitate the discovery of interrelated patterns."

(c) The rules focus on classes of sounds and the "feature changes" that account for the child's deviant patterns.

(d) Phonological rules "provide an objective way of evaluating the child's progress" in therapy.

Compton and Hutton give explicit instructions for administering their assessment procedure, e.g., eliciting two productions of each word, providing hints when a child does not give the desired response to a picture, obtaining samples of connected speech, assessing stimulability, etc. They note that the 50-item list is just the minimum sample required, and they advise clinicians to include additional productions in the analysis.

It is recommended that the clinician tape-record the first few evaluations so that on-the-spot transcriptions can be compared to the recordings. Tape-recording is also recommended for children with more severe problems or those who exhibit unusual misarticulations. When transcribing a child's responses, the examiner is told to focus on initial and final consonants (rather than transcribing the entire word) and to transcribe as "narrowly" as possible, using IPA symbols, supplemented by special diacritics and symbols provided in the manual.

According to the authors (p. 1), it takes approximately three-quarters of an hour to complete an evaluation: 20 to 25 minutes to elicit and transcribe the responses, 15 to 20 minutes for the pattern analysis, and 10 to 15 minutes for the optional phonological rule analysis (although an inexperienced clinician may need more time for the rule analysis). Compton and Hutton state that their assessment procedure was developed with children between 3 and 7 years of age. However, they claim that it also may be used with older children and adults.

The clinical application of the *Compton-Hutton Phonological Assessment* is said to be based on three principles (p. 14):

(1) A child's deviant productions do not represent "isolated sound errors," but rather are organized in a "system of interrelated deviant patterns."

(2) The correction of any particular deviant production that follows a specific pattern will "break down" that pattern (i.e., it will change the underlying principle).

(3) The effects of therapy will be maximized if "key patterns" and "key sounds" are selected that will have the greatest impact on the structure of the child's system.

The following guidelines are provided concerning the selection of (a) key patterns, (b) key sounds, and (c) key words:

(a) *key patterns*

(1) Unusual patterns should be given a high priority because they are likely to interfere with intelligibility.

(2) High priority should be given to patterns that affect a large number of words in the child's vocabulary.

(3) Patterns should be selected that are "appropriate for the child's age" (p. 17).

(b) *key sounds*

(1) At first, work on just one of the sounds that follows a deviant pattern. As this error is eliminated, there should be generalization to other sounds that follow the same pattern.

(2) When possible, select a key sound that will break down two or more patterns at one time.

(3) Choose sounds that occur in many words.

(c) *key words*

Therapy should start with words rather than isolated sounds. Words give a "meaningful context" for sounds, and they provide more chances for using "facilitating contexts." For instance (pp. 17–18):

(1) In training velar stops, choose words with high back vowels (such as *cool*).

(2) If a child uses [p, b] in place of /f, v/, select key words with unrounded vowels in order to reinforce the lip-spreading of /f, v/.

(3) If a child omits /s/ in blends, use alveolar consonants such as [t] and [n] (as in *stop* and *snow*) to reinforce the alveolar place of articulation of /s/.

Compton and Hutton stress the importance of periodic re-evaluations (every two or three months) to monitor changes in the child's phonological system and to update his or her therapy plan. Reevaluations also help the clinician detect what the authors call "therapeutic backfire" or "clinical backlash patterns" (p. 18). These are new and inappropriate patterns that result from an attempt to correct other patterns in a child's phonological system.

FOOTNOTES

[1]The authors state that they chose mainly one-syllable words to "minimize interference from complex phonetic sequences and multisyllabic words" (p. 2). However, this clearly limits their sample.
[2]It should be noted that although Compton and Hutton use the term "common deviant phonological rule," most of the rules that they list would not be considered deviant. What they apparently mean is that these rules are common in the speech of children with deviant speech.
[3]Although the authors point out that phonological rules should actually be specified in terms of distinctive features, they choose to abbreviate the rules by using more familiar phonological symbols "for the sake of brevity and ease of reading" (p. 11).

WEINER (1979)

Weiner's *Phonological Process Analysis* (PPA) was published in 1979. Weiner states that the PPA is not meant to be a test, but an analysis procedure. There are no norms, and it is not necessary to give the entire procedure to each child whose speech is being assessed. Weiner's analysis procedure is said to be useful for assessing the speech of unintelligible children between the ages of 2 and 5 years. "Action pictures" involving a character named Uncle Fred are used to elicit approximately 20 processes of three different types.[1] These processes are listed below, along with the initials that Weiner uses for each "test process" and an example of each. Although most of these processes are "natural," Weiner makes no claims about naturalness, and he appears to use *process* and *rule* interchangeably.

Processes Assessed
In Weiner's (1979)
Phonological Process Analysis

I. *Syllable Structure Processes*
    Deletion of Final Consonants (DFC)   book [bʊ]
    Cluster Reduction (CR)
      Syllable initial
        stop + liquid   block [bɑk]
        fricative + liquid   fly [fɑɪ]
        /s/ clusters   snake [nek]
      Syllable final
        /s/ + stop   mask [mæk]
        liquid + stop   milk [mɪk]
        nasal + stop   bump [bʌp]
    Weak Syllable Deletion (WSD)   telephone [tʰɛfon]
    Glottal Replacement (GR)   kitchen [kʰɪʔən]

II. *Harmony Processes*
    Labial Assimilation (LA)   thumb [wʌm]
    Alveolar Assimilation (AA)   skate [tet]
    Velar Assimilation (VA)   dog [gɔg]
    Prevocalic Voicing (PV)   pig [bɪg]
    Final Consonant Devoicing (FCD)   bed [bɛt]
    Syllable Harmony   water [wɔwɔ]

III. *Feature Contrast Processes*

Stopping (ST)	sun [dʌn]
Affrication (AF)	sun [tsʌn]
Fronting (F)	wagon [wædn̩] shoe [su]
Gliding of Fricatives (GF)	fish [wɪs]
Gliding of Liquids (GL)	red [wɛd] log [jɔg]
Vocalization (V)	table [tebo]
Denasalization (DN)	smoke [bok]
Neutralization	e.g., all vowels become [ə] or all fricatives become [θ]

Stimulus pictures (a total of 136) are organized by process rather than by sound; each stimulus item is designed to elicit a particular process (if that process is part of the child's system). Two elicitation procedures are used, *sentence recall* (R), which elicits the target word in a phrase or sentence, and *delayed imitation* (DI), which elicits the target word in isolation. To give an example, the child is shown a picture of Uncle Fred blowing a whistle. In the sentence recall task, the examiner says, "This is a whistle. Uncle Fred is blowing the whistle. What is Uncle Fred doing?" The child is expected to respond with something like "Blowing the whistle." In the delayed imitation task, the examiner says, "This is a whistle. Uncle Fred is blowing the _____?" The child is expected to fill in the blank by saying "whistle."² It is noted that these elicitation procedures are useful for young children who may be unintelligible or who may have little spontaneous speech. According to Weiner (1979, p. 1), the entire procedure takes approximately 45 minutes, with a cooperative subject. (In actual practice, it often takes considerably longer.)

Each child utterance is transcribed live in the "Response" column on the appropriate score sheet, but Weiner also recommends tape-recording for later verification. Weiner has attempted to control for the appearance of particular processes. Thus, the examiner simply has to recognize each response as either exemplifying or not exemplifying the process in question. Examples are given as an aid. For instance, one of the words that was chosen to elicit vocalization is *bottle*, and [bɑdo] is given as an example. If the child produces [bɑdo] or some other form with a vowel in place of the final syllabic liquid, the examiner checks (✓) the plus (+) column. If the final [l̩] is not replaced by a vowel, a check mark is written in the minus (−) column. So, a check in the + column indicates the presence (or application) of a process. If a process occurs when it is not specifically being tested, the appropriate initials are written beside the transcription. To illustrate, *moon* is one of the words chosen to elicit *denasalization*. If a child produces [bu] for *moon*, "DFC" is written beside the transcription of the child's production, and of course a check is also placed in the + column for denasalization.

In the section designed to elicit harmony (or assimilation) processes, Weiner includes control items. For example, if a child says [gʌk] for *duck*, the examiner presents the control item [dʌ]. If the child repeats [dʌ], then the [gʌk] response to *duck* is scored as a plus (+) under velar assimilation. However, if the child says [gʌ] in response to the control, then the [gʌk] response is scored as minus (−) under velar assimilation. (In this case, the child may have a backing process that affects alveolars.)[3]

The clinician ends up with a one-page "Process Profile" that shows which processes are operating and the percentage of application of each. The percentage of application or "proportion of test processes" is computed by dividing the number of times the process occurred (when tested) by the number of times it was sampled. The "frequency of nontest processes" is also indicated. That is, the examiner calculates the number of additional times each process occurred when it was not being sampled. In the column labeled "process decision," the examiner notes the extent to which each process is present by putting a + or − in that column. As there are no specific criteria, this decision is left up to the examiner. Effect on intelligibility is a prime consideration, however.

On the process profile sheet, it is also necessary to note any special "conditions of occurrence." For instance, if fronting affects only stops, this is noted by writing "stops only" to the right of the process decision column. (This information is said to be very important for therapy.)

Other processes that may be evident, such as nonfinal devoicing, are described at the bottom of the process profile page. There is also space on this sheet to summarize the child's phonetic inventory. According to Weiner, a sound has to be used four or more times in the sample before it is circled as "present." Sounds that occur less frequently are noted under the "absent" column.

Regarding therapy, Weiner recommends treating processes in all the major categories at once. The following "order of remediation" is proposed for processes in each major category, based on normal development, importance for intelligibility, and "ease of instruction" (p. 38).

Syllable structure processes: deletion of final consonants 〉 glottal replacement 〉 weak syllable deletion 〉 cluster reduction.

Harmony processes: prevocalic voicing 〉 final consonant devoicing 〉 velar assimilation 〉 labial assimilation 〉 alveolar assimilation.

Feature contrast processes: stopping ⟩ affrication ⟩ gliding of fricatives ⟩ fronting ⟩ denasalization ⟩ gliding of liquids ⟩ vocalization.

Some of Weiner's specific therapy suggestions are summarized below:

(1) Suggestions for eliminating syllable structure processes include:

(a) If several homonym pairs result from the application of a particular process, such as /s/-loss, Weiner (1979, p. 37) recommends using a sorting task called "conceptualization" (LaRiviere, Winitz, Reeds, & Herriman, 1974). The child is asked to sort pairs of words like *pill/spill, pot/spot,* etc. into two categories (e.g., by raising his or her hand). The child is then presented with pictures representing the words that are produced as homonyms and has to tell the clinician which picture to pick up. This is said to establish a meaning difference between the homonyms.

(b) Weiner also recommends using a "lexical approach" (Ferrier & Davis, 1973) to eliminate syllable structure processes that result in homonymy. For example, if a child produces *bow* and *boat* as [boʊ], due to deletion of final consonants, the clinician presents pictures representing the two words. The child then has to tell the clinician which picture to pick up. This approach should help the child to "realize that an articulatory change will affect a change in meaning" (Weiner, 1979, p. 37).

(2) Suggestions for eliminating assimilation or harmony processes include the following:

(a) Weiner (1979, p. 37) recommends a procedure based on "key words" to remediate assimilation processes. This is basically the paired stimuli approach discussed by Weston and Irwin (1971). For example, if a child produces *dog* as [gɔg] and *duck* as [gʌk] because of velar assimilation, these words are paired with words in which assimilation could not apply, such as *dime, date, day,* etc. (e.g., *dime/dog, date/duck*). This should help the child conceptualize the fact that both words in the pair begin with the same sound.

(b) Weiner (1979) also recommends using a modified sensorimotor approach (McDonald, 1964) to eliminate assimilation processes. For example, if a child produces [gɔg] for *dog* and [gʌk] for *duck*, due to velar assimilation, these words should be paired with (or presented directly after) words ending in [d], such as *mad, sad,* e.g., *mad duck, sad dog*. The final [d] in the first word should facilitate the initial [d] in the second word.

(3) Suggestions for remediating feature contrast processes include:
  (a) To remediate processes such as stopping, Weiner (1979, p. 38) suggests a distinctive feature-type approach (McReynolds & Bennett, 1972). The child is taught to produce two sounds that differ by just one distinctive feature (e.g., s-t, f-p). When the child has learned to produce the + and − aspects of the feature in a contrasting pair, he or she should generalize the correct feature to other similar sounds.
  (b) Another distinctive feature approach (Weiner & Bankson, 1978) focuses on helping the child develop an awareness of the phonetic characteristics of the + and − aspects of a feature (Weiner, 1979, p. 38). For example, [+ continuant] might be described as "flowing," and [− continuant] as "popping." First, the child would learn to identify these sounds and then produce the "flowing" sound, etc.

FOOTNOTES

[1]Weiner says that there are 16 "test processes," but the number is higher if the different processes that he groups under "cluster reduction" are counted separately.
[2]Although this procedure is supposed to be useful with children between the ages of 2 and 5, children as young as 2 (or older children with delayed development) may not understand that when the examiner's intonation rises, they are expected to "fill in the blank."
[3]The idea of including control items appears to be a good one, but it is possible that a child who exhibits a harmony process may be stimulable for the crucial sound in a CV syllable (such as [dʌ]) or that the harmony process may be optional (e.g., [dʌk] ~ [gʌk]). Weiner does not discuss these possibilities.

HODSON (1980)

Hodson's (1980) *The Assessment of Phonological Processes* is said to identify systematic patterns in children's speech. The stated goal of this procedure is to provide, as quickly as possible, information that will help clinicians plan more effective and efficient therapy for individuals with phonological disorders. The procedure was designed for use with preschool-aged children with multiple articulation errors. However, it has been used successfully with unintelligible children between the ages of 2 and 9 years and also with retarded and apraxic adults, according to Hodson. In this test, as it is called, 42 phonological processes are assessed. Some of the terms used by Hodson differ from those typically used, and her shorthand notation for the 42 target processes is also unique. However, all of the test processes are explained in the manual. Hodson's test processes are listed below. The shorthand notation for each is also given, along with at one example.

Basic Phonological Processes[1]

Syllable reduction	(1 Syl Re)	music box [mubɑ]
Cluster reduction		
Obstruent omissions	(2 Cl Re Ob)	screwdriver [kudɑ͡ɪvʊ]
Sonorant omissions	(3 Cl Re Son)	flower [fɑ͡ʊə]
Singleton obstruent omissions		
Prevocalic	(4 Pre→ϕ)	shoe [u]
Postvocalic	(5 Post→ϕ)	bed [bɛ]
Stridency deletion		
Omissions	(6 Str→ϕ)	star [tɑɚ], shoe [u]
Nonstrident substitutions	(7 Non Str)	soap [to͡ʊp], [ho͡ʊp]
Velar deviations		
Omissions	(8 Vel→ϕ)	gun [ʌn]
Fronting	(9 Vel Fr)	gun [dʌn]

Miscellaneous Phonological Processes

Prevocalic voicing	(10 Pre→V)	tub [dʌb]
Postvocalic devoicing	(11 Post→D)	page [pe͡ɪtʃ]
Glottal replacement	(12 Gl Re)	hat [hæʔ]
Backing	(13 Back)	tub [tʌg]
Stopping	(14 Stop)	soap [to͡ʊp]
Affrication	(15 Aff)	soap [tso͡ʊp]
Deaffrication	(16 Deaff)	chair [ʃɛɚ]
Palatalization	(17 Pal)	soap [sʲo͡ʊp], [ʃo͡ʊp]
Depalatalization	(18 Depal)	chair [tseə] shoe [su]
Coalescence	(19 Coal)	smoke [fo͡ʊk]
Epenthesis	(20 Epen)	tree [tᵊri]
Metathesis	(21 Meta)	mask [mæks]

Sonorant deviations

Liquid /l/

Omissions	(22/l/→φ)	leaf [if]
Gliding	(23→glide)	leaf [wif]
Vowelization	(24→vowel)	candle [kændo]
Other	(25 other)	leaf [tif] (Stopping)

Liquid /r, ɚ/

Omissions	(26/r/→φ)	rope [o͞up]
Gliding	(27→glide)	rug [wʌg]
Vowelization	(28→vowel)	zipper [zɪpə]
Other	(29 other)	rug [tʌg] (Stopping)

Nasals

Omissions	(30 Nas→φ)	spoon [pu]
Other	(31 other)	nose [do͞uz] (Denasalization)

Glides

Omissions	(32 glide→φ)	watch [ats]
Other	(33 other)	yellow [dɛwo͞u] (Stopping)

Vowel deviations	(34 Vowel De)	fish [fʌ]

Assimilation Processes

Nasal	(35 Nasal→A)	sun [nʌn]
Velar	(36 Vel→A)	gun [gʌŋ]
Labial	(37 Lab→A)	spoon [pum], smoke [fmo͞uk]
Alveolar	(38 Alv→A)	soap [to͞ut]

Articulatory Shifts

Substitutions of [f,v,s,z] for /θ,ð/	(39/θ,ð/→/f,v,s,z/)	thumb [fʌm], [sʌm]
Frontal lisp	(40 Fr Lisp)	nose [no͞uz̪]
Dentalization of /t,d,n,l/	(41 +/t,d,n,l/)	tub [t̪ʌb]
Lateralization	(42→Lat)	soap [ɬo͞up], [sᶩo͞up]

Any "deviations" that do not fall into the above categories are listed under "Other Patterns/Preferences." Such patterns would include reduplication, as in [kækæ] for *candle*, and diminutives, as in *ducky* or *dollie*. It is noted (p. 20) that these patterns are observed more often in the speech of normally developing young children than in older children with phonological disorders. "Other patterns" would also include nasalization and the use of nasal "snorts" (i.e., excessive nasal emission). Preferences (which Hodson calls "idiosyncratic rules") would include, for instance, the use of [θ] for all voiceless fricatives.

In *The Assessment of Phonological Processes*, all English consonants are assessed in prevocalic and postvocalic positions (with the exception of /w, j, h/), and 31 consonant clusters are also assessed. Fifty-five single words are elicited primarily by means of a spontaneous object-naming task. (Stimuli are not included.) Each stimulus item assesses more than one process. The elicitation procedure that is used is relatively "free." The child and the examiner sit on the floor, and the child chooses an object from a pile, holds it up high, and says its name loudly. It is then put aside, and another object is chosen. In a few cases, words have to be repeated (e.g., *rouge*) or elicited by means of questions (e.g., "If this feels *rough*, how does this feel?").

Hodson recommends transcribing live but also audio recording for later reference. Because the test words are not elicited in any particular order, it may be necessary to name each object after the child, particularly if his or her speech is unintelligible. Hodson reports that it takes about 20 minutes to elicit and transcribe the 55 test items. A shorter screening form, consisting of just 20 items, can be given in 5 minutes.

All 55 test words are listed on the recording sheet, and the adult transcription (or "model") of the word is also given. For instance, test item #50 is *truck*, and just below this word on the recording sheet is the adult form /trʌk/. In recording the child's production, the clinician works from this model. So if a child deletes the /r/ in *truck*, a slash is drawn through the r symbol in the model (/tɹ̸ʌk/). If a [ə] vowel is inserted between the elements of the cluster, the model is modified accordingly (/tᵊrʌk/). A substitution of [w] for /r/ would require writing a *w* above the r symbol. If the child's production is correct, the model is checked (✔). If, on the other hand, the child's production does not resemble the target, the entire utterance must be transcribed.

After all target words are transcribed, the transcriptions are transferred to the analysis sheet. The 42 test processes are listed across the top of this sheet, and the 55 target words are listed down the left side. Beside each target word is space for the transcription of the child's production.

Next, the data are scored. This takes about 30 minutes, according to Hodson, although the time is said to vary with the experience of the clinician and the severity of the disorder. The screening version, which is supposed to indicate if any of the most common processes are operating, takes only about 10 minutes. To "score" the sample, the clinician has to check the column for each process being used in each test word. If a process applies more than once in a given word, the box under that process (and across from the target word) will have more than one check mark in it. To illustrate, if a child says [ɪ] for *fish*, with deletion of both strident phonemes, there will be two checks in the square under column 6 (Str→ϕ) in row 14 (/fɪʃ/). The position of the target sound in the word is not considered here. Of course, there will also be checks under column 4 (Pre→ϕ) and column 5 (Post→ϕ). In some cases, as this example shows, one sound error may require checking more than one box. To illustrate further, if a child says [bɪʃ] for *fish*, the [b] for /f/ substitute would require checking boxes under column 7 (Non Str), column 10 (Pre→V), and column 14 (Stop).

After all sound errors are coded in the appropriate columns, the checks under each process are totaled. The total for each process is then entered on the appropriate line on the summary sheet. Next, a percentage of occurrence is derived for each "basic process" and each sonorant deviation. This is done by dividing the total number of occurrences of a process by the total number of possible occurrences of that process. These percentages are then used as a basis for identifying remediation priorities. Forty percent is the recommended cutoff score.

Hodson (1980, 31–32) discusses several "principles for the remediation of phonological disorders." First, she points out that a complete phonological evaluation must precede the planning of a therapy program. The order in which processes are remediated is said to depend on the individual's performance and on determining which processes are most "out of line" in comparison to those exhibited by other children with disorders. The specific order of remediation for sounds undergoing any particular process depends on stimulability. Hodson stresses that "auditory input is crucial." In her view, the clinician must help the child to develop new "kinesthetic images" and "articulatory skills" and to "match auditory and kinesthetic patterns." Although Hodson advocates presenting one target phoneme at a time, she says that it is not necessary to wait for one phoneme to be established before moving on to the next one. The clinician's task is to "facilitate the emergence of patterns." Like Weiner, Hodson argues that examples should be provided that illustrate semantic differences between the child's productions and the corresponding adult forms, such as *bow* vs. *boat*.

FOOTNOTE

[1]The processes that Hodson classifies as "basic" are said to be prevalent in the speech of children with severe phonological disorders.

SHRIBERG AND KWIATKOWSKI (1980)

Shriberg and Kwiatkowski's (1980) *Natural Process Analysis (NPA): A Procedure for Phonological Analysis of Continuous Speech Samples* differs in several ways from the other procedures discussed in this section. For one thing, it is based on continuous speech samples rather than naming responses, delayed imitation, or sentence recall. Also, Shriberg and Kwiatkowoski look for evidence of just eight "natural" processes. (See Stampe, 1969, 1972a.) In their view, a natural process has to fulfill two conditions: (1) it must involve simplification of a complex articulation, and (2) it must be widely attested in language change phenomena (such as dialect variation and historical sound change). The eight natural processes assessed by Shriberg and Kwiatkowski are listed here, along with their abbreviations. These eight natural processes were chosen from among many possibilities because they are seen frequently in children with delayed phonological development and they can be reliably coded.

(1) Final consonant deletion (FCD), including replacement by [?]

(2) Velar fronting (VF), including replacement by any front sound

(3) Stopping (S)

(4) Palatal fronting (PF), including replacement by any front sound

(5) Liquid simplification (LS), including replacement by a glide, vowel, or other liquid

(6) Assimilation, including cases in which the "culprit" is deleted:
Progressive (PA)
Regressive (RA)

(7) Cluster reduction (CR), including either deletion of one element of the cluster or replacement by another sound

(8) Unstressed syllable deletion (USD), including deletion of any syllable

Shriberg and Kwiatkowski provide information regarding their rationale and the theoretical background for their procedure. They differentiate "natural processes," which attempt to account for and explain children's sound errors, from "rules," such as s→t, which simply describe sound errors.

Natural Process Analysis involves five steps, some of which may be bypassed by an experienced examiner. Each step that is summarized here is discussed in detail by Shriberg and Kwiatkowski.

1. Sampling

Shriberg and Kwiatkowski give several reasons supporting their decision to use continuous speech samples as a basis for their Natural Process Analysis. For example, if this is done, then one sample can be used for all levels of analysis, including deriving an MLU (mean length of utterance). Although not every continuous speech sample is necessarily representative, the authors argue that such samples typically provide a more accurate picture of children's abilities than do imitation or picture-naming tasks. Shriberg and Kwiatkowski suggest getting children to tell stories or talk about objects and toys or about their interests. However, they note that it may be necessary to use more controlled tasks to elicit "rare" sounds. If continuous speech samples are used, it is essential that the clinician repeat the child's utterances, word for word, without "recoding" incorrect forms, such as, "He goed there." Otherwise, it may be impossible to interpret much of what the child is saying later on when the tape is played back.

2. Recording

Shriberg and Kwiatkowski emphasize the importance of using high-quality audio equipment and low-noise tapes and of recording the child in the quietest place available. Detailed suggestions for recording are provided.

3. Transcription

A sample of about 200 or 250 words should be transcribed as narrowly as possible, using the NPA Transcription Sheets. Shriberg and Kwiatkowski note that some combination of "on-line" transcription and transcription from tapes may provide the most reliable data. All the child's "glossable" utterances should be transcribed completely. (*Gloss* is defined as what the child attempted to say.) Although the whole sample is transcribed, only the first occurrence of each word is used in the analysis. Detailed transcription suggestions are provided.

4. Coding

Coding involves two operations. First, the words that are going to be analyzed are transferred from the transcription sheets onto the coding sheets. In a sample of 200–250 words, there will be about 80–100 different words to be coded. Three coding sheets are provided. Sheet A is for nasals, glides, and liquids; sheet B is for oral stop consonants, and sheet C is for fricatives and affricates. Each coding sheet is divided into columns. The first five are for words of five basic syllable shapes. For instance, (1) is for C̲V, (2) is for VC̲, (3) is for CVC̲, etc. Column 6 is for two syllable words, and column 7 is for words of three or more syllables. The target sounds are listed down the left side of the coding sheets. So, for example, coding sheet A has /m/, /n/, /ŋ/, /w/, /j/, /l/, /r/ down the left side. If a target sound does not occur in a particular position, that portion of the coding sheet is shaded. To illustrate, /ŋ/ does not occur in either C̲V or VC̲ syllables, so those parts of sheet A are shaded.

The underlined C̲ indicates "target consonant," and it determines where the gloss and the transcription of a word are entered on the coding sheet. For instance, if one of the words to be analyzed is *came*, produced by the child as [kēī], it would be entered on coding sheet A under column 3, CVC̲. The gloss *came* would be entered to the left under CVC̲, along with the item number (from the transcription sheet); the child's rendition of the word, in this case [kēī], would be entered beside the gloss under "transcription."

The next step is to assign a code to each consonant, consonant cluster, and polysyllabic word that is entered on the coding sheets. If the target sound in question is correct, a *C* is written under "code," and if the sound is deleted, a null sign (∅) is used. The eight natural processes assessed by Shriberg and Kwiatkowski are coded in a specific order—the order in which they are listed above. Each target consonant or consonant cluster is assigned just one code. However, in cases that involve both regressive assimilation and final consonant deletion, both processes are coded. For instance, if a child said [gɑ] for *dog*, regressive (velar) assimilation would be coded for the word-initial consonant /d/, and final consonant deletion would be coded for the word-final consonant /g/.[1]

For the word *came*, discussed above, the child's [kēī] production would be coded as follows. A *C* would be written in the left part of the code column to indicate that the initial /k/ is correct. In the right part of the code column would be written FCD because the child's production has no final consonant.

Note that many types of changes are not coded at all in *Natural Process Analysis*. For instance, voicing changes are not coded (because the authors have found that such changes cannot be reliably coded). Vowel-coloring (as in [kɑr] for *car*) is not coded, nor are additions or distortions. In addition, changes such as tʃ→ʃ (deaffrication) and tʃ→h are not coded in the NPA. The focus is on the eight "natural" processes discussed above. However, uncoded changes are noted on the summary sheet and can be used for an even closer analysis.

5. *Summarizing*

The "NPA Summary Sheet" is a one-page description of a child's use of eight natural processes in continuous speech. It also contains a description of the child's "phonetic inventory." The 24 consonant phonemes of English are displayed across the top of the Summary Sheet. For each phoneme, the examiner puts an *X* in the appropriate row out of the four rows under the phoneme symbols. The first row is labelled "Correct Anywhere." This row is marked if the phoneme in question is "correct" at all, even if it is distorted or if the voicing is wrong or if another sound is added. The second row, labelled "Appears Anywhere," is marked if the phoneme appears at all in the sample, even if it appears only as a substitute. The third row is labelled "Glossed; Never Correct; Never Appears." This row is marked if a phoneme is sampled in at least one word but is never produced correctly or as a substitute. The last row is marked if a phoneme is "Never Glossed" and "Never Appears."

The eight natural processes assessed by Shriberg and Kwiatkowski are listed on the bottom two-thirds of the summary sheet. These processes are arranged so that most of them appear directly under the phonemes that could be affected. If a process always affects the phoneme in question, the appropriate square is checked (✓). If the process sometimes affects the sound in question, a check is written in a circle (∅). A circle (O) alone indicates that the target sound is never affected by the process, and a dash (−) indicates that no relevant data are available.

On the summary sheet, there is space to list any examples of assimilation or cluster reduction. For unstressed syllable deletion, the number of two- and three-syllable target words is listed, and the number of words undergoing syllable deletion is indicated. A percentage is then computed. There is space at the bottom of the summary sheet for notes, including observations of potential clinical interest. Any distortions or uncoded sound errors are also listed.

In Part III of their book, Shriberg and Kwiatkowski present detailed guidelines for the interpretation of natural process analysis and for carrying out additional analyses using the total sample. First, Shriberg and Kwiatkowski (1980, p. 62) discuss three types of sound change. What they call *context-sensitive modifications* include allophonic and casual or fast speech changes, both of which are "normal and predictable"—not articulation errors. *Context-free modifications*, usually called distortions, on the other hand, are not normal occurrences. These sound changes occur in contexts where they would not be expected. For instance, a child might use a velarized /l/ in prevocalic position.

The third major type of sound change, referred to as *phoneme deletions and substitutions*, includes both natural processes and uncoded deletions and substitutions (some of which may actually be "natural" simplifications). When natural processes apply, it is assumed that either the affected sounds are not "available" in the child's phonetic inventory or some other factor (such as word complexity) requires the process to operate. In the latter case, the process analysis should attempt to determine what factor underlies the deletion or substitution.

After discussing these categories of sound change, Shriberg and Kwiatkowski present guidelines for phonetic analysis and process analysis. Phonetic analysis involves describing context-sensitive modifications, context-free modifications, and uncodable deletions and substitutions. Shriberg and Kwiatkowski (1980, p. 65) claim that phonetic analysis "is important diagnostically and is basic to an understanding of the natural process data." The clinician carefully examines the transcription sheet, the coding sheets, and the summary sheets and attempts to determine what articulatory features (e.g., nasality) are present in the child's sound inventory and to discover how these compare to normative data.

To illustrate the importance of phonetic analysis, Shriberg and Kwiatkowski provide an example of a child who nasalized all vowels, used [h] for fricatives, had no correct nasal-stop clusters, and used some glottal stops. On the basis of these errors, it was recommended that the child's velopharyngeal adequacy be assessed. Assessment results did suggest "marginal velopharyngeal insufficiency" (Shriberg & Kwiatkowski, 1980, p. 67).

In the natural process part of the analysis, the clinician has to determine, for each of the processes exhibited, the child's "developmental stage." In addition, if a process is used inconsistently, an attempt has to be made to find any associated context or function variables. The authors (1980, p. 68) point out that the developmental approach to assessment and remediation relies on developmental data of the type presented in their Appendix A.

To account for inconsistent process use, all the data on the transcription sheets and coding sheets are utilized. The clinician may simply scan the transcription sheets looking for context variables (e.g., canonical form or word-position) or function variables (e.g., pragmatic function) that might be associated with process use, or he or she may use work sheets. If work sheets are used, the clinician first scans the transcription and coding sheets to see if inconsistent process use seems to be related to context variables or function variables. Then, on a work sheet, the clinician writes down all the cases in which the process in question applied and the cases in which it could have applied but did not. In the third step, tabulations are made and percentages are calculated. Such calculations should show if there are linguistic context or function variables related to inconsistent process use.

In Part IV of their book, Shriberg and Kwiatkowski present four case studies that illustrate how natural process analysis (as well as additional types of analyses) may be used in planning therapy. These particular case studies were chosen to show the diversity found among children with delayed speech. The emphasis in the NPA is on differential diagnosis.

The first child discussed is Robby, age 7;1. He had moderately unintelligible speech. Although his productive language and vocabulary were delayed about one year, his language comprehension was approximately age-appropriate, as was his cognitive development. He had had frequent colds, with possible temporary hearing problems, and he was said to be "easily distractible."

Stimulability testing, along with the results on the summary sheet, showed that Robby could produce all the place, manner, and voicing features of English, and he correctly produced nasals, stops, liquids, and glides. He had no context-free or context-sensitive distortions, and he was stimulable for /s, z/. According to Shriberg and Kwiatkowski, Robby's sound changes appeared to be associated with phonological processes rather than with phonetic distortions.

Robby exhibited basically three natural phonological processes: final consonant deletion, stopping, and cluster reduction. For each of these processes, Shriberg and Kwiatkowski report the "stage" at which he was functioning, based on the tentative developmental data reported in their Appendix A. For example, only 7% of Robby's CVC words were reduced by final consonant deletion. This is said to indicate that FCD is "in the process of dissolution and does not require management" (Shriberg & Kwiatkowski, 1980, p. 85).

Robby was found to either stop or delete fricatives most of the time. Initial fricatives were stopped, and final fricatives were stopped or deleted or were produced correctly. According to Shriberg and Kwiatkowski, stopping is a process that should be targeted for therapy. For Robby, cluster reduction was limited primarily to deletion or stopping of fricatives. Sounds that were never said correctly as singletons were either stopped or deleted in clusters, while sounds just entering his phonetic inventory were either correct or stopped in clusters, as in [f] for /fl/ and [p] for /fr/. According to the authors, scanning the data indicates that there is no need to complete a context or function analysis.

For Robby, Shriberg and Kwiatkowski recommend a management program focusing on fricative production. Specifically, they state (p. 86) that the emphasis should be on when to produce fricatives, rather than how. That is, fricatives should be contrasted to stops. This is because Robby is already able to produce fricatives with stimulation. They also state that /s/ and /z/ should be taught in clusters, including cases in which they have a morphological function (e.g., to mark plurals). This should promote language development on several levels at once.

The second case study involves a child named Michael, aged 6;2, who was about 25% to 50% intelligible. He was a "late talker" with an unremarkable medical history. Each consonant of English that was attempted was produced correctly by Michael at least once. However, prominent lip rounding accompanied his production of sibilants. Sibilants were also produced with a posterior tongue position, and some sounded almost lateralized. In addition to sibilant distortions, Michael also exhibited sound changes affecting vowels and diphthongs. The authors (1980, p. 87) hypothesize that Michael's context-free distortions could have resulted from certain management techniques or could reflect his late speech onset, followed by a period of rapid phonetic development. Rather than delete sounds, he might simply have tried to "put something in." It is also hypothesized that his sibilant distortions could be related to his vowel errors.

Michael's natural sound changes involved primarily final consonant deletion, liquid simplification, and cluster reduction. Although Michael sometimes deleted /n, t, d, l/ in word-final position, the low incidence of FCD (22%) is said to indicate that this process is being resolved. Michael's liquid errors involved occasional [w] for /r/ substitutions, indicating that this process too should eventually be resolved without therapy. Michael was found to delete both marked and unmarked members of clusters. Thus context and function analyses were carried out. However, Shriberg and Kwiatkowski could not find a pattern in Michael's correct vs. incorrect clusters.

According to Shriberg and Kwiatkowski (1980, p. 98), Michael's therapy program should focus on "self-monitoring of vowel substitutions" and "elimination of lip rounding and tongue bunching" during the production of sibilants. Michael's vowel problems are considered to require an identification program in which he monitors his own productions and is reinforced for correcting himself. Regarding the elimination of lip rounding and tongue bunching on sibilants, Shriberg and Kwiatkowski recommend a program in which the child learns to discriminate lip rounding from non-lip rounding in increasingly complex linguistic environments. In addition, they recommend a response development program for /s/ in which more anterior tongue posture, proper tongue shape, and central air emission are stressed.

Toby, the subject of the third case study, was 5 years old and was said to be approximately 25% intelligible. He talked late and had an unremarkable medical/psychosocial history. Although his cognitive development and comprehension were within normal limits, his productive language was about one year delayed.

The phonetic analysis showed that Toby was producing at least one sound in each manner class. Because he was able to produce 79% of the consonants of English correctly, as well as all vowels and diphthongs, his intelligibility problem could not be due to a reduced phonetic inventory. Toby's "uncoded" errors included: initial consonant deletions (of /w, j, l, r, h/), use of a glottal stop for initial and final consonants, use of [tʃ] for selected fricatives and stops, substitution of [b] for /m/, and some substitutions of [k] for final /t/. The authors (1980, p. 101) note that these sound changes cannot be due to "ease of articulation." In addition, these data do not suggest a structural or functional problem. Instead, Toby's use of deletion is seen as a phonological process that simplifies all surface forms. Because Toby's sound changes shed light on certain methodological issues concerning the NPA, Shriberg and Kwiatkowski (1980) discuss all eight processes, as summarized below.

Final consonant deletion was pervasive for Toby. Some sounds in each manner class were "sometimes" or "always" deleted in final position, including front nasals, which are reportedly early developing sounds. However, Toby sometimes "marked" stops and nasals that he deleted by modifying the preceding vowel. Thus he showed an awareness of the final consonants. For instance, he sometimes lengthened vowels before voiced stops, even when those voiced stops were later deleted. Similarly, vowels preceding (deleted) nasal consonants were sometimes nasalized. Presumably such context-sensitive modifications have to take place before final consonants are deleted. Although the formal NPA procedures do not allow for ordered rules, the authors point out that additional analysis procedures can consider such possibilities.

Velar fronting sometimes affected initial velar stops, but final velars were usually omitted. Stopping was not used by Toby; rather, fricatives were often deleted. However, Shriberg and Kwiatkowski (1980, p. 112) speculate that stopping may show up at some point as final consonant deletion disappears.

Toby did not utilize palatal fronting. Instead he deleted palatals or used one in place of another (e.g., [tʃ] for /ʃ/). Toby did not exhibit liquid simplification because he deleted nearly all initial and final liquids.

However, he produced r-colored vowels ([ɚ] and [ɝ]) correctly. (These data are said to support the author's decision to symbolize final *r* in monosyllabic words as [r], rather than [ɚ] as in [faɪr] for *fire*.)

Only a few of Toby's one-syllable words contained two consonants, due to his extensive deletions. However, a few of his two-syllable words did show the effects of assimilation, as in [bʌbɚ] for *butter* (p. 113). Such examples would not show up in the formal analysis because two-syllable words are coded only for unstressed syllable deletion. The authors note that more instances of assimilation could appear as Toby's use of deletion decreases.

Although Toby correctly produced some word-initial stop + liquid clusters, most clusters were reduced to one element. Toby exhibited a fairly high percentage of unstressed syllable deletion, but he sometimes "marked" syllables by using glottal stops to replace various consonants. Shriberg and Kwiatkowski (1980, p. 113) state that Toby's data do not warrant a context-function analysis because his patterns are quite consistent.

Based on the results of the natural process analysis, along with additional analyses, Shriberg and Kwiatkowski recommended working on Toby's deletions and then on the /s/ phoneme. His progress during four months of therapy is summarized. Toby was placed in a program that focused on making him aware of final sounds and that taught him to recognize when he deleted them. The three target sounds selected were /m/, /n/, and /l/, all of which are said to occur early as children are resolving final constant deletion. All are also "salient" in final position. Stimulus words were simple CVC's. A type of /s/ morpheme program was used to aid Toby's morphophonological development. Awareness and identification were stressed, but position cues for /s/ were not specifically taught.

Shriberg and Kwiatkowski state that Toby's progress over a 4-month period showed up in the natural process analyses completed during this time. Changes were seen in four areas. His inclusion of word-final consonants increased from 27% to 63%. He began to use stopping for initial fricatives (rather than deletion). Correct /s/ began to appear in word-final position (where it had been trained). Finally, the occurrence of unstressed syllable deletion was reduced. These findings are said to support the construct validity of the NPA and to show its usefulness in planning therapy. Shriberg and Kwiatkowski (1980, p. 115) also claim that by "careful monitoring of continuous speech data" it is possible to address important clinical questions. For example, in Toby's case, it was possible to observe the effects of a change in one area of phonology on another area. Specifically, when he stopped deleting initial fricatives, he began stopping them, as predicted by developmental data.

The last case study (provided by Rhea Paul) involves Kirk, aged 5;9. It is said to illustrate the procedures that researchers need to use to understand associations between speech and language. It also represents one of the earliest attempts to use the NPA as a research tool. Although Kirk's phonetic inventory was nearly complete, he was found to use several phonological processes to "simplify" a variety of sounds. It was hypothesized that some grammatical contexts might be related to his variable process use.

Kirk did not have a significant cognitive delay, and his language comprehension also seemed to be within normal limits. The structure and function of the oral mechanism was found to be normal, and Kirk was reported to use language for a variety of functions. So, except for his language production, he appeared to be functioning normally.

Kirk's MLU of 4.75 morphemes was normal for his age. However, the results of the "structural analysis" were mixed. Most of Kirk's sentences contained structures typical of Stage IV, and Stage V structures also sometimes occurred. However, he had not mastered some Stage II and Stage III morphemes (e.g., plurals and possessives).

An attempt was made to use the information from the NPA to see if Kirk failed to use certain grammatical morphemes because he had not yet mastered the necessary syntactic rules or because his phonological system kept them from being realized. Data regarding the plural morpheme was not conclusive. Both words that should have had plural endings were polysyllabic and both should have taken the /z/ ending, but /z/ was not present in his inventory. Either factor (word length or absence of /z/) could have been the "primary limiting factor" (p. 119). Although Kirk produced two final /s/ clusters (in *last* and *what's*) and produced *there's* as [ɛɑd], with stopping of the final /z/, both instances of the possessive (*dad's*) were simplified (to [dæ]). So, although Kirk's phonological system would have allowed him to mark plurals and possessives, he did not do so.

A similar example is provided by Kirk's treatment of regular third person verbs. He did not produce the /s, z/ endings for these forms even though his phonological system alone did not prohibit such productions, and in fact, phonologically similar forms, such as *what's*, sometimes did have the appropriate final sound. Examples of this type are said to indicate that Kirk has a syntactic delay that interacts with his phonological delay and that prevents him from producing certain grammatical morphemes.

Paul, in this case study, also considered the interaction between language and speech by comparing grammatical complexity and phonological process usage. She found that for Kirk, increasing sentence complexity was not associated with an increase in the number of words simplified by phonological processes. Moreover, in most cases, a word was either always right or always wrong, regardless of the complexity of the sentence in which it occurred. Thus grammatical complexity did not seem to be a factor controlling his phonological production.

Next, the possible effects of canonical structure were examined. It was determined that although canonical structure may have some effect on the probability that a simplification process will be used, the particular target sounds have more of an effect. To illustrate, 81% of the CV words in Kirk's sample were never simplified. The three CV words that were simplified were found to contain relatively difficult sounds (e.g., velars and fricatives). Similar findings are reported for Kirk's VC's and CVC's. The processes that he used were likely to apply regardless of the canonical type.

To summarize, Kirk was found to make extensive use of processes affecting velars, liquids, and fricatives. Neither grammatical structures nor canonical types interacted very strongly with his process use. His phonological system was not found to be the only factor limiting his production of certain grammatical morphemes. Rather, he was found to have a language delay in addition to his phonological problem. This case study is said to demonstrate that the NPA provides a promising tool for investigating relationships between speech and language skills and for diagnosing language delay in phonologically disordered children.

FOOTNOTE

[1]Although Shriberg and Kwiatkowski do not discuss process ordering in detail, they note (p. 48) that examples such as [gɑ] for *dog* illustrate an ordering relationship. In this case, regressive assimilation has to apply before final consonant deletion. If final consonant deletion applied first, giving /dɑ/ for *dog*, regressive assimilation could not apply because there would no longer be a final consonant for the /d/ to assimilate to. The type of ordering illustrated by the [gɑ] example is called "counterbleeding" (see Appendix B) because if the processes applied in the opposite order, FCD would "bleed" RA.

INGRAM (1981)

In his *Procedures for the Phonological Analysis of Children's Language*, Ingram (1981) includes four related procedures or "levels of analysis." In his view, these four analyses provide a "complete description" of a child's developing phonological system. The four procedures proposed are: (1) phonetic analysis, (2) analysis of homonymy, (3) substitution analysis, and (4) phonological process analysis. Each analysis procedure is described in detail in a separate chapter and is illustrated in an appendix.

Ingram argues that his procedures should be useful with both normally developing and language disordered children. One of his goals is to provide a standard set of procedures for researchers so that their results can be compared. (As Ingram points out, one problem in this area is that different researchers have typically used very different procedures that are not necessarily comparable.) Any type of elicitation method can be used to obtain a speech sample; Ingram recommends using several elicitation techniques, if possible. Each of Ingram's analysis procedures is discussed briefly here; the focus, however, is on his procedures for phonological process analysis.

First, Ingram's *phonetic analysis* involves discovering the child's "phonetic inventory" for word-initial, medial, and final positions. A numerical count is derived that may, in Ingram's view, be useful as a "gross measure" of phonological acquisition, or a "phonological equivalent of MLU" (mean length of utterance). The frequency of preferred syllable shapes is also discovered. The question that is addressed in this part of the analysis is: What can the child produce, in terms of both segments and syllable types, regardless of the model?

Ingram (1981, p. 24) describes, in detail, six steps involved in phonetic analysis. First, the distribution of segments in the child's phonetic forms (in initial, medial, and final position) is recorded. Consonant inventory sheets are used for this purpose, with one sheet for each word position. Second, the child's "frequent syllable shapes" are determined. The child's syllable shapes are calculated separately for each initial segment, and then the totals are computed for each syllable shape. The total number of phonetic forms for each segment is also computed. Third, the frequency of each initial, medial and final consonant is determined. Fourth, the "criterion of phonetic frequency" is calculated. This involves adding together the number of lexical types (different words) and phonetic forms (tokens) and dividing by two. This number is then divided by 25. To illustrate, if a sample contains 120 lexical types (i.e, different words) and 100 phonetic forms, the criterion of frequency would equal 4.4 (120 + 100 = 220 ÷ 2 = 110   110 ÷ 25 = 4.4). Ingram considers the criterion of frequency to be a measure of "the child's ability to produce a sound and the tendency to use it" (p. 26). In the fifth step, the most frequently used segments are determined for each word-position and are entered on the Summary Sheet.

In step six, the examiner determines the child's phonetic ability. First the child's total number of consonant sounds is calculated. Ingram claims (p. 27) that this can be used as a "gross measure of phonetic development." Then, the child's "articulation score" is computed. This is said to be a more precise score in that points are assigned for sounds that the child uses, and frequently used sounds are worth more.

The child's two most frequent syllable shapes are also listed, along with their frequencies, and the "proportion of monosyllables" is then calculated. This gives an idea of the child's ability to produce multisyllabic forms. Finally, the "proportion of closed syllables" is calculated by dividing the number of CV plus CVC syllables into the number of CVC syllables. This is said (p. 28) to give an approximate idea of the child's ability to use final consonants.

Ingram's *analysis of homonymy* involves determing the extent of homonymy in a child's speech by measuring the proportion of homonymous words and homonymous phonetic forms. To give an example, Joan Velten (Velten, 1943) at 22 months of age had three homonymous phonetic forms, [bɑ], [but], [bu], each one representing several adult words. For instance, [bɑt] represented 12 different words (or homonymous words), including *blue* and *ball*. On the other hand, a child could have a large number of homonymous phonetic forms (as compared to three for Joan Velten), but each one might represent only two or three homonymous words. So, Ingram argues that it is necessary to measure both homonymous phonetic forms and homonymous words (or types). His procedure, therefore, includes computing the ratio and proportion of homonymous forms and also the ratio and proportion of homonymous types. For example, the proportion of homonymous forms is determined by dividing the number of homonymous forms by the number of phonetic forms, and the proportion of homonymous types is determined by dividing the number of homonymous types by the number of lexical types.

The examiner than enters these ratios and proportions onto the Summary Sheet. In Ingram's view, they provide an idea of the degree of homonymy in the data. There may be a low degree of both homonymous forms and types or a low degree of homonymous forms but a high degree of homonymous types, etc. As Ingram points out, some children exhibit much more homonymy than others, and if a child has a great deal of homonymy, communication may be impaired. However, Ingram also notes that we lack the normative data that would allow us to categorize a child's use of homonymy as "excessive."

In Ingram's third level of analysis, called *substitution analysis*, all of a child's substitutions that occur in each word-position are recorded, and the "extent of substitutions" is measured. As in the other sections of his book, Ingram discusses several methodological and theoretical issues; for instance, should the "unit of analysis" be the word (type) or phonetic form (token)? These problems arise when several tokens of one word are used (but they do not arise in a traditional articulation test). To illustrate, if a child substituted [g] for /k/ in two words and [t] for /k/ in two words, and if one of the words overlapped (i.e., was produced both ways), the picture would look somewhat different depending on whether phonetic forms (tokens) were considered or separate lexical items (types). For instance, velar fronting in this example affects two out of three lexical items (67%) but only two out of four phonetic forms (50%).

There are six steps in Ingram's substitution analysis. In the first, syllables in the adult words are isolated so that initial, final, and ambisyllabic sounds are determined.[1] In the second step, the examiner records the adult words and sounds that were attempted. The third step involves entering the child's substitutes for adult sounds on one of the forms provided. In step four the frequency of substitutions is determined; only those that occur at least twice for a particular sound and position are entered. This is done separately for adult initial, final and ambisyllabic consonants. When this step is completed, the examiner has one sheet (the Item and Replica Sheet) that summarizes all the substitution data for a child.

In step five, the most frequent substitutes are entered on the Summary Sheet. The Summary Sheet contains a list of all the consonants of adult English along with three rows designated as initial, ambisyllabic, and final. The two most frequent substitutes for each adult sound in each position are entered in the appropriate spaces. If a sound is correct, a check (✓) is placed in the proper box. A dash indicates that there is no available information. "Mismatches" are circled in red.

Finally, the degree of substitution is calculated. This last step represents an attempt to quantify the child's ability to match the adult model (Ingram, 1981, p. 61). First, the examiner determines the number and proportion of matches for each syllable position. To calculate the proportion of matches for each position, the number of matches for that position is divided by the number of sounds attempted. Second, the total number of matches and sounds attempted and the total "Proportion of Matches" are entered on the Summary Sheet. The "Proportion of Data" is calculated by dividing the number of consonants attempted by the total number of possible sounds. The number of acquired sounds (those checked in all positions) is entered on the summary sheet.

Ingram (1981, p. 77) defines a *phonological process analysis* as "an attempt to explain a child's substitutions by describing them in terms of general patterns of simplification." Ingram's phonological process analysis involves calculating the percentage of occurrence of 27 common phonological processes, as well as some that are not as common. As Ingram (1981, p. 77) defines the term phonological process, it refers to a "simplifying tendency on the part of the child to alter natural classes of sounds in a systematic way." Ingram states (p. 6) that phonological process analysis provides a more explanatory description of development and ties together surface substitutions. Thus, it logically follows substitution analysis. The major types of processes assessed by Ingram, as well as the specific ones under each type, are listed here:

SYLLABLE STRUCTURE PROCESSES

Deletion of final consonants (FCD)
(1) nasals, (2) voiced stops, (3) voiceless stops, (4) voiced fricatives, (5) voiceless fricatives

Reduction of consonant clusters (CR)
(6) liquids, (7) nasals, (8) /s/-clusters

Syllable deletion
(9) reduction of disyllables (RD)
(10) unstressed syllable deletion (USD)
(11) reduplication (R)

SUBSTITUTION PROCESSES

Fronting
(12) of palatals (PF), (13) of velars (VF)

Stopping (S)
(14) of initial voiceless fricatives
(15) of initial voiced fricatives
(16) of affricates

SIMPLIFICATION OF LIQUIDS AND NASALS
(17) liquid gliding (LG)
(18) vocalization (V)
(19) denasalization (DN)

OTHER SUBSTITUTION PROCESSES
(20) deaffrication (DA)
(21) deletion of syllable initial consonants (ICD)
(22) apicalization (AP)
(23) labialization (LB)

ASSIMILATION PROCESSES
(24) velar assimilation (VA)
(25) labial assimilation (LA)
(26) prevocalic voicing (PV)
(27) devoicing of final consonants (FS)

Ingram discusses each of these processes briefly and gives examples. He also presents a table containing all English consonant sounds, along with common substitutes for each sound and phonological processes that could result in those substitutes. To give an example, [b] is listed as the most common substitute for /m/, and the process that would account for this substitution is called denasalization.

Ingram outlines two somewhat different methods of deriving a phonological process analysis. In the first, the process analysis is based on the results of a substitution analysis. In the second, a process analysis is done without a substitution analysis. This procedure, therefore, combines the procedures for substitution analysis (discussed above) with those for phonological process analysis.

If the first method is followed, the examiner circles the appropriate general process that would account for each word-initial substitution and indicates the adult sounds affected. Before going on, the examiner also looks for other substitutes that fall under the same general process. If two or more processes together account for one substitute, that substitute is listed separately under each process. For example, if *key* is produced as [di], the [d] for /k/ substitution would be listed under both velar fronting and prevocalic voicing. This procedure is followed until all substitutes that occur in word-initial position have been "entered as processes." (Processes other than those listed may have to be postulated to account for some of a child's substitutions.) After all word-initial substitutes have been accounted for, ambisyllabic and then word-final substitutes are analyzed. Finally, the data are examined for evidence of processes affecting entire syllables.

The next step, if the first method is followed, is to decide whether to do a complete analysis of the child's processes or a partial analysis; according to Ingram, a partial analysis may be sufficient if a child uses just a few processes.

After all of a child's processes have been discovered, the frequency of each process is calculated. To compute the frequency of occurrence of a process, the number of lexical types (i.e., words) in which the process applies is divided by the number of lexical types in which it could have applied. A proportion is then calculated for the frequency of occurrence. For example, if word-initial /k/ is replaced by [t] three times and by [g] three times, out of a total of six attempts, the proportion for velar fronting (for /k/) would be 0.50. In a partial analysis, only those processes that account for a child's major substitutes are examined, while in a complete analysis, the frequency is calculated for each process and segment. Finally, the most frequent phonological processes—those occurring with a proportion of 50% or greater—are noted on the summary sheet, and the segments affected by each frequent process are indicated.

There is a set of eight forms, some of which have been mentioned here, designed for the four types of analysis just described. These forms, which "represent different ways to organize phonological data," are said to provide a complete record of a child's phonology. They also can be used for purposes of comparison, "to determine developmental advances and possible effects of intervention" (Ingram 1981, p. 7).

One chapter of Ingram's (1981) book is devoted to a discussion of preliminary norms of phonological development, based on the application of his procedures to phonological data from 15 normally developing and 15 language-delayed children (p. 97). Also each type of analysis that he presents is illustrated in an appendix, using actual data.

Ingram provides explicit and detailed instructions, and he defines and explains the many terms that are used. In his process analysis, he takes into consideration word and syllable position as well as types of sounds affected, making the results of his analysis more precise than the results of several other published procedures. However, the procedures are very detailed and complex, and they involve considerable paper work.

FOOTNOTE

[1]*Ambisyllabic* consonants are intervocalic consonants that belong with both the preceding and the following syllable. That is, they end one syllable and begin another.

References

Alajouanine, T., Ombredane, A., & Durand, M. *Le syndrome de disintegration phonetique dans l'aphasie.* Paris: Masson, 1939.

Albright, R. W., & Albright, J. B. The phonology of a two-year-old child. *Word,* 1956, *12,* 382–390. (Reprinted in A. Bar-Adon and W. F. Leopold, Eds., *Child language: A book of readings.* Englewood Cliffs, NJ: Prentice-Hall, 1971, 142–146.)

Allen, G. D., & Hawkins, S. The development of phonological rhythm. In A. Bell & J. B. Hooper (Eds.), *Syllables and segments.* Amsterdam: North Holland, 1978, 173–185.

Allen, G. D., & Hawkins, S. Phonological rhythm: Definition and development. In G. Yeni-Komshian, J. F. Kavanagh & C. A. Ferguson (Eds.), *Child phonology, Vol I: Production.* New York: Academic Press, 1980.

Allen, G. D., Hawkins, S., & Morris, M. Development of 'nuclear accent' marking in children's phrases. In H. Hollien & P. Hollien (Eds.), *Current issues in the phonetic sciences,* 1979, 919–926. (a)

Allen, G. D., Hawkins, S., & Morris, M. Rhythmic constraints in children's speech: Data for 3–6 year-olds. *Journal of the Acoustical Society of America,* 1979, *65,* (Supplement 1). (b)

Anderson, S. R. *West Scandinavian vowel systems and the ordering of phonological rules.* Bloomington: Indiana University Linguistics Club, 1969.

Anderson, S. R. On Grassman's Law in Sanskrit. *Linguistic Inquiry,* 1970, *1,* 387–396.

Anderson, S. R. On nasalization in Sudanese. *Linguistic Inquiry,* 1972, *3,* 257–268.

Anderson, S. R. *The organization of phonology.* New York: Seminar Press, 1974.

372   *References*

Atkinson-King, K. Children's acquisition of phonological stress contrasts. *Working Papers in Phonetics,* 1973, *25,* University of California, Los Angeles, Phonetics Laboratory.

Bach, E., & Harms, R. T. How do languages get crazy rules? In R. P. Stockwell & R.K.S. Macaulay (Eds.), *Linguistic change and generative theory.* Bloomington: Indiana University Press, 1972, 1–21.

Bailey, C.- J. N. Accented nuclei ending in underlying liquids. *Working papers in linguistics,* Department of Linguistics, University of Hawaii, 1969.

Bangs, J. A clinical analysis of the articulatory defects of the feebleminded. *Journal of Speech and Hearing Disorders,* 1942, *7,* 343–356.

Bar-Adon, A., & Leopold, W. F. (Eds.). *Child language: A book of readings.* Englewood Cliffs, NJ: Prentice-Hall, 1971.

Barton, D. *The role of perception in the acquisition of phonology.* Doctoral dissertation, University of London, 1976. (Also distributed by the Indiana Linguistics Club, Bloomington, IN, 1976.)

Berko, J., & Brown, R. Psycholinguistic research methods. In P. H. Mussen (Ed.), *Handbook of research methods in child development.* New York: Wiley and Sons, 1960.

Blanchard, I. Speech patterns and etiology in mental retardation. *American Journal of Mental Deficiency,* 1964, *68,* 612–617.

Bloch, B. Phonemic overlapping. *American Speech,* 1941, *16,* 278–284. (Also in V. B. Makkai (Ed.), *Phonological theory. Evolution and current practice.* New York: Holt, Rinehart & Winston, 1972, 66–70.)

Bloch, B., & Trager, G. L. *Outline of linguistic analysis.* Baltimore, Linguistic Society of America, 1942.

Bloomfield, L. *Language.* New York: Holt, Rinehart & Winston, 1933.

Blumstein, S. E. *Phonological implications of aphasic speech.* Doctoral dissertation, Harvard University, Cambridge, MA, 1970. (Revised as 1973b.)

Blumstein, S. E. *A phonological investigation of aphasic speech.* The Hague: Mouton, 1973. (a)

Blumstein, S. Some phonological implications of aphasic speech. In H. Goodglass & S. Blumstein (Eds.), *Psycholinguistics and aphasia.* Baltimore: Johns Hopkins University Press, 1973. (b)

Blumstein, S. E. Segment structure and the syllable in aphasia. In A. Bell & J. B. Hooper (Eds.), *Syllables and segments.* Amsterdam: North-Holland, 1978.

Bodine, A. A. phonological analysis of the speech of two Mongoloid (Down's syndrome) boys. *Anthropological Linguistics,* 1974, *16,* (1), 1–24.

Braine, M. D. S. The acquisition of language in infant and child. In C. E. Reed (Ed.), *The learning of language.* New York: Appleton-Century-Crofts, 1971, 7–95.

Branigan, G. Syllabic structure and the acquisition of consonants: The great conspiracy in word formation. *Journal of Psycholinguistic Research,* 1976, *5,* 117–133.

Bricker, W. Errors in the echoic behavior of preschool children. *Journal of Speech and Hearing Research,* 1967, *10,* 67–76.

Broca, P. *Extraits des Bulletins de la Societé Anatomique,* 1863.

Bruner, J. S. The ontogenesis of speech acts. *Journal of Child Language,* 1975, *2,* 1–19.

Buckingham, H. W. On correlating aphasic errors with slips-of-the-tongue. *Applied Psycholinguistics,* 1980, *1,* 199–220.

Bush, M. A. Articulatory proficiency and Fϕ control by profoundly deaf speakers. Presented at the Annual Convention of the American Speech-Language-Hearing Association, Atlanta, GA, 1979.

Cairns, H. S., & Williams, F. An analysis of the substitution errors of a group of standard English-speaking children. *Journal of Speech and Hearing Research,* 1972, *15,* 811–820.

Calvert, D. R. Speech sound duration and the surd-sonant error. *Volta Review,* 1962, *64,* 401–402.

Cantor, G. N., & Girardeau, F. L. Rhythmic discrimination ability in Mongoloid and normal children. *American Journal of Mental Deficiency,* 1959, *63,* 621–625.

Carr, J. An investigation of the spontaneous speech sounds of five-year-old deaf-born children. *Journal of Speech and Hearing Disorders,* 1953, *18,* 22–29.

Castro, A. *Lengua, enseñanza y literatura,* Madrid: Victoriano Suárez, 1924.

Chafe, W. L. The ordering of phonological rules. *International Journal of American Linguistics,* 1968, *34,* 115–136.

Chao, Y. R. The non-uniqueness of phonemic solutions of phonetic systems. *Bulletin of the Institute of History and Philology. Ac. Sinica IV,* 1934, *4,* 363–397. (Also in *Readings in Linguistics,* 1958, *1,* 38–54.)

Chomsky, N. *Syntactic structures.* The Hague: Mouton, 1957.

Chomsky, N. A transformational approach to syntax. In A. A. Hill (Ed.), *Proceedings of the Third Texas Conference on Problems of Linguistic Analysis in English.* Austin: University Texas Press, 1958. Also in J. A. Fodor, & J. J. Katz (Eds.), *The structure of language: Readings in the philosophy of language.* Englewood Cliffs, NJ: Prentice-Hall, 1964, 211–245.

Chomsky, N. Current issues in linguistics. In J. A. Fodor & J. J. Katz (Eds.), *The structure of language: Readings in the philosophy of language.* Englewood Cliffs, New Jersey: Prentice-Hall, 1964.

Chomsky, N. *Aspects of the theory of syntax.* Cambridge: M.I.T. Press, 1965.

Chomsky, N., & Halle, M. *The sound pattern of English.* New York: Harper & Row, 1968.

Clumeck, H. V. The acquisition of tone. In G. Yeni-Komshian, J. Kavanagh, & C. A. Ferguson (Eds.), *Child phonology, Vol I: Production.* New York: Academic Press, 1980.

Compton, A. J. Generative studies of children's phonological disorders. *Journal of Speech and Hearing Disorders,* 1970, *35,* 315–339.

Compton, A. J. Generative studies of children's phonological disorders: A strategy of therapy. In S. Singh (Ed.), *Measurements in hearing, speech, and language.* Baltimore: University Park Press, 1975.

Compton, A. J. Generative studies of children's phonological disorders: Clinical ramifications. In D. M. Morehead & A. E. Morehead (Eds.), *Normal and deficient child language: Selected readings.* Baltimore: University Park Press, 1976.

Compton, A. J., & Hutton, J. S. *Compton-Hutton Phonological Assessment.* San Francisco: Carousel House, 1978.

Contreras, H. Simplicity, descriptive adequacy, and binary features. *Language,* 1969, *45,* 1–8.

Critchley, M. Articulatory defects in aphasia. *Journal of Laryngology and Otology,* 1952, *66,* 1–77.

Crocker, J. R. A phonological model of children's articulation competence. *Journal of Speech and Hearing Disorders,* 1969, *34,* 203–213.

Cross, E. Some features of the phonology of a four-year-old boy. *Word,* 1950, *6,* 137–140.

Crothers, J. On the abstractness controversy. *Project on linguistic analysis,* Second Series 12. CR1–CR29. Berkeley: Phonology Laboratory, Department of Linguistics, University of California, 1971.

Cruttenden, A. Phonological procedures for child language. *British Journal of Disorders of Communication,* 1972, *7,* 30–37.

Cruttenden, A. An experiment involving comprehension of intonation in children from 7 to 10. *Journal of Child Language,* 1974, *1,* 221–231.

Crystal, D. Non-segmental phonology in language acquisition: A review of the issues. *Lingua,* 1973, *32,* 1–45.

Crystal, D. Prosodic development. In P. Fletcher & M. Garman (Eds.), *Language acquisition: Studies in first language development.* Cambridge: Cambridge University Press, 1979, 33–48.

Dale, P.S. *Language development: Structure and function* (2nd ed.). New York: Holt, Rinehart & Winston, 1976.

de Saussure, F. *Cours de linguistique générale* (4th ed.). Paris: Payot, 1949. (Originally published by Charles Bally & Albert Sèchehaye, 1916.)

Dew, D., & Jensen, P. J. *Phonetic processing: The dynamics of speech.* Columbus, OH: Charles E. Merrill Publishing Co., 1977.

Dinnsen, D. A. *Current approaches to phonological theory.* Bloomington, IN: University Press, 1979.

Dinnsen, D. A., Elbert, M., & Weismer, G. On the characterization of functional misarticulations. Prepared for the annual convention of the American Speech-Language-Hearing Association, Atlanta, GA, November 1979.

Dinnsen, D. A., Elbert, M., & Weismer, G. Some typological properties of functional misarticulation systems. In W. O. Dressler (Ed.), *Phonologica,* 1980. Paper presented at the Fourth International Phonology Meeting, Vienna, Austria, June 29–July 2, 1980.

Dodd, B. Recognition and reproduction of words by Down's syndrome and non-Down's syndrome retarded children. *American Journal of Mental Deficiency,* 1975, *80,* 306–311.

Dodd, B. A comparison of the phonological systems of mental age matched normal, severely subnormal, and Down's syndrome children. *British Journal of Disorders of Communication,* 1976, *11,* 27–42. (a)

Dodd, B. The phonological systems of deaf children. *Journal of Speech and Hearing Disorders,* 1976, *41,* 185–198. (b)

Donegan, P.J., & Stampe, D. The study of natural phonology. In D. A. Dinnsen (Ed.), *Current approaches to phonological theory.* Bloomington: Indiana University Press, 1979, 126–173.

Dore, J. Holophrases, speech acts, and language universals. *Journal of Child Language,* 1975, *2,* 21–40.

Dore, J., Franklin, M. B., Miller, R. T., & Ramer, A. L. Transitional phenomenon in early language acquisition. *Journal of Child Language,* 1976, *3,* 13–28.

Downs, M. P. Identification and training of the deaf child—birth to one year. *Volta Review,* 1968, *70,* 154–158.

Drachman, G. Generative phonology and child language acquisition. *Working Papers in Linguistics.* Ohio State University, 1973, *15,* 146–159. (Also in W. O. Dressler (Ed.), *Phonologica,* Munich:Finck, 1975, 235–251.) (a)

Drachman, G. Some strategies in the acquisition of phonology. In M. J. Kenstowicz & C. W. Kisseberth (Eds.), *Issues in phonological theory.* The Hague: Mouton, 1973. (b)

Dunlop, J. M., & Marquardt, T. P. Linguistic and articulatory aspects of single word production in apraxia of speech. *Cortex,* 1977, *13,* 17–29.

Edwards, M. L. The acquisition of liquids. *Working Papers in Linguistics.* Ohio State University, 1973, *15,* 1–54.

Edwards, M. L. Generative phonology and adult aphasia. Unpublished paper, Stanford University, Stanford, CA, 1977.

Edwards, M. L. Phonological aspects of adult aphasia: Evidence from three aphasic patients. Unpublished paper, Stanford University, Stanford, CA, 1978.

Edwards, M. L. *Patterns and processes in fricative acquisition: Longitudinal evidence from six English-learning children.* Unpublished doctoral dissertation, Stanford University, 1979.

Edwards, M. L. Characterization of deviant phonological systems. Evidence from a case study. Paper presented at the Annual Convention of the American Speech-Language-Hearing Association, Detroit, Nov. 22, 1980. (a)

Edwards, M. L. The use of "favorite sounds" by children with phonological disorders. Paper presented at the Fifth Annual Boston University Conference on Language Development. Boston, 1980. (b)

Edwards, M. L., & Bernhardt, B. H. Phonological analyses of the speech of four children with language disorders. Unpublished paper, Stanford University, 1973. (a)

Edwards, M. L., & Bernhardt, B. H. Twin speech as the sharing of a phonological system. Unpublished paper, Stanford University, 1973. (b)

Eilers, R. E. Suprasegmentals and grammatical control over telegraphic speech in young children. *Journal of Psycholinguistic Research,* 1975, *4,* 227–239.

Eisenson, J., & Ogilvie, M. *Speech correction in the schools,* (3rd ed.). New York: Macmillan Co., 1971.

Elbert, M., Dinnsen, D. A., & Weismer, G. (Eds.). *Linguistic theory and the misarticulating child.* To appear.

Farwell, C. B. Some strategies in the early production of fricatives. *Papers and Reports on Child Language Development,* Stanford University, 1977, *12,* 97–104.

Fee, J., & Ingram, D. Reduplication as a strategy of phonological development. *Journal of Child Languages,* 1982, *9,* 41–54.

Ferguson, C. A. Baby talk in six languages. *American Anthropologist,* 1964, *66,* 103–114.

Ferguson, C. A. Contrastive analysis and language development. *Georgetown University Monograph Series on Language and Linguistics,* 1968, *21,* 101–112.

Ferguson, C. A. Baby talk as a simplified register. Prepared for the SSRC Conference on Language Input and Acquisition. Boston, Sept. 6-8, 1974.

Ferguson, C. A. Fricatives in child language acquisition. *Proceedings of the Eleventh International Congress of Linguists.* Bologna-Florence, 1975, 647-664. (Earlier version in *Papers and Reports on Child Language Development,* Stanford University, 1973, *6,* 1-60. Also in V. Honsa & M. J. Hardman-de-Bautista (Eds.), *Papers on linguistics and child language.* The Hague, Netherlands: Mouton, 1978, 93-115.) (a)

Ferguson, C. A. Sound patterns in language acquisition. In D. Dato (Ed.), 26th annual *Georgetown University Round Table.* March 13, 1975. 1-16. (b)

Ferguson, C. A. New directions in phonological theory: Language acquisition and universals research. In R. W. Cole (Ed.), *Current issues in linguistic theory.* Bloomington: Indiana University Press, 1977, 247-299.

Ferguson, C. A. Learning to pronounce: The earliest stages of phonological development in the child. In F. D. Minifie & L. L. Lloyd (Eds.), *Communicative competence and cognitive abilities.* Baltimore: University Park Press, 1978, 237-297. (Earlier version in *Papers and Reports on Child Language Development*, Stanford University, 1976, *11,* 1-27.) (a)

Ferguson, C. A. Phonological processes. In J. H. Greenberg, C. A. Ferguson, & E. A. Moravscik (Eds.), *Universals of human language,* (Vol. 2). Stanford, CA: Stanford University Press, 1978. 403-442. (b)

Ferguson, C. A. Phonological development: Some cognitive aspects. Lecture given in the series, "Current Issues in Cognitive Science." Brown University, Providence, RI, 1979. (a)

Ferguson, C. A. Phonology as an individual access system: Some data from language acquisition. In C. J. Fillmore, D. Kempler, & W. S.-Y. Wang (Eds.), *Individual differences in language ability and language behavior.* New York: Academic Press, 1979. (b)

Ferguson, C. A., & Farwell, C. B. Words and sounds in early language acquisition. *Language,* 1975, *51,* 419-439. (Earlier version in *PRCLD,* 1973, *6,* 1-60.)

Ferguson, C. A., & Garnica, O. K. Theories of phonological development. In E. Lenneberg & E. Lenneberg (Eds.), *Foundations of language development.* New York: Academic Press, 1975, 153-180.

Ferguson, C. A., & Macken, M. A. Phonological development in children: Play and cognition. *Papers and Reports on Child Language Development,* Stanford University, 1980, *18,* 133-177.

Ferguson, C. A., Peizer, D. B., & Weeks, T. E. Model-and-replica phonological grammar of a child's first words. *Lingua*, 1973, *31*, 35-65.

Ferguson, C., & Slobin, D. (Eds.), *Studies of child language development*. New York: Holt, Rinehart & Winston, 1973.

Ferrier, E., & Davis, M. A lexical approach to the remediation of sound omissions. *Journal of Speech and Hearing Disorders*, 1973, *38*, 126-130.

Fey, M. E., & Gandour, J. Problem-solving in phonology acquisition. Presented at the 54th Annual Meeting of the Linguistic Society of America, Dec. 27-29, 1979, Los Angeles.

Fey, M. E., & Gandour, J. Rule discovery in phonological acquisition. *Journal of Child Language*, 1982, *9*, 71-81.

Firth, J. R. Phonological features of some Indian languages. In Firth, *Collected papers 1934-1951*, London: Oxford University Press, 1957. (Also in *Proceedings of the 2nd International Congress of Phonetic Sciences*, 1935.)

Firth, J. R. Sounds and prosodies. In V. B. Makkai (Ed.), *Phonological theory, evolution and current practice*. New York: Holt, Rinehart & Winston, 1972, 252-263. (Reprinted from *Transactions of the Philological Society*, 1948, 127-152.)

Firth, U., & Firth, C. D. Specific motor disabilities in Down's syndrome. *Journal of Child Psychology and Psychiatry*, 1974, *15*, 293-301.

Fischer-Jørgensen, E. *Trends in phonological theory: A historical introduction* (N. Davidsen-Nielsen, trans.). Copenhagen: Akademisk Forlag, 1975.

Fisher, H. B., & Logemann, J. A. *Therapists manual for the Fisher-Logemann Test of Articulation Competence*. Boston: Houghton Mifflin Co., 1971.

Fitzgerald, H. E., Brajović, C., Djurdjić, S., & Djurdjević, M. Development of articulatory competence in mentally retarded children. *Perceptual motor skills*, 1979, *48*, 1175-1182.

Foley, J. Phonological distinctive features. *Folia Linguistica*, 1970,2, *4*, 87-92.

Fromkin, V. A. The nonanomalous nature of anomalous utterances. *Language*, 1971, *47*, 27-52.

Fromkin, V. A., (Ed.). *Speech errors as linguistic evidence*. The Hague: Mouton, 1973. (a)

Fromkin, V. A. Slips of the tongue. *Scientific American*, 1973, *229* (6), 110-116. (b)

Fry, D. B. Phonemic substitution patterns in an aphasic patient. *Language and Speech*, 1959, *2*, 52–61.

Fry, D. B. The development of the phonological system in the normal and deaf child. In F. Smith & G. Miller (Eds.), *The genesis of language: A psycholinguistic approach*. Cambridge, Massachusetts: M.I.T. Press, 1966.

Fudala, J. B. *Arizona Articulation Proficiency Scale*. Los Angeles: Western Psychological Service, 1970.

Gamkrelidze, T. V. Sootnošenie smyčnyxi frikativnyx v fonologičeskoj sisteme (k probleme markirovannosti v fonologii). [Relation of stops and fricatives in the phonological system (on the problem of markedness in phonology)], 1974, Moskow: Institut Russkogo Jazyka AN SSSR.

Gandour, J. The nondeviant nature of deviant phonological systems. *Journal of Communication Disorders*, 1981, *14*, 11–29.

Garnica, O. K. The development of phonemic speech perception. In T. E. Moore (Ed.), *Cognitive development and the acquisition of language*. New York: Academic Press, 1973.

Goldman, R., & Fristoe, M. *Goldman-Fristoe Test of Articulation (GFTA)*. Circle Pines, MI: American Guidance Service Inc., 1972.

Goldstein, K. *Language and language disturbances*. New York: Grune & Stratton, 1948.

Greenberg, J. H. Synchronic and diachronic universals in phonology. *Language*, 1966, *42*, 508–518. (a)

Greenberg, J. H. *Language universals*. The Hague: Mouton, 1966. (Also in T. Sebeok (Ed.), *Current trends in linguistics*. The Hague: Mouton, 1966, *3*, 61–112.) (b)

Greenberg, J. H., Ferguson, C. A., & Moravscik, E. A. (Eds.), *Universals of human language*. Stanford, CA: Stanford University Press, 1978.

Greenberg, J. H., & Jenkins, J. J. Studies in the psychological correlates of the sound system of American English. *Word*, 1964, *20*, 157–177.

Greenlee, M. Some observations on initial English consonant clusters in a child two to three years old. *Papers and Reports on Child Language Development*, Stanford University, 1973, *6*, 97–106.

Greenlee, M. Interacting processes in the child's acquisition of stop-liquid clusters. *Papers and Reports on Child Language Development*, Stanford University, 1974, *7*, 85–100.

Grégoire, A. L'Apprentissage du language. II. La troisième anée et les années suivantes. Paris: Droz, Liege, 1947.

Grunwell, P. The phonological analysis of articulation disorders. *British Journal of Disorders of Communication,* 1975, *10,* 31-42.

Grunwell, P. *Clinical phonology.* Rockville, MD: Aspen Systems Corp., 1982.

Haas, W. Phonological analysis of a case of dyslalia. *Journal of Speech and Hearing Disorders,* 1963, *28,* 239-246.

Halle, M. *The sound pattern of Russian.* The Hague: Mouton, 1959.

Halle, M. Phonology in generative grammar. *Word,* 1962, *18,* 54-72.

Halle, M. On the bases of phonology. In J. A. Fodor & J. J. Katz (Eds.), *The structure of language: Readings in the philosophy of language.* Englewood Cliffs, NJ: Prentice-Hall, 1964, 324-333.

Halpern, H., Keith, R. L., & Darley, F. L. Phonemic behavior of aphasic patients without dysarthria or apraxia of speech. *Cortex,* 1976, *4,* 365-372.

Harris, J. *Spanish phonology.* Cambridge: M.I.T. Press, 1969.

Harris, Z. S. *Structural Linguistics.* Chicago: University of Chicago Press, 1963. (Reprint of *Methods in structural linguistics.* Chicago, 1951.)

Haynes, W. O., Haynes, M., & Jackson, J. The effects of phonetic context and linguistic complexity on /s/ misarticulation in children. *Journal of Communication Disorders,* 1982, *47,* 287-298.

Head, H. *Aphasia and kindred disorders of speech* (Vol. I). New York: Hafner. 1926.

Hinckley, A. A case of retarded speech development. *Ped. Sem.,* 1915, *22,* 121-146.

Hockett, C. *A manual of phonology.* Baltimore: Waverly Press, 1955.

Hodson, B. W. *The Assessment of Phonological Processes.* Danville, IL: The Interstate Printers & Publishers, 1980.

Hodson, B. W., & Paden, E. P. Phonological processes which characterize unintelligible and intelligible speech in early childhood. *Journal of Speech and Hearing Disorders,* 1981, *46,* 369-373.

Holmes, U. T. The phonology of an English-speaking child. *American Speech,* 1927, *5,* 219-225.

Honikman, B. Articulatory settings. *In honour of Daniel Jones.* Abercrombie et al. (Eds.), 1964.

Hooper, J. B. *Aspects of natural generative phonology.* Doctoral dissertation. University of California, Los Angeles, 1973. (Also distributed by the Indiana University Linguistics Club, Bloomington, IN, 1974.)

Hooper, J. B. *An introduction to natural generative phonology.* New York: Academic Press, 1976.

Hudgins, C. V. A comparative study of the speech coordination of deaf and normal subjects. *Ped. Sem.,* 1934, *44,* 3-48.

Hudgins, C., & Numbers, F. An investigation of the intelligibility of the speech of the deaf. *Genetic Psychology Monographs,* 1942, *25.*

Hughes, J. P. *The science of language: An introduction to linguistics.* New York: Random House, 1966.

Hyman, L. M. How concrete is phonology? *Language*, 1970, *46*, 58–76.

Hyman, L. M. *Phonology: Theory and analysis.* NY: Holt, Rinehart & Winston, 1975.

Ingram, D. Phonological analysis of a child. Unpublished paper, 1973. Also in *Glossa*, 1976, *10*, 1–27.

Ingram, D. Fronting in child phonology. *Journal of Child Language*, 1974, *1*, 233–241. (a)

Ingram, D. Phonological rules in young children. *Journal of Child Language*, 1974, *1*, 49–64. (b)

Ingram, D. Surface contrast in children's speech. *Journal of Child Language*, 1975, *2*, 287–292.

Ingram, D. *Phonological disability in children.* NY: American Elsevier Publishing Co., Inc., 1976.

Ingram, D. The production of word-initial fricatives and affricates in normal and linguistically deviant children. In. A. Caramazza & E. Zuriff (Eds.), *The acquisition and breakdown of language.* Baltimore: Johns Hopkins University Press, 1978.

Ingram, D. Phonological patterns in the speech of young children. In P. Fletcher & M. Garman (Eds.), *Language acquisition: Studies in first language development.* Cambridge: Cambridge University Press, 1979.

Ingram, D. *Procedures for the phonological analysis of children's language.* Baltimore: University Park Press, 1981.

Ingram, D. The assessment of phonological disorders in children: The state of the art. In M. Crary (Ed.), *Phonological intervention: Concepts and procedures.* San Diego, CA: College-Hill Press, Inc., 1982.

Ingram, D., Christensen, L., Veach, S., & Webster, B. The acquisition of word-initial fricatives and affricates in English by children between 2 and 6 years. In G. Yeni-Komshian, J. F. Kavanagh, & C. A. Ferguson (Eds.), *Child phonology, Vol 1: Production.* New York: Academic Press, 1980.

Ireland, J. V., Klich, R. J., & Panagos, J. M. Is there phonemic regression in aphasic speech? *Perceptual and Motor Skills*, 1977, *44*, 1042.

Irwin, O. C. The developmental status of speech sounds of ten feeble-minded children. *Child Development*, 1942, *13*, 29–39.

Jackson, J. H. *Selected Writings, II.* J. Taylor (Ed.), New York: Basic Books, 1958.

Jakobson, R. *Child language, aphasia and phonological universals.* (A. R. Keiler, trans.) The Hague: Mouton, 1968. (From *Kindersprache, Aphasie und allgemeine Lautgesetze.* Uppsala: 1941.)

Jakobson, R. Kindersprache, Aphasie und allgemeine Lautgesetze. In R. Jakobson (Ed.), *Selected writings* (Vol. 1). The Hague: Mouton, 1962.

Jakobson, R. The sound laws of child language and their place in general phonology. In A. Bar-Adon & W. F. Leopold (Eds.), *Child language: A book of readings.* Englewood Cliffs, NJ: Prentice-Hall, 1971, 75-82.

Jakobson, R. On the identification of phonemic entities. *Recherches Structurales, Travaux du Cercle Linguistique de Prague V,* 1949, 205-213. (Also in *Selected Writings I,* 1962.)

Jakobson, R., Fant, G., & Halle, M. *Preliminaries to speech analysis: The distinctive features and their correlates.* (Tech. Rep. 13, M.I.T. Acoustics Laboratory, 1952.) Cambridge: M.I.T. Press, 1963.

Jakobson, R., & Halle, M. *Fundamentals of language.* The Hague: Mouton, 1956.

Jespersen, O. *Language: Its nature, development and origin.* London: Macmillan, 1922.

John, J. E., & Howarth, J. W. The effect of time distortions on the intelligibility of deaf children's speech. *Language and Speech,* 1965, *8,* 127-134.

Johns, D. F., & Darley, F. D. Phonemic variability in apraxia of speech. *Journal of Speech and Hearing Research,* 1970, *14,* 131-143.

Johnson, C. E., & Bush, C. N. A note on transcribing the speech of young children. *Papers and Reports on Child Language Development,* Stanford University, 1972, *3,* 95-100.

Joos, M. Description of language design. *Journal of the Acoustical Society of America,* 1950, *22,* 701-708. (Also in M. Joos (Ed.), *Readings in linguistics I,* 1957.)

Kaplan, E., & Kaplan, G. The prelinguistic child. In J. Elliott (Ed.), *Human development and cognitive processes.* New York: Holt, Rinehart & Winston, 1971, 359-381.

Karlin, I. W., & Strazzula, M. Speech and language problems of mentally deficient children. *Journal of Speech and Hearing Disorders,* 1952, *17,* 286-294.

Khan, L. M. L. A review of 16 major phonological processes. *Language, Speech, and Hearing Services in the Schools,* 1982, *13,* 66-76.

Kiparsky, P. How abstract is phonology? Unpublished paper, 1968. Also in O. Fujimura (Ed.), *Three dimensions of linguistic theory.* Tokyo: TEC Co., Ltd., 1974. (a)

Kiparsky, P. Linguistic universals and linguistic change. In E. Bach & R. T. Harms (Eds.), *Universals in linguistic theory.* New York: Holt, Rinehart & Winston, 1968, 171-202. (b)

Kiparsky, P. Historical linguistics. In W. O. Dingwall (Ed.), *A survey of linguistic science,* Linguistics Program, University of Maryland, 1971, 576–649.

Kiparsky, P. Explanation in phonology. In S. Peters (Ed.), *Goals of linguistic theory.* Englewood Cliffs, NJ: Prentice-Hall, 1972, 189–227.

Kiparsky, P. "Elsewhere" in phonology. In S. R. Anderson & P. Kiparsky (Eds.), *Festschrift for Morris Halle.* New York: Rinehart & Winston, 1973.

Kiparsky, P., & Menn, L. On the acquisition of phonology. In J. Macnamara (Ed.), *Language learning and thought.* New York: Holt, Rinehart & Winston, 1973.

Kisseberth, C. W. On the abstractness of phonology: The evidence from Yawelmani. *Papers in Linguistics,* 1969, *1,* 248–282. 1974, *39,* 23–31.

Kisseberth, C. W. On the functional unity of phonological rules. *Linguistic Inquiry,* 1970, *1,* 291–306.

Kisseberth, C. W. Is rule ordering necessary? In B. B. Kachru et al. (Eds.), *Issues in Linguistics,* Papers in honor of Henry and Renee Kahane. Urbana: University of Illinois Press, 1973. (a)

Kisseberth, C. W. On the alternation of vowel length in Klamath: A global rule. In M. J. Kenstowicz & C. W. Kisseberth (Eds.), *Issues in phonological theory.* The Hague: Mouton, 1973, 9–26. (b)

Klich, R. J., Ireland, J. V., & Weidner, W. E. Articulatory and phonological aspects of consonant substitutions in apraxia of speech. *Cortex,* 1979, *15,* 451–470.

Klein, H. B. *The relationship between perceptual strategies and productive strategies in learning the phonology of early lexical items.* Doctoral dissertation, Brooklyn College of CUNY, 1977. (Also distributed by the Indiana University Linguistic Club, Bloomington, IN, 1978.)

Klein, H. B. Productive strategies for the pronunciation of early polysyllabic lexical items. *Journal of Speech and Hearing Research,* 1981, *24,* 389–405.

Koike, K. *A test of rhythm and intonation patterns for young, normal hearing children.* Unpublished master's thesis, University of Tennessee, Knoxville, 1977.

Koike, K. J., & Asp, C. W. *Test of Rhythm and Intonation Patterns*: A pilot study. Paper presented at the meeting of the Acoustical Society of America, Miami, 1977.

Kornfeld, J. R. Theoretical issues in child phonology. *Papers from the Seventh Regional Meeting of the Chicago Linguistics Society,* 1971, *454,* 468. (a)

Kornfeld, J. R. What initial clusters tell us about a child's speech code. *QPR, Research Laboratory of Electronics, M.I.T.,* 1971, *101,* 218-221. (b)

Kornfeld, J. R., & Goehl, H. A new twist to an old observation: Kids know more than they say. *Papers from the Parasession on Natural Phonology.* Chicago Linguistic Society, April 1974, 210-219.

Koutsoudas, A., Sanders, G., & Noll, C. The application of phonological rules. *Language,* 1974, *50,* 1-28.

Labov, W. The social motivation of a sound change. *Word,* 1963, *19,* 273-309.

Ladefoged, P. *Preliminaries to linguistic phonetics.* Chicago: University of Chicago Press, 1971.

Ladefoged, P. *A course in phonetics.* New York: Harcourt Brace Jovanovich, Inc., 1975.

LaRiviere, C., Winitz, H., Reeds, J., & Herriman, E. The conceptual reality of selected distinctive features. *Journal of Speech and Hearing Research,* 1974, *17,* 122-133.

Lecours, A. R., & Caplan, D. Review of S. Blumstein, *A phonological investigation of aphasic speech,* 1973. *Brain and Language,* 1975, *2,* 237-254.

Lecours, A. R., & Lhermitte, F. Phonemic paraphasias: Linguistic structures and tentative hypotheses. In. H. Goodglass & S. Blumstein (Eds.), *Psycholinguistics and aphasia.* Baltimore: Johns Hopkins, 1973, 69-105.

Lee, L. L. *Northwestern Syntax Screening Test.* Chicago: Northwestern University Press, 1971.

Lehiste, I. *Suprasegmentals.* Cambridge, MA: The M.I.T. Press, 1970.

Lenneberg, E. H. *Biological foundations of language.* New York: Wiley & Sons, 1967.

Lenneberg, E. H., Nichols, I. A., & Rosenberger, E. F. Primitive stages of language development in Mongolism. In D. McK.Rioch & E. A. Weinstein (Eds.), *Disorders of communication.* Research publications of the Association for Research in Nervous and Mental Disease, Vol. 62. Baltimore: Williams & Wilkins, 1964.

Leonard, L. B. The nature of deviant articulation. *Journal of Speech and Hearing Disorders,* 1973, *38,* 156-161.

Leonard, L. B., Miller, J. A., & Brown, H. Consonant and syllable harmony in the speech of language-disordered children. *Journal of Speech and Hearing Disorders,* 1980, *45,* 336-345.

Leonard, L. B., Newhoff, M., & Mesalam, L. Individual differences in early child phonology. *Applied Psycholinguistics,* 1980, *1,* 7-30.

Leonard, L. B., Schwartz, R. G., Morris, B., & Chapman, K. Factors influencing early lexical acquisition: Lexical orientation and phonological composition. *Child Development,* 1981, *52,* 882–887.

Leopold, W. F. *Speech development of a bilingual child: A linguist's record. Vol. II. sound-learning in the first two years.* Evanston: Northwestern University, 1947. *Vol. I. vocabulary growth in the first two years,* 1939.

Leopold, W. F. Pattering in children's language learning. In S. Saporta (Ed.), *Psycholinguistics: A book of readings.* New York: Rinehart & Winston, 1966.

Levitt, H., & Smith, R. Errors of articulation in the speech of profoundly hearing-impaired children. *Journal of the Acoustical Society of America,* 1972, *51,* 102–103.

Lieberman, P. On the development of vowel production in young children. In G. H. Yeni-Komshian, J. F. Kavanagh, & C. A. Ferguson (Eds.), *Child phonology, Vol 1: Production.* New York: Academic Press, 1980, 113–142.

Locke, J. L. Experimentally-elicited articulatory behavior. *Language and Speech,* 1969, *12,* 187–191.

Locke, J. L. The child's processing of phonology. In W. A. Collins (Ed.), *The Minnesota symposium on child psychology* (Vol. 12). Hinsdale, NJ: Erlbaum, 1979. (a)

Locke, J. L. Homonymy and sound change in the child's acquisition of phonology. In N. J. Lass (Ed.), *Speech and language: Advances in basic research and practice,* (Vol 2). New York: Academic Press, 1979. (b)

Lorentz, J. P. A deviant phonological system of English. *Papers and Reports on Child Language Development,* Stanford University, 1974, *8,* 55–64.

Lorentz, J. P. An analysis of some deviant phonological rules of English. In D. M. Morehead & A. E. Morehead (Eds.), *Normal and deficient child language: Selected readings.* Baltimore: University Park Press, 1976.

Lund, N. L., & Duchan, J. F. Phonological analysis: A multifaceted approach. *British Journal of Disorders of Communication,* 1978, *13,* 119–125.

Lund, N. J., & Duchan, J. F. *Assessing children's language in naturalistic contexts.* Englewood Cliffs, NJ: Prentice-Hall, 1983.

MacKay, I. R. A. Tenseness in vowels: An ultrasonic study. *Phonetica,* 1977, *34,* 325–351.

MacKay, I. R. A. *Introducing practical phonetics.* Boston: Little, Brown & Co., 1978.

Macken, M. A. Developmental reorganization of phonology: A hierarchy of basic units of acquisition. *Papers and Reports on Child Language Development,* Stanford University, 1977, *14,* 1–36. (Also in *Lingua,* 1979, *49,* 11–49.)

Macken, M.A. The child's lexical representation: The 'puzzle-puddle-pickle' evidence. *Papers and Reports on Child Language Development,* Stanford University, 1979, *16,* 26–41. Also in *Journal of Linguistics,* 1980, *16,* 1–17.

Macken, M. A. Aspects of the acquisition of stop systems: A cross-linguistic perspective. G. Yeni-Komshian, J. F. Kavanagh, & C. A. Ferguson (Eds.), *Child phonology, Vol. I: Production.* New York: Academic Press, 1980, 143–168.

Macken, M. A., & Barton, D. The acquisition of the voicing contrast in English: A study of voice onset time in word-initial stop consonants. *Journal of Child Language,* 1980, *7,* 41–74.

Macken, M. A., & Ferguson, C. A. Cognitive aspects of phonological development: Model, evidence and issues. In K. E. Nelson (Ed.), *Children's language* (Vol. 4). Gardner Press, 1982.

MacMahon, M. K. C. Modern linguistics and aphasia. *British Journal of Disorders of Communication,* 1972, *7,* 54–63.

Markides, A. The speech of deaf and partially-hearing children with special reference to factors affecting intelligibility. *British Journal of Disorders of Communication,* 1970, *5,* 126–139.

Martin, A. D., & Rigrodsky, S. An investigation of phonological impairment in aphasia, Part 1. *Cortex,* 1974, *10,* 317–328.

Maxwell, E. M. Competing analyses of a deviant phonogy. *Glossa,* 1979, *13,* 181–214.

McCarthy, D. Language development in children. In L. Carmichael (Ed.), *Manual of child psychology.* New York: Wiley, 1954, 452–630.

McDonald, E. T. *A Deep Test of Articulation: Picture Form, Sentence Form, and Screening Deep Test of Articulation.* Pittsburgh: Stanwix House, Inc., 1964, 1968.

McReynolds, L. V., & Bennett, S. Distinctive feature generalization in articulation training. *Journal of Speech and Hearing Disorders,* 1972, *37,* 462–470.

McReynolds, L. V., & Engmann, D. L. *Distinctive feature analysis of misarticulations.* Baltimore: University Park Press, 1975.

McReynolds, L. V., & Huston, K. A distinctive feature analysis of children's misarticulations. *Journal of Speech and Hearing Disorders,* 1971, *36,* 156–166.

Menn, L. Phonotactic rules in beginning speech. *Lingua,* 1971, *26,* 225-251.

Menn, L. Guck and beisuboru. Unpublished manuscript, 1972.

Menn, L. Note on the acquisition of fricatives and affricates. *Papers and Reports on Child Language Development,* Stanford University, 1973, *6,* 87-96.

Menn, L. Counter-example to 'fronting' as a universal of child phonology. *Journal of Child Language,* 1975, *2,* 293-296.

Menn, L. Evidence for an interactionist-discovery theory of child phonology. *Papers and Reports on Child Language Development,* Stanford University, 1976, *12,* 169-177. (a)

Menn, L. *Pattern, control and contrast in beginning speech: A case study in the development of word form and word function.* Doctoral dissertation, University of Illinois at Urbana-Champaign, 1976. (Also distributed by the Indiana University Linguistics Club, Bloomington, 1978.) (b)

Menn, L. An autosegmental approach to child phonology—First explorations. In G. N. Clements (Ed.), *Harvard studies in phonology I.* Linguistics Dept., Harvard University, 1977, 315-334.

Menn, L. Phonological units in beginning speech. In A. Bell & J. B. Hooper (Eds.), *Syllables and segments.* North-Holland Publishing Co., 1978, 157-171.

Menn, L. Phonological theory and child phonology. In G. Yeni-Komshian, J. F. Kavanagh, & C. A. Ferguson (Eds.), *Child phonology, Vol I: Production.* New York: Academic Press, 1980.

Menyuk, P. The role of distinctive features in children's acquisition of phonology. *Journal of Speech and Hearing Research,* 1968, *11,* 138-146. (Also in C. A. Ferguson & D. I. Slobin (Eds.), *Studies of child language development.* New York: Rinehart & Winston, Inc., 1973, 44-52.)

Menyuk, P. Clusters as underlying single segments: Evidence from children's production. Presented at the Seventh International Congress of Phonetic Sciences, Montreal, August 1971. *Proceedings,* 22-28.

Menyuk, P. *The development of speech.* New York: Bobbs-Merrill Studies in Communicative Disorders, 1972.

Menyuk, P., & Menn, L. Early strategies for the perception and production of words and sounds. In P. Fletcher & M. Garman (Eds.), *Language acquisition.* Cambridge: Cambridge University Press, 1979.

Miller, G. A., & Nicely, P. E. An analysis of perceptual confusions among some English consonants. *Journal of the Acoustical Society of America,* 1955, *27,* 338-352.

Miller, P. Some context-free processes affecting vowels. *Working Papers in Linguistics,* Ohio State University, 1972, *11,* 136–167.

Miller, P. Bleaching and coloring. In C. Corum et al. (Eds.), *Papers from the Ninth Regional Meeting of the Chicago Linguistic Society,* 1973, 386–397.

Moskowitz, A. I. The two-year-old stage in the acquisition of English phonology. *Language,* 1970, *46,* 426–441. (Reprinted in C. A. Ferguson & D. I. Slobin (Eds.), *Studies of child language development,* New York: Rinehart & Winston, 1973, 52–69.)

Moskowitz, A. I. Acquisition of phonology and syntax: A preliminary study. In I. Hintikka et al. (Eds.), *Approaches to natural language.* Dordrecht, Netherlands: Reidel, 1973.

Moskowitz, B. A. The acquisition of fricatives: A study in phonetics and phonology. *Journal of Phonetics,* 1975, *3,* 141–150.

Moskowitz, B. A. Idioms in phonology acquisition and phonological change. *Journal of Phonetics,* 1980, *8,* 69–83.

Mowrer, O. H. Speech development in the young child: The autism theory of speech development and some clinical applications. *Journal of Speech and Hearing Disorders,* 1952, *17,* 263–268.

Mowrer, O. H. *Learning theory and symbolic processes.* New York: Wiley & Sons, 1960.

Myers, L. M. *The roots of modern English.* Boston: Little, Brown & Co., 1966.

Naeser, M. A. The American child's acquisition of differential vowel duration *(Technical report No. 144* [2 parts]), Madison: Wisconsin Research and Development Center for Cognitive Learning, University of Wisconsin-Madison, 1970.

Newton, B. E. Ordering paradoxes in phonology. *Journal of Linguistics,* 1971, *7,* 31–53.

Oller, D. K. Regularities in abnormal child phonology. *Journal of Speech and Hearing Disorders,* 1973, *38,* 36–47.

Oller, D. K., & Kelly, C. A. Phonological substitution processes of a hard-of-hearing child. *Journal of Speech and Hearing Disorders,* 1974, *39,* 65–74.

Oller, D. K., Jensen, H. T., & Lafayette, R. H. The relatedness of phonological processes of a hearing-impaired child. *Journal of Communication Disorders,* 1978, *11,* 97–105.

Oller, D. K., Wieman, L. A., Doyle, W. J., & Ross, C. Infant babbling and speech. *Journal of Child Language,* 1976, *3,* 1–11.

Olmsted, D. A theory of the child's learning of phonology. *Language,* 1966, *42,* 531–535. (Also in A. Bar-Adon & W. F. Leopold (Eds.), *Child language: A book of readings.* Englewood Cliffs, NJ: Prentice-Hall, 1971, 360–364.)

Olmsted, D. *Out of the mouth of babes.* The Hague: Mouton, 1971.

Osthoff, H., & Brugmann, K. *Morphologische Untersuchungen* I, 1878.

Oyer, H. J. *Auditory communication for the hard of hearing.* Englewood Cliffs, NJ: Prentice-Hall, 1966.

Panagos, J. Persistence of the open syllable reinterpreted as a symptom of language disorder. *Journal of Speech and Hearing Disorders,* 1974, *39,* 23–31.

Panagos, J., & Prelock, P. Phonological constraints on the sentence productions of language-disordered children. *Journal of Speech and Hearing Research,* 1982, *25,* 171–177.

Passy, P. E. *Ètude sur les changements phonétiques.* Paris: Librairie Firmin-Didot, 1890.

Paul, H. *Principles of the history of language.* (H. A. Strong, trans, 1891). London: Swan Sonnenschein, Lowrey, & Co., 1888. (First ed., 1886.)

Paul, R., & Shriberg, L. Associations between phonology and syntax in speech-delayed children. *Journal of Speech and Hearing Research,* 1982, *25,* 536–547.

Pendergast, K., Dickey, S., Selmar, J., & Soder, A. L. *Photo Articulation Test.* Chicago: King, 1965.

Pike, E. G. Controlled infant intonation. *Language Learning,* 1949, *2,* 21–24. (Also in A. Bar-Adon & W. F. Leopold (Eds.), *Child language: A book of readings.* Englewood Cliffs, NJ: Prentice-Hall, Inc., 1971.)

Pike, K. L., & Pike, E. Immediate constituents of Mazateco syllables. *International Journal of American Linguistics,* 1947, *13,* 78–91.

Pollack, E., & Rees, N. S. Disorders of articulation: Some clinical applications of distinctive feature theory. *Journal of Speech and Hearing Disorders,* 1972, *37,* 451–461.

Poncet, M., Degos, C., Deloche, G., & Lecours, A. R. Phonetic and phonemic transformations in aphasia. *International Journal of Mental Health,* 1972, *1,* 46–54.

Poole, I. Genetic development of articulation of consonant sounds in speech. *Elementary English Review,* 1934, *11,* 159–161.

Prater, R. J. Functions of consonant assimilation and reduplication in early word productions of mentally retarded children. *American Journal of Mental Deficiency,* 1982, *86,* 399–404.

Prather, E. M., Hedrick, D. L., & Kern, C. A. Articulation development in children aged two to four years. *Journal of Speech and Hearing Disorders,* 1975, *40,* 179–191.

Priestly, T. M. S. One idiosyncratic strategy in the acquisition of phonology. *Journal of Child Language,* 1977, *4,* 45–66.

The principles of the International Phonetic Association. London: University College Department of Phonetics, 1949; revised, 1978. Revised chart in *Journal of the International Phonetic Association, 8,* 1978.

Pulgram, E. *Syllable, word, nexus, cursus.* The Hague: Mouton, 1970.

Pullum, G. K. On a nonargument for the cycle in Turkish. *Linguistic Inquiry,* 1975, *6,* 494–501.

Quigley, S. P. Language research in countries other than the United States. *Volta Review,* 1966, *68,* 68–83.

Rees, N. S. The role of babbling in the child's acquisition of language. *British Journal of Disorders of Communication,* 1972, *7,* 17–23.

Robins, R. H. *A short history of linguistics.* Bloomington: Indiana University Press, 1967.

Ross, A. S. C. An example of vowel-harmony in a young child. *Modern Language Notes,* 1937, *52,* 508–509.

Roussey, C. Notes sur l'apprentissage de la parole chez un enfant. *La Parole,* 1899–1900, *1,* 870–880, *2,* 23–40.

Sander, E. When are speech sounds learned? *Journal of Speech and Hearing Disorders,* 1972, *37,* 55–63.

Sapir, E. *Language.* New York: Harcourt Brace, 1921.

Sapir, E. The psychological reality of phonemes. In D. G. Mandlebaum (Ed.), *Selected writings of Edward Sapir.* Berkeley, CA 1951.

Schane, S. A. *Generative phonology.* Englewood Cliffs, NJ: Prentice-Hall, 1973.

Schlanger, B. Speech measurements of institutionalized mentally handicapped children. *American Journal of Mental Deficiency,* 1953, *58,* 114–122. (a)

Schlanger, B. Speech examination of a group of institutionalized mentally retarded handicapped children. *Journal of Speech and Hearing Disorders,* 1953, *18,* 339–349. (b)

Schlanger, B. & Gottsleben, R. H. Analysis of speech defects among the institutionalized mentally retarded. *Journal of Speech and Hearing Disorders,* 1957, *22,* 98–103.

Schmauch, V., Panagos, J., & Klich, R. Syntax influences the articulation performance of language-disordered children. *Journal of Communication Disorders,* 1978, *11,* 315–323.

Schnitzer, M. L. Generative phonology—evidence from aphasia. *The Pennsylvania State University Studies No. 34,* University Park, PA: Pennsylvania State University, 1972.

Schwartz, R. G., & Folger, M. K. Sensorimotor development and descriptions of child phonology: A preliminary view of phonological analysis for Stage I speech. Paper presented at the Stanford Child Language Research Forum, Stanford, CA, 1977.

Schwartz, R. G., & Leonard, L. B. Do children pick and choose? An examination of phonological selection and avoidance in early lexical acquisition. *Journal of Child Language,* 1982, *9,* 319–336.

Schwartz, R. G., Leonard, L. B., Folger, M. K., & Wilcox, M. J. Early phonological behavior in normal-speaking and language disordered children: Evidence for a synergistic view of linguistic disorders. *Journal of Speech and Hearing Disorders,* 1980, *45,* 357–377.

Schwartz, R. G., Leonard, L. B., Wilcox, M. J., & Folger, M. K. Again and again: Reduplication in child phonology. *Journal of Child Language,* 1980, *7,* 75–87.

Shadden, B. B., Asp, C. W., Tonkovich, J. D., & Mason, D. Imitation of suprasegmental patterns by five-year-old children with adequate and inadequate articulation. *Journal of Speech and Hearing Disorders,* 1980, *45,* 390–400.

Shankweiler, D., & Harris, K. An experimental approach to the problem of articulation in aphasia. *Cortex,* 1966, *2,* 277–292.

Sheehan, J., Martyn, M. M., & Kilburn, K. L. Speech disorders in retardation. *American Journal of Mental Deficiency,* 1968, *73,* 251–256.

Shelton, D. *Acoustic and perceptual analyses of segmental and suprasegmental features in verbal responses of four-year-old children with adequate or inadequate articulatory development.* Unpublished doctoral dissertation, University of Tennessee-Knoxville, 1976.

Shibatani, M. The role of surface phonetic constraints in generative phonology. *Language,* 1973, *49,* 87–106.

Shriberg, L. D. Programming for the language component in developmental phonological disorders. In J. Panagos (Ed.), Children's phonological disorders in language contexts. *Seminars: Speech Language Hearing,* (Vol. 3), May 1982, *2,* 115–137. (a)

Shriberg, L. *PEPPER (Programs to Examine Phonetic and Phonologic Evaluation Records),* 1982, Waisman Center Computing Facility, Madison, WI. (b)

Shriberg, L. D., & Kent, R. D. *Clinical phonetics.* New York: John Wiley & Sons, Inc., 1982.

Shriberg, L. D., & Kwiatkowski, J. *Natural Process Analysis (NPA): A procedure for phonological analysis of continuous speech samples.* New York: John Wiley & Sons, Inc., 1980.

Silverman, S. R. Clinical and educational procedures for the deaf. In L. E. Travis (Ed.), *Handbook of speech pathology.* London: Peter Owen, 1963.

Singh, S., & Frank, D. C. A distinctive feature analysis of the consonantal substitution pattern. *Language and Speech,* 1972, *15,* 209–218.

Singh, S., Hayden, M. E., & Toombs, M. S. The role of distinctive features in articulation errors. *Journal of Speech and Hearing Disorders,* 1981, *46,* 174–183.

Sirkin, J., & Lyons, W. F. A study of speech defects in mental deficiency. *American Journal of Mental Deficiency,* 1974, *46,* 74–80.

Skousen, R. On capturing regularities. In P. M. Peranteau et al. (Eds.), *Papers from the Eighth Regional Meeting of the Chicago Linguistic Society,* 1972.

Sloat, C., Taylor, S. H., & Hoard, J. E. *Introduction to phonology.* Englewood Cliffs, NJ: Prentice-Hall, 1978.

Smith, M. D., & Brunette, D. Early rampant homonymy: Problem or strategy? *Papers and Reports on Child Language Development,* Stanford University, 1981, *20,* 133–139.

Smith, N. V. *The acquisition of phonology: A case study.* Cambridge University Press, 1973.

Snow, K. A detailed analysis of articulation responses of "normal" first grade children. *Journal of Speech and Hearing Research,* 1963, *6,* 277–290.

Sommerstein, A. H. *Modern phonology.* Baltimore: University Park Press, 1977.

Sparks, R. W., & Holland, A. L. On: Melodic intonation therapy for aphasia. *Journal of Speech and Hearing Disorders,* 1976, *41,* 298–300.

Stampe, D. The acquisition of phonetic representation. In R. T. Binnick et al. (Eds.), *Papers from the Fifth Regional Meeting, Chicago Linguistic Society,* 1969, 433–444.

Stampe, D. How I spent my summer vacation. Mimeo. Ohio State University, 1972. (Revised, 1973.) (a)

Stampe, D. On the natural history of diphthongs. In P. M. Peranteau et al. (Eds.), *Papers from the Eighth Regional Meeting of the Chicago Linguistic Society,* 1972, 578–590. (b)

Stampe, D. *A dissertation on natural phonology.* Unpublished doctoral dissertation, University of Chicago, 1973. Revised version of 1972a, How I spent my summer vacation. (Also published as *A dissertation on natural phonology,* Garland Publishing, New York, 1979.) (a)

Stampe, D. On chapter nine. In M. J. Kenstowicz & C. W. Kisseberth (Eds.), *Issues in phonological theory.* The Hague: Mouton, 1973. (b)

Stark, J., Poppen, R., & May, M. Effects of alteration of prosodic features on the sequencing performance of children. *Journal of Speech and Hearing Research,* 1967, *10,* 849–855.

Stark, R., Rose, N., & McLagen, M. The features of infant sounds: The first eight weeks of life. *Journal of Child Language,* 1975, *2,* 205–221.

Stoel-Gammon, C. Phonological analysis of four Down's syndrome children. *Applied Psycholinguistics,* 1980, *1,* 31-48.

Strazzula, M. Speech problems of the Mongoloid child. *Quarterly Review of Pediatrics,* 1953, *8,* 268-273.

Sweet, H. *Handbook of phonetics.* Oxford, 1877.

Sweet, H. *Primer of phonetics.* Oxford, 1880.

Templin, M. C. *Certain language skills in children, their development and interrelationships.* Institute of Child Welfare, *Monograph Series,* 1957, *26.* Minneapolis: University of Minnesota Press.

Templin, M. C., & Darley, F. L. *The Templin-Darley Tests of Articulation.* Iowa City: Bureau of Educational Research and Service, Extension Division, State University of Iowa, 1960.

Timm, L. A. A child's acquisition of Russian phonology. *Journal of Child Language,* 1977, *4,* 329-339.

Tonkova-Yampol'skaya, R. V. Development of speech intonation in infants during the first two years of life. *Voprosy psikhologii,* 1968, *14* (3), 94-101 (M. Vale, trans. & D. I. Slobin, Ed.) Translation reprinted from *Soviet Psychology,* 1969, *7 (3),* 48-54 in C. A. Ferguson & D. I. Slobin (Eds.), *Studies of child language development.* New York: Holt, Rinehart & Winston, 1973, 128-138.

Toombs, M. S., Singh, S., & Hayden, M. E. Markedness of features in the articulatory substitutions of children. *Journal of Speech and Hearing Disorders,* 1981, *46,* 184-191.

Trager, G., & Bloch, B. The syllabic phonemes of English. *Language,* 1941, *17,* 223-246.

Trost, J. E., & Canter, G. J. Apraxia of speech in patients with Broca's aphasia: A study of phoneme production accuracy and error patterns. *Brain and Language,* 1974, *1,* 63-79.

Trubetzkoy, N. S. *Grundzüge der phonologie. Travaux du Cercle linguistique de Prague,* II, 1939. Trans. C. A. M. Baltaxe, *Principles of phonology.* Berkeley, 1969.

Velten, H. V. The growth of phonemic and lexical patterns in infant language. *Language,* 1943, *19,* 281-292. Also in A. Bar-Adon & W. F. Leopold (Eds.), *Child language: A book of readings.* Englewood Cliffs, NJ: Prentice-Hall, 1971, 82-91.

Vennemann, T. On the theory of syllabic phonology. *Linguistiche Berichte,* 1972, *18,* 1-18. (a)

Venneman, T. Rule inversion. *Lingua,* 1972, *29,* 209-242. (b)

Vihman, M. M. From pre-speech to speech: On early phonology. *Papers and Reports on Child Language Development,* Stanford University, 1976, *12,* 230-243.

Vihman, M. M. Consonant harmony: Its scope and function in child language. In J. Greenberg, C. A. Ferguson, & E. A. Moravscik (Eds.), *Universals of human language: Vol 2, phonology*. Stanford, CA: Stanford University Press, 1978.

Vihman, M. M. Homonymy and the organization of early vocabulary. Paper presented at the Stanford Child Language Research Forum, Stanford, CA, 1979.

Vihman, M. M. Phonology and the development of the lexicon: Evidence from children's errors. *Journal of Child Language*, 1981, *8*, 239-264.

von Raffler-Engel, W. The development from sound to phoneme in child language. In C. A. Ferguson & D. I. Slobin (Eds.), *Studies in child language development*. New York: Holt, Rinehart & Winston, 1965.

Walsh, T. On the necessity of rule ordering in Natural Generative Phonology. Presented at the VII Linguistic Symposium on Romance Linguistics, Cornell University, 1977.

Wang, W. S.-Y. Vowel features, paired variables, and the English vowel shift. *Language*, 1968, *44*, 695-708.

Wardhaugh, R. *Introduction to linguistics*. New York: McGraw-Hill Book Co., 1972.

Waterson, N. Some speech forms of an English child: A phonological study. *Transactions of the Philological Society*, 1970, 1-24.

Waterson, N. Child phonology: A prosodic view. *Journal of Linguistics*, 1971, *7*, 179-211. (a)

Waterson, N. Child phonology: A comparative view. *Transactions of the Philological Society*, 1971, 34-50. (b)

Waterson, N. Some views on speech perception. *Journal of the International Phonetic Association*, 1971, *1*, 81-96. (c)

Waterson, N. Perception and production in the acquisition of phonology. In W. von Raffler-Engel & Y. Lebrun (Eds.), *Baby talk and infant speech*. Amsterdam: Swets and Zeitlinger, 1976.

Waterson, N. Growth of complexity in phonological development. In N. Waterson & C. Snow (Eds.), *The development of communication*. New York: Wiley & Sons, Inc., 1978.

Weber, J. L. Patterning of deviant articulation behavior. *Journal of Speech and Hearing Disorders*, 1970, *35*, 135-141.

Weiner, F. F. *Phonological process analysis*. Baltimore: University Park Press, 1979.

Weiner, F. F. Systematic sound preference as a characteristic of phonological disability. *Journal of Speech and Hearing Disorders*, 1981, *46*, 281-286.

Weiner, F. F., & Bankson, N. Teaching features. *Language, Speech and Hearing Services in the Schools,* 1978, *9,* 29–34.

Weir, R. H. *Language in the crib.* The Hague: Mouton, 1962.

Wellman, B. L., Case, I. M., Mengert, I. G., & Bradbury, D. E. Speech sounds of young children. *University of Iowa Studies in Child Welfare,* 1931, *5* (2).

West, J. J., & Weber, J. L. A phonological analysis of the spontaneous language of a four-year-old hard-of-hearing child. *Journal of Speech and Hearing Disorders,* 1973, *38,* 25–35.

Weston, A., & Irwin, J. Use of paired stimuli in modification of articulation. *Perceptual Motor Skills,* 1971, *32,* 947–957.

Whitaker, H. A. On the representation of language in the human brain. *Working Papers in Phonetics, No.* 12. University of California at Los Angeles, 1969.

Whitaker, H. A. *A model for neurolinguistics.* Occasional Papers 10, University of Essex, Language Centre, 1970.

Willbrand, M. L., & Kleinschmidt, M. J. Substitution patterns and word constraints. *Language, Speech, and Hearing Services in the Schools,* 1978, *9,* 155–161.

Winitz, H. *Articulatory acquisition and behavior.* Englewood Cliffs, NJ: Prentice-hall, 1969.

Wolff, P. H. The natural history of crying and other vocalizations in early infancy. In B. M. Foss (Ed.), *Determinants of infant behavior* (Vol. 4). London: Methuen, 1969.

Working Papers in Language Universals (WPLU), Stanford University, Stanford, CA.

Zisk, P. K., & Bialer, I. Speech and language problems in Mongolism: A review of the literature. *Journal of Speech and Hearing Disorders,* 1967, *32,* 228–241.

Author Index

Subject Index